ANARCHA

ANARCHAFEMINISM

Chiara Bottici

BLOOMSBURY ACADEMIC
LONDON • NEW YORK • OXFORD • NEW DELHI • SYDNEY

BLOOMSBURY ACADEMIC
Bloomsbury Publishing Plc
50 Bedford Square, London, WC1B 3DP, UK
1385 Broadway, New York, NY 10018, USA
29 Earlsfort Terrace, Dublin 2, Ireland

BLOOMSBURY, BLOOMSBURY ACADEMIC and the Diana logo are
trademarks of Bloomsbury Publishing Plc

First published in Great Britain 2022
Reprinted in 2024

A catalogue record for this book is available from the British Library.

Library of Congress Cataloging-in-Publication Data
Names: Bottici, Chiara, author.
Title: Anarchafeminism / Chiara Bottici.
Description: London ; New York : Bloomsbury Academic, 2022. |
Includes bibliographical references and index.
Identifiers: LCCN 2021023323 (print) | LCCN 2021023324 (ebook) |
ISBN 9781350095878 (paperback) | ISBN 9781350095861 (hardback) |
ISBN 9781350095854 (ebook) | ISBN 9781350095885 (epub)
Subjects: LCSH: Anarchafeminism.
Classification: LCC HQ1193 .B68 2022 (print) | LCC HQ1193 (ebook) |
DDC 320.5/7082—dc23
LC record available at https://lccn.loc.gov/2021023323
LC ebook record available at https://lccn.loc.gov/2021023324

ISBN: HB: 978-1-3500-9586-1
        PB: 978-1-3500-9587-8
        ePDF: 978-1-3500-9585-4
        eBook: 978-1-3500-9588-5

Typeset by RefineCatch Ltd, Bungay, Suffolk
Printed and bound in Great Britain

To find out more about our authors and books, visit www.bloomsbury.com
and sign up for our newsletters.

To Elena Pulcini, *maestra e amica*,
philosopher of the care of the world.
In memoriam.

Contents

Figures

Acknowledgements

I began writing this book many years ago and, as often happens with books that have long been in the making, it is hard to acknowledge all the people and encounters that have been influential for its development. Furthermore, the last part of the writing process coincided with the Covid-19 pandemic. During these times of segregation, not only I did not have "a room of my own," which, as Virginia Woolf reminds us, is the necessary condition for writing: living in a small New York apartment with two children, I did not even have a "desk of my own." This, among other issues, meant that I did not have access to my New School office, where all my books are located. Without the support of my family, who let me occupy a desk often at their expense, and of the incredible research assistance of Austin Burke, who shared with me their personal electronic sources, and who always provided intelligent and prompt feedback along with them, the writing process would not have been materially possible. For a constant dialogue and invaluable support, I am indebted to them in a degree that can hardly be expressed in words.

I am grateful to Lizabeth During for her friendship and for lending me her own home library, where I found a physical copy of many of the feminist books that, at the moment of writing, were stuck in my office, as well as the quiet necessary for writing. Thinking is always a collective process, but you need silence to hear the many voices in your head. I am incredibly thankful to her for providing me with that space and for the many feminist conversations which often took place along with, and as, a delicious meal. Other friends and colleagues who have deeply influenced this work in a way that goes well beyond the practice of quoting explicit sources include: María Pía Lara, my sister in imagination, whose support and feedback on my work has been invaluable throughout the years; Elena Pulcini, who taught me what to "care for the world" means; Patricia Gherovici and Jamieson Webster, my psychoanalytic and dancefloor soul-mates; Simona Forti, *amica da sempre*; my friend, and psychoanalyst of the feminine, Jill Gentile; my New School colleagues, Cinzia Arruzza,

Nancy Fraser, and McKenzie Wark, from whom I have learned more than what could ever come out from the works I quoted in this book. I am particularly grateful to Benoît Challand, co-teacher and co-author (among many other things), who, more than twenty years ago, woke me up from the Eurocentric slumber I had inherited from my European (and Eurocentric) education, and who has been a continual source of exchange and truly transindividual thinking.

Among my New School colleagues, I also thank Lisa Rubin, with whom, during the process of finishing this book, I have begun building a new "Gender and Sexualities Studies Institute" (GSSI). This institutional space has been an incredible framework for bringing together all the exciting and path-breaking work on gender and sexuality currently being done at the New School. I am incredibly grateful to all those who supported its creation and to the colleagues and students who make its daily life. Among them, I should mention all the GSSI student assistants with whom I am in constant conversation: Austin Burke, K. Eskin, Elijah Sparrow, and Giuseppe Vicinanza.

Besides the direct intellectual sources of this book, I would like to acknowledge the practical sources of inspiration, which come from the many feminist battles and social movements of the last forty years, but also from the personal struggles of the *femina* who have been the closest to me since when I was born. Among them, I have to mention all the women in my own family, who struggled to survive in a very patriarchal Italian small town, and in particular: my grandmothers, who overcome the violence of the war, included that which took their partners away and forced them to raise four and five children respectively on their own; my mother, Pedrini Alvarina, who had to abandon her studies to become a door-to-door vendor to support her three children, and whose love for and dedication to us taught me very early on what it means to "care"; and my sister, Elena Bottici—also known by her musician name "El Conchitas"—who, even though just two years older, paved the way for me and other women of our generation who left and found themselves elsewhere. It is thanks to her that, from a very early age, I realized that another way of being woman was not just possible, it was *real*, because she was there.

A note on style. This book was written originally using the Harvard quotation system, one that references sources by naming only the author and the date of the publication in question. That is the system I used in all of my previous philosophy books. While writing this book, I progressively realized the tension between an anarchafeminist philosophy and a quotation system that reduces sources to their "family name," which in most cases also means "the name of the father." I lived with that tension until Chapter 8, when I finally decided to switch to a modified version of the Chicago style, one where author(ities) are quoted with both their first and their family name. I am grateful to my research assistant Lucas Ballestin, who took on the burden of revising all the chapters that had already been written, and to Austin Burke, who continued that process.

As I wrote this book, I developed an anarchafeminist lens that, among other things, made me aware that, in mainstream writing practices, whenever we want to summarize the name of an author, and avoid repetition, we consistently reduce it to their "family name": why the last and not the first name? Why should Simone de Beauvoir become "de Beauvoir," and thus be subsumed into the name of her father? We want a short cut, and we find one in the "family," which, in most cases—in the West at least—also means the patrilinear and patriarchal family. In this book I have tried to resist this reduction and, particularly after the discussion of naming in Chapter 6, decided to quote sources with their full name. When that became too repetitive, I alternated quoting the first and the family name. This may disorient some readers, while others may feel this looks "unprofessional;" other still may reflect on how such a state of affairs is the result of a few millennia of patriarchy. The form is the content. It is the same anarchafeminist philosophy that made me reluctant to assume any of the authors' gender, except in cases where the self-identification was clear. I have therefore used specific pronouns where such self-identification was evident, but made recourse to "they" when I could not, and did not want to, guess.

The earliest formulation of ideas exposed in this book were presented in a keynote lecture for the *2nd Annual "Thinking the Plural"—Richard J. Bernstein Symposium* (Muhlenberg College, September 25, 2015) and, in a subsequent version, as *Thesis Eleven Annual Lecture* (La Trobe University, Melbourne, July 26, 2016). I started thinking about this book even before, but the key idea came to me in 2015 while preparing the lecture for the Richard J. Bernstein Symposium: as I pondered over the meaning of the plural in Bernstein's work, I realized that, in my long-standing engagement with Spinoza's philosophy, I was actually trying to find an ontological framework that would allow me to think the plural in a similar way through a feminist lens. There is more of the relationship between the philosophy of transindividuality and pragmatism that I need to explore in the future. But first I had to find my own voice, so here is a first step in that direction.

Parts of Chapters 6 have been published in "Bodies in plural: Towards an Anarchafeminist Manifesto", *Thesis Eleven*, Vol. 142 (2017): 99–111 (Spanish translation: "Cuerpos en plural: hacia un manifiesto anarca-feminista," in *FEMERIS: Revista Multidisciplinar de Estudios de Género*, no. 3 (2019): 224–45; French translation: "Anarcha-féminisme et l'ontologie du transindividuel," in *La Deleuziana*, Dec 2018, no. 8: 88–104; Portuguese translation: "Corpos no plural: em direção à um manifesto anarca-feminista" in *Psicologia em Revista*, 2020). An earlier version of the "Stabat Mater" intermezzo has been published with the title "Stabat Matter Tryptic," in *Fence,* Spring–Summer 2021: 37–8.

A first version of the introduction was presented at the Night of Philosophy in New York City on January 26, 2018, and then at the UNESCO Night of Philosophy on November 15, 2018. An extract of the talk was published in *Libération* on November 15, 2018,[1] whereas a full version appeared on *Public Seminar* on March 7, 2018.[2] A Spanish translation of the latter appeared on September 12, 2018 in *Reporte Sexto Piso*[3] and an Italian translation in *Per cosa lottare. Le frontiere del progressismo*, edited by Enrico Biale and Corrado Fumagalli (2019), Milan: Fondazione Giacomo Feltrinelli.

Other talks and conferences where parts of this book have been presented and discussed include: the lecture "Rethinking the Human Through the Philosophy of Transindividuality," at the International Conference *Reimagining the Human*, Institute of Philosophy, Vilnius University, September 19, 2021; "Anarchafeminism and Transindividuality," a paper delivered at the International Conference *New Materialisms*, Center March Bloch & ICI, Berlin, April 8–9, 2019; "Anarchafeminism," Guest Lecture, Philosophy Department, Clemson University, March 7, 2019; "Anarchaféminisme," Guest Lecture, École des Hautes Études en Sciences Sociales, November 23, 2018; "Anarcofemminismo," Guest Lecture, Philosophy Department, Università La Sapienza di Roma, October 22, 2018; "Anarcofemminismo ed ontologia del transindividuale," Invited Guest Lecture, Centro di Ricerca Politiche e Teorie della Sessualità, Università di

[1] https://www.liberation.fr/debats/2018/11/15/nuitisede-la-philo-pour-un-anarcha-feminisme_1692047, accessed on March 25, 2020.

[2] http://www.publicseminar.org/2018/03/anarchafeminism/, accessed on March 25, 2019.

[3] http://reportesp.mx/anarcafeminismo-chiara-bottici, accessed on March 25, 2019.

Verona, March 2, 2018; "The imaginal and the transindividual," lecture at the international conference *Zooethics,* MIT Program in Art, Culture, and Technology, April 27–8, 2018; "Anarchafeminism and the ontology of the transindividual," Invited Guest Lecture, Philosophy Department, University of San Diego, April 2018; "Bodies in plural," Guest Lecture at IBERO University, Mexico City, February 20, 2018; "Anarcofeminismo," Guest Lecture at the Universitad Autonoma Metropolitana, February 19, 2018; "Imaginal economies and feminist subversions," Invited Lecture at the international conference *Imagining the Future: Financial Capitalism and the Social Imagination,* University College London, July 11, 2017; "Feminist struggles and insurrectionary memory: A Panel," *Documenta 14,* Athens, June 30, 2017; "Feminist imagination," an Invited Lecture, Sydney University, July 25, 2016. I am grateful to all the colleagues who invited me to present my work and for all the comments and feedback received on these occasions.

Last, but certainly not least, for reading and commenting on parts, or the entirety, of this manuscript, I am grateful to Richard Bernstein, Austin Burke, Benoît Challand, Simten Cosar, Robert Cremins, Nancy Fraser, Jill Gentile, Todd May, Maura McCreight, María Pía Lara, Ross Poole, Dimitris Vardoulakis, McKenzie Wark, and Jamieson Webster. My thanks to Maura McCreight and Laura Anderson Barbata for their help with images and solving related copyright issues. A special thanks to my Bloomsbury editor, Liza Thomson, for her enthusiasm and support, to her assistant, Lucy Russell, for her relentless patience, and to Lisa Carden for her careful and beautiful copy-editing.

Introduction: feminism as critique

It has become something of a commonplace to argue that in order to fight the oppression of women, it is necessary to unpack the ways in which different forms of oppression intersect with one another. No single factor, be it nature or nurture, economic exploitation or cultural domination, can be said to be the *single* cause sufficient to explain the multifaceted sources of patriarchy and sexism. Intersectionality has consequently become the guiding principle for an increasing number of feminists, both from the global north and from the global south. Some have even claimed that intersectionality is the most important contribution by women's studies so far.[1] As a result, while intersectionality is embraced as a buzzword by many actors on the ground, most publications in gender theory have engaged with the concept in one way or another—whether to promote it, to criticize it, or simply to position oneself with regards to it.

Yet, strikingly enough, in all the literature engaging with intersectionality, there is barely any mention of the feminist tradition of the past that has been claiming the same point for a very long time: anarchist feminism or, as we prefer to call it, "anarchafeminism." The latter term has been introduced by social movements trying to feminize the concept, and thereby give visibility to a specifically feminist strand within anarchist theory and practice. This anarchafeminist tradition, which has largely been neglected both in academia and in public debate, has a particularly vital contribution to offer today. Recovering that tradition is the reason why we started writing this book.

To begin, along with queer theory's path-breaking work aimed at dismantling the gender binary of "men" *versus* "women," it is pivotal to

---

[1] See, for instance, Leslie McCall, "The Complexity of Intersectionality," *Signs: Journal of Women in Culture and Society* 30, no. 3 (2005), 1771.

vindicate once again the need for a form of feminism that opposes the oppression of people who are *perceived as* women and who are discriminated precisely on that basis. Notice here that we are using the term "woman" in a way that includes all types of women: women who have been assigned the female sex at birth (AFAB),[2] women who have been assigned the male sex at birth (AMAB), not less than feminine women, masculine women, lesbian women, trans women, queer women, and so on and so forth. Despite the alleged equality of rights, women, and all of those who are perceived as belonging to that category, are still the object of consistent discrimination. The most striking sign of the continued oppression of women is the data about gender violence, that is, the sheer amount of violence constantly inflicted on women and bodies that are perceived as such.[3] According to some estimates, there are somewhere between 140 to 160 million women missing from the global population—meaning that, as a consequence of sex-selective abortion, infanticide, and inequalities of care, the world population is characterized by a macroscopic hole: that of all the "girls" who went "missing."

Far from being an issue of the past, feminism, the struggle against the oppression of all "*femina*", is therefore more imperative than ever. By "*femina*," the Latin term from which feminism derived, we mean all those who are excluded from the "first sex," that is from the category of "man" (*homo*), as defining both a specific sex and the gender neutral position for humans in general.[4] In comparison to cisgendered males, all other sexes and genders are "second" because none of them can aspire to be both one specific position and the neutral term. For instance, in the US alone,

---

[2] We use the term Assigned Female At Birth (AFAB) and Assigned Male At Birth (AMAB) to signal the fact that by speaking about "male" and "female," we implicitly accept the state-sanctioned view according to which our gender corresponds to the sex assigned to us at birth. Notice here how the (almost always binary) gender system and the state apparatus are tightly linked, since it is through our state-issued ID, such as passports, that a gender identity is attached to our lives.

[3] See "Gender-biased sex selection," United Nations Population Fund, https://www.unfpa.org/gender-biased-sex-selection (accessed on March 24, 2021) and Anna Higgins, "Sex-Selection Abortion: The Real War on Women," Charlotte Lozier Institute, 2016-04-13, https://lozierinstitute.org/sex-selection-abortion-the-real-war-on-women/ (accessed on March 24, 2021).

[4] In this sense, *homo* works like the Italian term "*uomo*," the French "*homme*," and the English "*man*." We borrow the term "second sex" from Simone de Beauvoir's influential book of the same name, which insists on this peculiar position of men, who can be both one single sex and the unsexed humanity more in general: "The relation of the two sexes is not that of two electrical poles: the man represents both the positive and the neuter . . ." Simone de Beauvoir, *The Second Sex* (New York: Vintage, 2011), 5.

nearly one out of six transgender people have been incarcerated at least once in their life time.[5] Gender violence affects not only women who were assigned female at birth, but also includes transwomen and other gender-nonconforming bodies who are the target of a worldwide feminicide. The term "transmisogyny"[6] has been coined, for instance, in order to point out how transphobia and misogyny can go hand in hand and actually mutually reinforce each other. Along with "femicide," that is, the killing of single females, there is an ongoing "feminicide," that is, a comprehensive and systematic discrimination and outright killing of *femina* that often takes place with state complicity, either in the form of delayed punishment or through impunity.[7]

There is, therefore, an urgent need for feminism, but the latter must be supported by an articulation of women's liberation that does not create further hierarchies, and this is precisely where anarchafeminism comes in. While other feminists from the left have been tempted to explain the oppression of women on the basis of a single factor, or have imprisoned women's liberation into the framework of a narrow understanding of "womanhood," anarchists have always been clear in arguing that, in order to fight patriarchy, we have to fight the multifaceted ways in which multiple factors—economic, cultural, racial, political, sexual, etc.—converge to foster it. Including, we might say, the very factors that lead us to privilege certain notions of womanhood over others.

This neglect, if not outright historical amnesia, of an important leftist tradition is certainly the result of the ban that anarchism suffered within academia in particular and within public debates in general, where

---

[5] Nearly one in six transgender people (16 percent) have been incarcerated at some point in their lives—this rate is far higher than that for general population. For transgender women, the figure raises to 21 percent, while nearly half of Black transgender people (47 percent) have been incarcerated at some point (https://transequality.org/sites/default/files/docs/resources/NCTE_Blueprint_for_Equality2012_Prison_Reform.pdf, accessed on May 21, 2021).

[6] See Julia Serano, *Whipping Girl: A Transsexual Woman on Sexism and the Scapegoating of Femininity* (Berkeley: Seal Press, 2016).

[7] By drawing inspiration from Latin American movements, the Kurdish women's movement has for instance used "feminicide" to mean a comprehensive, structurally anchored war against women, both in armed conflicts and in everyday life. See, for instance, "100 reasons to prosecute the dictator," Kurdish Women's Movement of Europe" (TJK-E), https://100-reasons.org/call/ (accessed on March 24, 2021). It is a war that takes place on a physical, military level as well as on an ideological and psychological level. See also the extraordinary flash mob called "un violador en tu camino" / "a rapist in your path," which has been created by the Chilean collective Las Tesis and has subsequently become a feminist anthem worldwide (https://www.youtube.com/watch?v=aB7r6hdo3W4, accessed on March 25, 2021).

anarchism has most often been deceitfully portrayed as a mere call for violence and disorder. This ban is based on a semantic conflation between "anarchy" as absence of government and "anarchy" as disorder. Anarchy does not mean disorder; it means searching for an order without an "orderer," that is, for a form of spontaneous sociality that does not issue from a command. Those who understand anarchy as merely synonymous with disorder conflate the meaning of "order" as the existence of some patterns of behavior (without which no society is possible) with that of order as "command," without which societies are not just possible—they are also desirable. The neglect of the anarchafeminist tradition has thus been enacted to the detriment of conceptual accuracy, inclusiveness, and, as we will see, political efficacy.

Our proposal is to remedy such a gap by formulating a specific anarchafeminist approach adapted to the challenges of our time. The point is not simply to give visibility to an anarchafeminist tradition, which has been an important component of past women's struggles, and thereby to reestablish some historical continuity—although this alone would certainly be a worthwhile endeavor. Besides historical accuracy, recovering anarchafeminist insights has the crucial function of enlarging feminist strategies precisely in a moment when different factors increasingly converge to intensify the oppression of women by creating further class, racial, and cultural cleavages among them.

At a time when feminism has witnessed bitter divisions between cis- and transfeminism,[8] when feminism as a whole has been accused of being mere white privilege, this task is more crucial than ever. The emancipation of (some) women from the global north can indeed happen at the expense of other women from the global south, whose reproductive labor within the household is often used to replace the labor previously performed by the now allegedly "emancipated" women. It is precisely when we adopt such a global perspective, all the more necessary today because of the global entanglements of social reproduction, that the chain linking gendered labor across the globe becomes visible and the timeliness of anarchafeminism all the more manifest. We need a

---

[8] See Jack Halberstam, *Trans*: A Quick and Quirky Account of Gender Variability* (Oakland: University of California Press, 2018) for a reconstruction of some of these controversies, as well for an invitation to overcome them. Cis- is the term opposite to trans- and thus the term used in LGBTQI+ communities to mean those women who have not transitioned from the gender that was assigned to them at birth.

multifaceted approach to domination. In particular, we need an approach able to incorporate different factors as well as different voices coming from all over the globe. As Chinese anarchafeminist He Zhen wrote at the dawn of the twentieth century in her *Problems of Women's Liberation*:

> The majority of women are already oppressed by both the government and by men. The electoral system simply increases their oppression by introducing a third ruling group: elite women. Even if the oppression remains the same, the majority of women are still taken advantage of by the minority of women. [. . .] When a few women in power dominate the majority of powerless women, unequal class differentiation is brought into existence among women. If the majority of women do not want to be controlled by men, why would they want to be controlled by women? Therefore, instead of competing with men for power, women should strive for overthrowing men's rule. Once men are stripped of their privilege, they will become the equal of women. There will be no submissive women nor submissive men. This is the liberation of women.[9]

The relevance of these words, written in 1907, shows how prophetic anarchafeminism has been. Liberation does not mean that women should come to share the privileges that some men enjoy, but it means "no submissive women nor submissive men." In these words lies thus a first answer to our question: why anarchafeminism? Because it is the best antidote against the possibility of feminism becoming a privilege and, thus, a tool in the hands of a few women who dominate the vast majority of them. In an epoch when the election of a woman president is presented as liberation for *all* women, when feminism can become a tool for corporate branding, the fundamental message of anarchafeminists of the past is more urgent than ever: "Feminism does not mean female corporate power or a woman president: it means no corporate power and no president."[10] In other words, it means the liberation of all women.

Although recovering forgotten anarchafeminist voices of the past is an important task for today's feminists, this is not our central aim. This book

---

[9] He Zhen, "Women's Liberation," in *Anarchism: A Documentary History of Libertarian Ideas – Volume I*, ed. Robert Graham (Montreal: Black Rose Books, 2005), 341.
[10] Peggy Kornegger, "Anarchism: The Feminist Connection," in *Quiet Rumors* (California: AK Press, 2012), 25.

began as an attempt to recover the anarchafeminist tradition, but ended up becoming something else. The more we searched for the "anarchafeminist tradition," and the more we tried to identify the "anarchafeminist canon," the less interested we were in it. While researching for this book, it became clear that the concept of an "anarchafeminist tradition," let alone that of an "anarchafeminist canon," is fraught with internal tensions, if not with an outright contradiction. The idea of a "tradition" implies the intentional transmission of a certain body of thought from one generation to the other, which, in turn, implies the existence of a relatively stable body of works that are meant to be "classical" and thus worth transmitting. Even more so, the idea of a "canon" implies that such a body of thought and practices has been transcribed into a series of books, which are accepted as genuine and foundational, if not as sacred. But the term "anarchy" gestures at the getting rid of hierarchies, whether they are political, canonical or ideological. Even the notion of a "classical anarchism," as we will see, often becomes a tool to perpetrate exclusions and policing a supposed anarchist "canon," which ends up being largely Eurocentric and androcentric.[11] Is there not a performative contradiction in trying to construct an anarchafeminist tradition, let alone a canon?

The more we delve in that space, the more such a tension becomes evident. The "anarchafeminist" philosophy is scattered in a constantly shifting set of books, works and ideas that can hardly be enclosed into a given canon. Furthermore, many anarchafeminist authors are not even primarily interested in branding themselves as such. Some simply focus on specific issues, while others chose opacity as a strategy. As a consequence, whereas reading and engaging with groups that identify themselves as anarchafeminist is always useful, we have actually found some of the most productive anarchafeminist insights in writers, philosophers and activists who do not identify themselves as such. The same holds for the many and varied other forms of anarchism. For

---

[11] For instance, in George Crowder's reconstruction of "*Classical Anarchism*," the term "classical" become the justification for limiting his reconstruction of anarchism to the ideas developed by four men (Godwin, Proudhon, Bakunin, and Kropotkin), thereby completely erasing the contribution of all other genders to what is "classical" in anarchist thought. See: George Crowder, *Classical Anarchism: The Political Thought of Godwin, Proudhon, Bakunin, and Kropotkin* (Oxford: Clarendon Press, 1992). It is indeed significant—yet all too often forgotten—that "classical" and "class" derive from the same Latin root "*classis*," a term initially denoting simply any class, but, increasingly, and particularly through the French term "*classique*," denoting whatever belongs to the class *par excellence*.

instance, while there are relatively few self-identified "Black anarchists," so much of the literature in the Black radical tradition and in Black feminism expresses anarchist ideals and sentiments, as some have noted.[12] So how to reconcile such a tension? How can the two possibly go together?

The tension disappears when we ponder over the meaning of "anarchy" itself, and over "anarchism" as the philosophy and praxis of anarchy. If anarchy means, as we will see, absence of an *archē,* that is of a ruler and of an overarching principle, and thus invites us to search for an order without an orderer, then it is clear why most anarchists are not primarily interested in classifying themselves in one way or another, let alone in constructing an anarchist "canon." Most anarchist thinkers were mainly interested in dismantling any *archē* and thus they fought on the specific battlegrounds of their time and space, without necessarily engaging in the (academic) exercise of identifying traditions and canonical texts. It is therefore perfectly possible to develop a form of "anarchoblackness" and not desire to identify a specific "Black-anarchist tradition," in as much as it is possible to develop anarchafeminist ideas without calling oneself as such, nor being aware of the existence of such a tradition. This is probably the strength of anarchafeminism, because it protected it from the ossification into an orthodoxy, but also its weakness, because many of its contributors have more easily fallen into oblivion.

In this book, we want to transform the weakness into a strength, that is use the versatility of the anarchafeminist philosophy as a way to create a dialogue between texts, political projects, and philosophical ideas that are not usually associated. In doing so, we will refer to both theorists and activists who define themselves as anarchafeminists, but also to others who do not so. This book is thus less a faithful reconstruction of all anarchafeminist theories than an attempt to individuate an anarchafeminist philosophy that responds to the challenges of our time. More than a label to classify texts or people, or a philosophico-political program to be written once and for all, anarchism is a *method,*[13] one that questions all forms of hierarchy and therefore invites us to investigate the way in which they mutually reinforce each other. When applied to

---

[12] As Marquis Bey observes, this is also true for Black anarchism: while there are relatively few self-identified "Black anarchists," so much of the literature in the Black radical tradition and in Black feminism expresses anarchic sentiments. See, in particular, Marquis Bey, *Anarcho-Blackness: Notes Towards a Black Anarchism* (California: AK Press, 2020), 8.

[13] Errico Malatesta, *L'anarchia* (Rome: Datanews, 2001), 39.

feminism, the prefix *anarcha* has the function of underlining that neither sex, nor class or race, nor cis- or heteronormativity, nor whatever other single item we can pick from our gender bookshelves, can ever aspire to be the unique factor, the decisive origin, the *archē* that explains, and thus also explains away, the pluralistic nature of the oppression of women.

This is the meaning of "anarchafeminism" that we find in historical texts by anarchists who considered themselves feminist, but also in those by theorists and activists that have embraced these ideas without necessarily using that label: what they had in common was the awareness that there is something specific in the oppression of women, but also that different forms of oppression reinforce each other, so one cannot get rid of one of them without addressing all others. In sum, they share the conviction that one cannot be free, unless everybody else is also equally free.

It is this anarchafeminist awareness, for instance, that led Emma Goldman, one of the sources of inspiration for this book, to reject the label "feminism" and only embrace that of "anarchism." For her, as we will see, anarchism was the teacher of the unity of life, and thus of the fact that all forms of oppression meet in a single point, whereas "feminism," in the New York of the early twentieth century, was mainly associated with a movement made up of middle-class women who had no vested interest in overcoming class exploitation, and other forms of domination. Hence, Emma Goldman's philosophy addresses the question of the liberation of women through the concept of anarchism, refuses the label of "feminism," but, as we will see, nevertheless harbours clear anarchafeminist insights.

The term "anarcha-feminism" was, on the contrary, used explicitly in 1970s by feminist social movements who looked at a different type of feminism, and saw themselves as anarchist, emphasizing the important convergence between the two—a convergence perceived as so poignant that some activists argued that "feminism practices what anarchism preaches."[14] Indeed, many feminists of the 1970s shared anarchist goals such as ending all forms of hierarchy, capitalism, gender stereotypes, and interpersonal violence, and often used techniques traditionally used by anarchists, from the recourse to consensus building in affinity groups to

---

[14] Julia Tanenbaum, "To Destroy Domination in All Its Forms: Anarchafeminist Theory, Organization and Action, 1970–1978," in *Anarchafeminism: A Special Issue of Perspectives on Anarchist Theory*, ed. Perspectives Editorial Collective (Portland: Eberhardt Press, 2016), 13.

the emphasis on "the personal is political" or what anarchists traditionally called "prefigurative politics."[15]

However, as we will see, it is undeniable that not all forms of feminism have historically been anarchist. For many self-defined feminists, feminism means reaching equality between men and women, and thus searching for the legal and political conditions necessary for women to come to enjoy the same position of power enjoyed by men. But not all men are equally placed in the hierarchy of power, so when feminism aims at reaching equality with men, what is meant is actually a few of them. In this way, feminism can easily become a form of elitism, that is an attempt by (some) women to come to enjoy the same privileges of some men. On the contrary, in this book we understand feminism not as struggle for equality with some men, but as a struggle against the oppression of all women,[16] as well as a struggle against the oppression perpetrated through the imposition of a narrow understanding of "womanhood."

As a consequence, feminism is not a movement concerned just with women's issues, but rather a form of critique of the entire social order, one that in the current predicament is inseparable, as we will see, from the "modern/colonial gender system"[17] that reduces gender roles to biological dimorphism and pathologizes those who deviate from it. Gender norms and binary dichotomies of "men" *versus* "women" are oppressive for everybody, not just for those assigned the female sex at birth, despite the fact that men can profit from a gender binary system with men on top much more than women can. This is because everybody participates in the production and reproduction of gender roles.

Considering feminism as a lens for a general critique of the social order also has the function of deepening our understanding of oppression through an analysis of internalized modes of domination. Feminist theorists of the past have been able to unpack the mechanisms of domination in a very subtle way. While it is certainly true that there is something unique about the oppression of women, it is also true that discerning such peculiarity can illuminate the mechanisms of domination more generally. For some feminists, the insidious nature of domination is

---

[15] Julia Tanenbaum, "To Destroy Domination in All Its Forms," 13–14.
[16] On the definition of feminism as a movement to end sexist oppression, we follow bell hooks, *Feminist Theory from Margin to Center* (Boston: South End Press, 1984), 17–31.
[17] Maria Lugones, "The Coloniality of Gender," in *The Palgrave Handbook of Gender and Development*, ed. Wendy Harcourt (London: Palgrave Macmillan UK, 2016), 14.

derived from the erotic dimension of power or what other anarchists have called "the dilemmas of voluntary servitude." As Étienne de La Boétie once observed, the main reason certain rulers remain in power for so long is that the multitude willingly obey.[18] It would be enough for the majority of people to simply stop obeying in order to bring about the dissolution of such a power. Why do people keep submitting to them? Why does patriarchy persist? If we look at feminist literature, we can find various insights as to the mechanisms whereby women have willingly reproduced the very same gender roles and stereotypes that have oppressed them for so long. Simone de Beauvoir, for instance, more than seventy years ago, pointed to this problem: there have been other cases where, for a shorter or longer period of time, one category of humans managed to prevail over another, and most often it was numerical inequality that enabled this privilege to come into being and persist over time, but in the case of women that is clearly not the case. It is not that women are a numerical minority and therefore become oppressed, but the other way around: because of widespread feminicide and inequalities, a significant number of women went missing from the global population. Thus, the reason why such oppression persists must lie elsewhere. For Simone de Beauvoir, it is because "the man who sets the woman up as an *Other* will find in her deep complicity": "refusing to be the Other, refusing complicity with man, would mean renouncing all the advantages an alliance with the superior caste confers on them."[19] There is thus something peculiarly insidious in gender domination, so unpacking the way it works can also act as a magnifying glass to help unpack mechanisms of domination more generally, and thus to prepare the ground for their subversion. Feminism should not be just an addendum to a more general critique of the social order, but rather one of its starting points.[20]

---

[18] Étienne de La Boétie, *The Politics of Obedience: The Discourse of Voluntary Servitude* (Auburn: Mises Institute, 2015).

[19] Simone de Beauvoir, *The Second Sex*, 11.

[20] We follow here Karl Marx's 1843 definition of critical theory as the "self-clarification of the struggles and wishes of the age," but, following Nancy Fraser, we consider feminist struggles as a crucial component of them, and thus not as something that can be added later on, when general theory has done its work. See, in particular, Nancy Fraser, *Fortunes of Feminism: From State-Managed Capitalism to Neoliberal Crisis* (London: Verso, 2013), 19–51. As we will see later on, we combine historical materialism with a transindividual philosophy and a monist ontological framework that enable us to formulate critique as a form of immanent critique. On critique and a Spinozist philosophy of immanence, see also Martin Saar, *Die Immanenz der Macht. Politische Theorie nach Spinoza* (Berlin: Suhrkamp, 2013), in particular 424–6.

A variety of critical theorists who combined an historical materialist analysis with a psychoanalytic lens did important work in unpacking how structures of dominations can be internalized and reproduced, even by those who are most oppressed by them. To paraphrase Erich Fromm, both historical materialism and psychoanalysis are very helpful in this enterprise because they both converge in "deposing consciousness from its throne."[21] Whereas most of the canonical works in critical theory have done so through a Eurocentric philosophical framework and an androcentric psychoanalysis, the type of critique that we will pursue in this book must be understood as an exercise in an "interstitial global critical theory."[22] The latter is a form of critique that is global in the sense that it takes the globe as it horizon, but also interstitial because it focuses on how the global intersects with regional, national, and even microlocal forces in creating specific configurations of oppression. The metaphor of the "interstices" is a way to move beyond the logic of binaries that counterpoises universalism *versus* particularism, the global *versus* the particular, while also keeping in mind the performative contradiction one may risk when doing critical theory by taking only European or Western experiences and sources as the basis for critical theory. We can still retain some lessons from European histories and intellectual traditions, but they have to be put in a *global* context, that is, one where, as we will see, relations of colonialism, imperialism, and the "coloniality of gender"[23] emerge. Notice also that "global" does not mean "universal": the point of an "interstitial global critical theory" is precisely to argue that one can combine a global gaze, focused on the inequalities rooted in global phenomena such as capitalism and colonialism, with a focus on interstices, where a number of different factors can intervene, thus creating specific intersections of oppressions that are not universal. "Critical theory" without qualification would be a universal. The idea of a "global critical theory" already introduces a qualification, because it suggests that theory is done from a certain perspective, i.e. that of the

---

[21] Erich Fromm, "Psychoanalysis and Sociology" and "Politics and Psychoanalysis," in *Critical Theory and Society: A Reader,* eds. Stephen Eric Bronner and Douglas MacKay Kellner (New York: Routledge, 1989).

[22] We have elaborated this methodology more at length in Chiara Bottici and Benoît Challand, "Towards an Interstitial Global Critical Theory," in *Globalization* (forthcoming, 2021).

[23] Maria Lugones, "The Coloniality of Gender," 14.

globe as its horizon of operation, while not claiming or implicitly assuming any universality. Global does not mean "total" either, because an interstitial global critical theory is not meant to address all current and possible forms of oppressions at once. No emancipatory theory can ever be all-encompassing, because any theory cannot but reflect the positionality and the limits of the knowledge available to the theorists in that moment in space and time.

The approach used in this book is thus best described as "critical-colonial," thereby meaning that no critique of the social order can today be effective without taking into account insights from the de-, post-, and settler-colonial studies.[24] Being critical involves questioning the conditions in which theory is produced. And that is where the contribution of post-colonial, de-colonial, and settler-colonial theories, with their emphasis on the persistence of the "racial schema" and the "psychology of colonialism,"[25] become crucial: presenting a form of critical theory that does not take into account the extent to which theorizing itself is influenced by the persistence of colonial modes of thought and unconscious patterns of feeling means falling into a performative contradiction, where one professes to exercise a critique, but fails to do so because, by systematically ignoring the unconscious racial schemes shaping one's own theorizing, one cannot avoid reproducing them. This is the reason why decolonization cannot be done all at once, but requires a "decolonial attitude"[26] that is relentless in progressively unpacking the different layers of domination accumulated over time. Furthermore, for us theorists of European descent operating in the Americas, we also deem it crucial to add a critical settler-colonial perspective to the de- and post-colonial emphasis. Being located in the United States, a country marked by the overall "coloniality of power" generated by "the colonial/modern Eurocentred capitalism,"[27] but also by the specific settler-colonial history and present-day context of the

---

[24] We have elaborated the concept of a "critical-colonial approach" in Chiara Bottici and Benoît Challand, "Europe after Eurocentrism?," *Crisis & Critique* 7, no. 1 (2020), 59.

[25] Ashis Nandy, *The Intimate Enemy: Loss and Recovery of Self Under Colonialism* (Delhi: Oxford University Press, 1983).

[26] Nelson Maldonado-Torres, "Outline of Ten Theses on Coloniality and Decoloniality," available at http://fondation-frantzfanon.com/outline-of-ten-theses-on-coloniality-and-decoloniality/.

[27] Aníbal Quijano, "Coloniality of Power, Eurocentrism, and Latin America," *Nepantla: Views from South* 1, no. 3 (2000a), 533.

United States,[28] we believe it is pivotal that a critical theory produced in these conditions begins by addressing them first hand. How is the settler-colonial structure of the United States impacting the way in which knowledge is produced? How does that structure shape what gets to count as "critique"[29] and what does not? Why are Indigenous philosophies so systematically excluded from critical theory? These are questions that should in our view be addressed by any critical theorist operating in a settler-colonial context, but also by whoever cares about the globe as the horizon for rethinking the critical project. As Eduardo Mendieta puts it, critical theory is inseparable from decolonial thinking, understood as "an exercise in *epistemic insubordination* that challenges the *epistemic privilege* that has been accorded and delegated to certain knowledge producers and withdrawn and refused to other knowledge producers."[30]

Consequently, an interstitial global critical theory cannot prescind from a critique of the Eurocentric biases that so much radical theory still carries within itself. As Ina Kerner, among others, argued, methodological Eurocentrism (or Occidentalism) is what automatically leads to posit a more or less autonomous European (or Western) history of progress and to implicitly use that history and developments as the global norm or yardstick to approach all others around the globe.[31] In this sense, Eurocentrism does not simply imply ethnocentric universalism, that is, presenting claims that only hold for a particular ethnos as if they were universal. It also implies neglecting that such ethnocentric universalism relies in turn on the opposition between universalism and particularism, and thus forgetting that cultural relativism is not the opposite of Eurocentrism but the *other* side of it: they both share the implicit assumption of a globe divided into essentialized group differences (whether they are national or geo-political), as well as their hierarchical

---

[28] Roxanne Dunbar-Ortiz, *An Indigenous Peoples' History of the United States* (London: Beacon Press, 2014).

[29] Nelson Maldonado-Torres, for instance, emphasized that in *The Wretched of the Earth* Frantz Fanon refers to the African tradition of public self-criticism and builds on it; and yet, Fanon is rarely mentioned in the canon of critical theory thinkers. Nelson Maldonado-Torres, "What is Decolonial Critique?," in *Philosophy and Coloniality*, a special issue of the *Graduate Faculty Philosophy Journal*, Vol. 41, no.2 (2020), 162.

[30] Eduardo Mendieta, "Critique of Decolonial Reason: On the Philosophy of the Calibans," in *Philosophy and Coloniality*, a special issue of the *Graduate Faculty Philosophy Journal*, 41. No.1, (2020), 146.

[31] Ina Kerner, "Postcolonial Theories as Global Critical Theories," *Constellations* 25, no. 4 (2018).

organization, with some of them portrayed as universal and other as merely particular.[32] Thus it is possible to find Eurocentric theories being produced in Europe, or the West, as well as in the peripheries of it, where, given the hegemony exercised by Europe over the past 500 years, Eurocentric modes of thinking can very well be internalized even by those who are most oppressed by it. Unpacking methodological Eurocentrism is thus pivotal for an anarchafeminist philosophy aimed at addressing the liberation of not only some (white) women, but all the *femina* around the globe, despite their interstitial differences.

Adopting an anarchafeminist lens entails taking the entire globe as the framework for thinking about the liberation of women, but also questioning any form of methodological ethnocentrism, that is, privileging certain women and thus certain national or regional contexts. If fighting the oppression of women means we have to fight all forms of oppression, then statism, nationalism, and Eurocentrism are no exceptions. If one begins by looking at the dynamics of exploitation by taking state or geopolitical boundaries as an unquestionable fact, one ends up reinforcing one of the greatest sources of the very oppression one was meant to question in the first place. Today, adopting anything less than the entire globe as our framework is at best naïve provincialism, and at worst obnoxious ethnocentrism. But such global gaze must be accompanied by a decolonial and deimperial[33] attitude that takes into account how differences have been constructed and how universalist claims have most often worked as mere ideological cover for "Eurocentrism," and thus as a justification for the narcissism of those still caught in the missionary position of the "white man's burden."

Whereas several feminist theories produced in the global north have failed to understand the extent to which the emancipation of white, middle-class women happened at the expense of a renewed oppression of working-class people of color, and have thus elaborated their own models for women's liberation without giving voice to those placed in the margins of modern/colonial gender system, anarchafeminists are by definition called to adopt an inclusive perspective. Although some individuals who

---

[32] Ina Kerner, "Postcolonial Theories as Global Critical Theories," 615.
[33] We use "deimperial," instead of "non-imperial" or "anti-imperial," for reasons that will become clear in the course of this book. For now, notice that, like "decolonial," the term suggests an attitude of progressively turning away from imperial cognitive scheme, including internalized ones.

defined themselves as "anarchist" in the past may have failed to so do, as a concept and as a method, "anarchism" calls for a focus on the processes of production and reproduction of life independently of all hierarchies, including state boundaries, with their racial and colonial cleavages.

A side remark: note that, although one can use labels such as Latin American or Chinese anarchafeminism, we believe that those labels must be used as ladders to be abandoned in the process of thinking through them. The vitality of the anarchafeminist tradition consists precisely in its capacity to transcend state boundaries, methodological nationalism, and even the Eurocentric biases that persist throughout a lot of the radical theory produced in the global north. It is very revealing, for instance, that most of the feminist tools circulating in Western academia, whether rooted in post-structuralist feminism, radical feminism, or even socialist feminism, derive from theories produced in a very small number of countries. To combat this Eurocentric trend, it is pivotal to bring to the center of the discussion texts produced by anarchists worldwide. This alone can insure a form of feminism beyond Eurocentrism, and beyond ethnocentrism.

As Chandra Tolpade Mohanty argued, it is crucial for feminism to flag up the experiences, texts, and struggles produced by the most marginalized communities within global capitalism, and thus by poor women of all colors in both affluent and neocolonial nations.[34] Although oppression can be internalized even by those who are most oppressed, it still remains that the voices of those who are most marginalized enjoy the "epistemic privilege" of being able to provide the most inclusive viewing of systematic power: we need perspectives that enable us to "study up" the global structures of power, and not simply to "study them down."[35] By focusing on the micro-politics of marginalized women anti-capitalist struggles, one can indeed come to grasp the macro-politics of global capitalism through a bottom up, interstitial approach.

This also implies reading and engaging with theories and praxes produced outside of the West, but cannot be reduced to a mere politics of diversity. Adopting a decolonial and a deimperial attitude does not mean to simply invite "diverse" people to the dinner table, that is, to an already predetermined set of questions, issues, and authors: it means opening up

---

[34] Chandra Tolpade Mohanty, *Feminism Without Borders: Decolonizing Theory, Practicing Solidarity* (Durham: Duke University Press, 2003).

[35] Chandra Tolpade Mohanty, *Feminism Without Borders*, 231–6.

the possibility of changing those dinner plans completely.[36] In other words, it does not mean to just add exotic names as "multicultural add-on" to our already established theoretical endeavors. It means to follow a "bottom-up epistemology" and thus not only to invite a plurality of voices to the table but also to grant them the opportunity to create a different menu. We take the notion of bottom-up epistemology from Boaventura de Sousa Santos, who emphasized how epistemologies of the South can help us to affirm and valorize the differences that remain after the hierarchies between centers and peripheries, north and south, affluent and non-affluent countries, have been eliminated. As such, rather than an abstract universality, "bottom-up epistemologies" promote a "pluriversality," that is, a kind of thinking that encourages decolonization, creolization, or *mestizaje* through intercultural translation, and that thereby also questions the dichotomy of "universal" versus "particular."[37]

If we take the globe as our framework, and adopt a decolonial and deimperial attitude, the first striking datum to emerge is that people across the globe have not always been *doing* gender, and, moreover, even if they did *do* it, they have *done* it in very different terms. It is only with the emergence of a worldwide capitalist system that the gender binary of (masculine) "men" *versus* (feminine) "women" became so hegemonic worldwide. This does not mean that sexual difference did not exist before capitalism, nor does it imply that we should indulge in the nostalgia of a gender-fluid past. It simply means taking note of the historically situated nature of the current gender regime, and, in particular, of the fact that binary gender roles were not as universally accepted as the primary criteria by which to classify bodies as they are today. Modern colonialism and capitalism made the mononuclear bourgeois family, with its binary gender roles, hegemonic, while it endowed the modern sovereign state with a formidable bureaucratic apparatus able to inscribe that gender binary on us through state ID, passports, demography, and healthcare systems, among others.

---

[36] In his "Outline of Ten Theses on Coloniality and Decoloniality," Nelson Maldonado-Torres insists that we need to decolonize every building block of what gets to count as knowledge (18–21). See also his critique of the neoliberal politics of diversity in the academy in Nelson Maldonado-Torres, "What is Decolonial Critique?," 157.

[37] Boaventura de Sousa Santos, *The End of the Cognitive Empire: The Coming of Age of Epistemologies of the South* (Durham: Duke University Press, 2018), 8–9.

Socialist feminists have long been emphasizing how capitalism needs a gendered division of labor because, being predicated on the endless expansion of profit, it needs both the extraction of surplus value from waged productive labor as well as unpaid reproductive labor, which is still largely performed by gendered bodies.[38] Put bluntly, capitalism needs "women." It relies on the assumption that when women are washing their husband's and children's socks, they are not "working" but merely performing their nature-ordained function. As anarchafeminist Maria Mies, among others, has emphasized, perceiving women's labor as simply the necessary calling of their "womanhood" instead of seeing it as the actual work it is, is pivotal to keeping the division between "waged labor," subject to exploitation, and "unwaged labor," subject to what she called "super-exploitation."[39] This form of gendered exploitation is "super" because, whereas the exploitation of waged labor takes place through the extraction of surplus value, the exploitation of women's domestic labor takes place via denying their work *the very status of* work.

By building on socialist-feminist insights, and combining them with Aníbal Quijano's thesis of a "coloniality of power," Maria Lugones put forward the very useful concept of the "coloniality of gender."[40] With this concept, Lugones emphasizes how the "men/women" binary and the racial classification of bodies went together, both systems having been developed by Europeans through the colonial expansion that accompanied the formation of global capitalism. Within the American context, Lugones shows how gender roles were much more flexible and variegated among Native Americans before the arrival of European settlers. Different Indigenous nations possessed, for instance, a third gender category to positively recognize intersex and queer subjectivities, whereas others, such as the Yuma, attributed gender roles on the basis of dreams, so that

---

[38] See, for instance, Silvia Federici, *Revolution at Point Zero: Housework, Reproduction, and Feminist Struggle* (Oakland: PM Press, 2012); Nancy Fraser, *Fortunes of Feminism* (London: Verso, 2013); Cinzia Arruzza, *Le Relazioni Pericolose: Matrimoni e Divorzi Tra Marxismo e Femminismo* (Rome: Alegre, 2010), and the recent anthology *Marxism and Feminism*, ed. Shahrzad Mojab (London: Zed Books, 2015).

[39] Maria Mies, *Patriarchy and Accumulation on a World Scale: Women in the International Division of Labour* (London: Zed Books, 1986). Maria Mies does not use the expression "anarchafeminism," but defines feminism itself as "an anarchist movement which does not want to replace one (male) power elite with another (female) power elite, but which wants to build up a non-hierarchical, non-centralized society where no elite lives on the exploitation and dominance over others" (ibid., 37).

[40] Maria Lugones, "The Coloniality of Gender."

a female-born woman who dreamed of weapons was considered and treated, for all practical purposes, as a man. As we will see, there is today large evidence showing that there has been a systematic intertwinement among capitalist economy, racial classification of bodies, and gender oppression. In other words, although cultures have varied significantly in their attitudes towards homosexual behavior and different gender embodiments, queer *eros* flowered in a variety of forms before the era of European colonialism and imperialism started to promote the binary gender system.[41] Although there have been, and there still are important site of resistance to such a system, we now live in a world in which it is possible for the Uganda's Christian president to condemn homosexuality as a foreign import, despite the fact that Christianity is not indigenous to Uganda, whereas the country's indigenous Langi people actually allowed marriages between males and *mudoko dako*, effeminate men who were considered to be a gender in themselves.[42] It is therefore imperative to systematically explore the link between patriarchy, homophobia, and colonialism. This is what we will do by investigating the different forms and shapes of the "coloniality of gender."

It is manifest, and yet all too often forgotten, that to classify people on the basis of their skin color or their genitalia is not an *a priori* of the human mind. Classifying bodies on the basis of their sex, as well as classifying them on the basis of their race, implies (among other things) a primacy of the visual register. The emergence of modernity is inseparable from the emergence of both the racial and the gender system, so the two cannot be separated. According to Oyèrónké Oyěwùmí, both gender and racial classification rely on a form of "oculocentrism," on a primacy of sight as the major source of information gathering, that is typical of the West, particularly when looked at from the perspective of the Yoruba pre-colonial cultures. As Oyěwùmí points out in *The Invention of Women*, the Yoruba cultures, for instance, relied much more on the oral transmission of information than on its visualization, and they valued age over all other criteria for social hegemony.[43] For the Yoruba *obinrin* (or "anatomical

---

[41] pattrice jones, "Eros and the Mechanisms of Eco-Defense," in *Ecofeminism: Feminist Intersections with Other Animals and the Earth*, eds. Carol Adams and Lori Gruen (New York: Bloomsbury Academic, 2014).

[42] pattrice jones, "Eros and the Mechanisms of Eco-Defense," 98.

[43] Oyèrónké Oyěwùmí, *The Invention of Women: Making an African Sense of Western Gender Discourses* (Minneapolis: University of Minnesota Press, 1997).

females," as Oyěwùmí translates it), colonization meant being inferiorized as a race, as a gender, and, through the exclusion from waged work, as a class. Whereas before colonization, the Yoruba language did not even have the terms to classify people into "men" *versus* "women," with the consequent inferiorization of the latter, after the arrival of the European colonizers Yoruba *obinrin* started to be relegated to a position of systematic inferiority, and thus perceived as "women." "Women" are those who do not have a penis, those who do not have power, and those whose role is defined in relation to men, who are both a specific gender but also the neutral. None of this was true of Yoruba *obinrin* prior to European colonization.[44]

Therefore, questioning the coloniality of gender also means questioning the primacy of biological determinism as well as that of the visual classification of bodies: it is by seeing bodies that we say "here is a woman!" or "that is a man!" But it is also within such a visual register that we have to operate to question narrow heteronormative and cisnormative views of womanhood and thereby open new paths toward subverting them. To summarize the content of this book in one sentence, we could say: "Another woman is possible; another woman has always already begun."

At this point of the argument, one may already object: why insist on the concept of feminism and not just call this anarchism? Why focus on women? If the purpose is to dismantle all types of oppressive hierarchies, should we not also get rid of the gender binary which, by opposing "women" to "men," imprisons us in a heteronormative matrix?

We should be immediately clear that when we say "women," we are not speaking about some supposed object, about an eternal essence, or, even less so, about a pre-given object. Indeed, to articulate a specifically feminist position while maintaining a multifaceted understanding of domination, we need a more nuanced understanding of "womanhood." By drawing insights from feminist readings of Baruch Spinoza's philosophy of the unique substance and from an ontology of the transindividual, we will argue that bodies in general, and women's bodies in particular, must not be considered as objects given once and for all, but rather as processes. We are not things, we are relations. Women's bodies are bodies in plural because they are processes, processes that are constituted by mechanism of

---

[44] Oyèrónkẹ́ Oyěwùmí, *The Invention of Women,* 34.

affecting and associating that occur at the *inter-*, *supra-*, and the *infra-*individual level. To give just a brief example of what we mean here, think of how our bodies come into being through an *inter-*individual encounter, how they are shaped by *supra-*individual forces, such as their geo-political locations, and how they are made up by *intra-*individual bodies such as the air we breathe, the food we eat, or the hormones one may take. And, in their turn, think of how such infra-individual bodies connect us with supra-individual ecosystems, modes of production, and structures of (re)productions.

Notice here the benefits of such an ontological shift towards transindividuality as the prism through which individuality must be understood. First, instead of elaborating a form of feminism and then adding ecology as something different from feminism itself, here the two positions are unified from the beginning because, in a philosophy of the transindividual, the environment is not something separated from us, but rather, the environment is us[45]—literally something constitutive of our individuality. It is not that such a transindividual philosophy is new, since, as we will see, it has been circulating for a while. But we can no longer ignore our transindividual nature, and thus the chains of inter- and infra-actions between different species and ecosystems. The price that we may now pay for such ignorance is going extinct as a consequence of global warming or the next pandemic created by a zoonotic disease. If there is one thing that the Covid-19 catastrophe made patent is that we cannot be healthy on our own, because our being is intimately *inter*, *supra-*, and even *infra-*dependent on that of all others—including other living organism, such as other animals and plants, or non-living ones, such as viruses.

Second, when women's bodies are theorized as processes, as sites of a process of becoming that takes place at different levels, we can speak about "women" without incurring the charge of essentialism or culturalism. As we will see, in this monist ontology, there is no place for the opposition between sex (nature) and gender (culture), an opposition that has plagued so much of the feminist debates in the West, because there is no place for

---

[45] We borrow this expression from Stacy Alaimo's *Bodily Natures: Science, Environment, and the Material Self* (Indianapolis: Indiana University Press, 2010), 11, who, in turn, takes it from Harold Fromm.

body–mind dualism, and for "nature" to be conceived as static and inert, and thus opposed to an always changing "nurture."[46]

Third, by adopting this transindividual ontology, we can also situate the concept of woman outside of a hetero- or cisnormative framework, and thus use the term in such a way that it includes all types of women: feminine women, masculine women, AFAB women, AMAB women, lesbian women, bisexual women, transwomen, ciswomen, asexual women, queer women, and so on and so forth. In sum, "women" come to encompasses all bodies that identify themselves and are identified through the always changing narrative of "womanhood."

To conclude this point, the transindividual framework will allow us to answer the question "what is a woman?" in pluralistic terms, while also defending a specifically feminist form of anarchism. Developing the concept of women as processes also means going beyond the individual *versus* collectivity dichotomy: if it is true that all bodies are transindividual processes, then the assumption that there could be such a thing as a pure individual, separate, or even opposed, to a given collectivity, is at best a useless abstraction and at worst a deceitful fantasy.

This is also the reason why we used the pronoun "we" in writing this book: we want to signal from the very beginning that the thinking recorded in these pages is not the result of an individual mind. It is the result of a transindividual life, a life which began almost a half a century ago in a small town of the Italian peninsula and is currently continuing in a big city in the Americas, a geographical location also known as the territory of Turtle Island according to its pre-colonial name. We use the "we" to signal the transindividual nature of the process of thinking deposited in these pages, but also to recover a practice of writing that is typical of our native language, Italian, where the use of the plural is a common practice.

Most of this book is written through the rhetorical devise of the "transparent subject,"[47] that is, it is written as if the subject who is writing

---

[46] The rejection of such a dichotomy of sex (nature) *versus* gender (nurture) does not imply that the two terms could not be transformed and used in a different context. For instance, within certain LGBTQI+ communities, the distinction can be used to mean the difference between sexual orientation or sexualities (thus lesbian, gay, queer, etc) and atypical gendered forms of embodiment, such as that of trans-women or trans-men. This usage, however, questions even further the traditional dichotomy of sex (nature) *versus* gender (nurture).

[47] Maria Lugones, "Purity, Impurity, and Separation," *Signs* 19, no. 2 (1994).

were not an embodied, gendered, and racialized being. That is the writing strategy used by mainstream philosophical writings today, at least in the West. In this book, we will use that writing mode, but also disrupt it through "intermezzos," where an embodied, gendered, and culturally located voice comes through language itself. The purity of the "transparent subject" performed in the first three chapters will thus be interrupted by a *Stabat mater* fragment that will both make that performance evident, as well as glance at another possible type of writing. Whereas the chapters of this book follow the common order of an already established syntax, intermezzos will follow the free writing of a body in search of meaning beyond the conventional syntax. This reflects our belief that an anarchafeminist philosophy should be able to recognize the philosophical legitimacy of a multiplicity of writing styles, including those that are most alien to the (Eurocentric) model of the philosophical treatise, and that some may consequently deem as not proper theory or philosophy.

The first part of this book will introduce anarchafeminism as the philosophy that is able to keep together two fundamental claims: that there is something specific in the oppression of women, and of *femina* more in general, and that in order to address that oppression we need to tackle all other forms of oppression. To this end, we will discuss the Black feminist literature on intersectionality and analyze its relationship with anarchafeminist theories and ideas (Chapter 1), we will delineate the sort of anarchism "beyond Eurocentrism and sexism" that will accompany such a project (Chapter 2), and finally situate anarchafeminism between feminism and queer and trans-theory (Chapter 3).

The *Stabat mater* intermezzo will open Part II, which will tackle the question of how one can develop an expansive concept of womanhood, and thereby invoke a monist philosophy of transindividuality as the best philosophical framework to do so. Chapter 4 will explore how the philosophical outlook provided by the feminist interpretations of a seventeenth-century Marrano philosopher, Baruch Spinoza, can provide insights as to the transindividual nature of all bodies as well as to the monist philosophy that they presuppose—one where there is no opposition between bodies and minds, both being expressions under different attributes of the same unique and infinite substance. This will in turn provide the basis for arguing that there cannot be any strict separation between the subject and the object of knowledge, and that therefore a philosophy of transindividuality is also a transindividual philosophy (Chapter 5), that is, one where the philosophical discourse individualizes itself—thus explaining why we began writing this book through the pronoun "I," but moved to "we" in the very process of doing so. Chapter 6 will tackle the question of what enables us to speak about a single "woman" out of this transindividual ongoing process, and with the help of philosophical theories and artistic practices we will respond that it is through a process of story-telling.

After the intermezzo *Itinerarium in semen*, showing how at the beginning was movement, Part III will explore the process of ontogenesis of gendered and sexuated bodies by looking at the *supra-*, *inter-*, and *infra*-individual levels and thus focusing on the interstices available to us currently to do so. Whereas the *supra*-individual level will lead us to explore the global geopolitics of ontogenesis and thus claim for a form of "de-colonial" and "de-imperial" feminism (Chapter 7), the examination of the *inter*-actions between gendered bodies will lead to an analysis of the capitalist mode of (re)production, where the prefix "re" in parentheses is meant to signal how there cannot be capitalist production without the reproduction of the laborers themselves, despite the fact that the very putting between parentheses of the "reproduction" has been one of the tools whereby gendered bodies were created. Finally, Chapter 9 will look at the *infra*-actions, and thus at how gendered beings come into being through the (re)productive capacity of animals, plants, and even inanimate matter, thus arguing that a transindividual ecology cannot but question the hierarchy of man(on top of)>woman(on top of)> animals (on top of)>plants(on top of)>inanimate matter. In sum, a transindividual ecology cannot but be a queering of ecology.

This book stems from a utopian vision, that of a society where people will pursue their liberation without creating further hierarchies for other people and for the other-than-human life forms. Utopias are realist because they tell us where we (do not) stand. An anarchafeminist utopia tells us that a society where all and every woman is free is still far from coming, but it also tells us that it is the many of us who are working in that direction. Some call it intersectional feminism, others call it ecofeminism, other still call it queer struggles, or feminism without borders: the name changes and so do the political agendas, but the fundamental message remains the same—feminism does not mean the liberation of a few privileged women: it means liberation for all of us.

PART ONE

Bodies in plural and their oppression

In 2015, the New York State Education Department (NYSED) launched a new disability awareness campaign. As part of the effort to encourage differently abled people to work, the NYSED circulated a subway advertisement entitled "Do you have a disability? Do you want to work?" and enriched it with a number of images, representing, presumably, people who had some type of physical or mental challenge. The message communicated by words is clear enough: It tells you that if you have a disability, and you want to work, you can take advantage of the benevolent NYSED (how happy this can make you is underlined by the fact that the people represented are smiling). But, besides words, what is being communicated at what we can call the imaginal level, that is, at the level of images that are (re)presentations and thus also presences in themselves? What are images, particularly as they work both at the conscious and unconscious level,[1] telling us? And perhaps most importantly: what are they not telling, yet surreptitiously communicating?

The images on display showed, beginning from the top right, a Latino construction worker, an African American student, a (possibly Latina)

---

[1] We use the term "imaginal" in the sense discussed in Chiara Bottici, *Imaginal Politics: Images Beyond the Imagination and Beyond the Imaginary* (Columbia University Press: New York, 2014). We will come back to the philosophy of the imaginal later on in the book.

middle-class woman who is being helped by another woman, an African American mechanic in front of a car, and, finally, an elderly white middle-class woman using a computer.[2] For the typical New York subway user, the images cannot but convey a very clear message: disability is likely to concern racialized working-class bodies, racialized youth, and women, because, even when comfortably sitting at a desk, they are still likely to need some help. This is what is visible in those images. Let us now ask what remains *invisible*. What is absent and yet perhaps still powerfully present? Who is the conspicuous absence in these images, the one who supposedly does not need to be addressed by a disability campaign, the one who precisely because of this conspicuous absence is implicitly represented as immune from disability? The cisgendered white middle-class male. This is his invisible privilege: he is the exception to the disability that can normally happen to people of an inferior status.

Conversely, notice, how race, gender, and class intersect with one another in the images above mentioned. In the top-right image, we have someone who is both a Latino and a construction worker: would he be less likely to be differently abled had he been a white working-class man? The young school boy is an African American: are white youths immune from disability? Last, but not least: the only possibly white and middle-class representatives are both women, and significantly, both are being helped, either by a computer or by another woman. Are white middle-class men immune to the need for help? Why has it not occurred to the designer of the advertisement to insert a white man, among all of these diverse bodies?

One could continue the analysis of the imaginal side of the campaign and highlight other features, such as the hetero- and cisnormative[3] framework of the advertisement. All bodies represented are cis-bodies who are performing rather stereotyped gender roles: men are doing the hard physical work (mechanic and construction), while lightly dressed women are all sitting in front of tables (and being helped). By excluding gender non-conforming bodies and simultaneously insisting on the

---

[2] On this image, see Chiara Bottici, "Bodies in Plural: Towards an Anarchafeminist Manifesto," *Thesis Eleven*, 142 (2017), 99–11.

[3] We use the term "cisnormativity" to mean the view that projects "cis-bodies" as the social norm, and which implicitly, or explicitly, presents "trans-bodies" as an anomaly. Similarly, we use "heteronormativity" to mean the view according to which "homo-sexuals" are an anomaly. We will discuss this notion in Chapter 3.

stereotypical male *versus* female roles, the advertisement turns the male/ female binary into a dichotomy, that is, into an opposition that is both mutually exclusive but also jointly exhaustive of the gender possibilities. Finally, notice that only men are represented as looking straight at you, while women's gaze is always directed elsewhere: presumably towards the source of help for which they display a need. Could this subtle, yet unspoken, lowering of women's gazes be linked to the fact that, despite all the talk about the alleged equality between men and women, the latter are still subject to systematic discrimination? Is being exposed to such images when we enter the subway affecting the way in which bodies are perceived as well as the way in which they perceive themselves?

More could be said in that respect, but for now notice that, when it comes to representing bodies—and in particular bodies who are likely to be affected by disability, gender, sexuality, class, and race—all of these factors intersect with one another. But if that is the case, does it even make sense to put forward a specifically feminist proposal? If different axes of oppression are always meant to intersect, why focus on feminism to the detriment of all others?

In Chapter 1, we address this question by first showing the usefulness, but also the limits, of the notion of intersectionality, and thus arguing for the need to combine it with an anarchafeminist philosophy. In the following two chapters, we will argue that the latter can unite the insights of anarchism, according to which in order to fight one form of oppression one needs to fight all of them, with the feminism insistence on the need to fight against the oppression of women *qua* women. Feminism alone is not enough, since it has proved to be compatible with domination, hence the need for an anarchafeminist philosophy.

1 Intersectional struggles, interlocking oppressions

There exists now a great deal work showing how different forms of oppression reinforce and sustain each other. In the English language, the term "intersectionality" has gained traction in the last few decades precisely for its capacity to convey this message in a single word: from the closed spaced of academic feminism, "intersectionality" has now reached a wide popularity in the anglophone public sphere.

While the term originated from the field of Black feminism, where it was first coined in 1989 by Kimberlé W. Crenshaw to address the specific oppression faced by women of African American descent in the United States, it has subsequently generated a very heightened debate outside of those boundaries.[1] Despite controversies around the term, its popularity is such that some have, as already mentioned, declared it "the most important contribution that women's studies has made so far."[2] The main

---

[1] Kimberlé Crenshaw, "Demarginalizing the Intersection of Race and Sex: A Black Feminist Critique of Antidiscrimination Doctrine, Feminist Theory and Antiracist Politics," *University of Chicago Legal Forum* (1989): 139–67. Kimberlé Crenshaw used the term 'intersectionality' in 1989, but its intellectual origins go much further back in time. While some have traced its origins in Black feminism in the US (Elena Ruíz, "Framing Intersectionality," in *The Routledge Companion to the Philosophy of Race*, eds. Linda Martin Alcoff, Paul C. Taylor, Luvell Anderson [London: Routledge, 2017]), we will emphasize its convergence with ideas circulating in anarchist movements. From Bakunin's early remarks on how patriarchy intersected with authoritarianism (Mikhail Bakunin, "Against Patriarchal Authority," *Anarchism: A Documentary History of Libertarian Ideas, Vol. 1*, ed. Robert Graham [Montreal: Black Rose Books, 2005]) to Emma Goldman's anarchafeminist writings, we see a recurring emphasis on how different forms of oppression intersect with one other (Emma Goldman, *Anarchism and Other Essays* (New York: Dover, 1969).
[2] Leslie McCall, "The Complexity of Intersectionality," *Signs: Journal of Women in Culture and Society* 30, no. 3 (2008): 1771–1800.

insight behind this keyword is that if we want to understand how the oppression of women works, we cannot limit ourselves to one single factor (be it gender, race, class, or heterosexism), but need to investigate the way in which a plurality of such factors intersect with one another in order to reinforce and reproduce the inferior position of women. Once we are equipped with such an intersectional lens, we can perceive the specific form of oppression that intersections create, which changes in every context for different social groups.

While feminists have used the term to denote all sorts of intersections but also the complexity of identities in general, Black feminists and women of color criticized the "academization" of the concept and tried to re-appropriate its initial critical impetus.[3] In her original usage of the term, Crenshaw coined the term "intersectionality" to address a problem she perceived within the very specific context of US discrimination laws during the 1980s: whereas the latter recognized harms done on the basis of gender *and* those done on the basis of race discrimination, they did not recognize the discrimination against "Black women" as a distinct category, because by doing so interpreters of those laws feared they would end up creating a super-category of "Black womanhood." Against this tendency to treat race and gender as mutually exclusive categories of experience, enabling us to consider harms done on the basis of gender *or* race only at once, Crenshaw argued that, in the case of Black women, race and gender intersect in such a way that they create a situation that is unique and that cannot be reduced to the simple sum of its elements.[4] For Crenshaw, this is because human experience is not additive, but temporally thick with the simultaneous intersection of different socio-historical identity categories: Black women experience discrimination as a compound harm against them as "Black women"—and not as the sum of the harm being done to them as "women" *plus* those done to them as "Black."[5] Black women can indeed suffer discrimination in ways that are both similar and different from those experienced by white women and by Black men respectively. Although there are occasions when Black women experience discrimination along one single axis, and can consequently decide to

---

[3] Elena Ruíz, "Framing Intersectionality," 335.
[4] Kimberlé Crenshaw, "Demarginalizing the Intersection of Race and Sex," 140.
[5] Ibid, 149.

mobilize under the respective banner of "Blackness" or "womanhood," it is never clear for subjects who are at the intersection between different axes of oppression to determine where discrimination comes from. Like in a traffic intersection, one cannot a priori know whether the harm is coming from one side or another: it is being positioned in a specific location, created by the thickening over time of multiple historical discriminatory practices, that determines the peculiarity of that form of oppression.[6] Erasing the specificity of the harm done to Black women means not only that their experience is made unaccountable, and that they are thus deprived of the legal means of reclaiming reparations, but also that that they are epistemologically subordinated to the centrality of white women's and Black men's experiences in the conceptualization of discrimination.[7]

This was the rationale for the introduction of the term "intersectionality." However, through its increasing popularity, the concept has been generalized and turned into a tool for analyzing the oppression of all women. At times, it even left women's studies and became just a metaphor for the complexity of identity in general, including not only white women, but also white men, who are also said to be inevitably placed at some type of gender and race crossroads.[8] In a sort of perverse, albeit probably unintended, turn of the wheel, the success of the concept ended up replicating the harm that it was supposed to remedy: the erasure of the specific position of Black women. It is therefore not by chance that so many feminists of color have decried this development in an attempt at "saving intersectionality from feminist intersectionality studies."[9] In their view, by applying the intersectional models to any sort of identity, the

---

[6] For instance, in a significant passage explaining why oppression is analogous to a four-way traffic intersection where danger can come from a number of directions, she writes: "[It] may flow in one direction, and it may flow in another. If an accident happens in an intersection, it may be caused by cars traveling from any number of directions and, sometimes, from all of them. Similarly, if a Black woman is harmed because she is in an intersection, her injury could result from sex discrimination or race discrimination" (ibid).

[7] Elena Ruíz, "Framing Intersectionality," 339.

[8] Ibid, 341–4.

[9] Sirma Bilge, "Intersectionality Undone: Saving Intersectionality from Feminist Intersectionality Studies," *Du Bois Review* 10, no. 2 (2013), 405–24.

term went through a process of "whitening" and dilution that deprived it of its original critical impetus.[10]

Yet, there seems to be something very promising about the concept itself that has understandably led many feminists to make recourse to it. According to Jennifer Nash, for instance, as intersectionality has become a central tool for feminist analysis, Black feminists have shown an excessive defensiveness towards the concept, as manifested by multiple attempts to police intersectionality's usages and circulation. On the contrary, according to Nash, Black feminists should let go of their protectionist stance towards the concept and rather embrace its visionary world-making possibilities as testified by its fortune in the field.[11]

Jennifer Nash's critique, however, does not seem to take into sufficient account that the question is not just one of (academic) ownership of one concept. Given the history of erasure of the contribution of women of color to feminism, it is all too understandable that Black feminists resist the whitening of the concept and its transformation into just another metaphor for the complexity of identity, including that of their oppressors. Indeed, the re-appropriation of this term by white feminists risks providing them *with an appearance* of inclusiveness ("we are using a concept coming from our Black sisters") without any concrete change in the substance of the conceptual and political attitude that underlies the theories for the purpose of which they are invoked. If the only result of an engagement with the Black feminist intersectional literature is the insight that we are all intersectional, then there is no need to take seriously the challenge of Black feminism, and white feminists can continue to do business as usual.

---

[10] The term has even been taken up by normative analytic anglophone philosophy to propose a so-called "metaphysics of intersectionality": According to Sara Bernstein, for instance, intersectionality should not only be thought about through the metaphor of traffic intersections, but also through contemporary "analytic metaphysics" as a way to show that, as certain strands of anglophone analytic philosophy have argued, it is not the conjuncts that explain the conjunction, but the conjunction that explains the conjuncts (Sara Bernstein, "The Metaphysics of Intersectionality," *Philosophical Studies* 177, no. 2 (2020), 331). This brought the concept to a metaphysical level of abstraction where it can apply to any sort of identity. Among those who defended the original critical impetus of the concept of intersectionality, see, for instance, Sirma Bilge, "Intersectionality Undone," 2013; Elena Ruíz "Framing Intersectionality," 2017; Patricia Hill Collins, *Intersectionality as Critical Social Theory* (Durham: Duke University Press, 2019); and Patricia Hill Collins and Sirma Bilge, *Intersectionality* (Cambridge: Polity, 2016).

[11] Jennifer C. Nash, *Black Feminism Reimagined: After Intersectionality* (Durham: Duke University Press, 2018), 137.

However, in the words of Audre Lorde: "as white women ignore their built-in privilege of whiteness and define *woman* in terms of their own experience alone, then women of Color become *other,* the outsider whose experience and tradition is too 'alien' to comprehend."[12] Or, we can now add, too familiar, which is what happens when intersectionality is turned into a general theory of identity. In both ways, difference is swept under the carpet: either into a false universal "woman" category, or into an inassimilable "Black" difference. This, according to Lorde, explains the marginality of Black women's experiences and literature in women studies courses and literature in the academy. To this remark, we must add the fact that, being placed at the intersection between racial and class oppression, many Black women simply cannot afford the luxury of writing long treatises to be published in academic presses—books that can pair with those of their white counterparts. Therefore, as Audre Lorde points out, in order to be really inclusive of different theories one has to look also in those places and formats "alien" to mainstream academic presses, such as poetry and even songs.[13]

Yet, at this point of the argument one may further ask: is re-appropriating the term "intersectionality" and defending its "Blackness" the best tool to prevent erasure of the experience of Black women? Is the problem only that of the "academization" of the concept? In the end, the term itself first appeared in an academic publication where it was used by an activist academic.[14] Some have argued that the term has itself popularized an idea that was already circulating in other Black feminist movements, but non-academic ones. For instance, according to Rogue and Volcano, the birth of intersectionality should be placed in the statement by the Combahee River Collective, a collective of Black, lesbian, working-class women, who did not use the term "intersectionality" but provided the very conceptual apparatus for its appearance.[15] The first

---

[12] Audre Lorde, *Sister Outsider: Essays and Speeches* (Berkeley: Crossing Press, 1984), 117.

[13] The hierarchy between different modes of "theory making" has often worked as a tool for silencing some voices while systematically privileging others. Ibid, 116; Audre Lorde, *The Master's Tools Will Never Dismantle the Master's House* (London: Penguin, 2017), 4; Patricia Hill Collins, *Black Feminist Thought: Knowledge, Consciousness, and the Politics of Empowerment* (New York: Routledge, 2000), 268–9.

[14] The first academic text in which it appeared is the already quoted Kimberlé Crenshaw, "Demarginalizing the Intersection of Race And Sex."

[15] J. Rogue and Abbey Volcano, "Insurrection at the intersections," in *Quiet Rumors: Anarcha-feminist Reader*, eds. Dark Star Collective (Oakland: AK Press 2012), 43. Elena Ruíz also insists that the Combahee River Collective's 1977 statement contains what is "arguably the first methodological account of intersectionality" (Elena Ruíz, "Framing Intersectionality," 337).

paragraph of their April 1977 statement, which has subsequently been anthologized numerous times, ends indeed as follows: "The most general statement of our politics at the present time would be that we are actively committed to struggling against racial, sexual, heterosexual, and class oppression, and see as our particular task the development of integrated analysis and practice based upon the fact that the major systems of oppression are interlocking."[16]

In this document, we can perceive a clear awareness that as lesbian, Black, working-class women, they faced a unique combination of challenges, one where it was not just the two factors mentioned by Crenshaw in 1989 that intersected, but rather a multiplicity of them. By focusing only on race and gender, one risks erasing the experience of other Black women who also suffer from class and heterosexist discrimination. For Black lesbians, heterosexism is a particularly salient axis of oppression because, given the perceived link between heterosexuality and white patriarchy, lesbian Black women also have to struggle with the "belief in the protective coloration of heterosexual relationships."[17] The latter, in its turn, is inseparable from class oppression, because many working-class Black women in that intersection feel that they cannot afford the privilege of sexual fluidity. In sum, they felt they were at the bottom of the society they lived in, so much so that, they hyperbolically conclude: "If Black women were free, it would mean that everyone else would have to be free since our freedom would necessitate the destruction of all systems of oppression."[18] This sentence could be used as epigraph for this chapter, since it provides an important clue into the entire argument of the book.

Hence also their emphasis on the importance of what they termed "identity politics," an expression that meant for them something very different from what is today commonly associated with the term. For them, it meant pointing towards the overwhelming layers of oppression they had to face in a daily life and death struggle: "we believe that the most profound and potentially most radical politics come directly out of our own identity, as opposed to working to end somebody else's

---

[16] The Combahee River Collective "A Black Feminist Statement," in *But Some of Us Are Brave: Black Women's Studies*, eds. Gloria T. Hull, Patricia Bell Scott, and Barbara Smith (New York: The Feminist Press, 1982), 13.

[17] Audre Lorde, "Age, Race, Class, and Sex," in *Sister Outsider: Essays and Speeches* (Berkeley: Crossing Press, 1984), 121.

[18] Combahee River Collective, "A Black Feminist Statement," 18.

oppression."[19] As Black, lesbian, working-class women in US society, in a context where Black women were the lowest-paid workers in the country, and where, as feminist and lesbians, they were often deemed betrayers of the united Black struggles, since lesbianism was perceived by many as just another white privilege, placing their struggles on their specific identity meant indeed to call for a total revolution, and thus for "the most radical politics" one could have imagined at the time. But when the term "identity politics" is taken out of this context and placed within a liberal understanding of intersectionality, where *everybody's* identity is said to be multiple, intersectional and thus in need of recognition, then we are led once again to a loss of the critical potential of such a concept.

Against this tendency, one can always go back to the supposed origins of a concept, when it possessed a critical momentum, and thus reclaim, as Elena Ruíz does, the pre-history of intersectionality. Ruíz's strategy consists in identifying a specific "proto-intersectionality" in nineteenth-century authors and activists and emphasize the centrality of the work of Black women such as Maria Stewart, Sojourner Truth, Anna Julia Cooper, Ida B. Wells, Elise McDougald, Sadie Alexander, and Frances Beale.[20] But would that be enough, or should we not instead follow the warning of the historian Roxanne Dunbar-Ortiz and remember the vast majority of anarchafeminist women, who may not have called themselves "anarchafeminist" or "intersectional feminists," but yet have been fighting their battles under the claim that different systems of oppression reinforce each other and so we cannot fight one without fighting all of them?[21] There is a veritable historical amnesia surrounding the foremothers of

---

[19] Ibid, 16.

[20] Elena Ruíz, "Framing Intersectionality," 336.

[21] Elena Ruíz addresses the question of the history and even prehistory of intersectionality, but never mentions the convergence with anarchafeminist struggles. Significantly, though, the summary she gives of the Black feminist articulations of intersectionality bears a striking resemblance to anarchafeminism. She writes: "Over time, five key features emerged from black feminist intellectual traditions and their various articulations of the intersectionality paradigm: (1) an emphasis on lived experience as the starting point of critical inquiry; (2) an emphasis on the multidimensionality of experience; (3) a diagnostic acumen for the role of *power*; (4) a focus on the systematic, multivalent, and interlocking nature of oppression; and (5) an emphasis on the emancipatory aims of critical analyses of structural oppression" (Elena Ruíz "Framing Intersectionality," 337). As we will see in this book, all five key features can also be applied to the anarchafeminist movement. See also: Roxanne Dunbar-Ortiz, "Quiet Rumors: An Introduction to this Anthology," in *Quiet Rumors*, 11.

anarchafeminism, of whom only a handful are known. And yet, as Dunbar-Ortiz puts it: "the historical amnesia we suffer serves well the state authorities, military-industrial civilization, and the capitalist thieves that control our lives and destinies."[22] And, we may add, it serves them well, because it helps us to forget, for instance, that a dismantling of the sexism, classism, racism, and heterosexism that the Combahee River Collective well identified can hardly be achieved without criticizing the state, a formidable apparatus where a tiny minority of people rules the overwhelming majority of them.[23] It is indeed through state apparatuses and identity papers, that, as we will see later on, gender identity is attached to every citizen from birth, and thus inscribed into their lives, not to mention the central role states play in perpetrating the coercive apparatus that implement a market economy, the prison complex and racial policies.

The choice between "intersectionality" and the "interlocking systems of oppression" seems to be one between what is the best metaphor one can use to describe the idea that systems of oppression reciprocally reinforce each other so you cannot fight one without fighting all the others. One could complicate things further, and add to the list of potential good metaphors Gloria Anzaldúa's Chicana "borderland theory," which depicts borders as an open wound, or Maria Lugones' "curdling," an intersectional practice of resistance that works against the logic of purity, considered oppressive by itself, and includes therefore practices such as gender transgression, code-switching, and multilingual experimentation.[24] Or perhaps Hillary Lazar's anarchafeminist metaphor of the tangled knot, containing countless strands, each one representing a different axis of oppression and all tightly bound together.[25] Given their entanglement, it is necessary to loosen all the strands if the knot is to be undone. But, as Lazar points out in *Until All Are Free: Black Feminism, Anarchism and Interlocking Oppressions*, in some contexts, one strand may need more immediate attention and loosening, while in others it may be necessary to pull multiple strands at once.[26] "While the knot of oppression will remain

---

[22] Roxanne Dunbar-Ortiz, "Quiet Rumors: An Introduction to this Anthology," 11.

[23] We will come back to the question of the state in Part III.

[24] Gloria Anzaldúa, *Borderlands/La Frontera: The New Mestiza* (San Francisco: Aunt Lute Books, 2012); Maria Lugones, "Purity, Impurity, and Separation," *Signs* 19, no. 2 (1994).

[25] Hillary Lazar, "Until All Are Free: Black Feminism, Anarchism, And Interlocking Oppression," in *Perspectives on Anarchist Theory* 29 (2016).

[26] Hillary Lazar, 48.

ensnared until all strands are free, it is vital to understand that interdependent as the threads may be, each must be attended to both as an individual strand and as part of the collective struggle."[27] The tangled knot is indeed a conceptualization that helps us avoid the totalizing false universality of the "alls" (be they all "Black women," or all "women") that erase distinct experiences of subjugation, while still allowing to struggle for the untying of the entire knot because none of us will be free until everybody else is.

That is indeed the terrain where the history of intersectional Black feminism and that of anarchafeminist struggles converge, while retaining their distinctiveness. The awareness that systems of oppression are interconnected, and hence requiring the concurrent rooting out of all forms of domination, is at the heart of anarchist theory, as much as it is at the center of the work of intersectional Black feminist thinkers such as Audre Lorde and bell hooks.[28] As bell hooks underlined, what different systems of oppression have in common is indeed a "politic of domination." If we look at the multiple axes of oppression of race, class, and gender (but we should add heterosexism, among others), it becomes evident that this is their shared ideological ground: they all exhibit a belief in domination, that is, the belief that some people are superior to others, and thus entitled to dominate them.[29] They may appear, and be experienced, as different systems of oppression, but they all inhabit the same house.

Indeed, what is racism if not the belief in the inherent superiority of one race over all others and the right to dominance that ensues from such superiority? "Sexism, the belief in the inherent superiority of one sex over the other and thereby the right to dominance. Ageism. Heterosexism. Elitism. Classism."[30] The list goes on. All of these different axes of oppression converge in the belief that some bodies are superior to others, which in turn justifies and perpetrates a politics of domination.[31] Whereas the concept of oppression points to a systemic impediment to the free

---

[27] Ibid, 48.

[28] Ibid, 41.

[29] bell hooks, *Talking Back: Thinking Feminist, Thinking Black* (New York: Routledge, 2015), 294.

[30] Audre Lorde, "Age, Race, Class, and Sex," 115.

[31] Similarly, Black feminist Patricia Hill Collins speaks about "the matrix of domination" (Patricia Hill, *Black Feminist Thought: Knowledge, Consciousness, and the Politics of Empowerment*, 227–8, 274–6). For a discussion of the politics of domination from the point of view of contemporary anarchafeminism, see Hillary Lazar, "Until All Are Free," 40.

development of certain people and social groups, that of domination also points to the much more insidious and pervasive "piece of the oppressor which is planted deep inside each of us," as Audre Lorde put it.[32] We can therefore conclude that systems of oppression reinforce each other because they inhabit the same house whose foundation is a politics of domination, that is a politics based on the assumption that some people are superior to others and therefore have a right to dominate them. This is a belief that is (re)produced both by institutions such as capitalism and statism, and by individuals themselves in their daily life. Without the internalization of such a belief, and thus the collaboration of the internal oppressor, no institution would ever be able to sustain itself for a long period of time.[33]

Hence Audre Lorde's warning that "the master's tools will never dismantle the master's house," which does not simply mean that white theory cannot dismantle white privilege, but rather, and much more radically, that theoretical tools imbued with sexism, racism, classism, and heterosexism cannot dismantle the master's house, that is, his politics of domination.[34] You can fight one axis of oppression, and even be apparently successful at that, but until that entire house is shaken to foundations, it will keep replicating and even inventing other forms of oppression. Indeed, as we read in the often-forgotten continuation of that passage: "The master's tools will never dismantle the master's house. They allow us temporarily to beat him at his own game, but they will never allow us to bring about genuine change. And this fact is only threatening to women who still define the master's house as their only source of support."[35]

Emphasizing this convergence between Black feminism and anarchist theory does not mean to deny the independence of the two feminist traditions, but rather insisting on the importance of a "politics of solidarity" as the only possible remedy against the politics of domination.[36] As Audre Lorde observed: "Our future survival is predicated upon our ability to relate within equality. As women, we must root out internalized

---

[32] Audre Lorde, "Age, Race, Class, and Sex," 123.

[33] As we already mentioned, anarchist theorists called this the "dilemma of voluntary servitude," a dilemma that Étienne de la Boétie formulated in quite useful terms as early as 1553 in the "Discourse on voluntary servitude" (Étienne de La Boétie, *The Politics of Obedience: The Discourse of Voluntary Servitude* (Auburn: Mises Institute, 2015).

[34] Audre Lorde, "Age, Race, Class, and Sex: Women Redefining Difference," 123.

[35] Audre Lorde, *The Master's Tools Will Never Dismantle the Master's House*, 19.

[36] Hillary Lazar, "Until All Are Free," 39.

patterns of oppression within ourselves if we are to move beyond the most superficial aspect of social change. Now we must recognize differences among women who are our equals, neither inferior nor superior, and devise ways to use each other's difference to enrich our visions and joint struggles. The future of our earth may depend upon the ability of all women to identify and develop new definitions of power and new patterns of relating across difference."[37]

Looking for a new definition of power and a new terrain that will enable us to "relate within equality" is the main task of this book. Not just the liberation of women, but the entire future of the earth, Lorde lucidly points out, depends on this. But if that is the aim, can intersectionality alone provide such a new definition of power and a new pattern for relating across differences? It is a crucial tool to emphasize that each intersection is different, and thus that each thread of the knot needs to be analyzed with an intersectional lens.[38] As a consequence, it can tell us how specific configurations of oppression work, but not yet how and why domination as such should be abolished. For instance, there have also been quite misleading liberal interpretations of intersectional feminisms, which generated a strategy of "respecting diversity" aimed at recognizing the multifaceted features of identity but incapable of addressing the persistence of a politics of domination in general.[39] According to this view, we all experience race, gender, heterosexism, and class divisions, and therefore the solution is to recognize each other's diversity. This has for instance led to the "gravely confused notion that class oppression needs to be rectified by rich people treating poor people 'nicer' while still maintaining class society."[40] Respecting diversity may be important in disentangling some of the threads of the knot, but is certainly alone insufficient to abolish class exploitation, one of the most pervasive form of domination in global capitalism. Furthermore, if we merely have to respect each other's differences, how will we find an end to the items to be added to our intersectional list?

It is in the attempt to render a plurality of axes of oppression that publication titles have started to grow: from Angela Davis' path-breaking

---

[37] Audre Lorde, "Age, Race, Class, and Sex," 123.
[38] On intersectionality as an "open-ended hermeneutic lens" see: Elena Ruíz, "Framing Intersectionality," 346.
[39] J. Rogue and Abbey Volcano, "Insurrection at the Intersections," 44.
[40] Ibid, 44.

Women, Race and Class (1981) we moved to David Newman's *Identities and Inequalities: Exploring the Intersections of Race, Class, Gender and Sexuality* (2001), which adds to the list of factors the then still-common, but now contested, distinction between sex and gender.[41] It is however in the last few decades that intersectionality blossomed in the academia— and title length of the corresponding publications consequently expanded. Under the influence of postcolonial feminists, who underlined that the emancipation of women in the global north may happen at the price of further oppression of women from the global south, and thus pushed white feminism to rethink its intrinsic ethnocentric biases, the term "empire" has become an inevitable addendum to the list: it is not sufficient to speak about "Black women" because where one is placed within the imperial cartography of power also creates significant differences.[42] The latter, however, does not stop there, as other forms of oppression have rightly been brought to the scene. For instance, Brooke Holmes entitled her work "Marked Bodies: Gender, Race, Class, Age, Disability, Disease."[43] Although she overlooked sexuality (which is different from gender)[44] and empire (which is different from race), it is to her credit that she highlighted other important items such as age, disability, and disease.

Despite the fact that very important empirical work has been done under the heading of "intersectionality," there remain a few problems which go beyond the editorial challenge of how to accommodate books with excessively long titles. First, any list is open to the objection

---

[41] Angela Davis, *Women, Race and Class* (New York: Random House, 1981); David M. Newman, *Identities and Inequalities: Exploring the Intersections of Race, Class, Gender, and Sexuality* (New York: McGraw Hill, 2001). More recently see, Patricia Hill Collins and Margaret L. Andersen, *Race, Class & Gender: An Anthology* (Belmont: Wadsworth, 2012); Susan J. Ferguson, *Race, Gender, Sexuality, and Social Class: Dimensions of Inequality and Identity* (London: Sage, 2013). For a succinct summary of recent critiques of the distinction between sex and gender, see: Tina Chanter, *Gender: Key Concepts in Philosophy* (London: Continuum, 2006), 1–7.

[42] See for instance: Laura E. Donaldson, *Decolonizing Feminisms: Race, Gender, and Empire Building* (Chapel Hill: UNC Press, 1992). We will come back to the question of empire and cartography later on.

[43] Brooke Holmes, "Marked Bodies (Gender, Race, Class, Age, Disability, Disease)," *A Cultural History of the Human Body, Vol. 1: In Antiquity*, ed. Daniel H. Garrison (Oxford: Berg, 2010), 159–83.

[44] We mean here to note that questions of sexual orientations (gay, lesbian, bisexual etc) are different from those of gender embodiment (cis, trans, trans-woman, etc), not to retrieve the sex (nature) *versus* gender (nurture) dichotomy, which, as we will see, is incompatible with a transindividual philosophy.

that it cannot be anything other than incomplete: if it is the case that you cannot understand the oppression of women in our societies without looking at the way in which different factors intersect with one another, why stop with the items discussed above? Why not include "beauty," for instance? One can hardly ignore how capitalism, class, heterosexist, and race expectations coalesce with images of beauty in transmitting hegemonic views of womanhood. Just measure the space devoted to women's beauty products with those reserved for men's in a supermarket and you will get a spatial representation of the different degrees to which beauty expectations impact men and women.[45] But would it be enough to add yet another item? Will there ever be an end to it? The problem with lists is actually twofold: that they are necessarily incomplete, while at the same time being necessarily closed. By naming certain items, any list operates an implicit selection, privileging some factors over others that are left out of it. And we have to remind ourselves that the oppressed can always in turn become the oppressors. To put it bluntly: Any intersectional list is deemed to tell us, at the same time, too much and too little. How to avoid them, though, if we want to render a plurality?

Second, while intersectionality is a good tool via which to orient empirical analysis since it prevents any sort of reductionism (e.g. culture being *the* factor that explains everything), there is the risk of losing something about the specificity of women's oppression. Intersectionality is a crucial advocacy and activist tool for addressing the specificity of certain forms of oppression, and thus an invaluable platform on which to build specific political programs and demands. But it cannot be turned into a general feminist theory able to provide not simply a diagnosis of specific forms of oppression, but also a positive proposal on how to move forward in the feminist movement. Indeed, if we take intersectionality as the only basis for theory-making, and keep insisting that all forms of oppression are meant to intersect with one another, does it even make sense to speak about "feminism"? If lists are ever expanding, what is so specific about women's condition? What are we saying when we say "women"? Is that word not in itself surreptitiously suggesting a cis- and

---

[45] An example of empirical analysis of discrimination is provided by Marco Castillo, Ragan Petrie, and Maximo Torero, "Beautiful or White? Discrimination in Group Formation," *GMU Working Paper in Economics*, no. 12–29 (2012), whereas Johanna Oksala makes a similar point at the philosophical level, by analyzing how techniques of beauty contributed to the creation of a specifically neo-liberal subject of feminism. See: Johanna Oksala, "The Neoliberal Subject of Feminism," *Journal of the British Society for Phenomenology* 42, no. 1 (2011), 104–20.

heteronormative gender distinction between "women" and "men" that can itself be a source of oppression for those who identify themselves as neither of them? Can we talk about the specific condition of women, and justify a distinctively *feminist* position, without falling into the trap of heteronormativity or, even worse, essentialism?

In order to respond to this criticism, this book puts forward a call for an anarchafeminist philosophy. Doing so means keeping together the two claims: that there is something *specific* in the oppression of women and that in order to fight it you have to fight *all* other forms of oppression. In other words, it means defending a position that is both feminist and anarchist at the same time. In what follows, we will defend such a position at both the methodological and the substantive level (although, as it will become clearer later on, this is only a distinction that holds in theory since in practice the two levels converge). At the substantive level, defending an anarchafeminist approach means arguing that there is no *archē*, that is, no unique principle or origin of the subjugation of women, because freedom is indivisible, so we cannot be free unless everybody else on Earth is also free. At the methodological level, it implies insisting on the plurality of the axes of oppression and thus investigating how they intersect with each other in each context, while at the same time looking into how they inhabit the same common house of a politics of domination.[46] It is at this level that, as it has been argued, intersectionality can be particularly insightful towards the development of an "intersectional anarchafeminism," that is, an anarchafeminist philosophy that recognizes the independence of individual struggles, but also opens the path for a politics of solidarity between them on a global level.

---

[46] Among those who emphasized the importance of developing an intersectional anarchafeminist philosophy, see: Deric Shannon, "Articulating a Contemporary Anarcha-Feminism," *Theory in Action* 2, no. 3 (2009), 58–74; J. Rogue and Abbey Volcano, "Insurrection at the Intersections;" and Hillary Lazar, "Until All Are Free: Black Feminism, Anarchism, And Interlocking Oppression."

2 Anarchism beyond Eurocentrism and beyond sexism

"Anarchafeminism" is an expression that combines "anarchism" and "feminism." Similar expressions are "anarcho-feminism" or "anarchist feminism" or, more recently, "anarchistix-feministix." When approaching the term "anarchy," given that it is often used as mere synonym of "chaos," it is useful to look at its genealogy. The purpose of this genealogical work is not to provide a systematic reconstruction of the history of anarchism, but to identify those conceptual movements that are deposited in the meaning of the term "anarchy" (and "anarchism") so that we can situate our usage of the term within that genealogy, but also possibly move beyond it.

"Anarchy" derives from the assemblage of the Ancient Greek privative *alpha* and the noun *archē*, which means "beginning, first cause, first principle, supreme power, dominion and empire."[1] Despite its derivation from Ancient Greek roots, the first attested appearance of "anarchy" in English is from 1539, when it was probably imported into that language from the Medieval Latin "*anarchia*."[2] Although the appearance of the

---

[1] Henry George Liddell and Robert Scott, *Liddell and Scott's Greek–English Lexicon, Abridged* (Mansfield Centre, CT: Martino, 2015). On the meaning of *archē* in ancient Greek sources, see Stathis Gourgouris, "archē," *Political Concepts: A Critical Lexicon,* 2013. Gourgouris emphasized that the term meant both origin and rule, and uses his reading of Ancient Greek sources to argue that anarchy is the *archē* of democracy.

[2] For instance, the 1936 edition of *The Shorter Oxford English Dictionary on Historical Principles* provides the following entry for anarchy: "Anarchy: 1539. [ad. Gr. ἀναρχία, or med. L. *anarchia*; cf. Fr. *anarchie*.] 1. Absence of government; a state of lawlessness due to the absence or inefficiency of the supreme power; political disorder. 2. *trans.* Absence or

word in English is therefore a modern phenomenon, it is important to note that it was formed with a creative appropriation of Ancient Greek roots. Like the corresponding verb *archein*, the noun *archē* came to mean both the "beginning" and "rule," and in particular the idea of an "imperial," "supreme rule." The unification of the two semantic areas of "inception" and "domination" into the abstract concept of *archē* was, however, not present in the term from the very beginning. As Reiner Schürmann emphasized, it was indeed an innovation by Aristotle to connect the two meanings systematically and thereby turn *archē* into a philosophical concept that was destined to deeply influence Western metaphysics.[3] This unification and the formation of the abstract notion happen because, in the construction of his metaphysical system, Aristotle looked back at what he considered to be the first philosophers and identified them as those who first set up for a search of the *archē*. According to the Aristotelian reconstruction, which may reflect more closely Aristotle's own definition of philosophy than the intent of the so-called "first philosophers," philosophy was indeed born when thinkers such as Thales of Miletus began their search for the *archē*, that is, for the first origin and unique ruling principle of being. Some, like Thales, found it in water, while others like Anaximander, in the *apeiron*—literally what is without borders, and thus limits.[4]

---

non-recognition of authority in any sphere 1667; moral or intellectual disorder 1656." (William Little, H. W. Fowler, and J. Coulson, *The Shorter Oxford English Dictionary on Historical Principles*, ed. C. T. Onions (Oxford: Clarendon Press, 1936), 62. Similarly, the 2007 edition points to the origin of the term in medieval Latin, and to the conflation between the two meanings of "absence of government" and "disorder": "Anarchy noun. [origin: medieval Latin *anarchia* from Greek *anarkhia*, formed as anarch] 1. Absence of government in a society (orig. as a source of civil disorder, later also as a political ideal); a state of political or social confusion; absolute freedom of the individual. 2. transf. and fig. Absence or non-recognition of authority in any sphere; moral or intellectual conflict; a state of disorder; chaos." (Angus Stevenson and Lesley Brown, *Shorter Oxford English Dictionary on Historical Principles* [Oxford: Oxford University Press. 2007]). From the same 2007 edition, the entry "anarch" reads: "Anarch noun. [origin: Greek *anarkhos* without a chief, formed as an- + -arch.] 1. An instigator of anarchy, a leader of revolt. *poet.* 2. An anarchist. (Angus Stevenson and Lesley Brown, *Shorter Oxford English Dictionary on Historical Principles*).
[3] Reiner Schürmann, *Heidegger on Being and Acting: From Principles to Anarchy*, trans. Christine-Marie Gros (Bloomington: Indiana University Press, 1987), 47.
[4] On this point see, "Introduction" and "The Milesians" in Patricia Curd, *A Presocratics Reader: Selected Fragments and Testimonia* (Indianapolis: Hackett, 2011), 1–22. For a critique of the idea that the Milesian philosophers were the first "philosophers," see Giorgio Colli, *La nascita della filosofia* (Milan: Adelphi 1975), and *La sapienza greca. I, II, III*

Whether there could ever be any such thing as the "birth" of philosophy, and whether one could possibly exclusively locate it into Ancient Greece, must be left for another discussion.[5] For the time being, note that, in the Western philosophical terminology, *archē* came to mean both an overarching principle and a government. This, among other things, explains the possible conflation between philosophical and political anarchism: whereas the former insists there is no unique philosophical principle, the latter claims there is no legitimate government or leader. Although the two types of anarchism can converge, they can also proceed separately, so it is important to keep them distinct from one another. One can believe there is no philosophical *archē*, and still call for political leaders to provide a political one.[6] Conversely, one can argue that there should be no government, and thus be a political anarchist, but believe there is a philosophical *archē,* that is some form of principle organizing or even governing being.[7]

In both cases, though, "anarchism" presupposes the meaning of "absence of government," a meaning that, in common parlance, is often conflated with the extended, polemical meaning of "absence of order."[8]

(Milan: Adelphi 1977–8). According to Colli, the first so called "philosophers' were actually "*sapienti*," something more akin to shamans, upon whom Aristotle projected his own definition of what philosophy is, thereby turning them into the "first philosophers."

[5] For a critique of the narrative of the Greek birth of philosophy as a political myth, see: Chiara Bottici, *A Philosophy of Political Myth* (Cambridge, Cambridge University Press, 2007), 21–31. For a critique of the role that this narrative of Ancient Greece as the cradle of European civilizations played in the construction of a specific European identity, see: Chiara Bottici and Benoît Challand, *Imagining Europe: Myth, Memory, and Identity* (Cambridge: Cambridge University Press, 2013), and in particular pp. 87–110.

[6] As an example of a philosophical anarchism that does not automatically imply political anarchism, see Paul Feyerabend, who began his influential *Against Method* in this way: "The following essay is written in the conviction that *anarchism*, while perhaps not the most attractive *political* philosophy, is certainly excellent medicine for *epistemology*, and for the *philosophy of science.*" Paul Feyerabend, *Against Method* (London: Verso, 1993), 9.

[7] An example of political anarchism which does not imply philosophical anarchism is Pyotr Kropotkin, who based his anarchism on the principle of mutual aid, and who argued that cooperation between life species is the driving force of evolution, and is therefore committed to arguing for the existence of a philosophical principle as the basis of life. See: Pyotr Kropotkin, *Mutual Aid: A Factor in Evolution* (London: William Heinemann, 1902).

[8] Both the 1936 edition of *The Shorter Oxford English Dictionary on Historical Principles* and its 2007 edition register this conflation (William Little, H. W. Fowler, and J. Coulson, *The Shorter Oxford English Dictionary on Historical Principles*, 62; Angus Stevenson and Lesley Brown, *Shorter Oxford English Dictionary on Historical Principles*).

Interestingly, however, the Ancient Greek term "*anarchos*" simply meant "not governed or subject," "not submitting to be governed," so it did not automatically mean also an *absence* of order, or chaos.[9] Classical Latin, which imported so many words from Classical Greek, did not feel the need to import "*anarchos,*" nor did it use any term close to "anarchy" to denote pure chaos.[10] In sum, it does not seem an exaggeration to state that in classical Latin, there was no "*anarchia,*" and thus no "anarchy."

This conspicuous absence in Latin confirms that it is only in modern times that "anarchy" came to the fore as a word and started to systematically assume the further connotation of chaos.[11] The reason why anarchy came to mean absence of order in more general terms is linked to the vicissitudes of the modern sovereign state and the European political theory that accompanied its birth. "Anarchy" came to be synonymous with "chaos" and "disorder" because the European theorists of modern state sovereignty, such as Jean Bodin or Thomas Hobbes, argued that without a sovereign power, there would be a pure state of chaos, or, as Hobbes famously put it, a war of all against all.[12] Since then, the modern sovereign state has progressively come to be perceived as the necessary condition of an ordered political life, the alternative to it being mere chaos and war.[13] The degree to which the sovereign state is still perceived as the ultimate manifestation of political life is signaled by the fact that the entire field of political science is structured around the separation

---

[9] Henry George Liddell and Robert Scott, *A Lexicon. Abridged from Liddell and Scott's Greek-English Lexicon* (Mansfield center: Martino Publisher, 2015), 54.

[10] According to Castiglioni and Mariotti, the classical Latin terms that most closely approximate anarchy in our contemporary meaning are: "*licentia,*" "*nullae leges,*" "*nulla iudicia.*" These terms convey the sense of licentiousness, absence of laws and judgment, but none of them uses the root of "an- + arch-." See: Luigi Castiglioni and Scevola Mariotti, *Vocabolario della lingua latina* (Turin: Loescher, 1966), 1670.

[11] Note that according to the 1936 edition of *The Shorter Oxford English Dictionary on Historical Principles*, the first attested appearance of the word "anarchy" in English is put at 1539 (William Little, H. W. Fowler, and J. Coulson, *The Shorter Oxford English Dictionary on Historical Principles*, 625).

[12] We have dealt more extensively with this aspect of Hobbes' philosophy in *Men and States* (see in particular: Chiara Bottici, *Men and States: Rethinking the Domestic Analogy in a Global Age*, trans. Karen Whittle (London: Palgrave Macmillan, 2009), 39–51.)

[13] For a critique of sovereignty that covers the modern theorists of sovereign state, from Bodin to Kant, via Hobbes and Rousseau, see: Daniel Loick, *A Critique of Sovereignty* (London: Rowman & Littlefield, 2019). Loick carefully reconstructs the aporias in modern theories of sovereignty, in order to argue, along with a plethora of other sources among contemporary critical theorists, that law without state coercion and politics without state sovereignty, are both possible and desirable.

between "political *theory*" and "international *relations*" (emphasis added): only within the boundaries of the sovereign state can there be proper "theory" about "politics", whereas outside those boundaries we are left with mere "relations."[14]

This is clear not only in Hobbes, but also in other social contract theorists who counterpoise the "civil society" to a hypothetical "state of nature," thereby supporting the idea that "absence of a sovereign power" means lack of "civility," and thus being confined to a mere "state of nature"—as if there could ever be one.[15] Such an opposition is, however, more an idealized and therefore disputable model of social order than a description of the actual origins of the state. However, it signals how much the imagination of modern European political theorists has been saturated ever since with the idea of the state as the condition of order and civility. Since the model of state sovereignty expanded outside of Europe, being exported via European colonialism to the rest of the world, it progressively came to be perceived as the default form of political arrangement—not only in Europe but also worldwide. Whereas the beginning of the system of sovereign states is usually located in 1648, with the Peace of Westphalia, it is rarely noted that such a system came to be extended to the entire globe only after the Second World War. Strikingly enough, even international relations theorists, imbued as they are with the myth of a Westphalian system of sovereign states dating back to mid-seventeenth century, tend to neglect the fact that we lived in a world dominated by formal empires until very recently. Not only was the Westphalian system an experience limited to Europe for a long time, but even for European history, the image of a sovereign state system is misleading, because countries like France and England were not sovereign

---

[14] This separation has been strongly criticized within the discipline, but it is relevant to note that, in 1960, one of its most distinguished theorists could still ask the question "why is there no international theory?" and respond by saying that it is because the sovereign state is all too often implicitly taken as the culminating point of political life. See: Martin Wight, "Why Is There No International Theory?," *International Relations* 2, no. 1 (1960).

[15] For an account of the way in which the dichotomy "civil society" *versus* "state of nature" has served to exclude "as uncivilized" certain peoples deemed as "primitive" during the heyday of European colonialism, and how that exclusion still reverberates today in contemporary theories of "civil society," see: Benoît Challand, *Palestinian Civil Society* (London: Routledge, 2009), 25–8.

states, but rather imperial ones.[16] And yet, we are now so used to live in a world divided into sovereign states, and imbued by its ideology, that we have lost sense of the fact that things could be—and have been— otherwise.

In the course of this book, we will use the term "anarchy" in its sense of absence of government or any other supreme power. The reason why such a meaning remains crucial is that it enables us to articulate a conceptual space for thinking about the possibility of an order even in the absence of an orderer: to denote "anarchy" in the extended polemical meaning of "disorder," we do possess synonyms, such as "chaos," "disarray," etc, but the meaning of absence of *archē* understood as government is the only one at our disposal to denote social organizations that display order despite the absence of an "orderer," that is of a government. If we conflate the two meanings, as often happens in common parlance, not only do we implicitly reproduce the historically situated idea that there cannot be order without an orderer, but we also lack a term to describe all those societies that are anarchical, i.e. all those human groups characterized by a social order despite the absence of a leader and a government. Whilst the enlarged meaning of "anarchy" as disorder is superfluous, the strict meaning is necessary because we otherwise lack a single word to denote the third possibility between the existence of a government and pure chaos.

This definition has three main corollaries. First, anarchy does not mean lack of organization, although disputes may arise as to the degree of centralization that is compatible with anarchy. For instance, even in the case of the so-called "society of sovereign states," we can argue that it is anarchical in the technical sense of the term of absence of a formal government, and yet still exhibits a high degree of organization and institutionalization.[17] There is no *archē* ruling the society of sovereign states, because there is no formal world government, but there remains a large variety of institutions and powers that regulate it. Anarchy, in this technical sense, is a key concept of international politics, with realists

---

[16] Among those political theorists who emphasize this fact, see Tarak Barkawi, who acutely observes that "International Relations" as a discipline "was founded amidst empire, but discovered instead only a world of sovereign states and their collective action problems." Tarak Barkawi, "Empire and Order in International Relations and Security Studies," *Oxford Research Encyclopedia of International Studies* (2010), 1360.

[17] Hedley Bull, *The Anarchical Society* (New York: Columbia University Press, 1977).

arguing that international anarchy is a structural issue and there is no way to overcome it, and those who insist that international anarchy is what states make of it, and that the existence of a technically anarchical condition between sovereign states does not mean absence of power.[18]

Second, anarchy does not mean absence of a political community either. Anarchy means absence of a hierarchical and centralized government, of which the modern sovereign state is only one possible form (other examples being traditional empires or hierarchically ordered tribes). The modern state is defined by the existence of a firm dominion over a population and a territory, with borders clearly indicating its extent, and by the existence of a monopoly over the use of legitimate coercion within such boundaries.[19] This was the novelty of the modern state, in comparison with European medieval political formations, characterized as they were by overlapping systems of authorities. For some authors, even the state form would be compatible with anarchist ideals, particularly in cases where state sovereignty is decentralized and organized according to radical federalist principles.[20] One can even argue the more general point that any non-coercive type of political organizations, such as those based on direct democracy and consensus decision-making, are compatible with anarchy.

---

[18] An example of a realist approach to international anarchy is Kenneth Waltz's, *Theory of International Politics* (Long Grove, IL: Waveland Press, 1979), whereas an example of constructivist approaches to the issue is that of Alexander Wendt's 1992 essay, significantly entitled "Anarchy Is What States Make It: The Social Construction of Power Politics" (Alexander Wendt, "Anarchy Is What States Make It: The Social Construction of Power Politics," *International Organization* 46, no. 2 (1992), 391–425).

[19] This is the classical Weberian definition of the state, according to which the state is a human *Gemeinschaft* that has successfully reclaimed the monopoly of legitimate coercion. See for instance the following passage: "*Staat ist diejenige menschliche Gemeinschaft, welche innerhalb eines bestimmten Gebietes – dies: das „Gebiet", gehört zum Merkmal – das Monopol legitimer physischer Gewaltsamkeit für sich (mit Erfolg) beansprucht*" in Max Weber, *Politik als Beruf* (Munich und Leipzig: Duncker and Humblot, 1958), 8. More recently, in a definition that begins with Weber, but also takes into account more recent scholarship, Gianfranco Poggi writes that "an organization which controls the population occupying a definite territory is a state insofar as 1) it is differentiated from other organizations operating in the same territory 2) it is autonomous 3) it is centralized and 4) its divisions are formally coordinated with one another." See: Gianfranco Poggi, *The State: Its Nature, Development, and Prospects* (Cambridge: Polity, 1990), 19.

[20] For instance, Pierre-Joseph Proudhon, in his *Principle of Federation*, argues for a form of state federalism that combines the state form with the anarchist principle of free agreement and federation. See: George Woodcock, *Pierre-Joseph Proudhon: A Biography* (Montreal: Black Rose Books, 1987), 249–50.

Anarchists have traditionally been involved in building these types of political organizations, as it can be seen in the history of workers' cooperatives, mutual aid societies, and workers' syndicates.[21] Indeed, all acephalous societies that do not have a formal government and an established political hierarchy are (technically speaking) anarchical. This is the case of most stateless societies, organized by principles other than the sovereign dominion of a territory through clear-cut boundaries and a centralized authority presiding over the distribution of wealth and social rank.[22] As David Graeber, among others, has emphasized, this does not mean that in acephalous societies there are no individuals who try to accumulate power and wealth for themselves, but that the social structure is itself organized in such a way as to make such accumulation inconvenient and thus not systematic. In societies based on a gift economy, for instance, those who possess most are also those who are expected to give most to others; similarly, the task of chiefs is made so burdensome that nobody could do much with the accumulated power.[23] Thus, despite any individual attempt to accumulate power and wealth, gift-economy societies tend to remain "anarchical" because they are structurally acephalous.

Third, "anarchy" is both a descriptive and a prescriptive concept. In the first sense, it denotes an already existing state of things, such as all the examples of anarchical societies mentioned above; in the second, it means an ideal that must be pursued. "Anarchism" is the doctrine that explores possible anarchic ideals. The anarchic ideal is defined by the central emphasis it puts on the concept of freedom, so much so that some have claimed that this word summarizes the sense of the entire anarchic doctrine. Emma Goldman makes this point explicit when she writes that

---

[21] Ruth Kinna, "Anarchism," in *Encyclopedia of Political Theory*, ed. Mark Bevir (London: Sage, 2010), 36.

[22] For a discussion of acephalous societies, see Brian Morris' essay "People Without Government," in Brian Morris, *Anthropology, Ecology, and Anarchism* (Oakland: PM Press, 2014), 109–30; and H.S. Daannaa, "The Acephalous Society and the Indirect Rule System in Africa," *Journal of Legal Pluralism and Unofficial Law* 26, no. 34 (1994), 61–85. In this article, H.S. Daanaa analyzes the different impacts that colonial rule had respectively on societies that already possessed some form of centralized authority, and those that were literally "acephalous," that is, without a head. David Graeber's *Fragments of an Anarchist Anthropology* (Chicago: Prickly Paradigm, 2004) also focuses on examples of stateless societies from an anthropological point of view (see in particular 21–37), while James Scott provides an account of the Zomie Highlands as an example of anarchical society in Southeast Asia. See: James C. Scott, *The Art of Not Being Governed* (New Haven: Yale University Press, 2009).

[23] David Graeber, *Fragments of an Anarchist Anthropology*, 22–3.

"anarchism stands for a social order based on the free grouping of individuals for the purpose of producing real social wealth; an order that will guarantee to every human being free access to the earth and full enjoyment of the necessities of life, according to individual desires, tastes, and inclinations."[24]

Although the anarchic ideal is recurrent in different cultures and epochs, most accounts of it place its origins in the Western socialist movements of the nineteenth and twentieth centuries, when a number of revolutionary movements started defining themselves as "anarchist."[25] Pierre-Joseph Proudhon is often identified as the "father" of anarchism, because he is said to be the first philosopher to define himself as an "anarchist."[26] It is in his very influential *What is property* that, after putting forward the argument that property is theft, he also explicitly calls himself an "anarchist" and provides a definition of anarchy as "absence of a master."[27] With Proudhon, as we will see later on, it becomes clear that anarchism opposes equally political and economic forms of hierarchy and subordination, as it sees them as mutually constitutive and thus inseparable.

Although this account of anarchism helps identify an historical moment when anarchist ideals flourished into a self-identified social and political movement, it also reflects a Eurocentric model of the history of anarchism, one the privileges European history and experiences as the prism through which to reconstruct the history of anarchist ideals as such. Although a number of histories of anarchism still reflect this

---

[24] Similarly, in his article for the *Encyclopedia Britannica*, Pyotr Kropotkin defines anarchism as a form of social organization based on free agreement: "Anarchism (from the Gr. an-, and *archē*, contrary to authority), is the name given to a principle or theory of life and conduct under which society is conceived without government—harmony in such a society being obtained, not by submission to law, or by obedience to any authority, but by free agreements concluded between the various groups, territorial and professional, freely constituted for the sake of production and consumption, as also for the satisfaction of the infinite variety of needs and aspirations of a civilized being" (Pyotr Kropotkin, *Anarchism: A Collection of Revolutionary Writings* (2002), 284. See also: Emma Goldman, *Anarchism and Other Essays* (New York: Dover Publications, 1969), 62.

[25] Nicola Abbagnano, *Dizionario di Filosofia* (Turin: UTET, 1971), 41; Giorgio Rovida, "Anarchismo," in *Enciclopedia di Filosofia,* eds. Gianni Vattimo, Maurizio Ferraris, Diego Marconi (Milan: Garzanti, 1993); Ruth Kinna, "Anarchism," 36.

[26] Giorgio Rovida, "Anarchismo," 30; Nicola Abbagnano, *Dizionario di Filosofia*, 41.

[27] Pierre-Joseph Proudhon, *What is Property?* (Cambridge: Cambridge University Press, 1994), 205, 209.

Eurocentric bias, a lot of work has been done to provide genealogies of anarchism beyond this prism.[28] In this respect, it is particularly useful to distinguish between anarchism as a formally organized social movement, with its self-identified banners and institutions, which, in many senses, does not predate European modernity, and anarchism as a set of ideals, which go far back in time and extend globally. In this book, we are more interested in the latter than in the former. The reason why the formally organized anarchist political movements were absent in antiquity is due to the specifically modern nature of that type of institutionalized political mobilization: we cannot identify formally organized anarchist political movements in the antiquity because there were not formally organized political movements *per se*, but this should not be mistaken for an absence of anarchism as such.

Another reason for the lack of such movements, and thus for the specifically modern flourishing of the term "anarchism," is that for a great number of premodern societies anarchy was a lived experience—and thus not something to be theorized as a desirable condition. It is indeed an historical truism to state that the human species lived in societies

---

[28] Examples of the former are found in the often quoted anthology by Daniel Guérin, *Ni Dieu, ni Maître: Anthologie de l'anarchisme* (Paris: La Découverte, 1999); but also in: Ruth Kinna, "Anarchism," 36; Nicola Abbagnano, *Dizionario di Filosofia*, 41; Giorgio Rovida, "Anarchismo," 30; while the anthology *Anarchism: A Documentary History of Libertarian Ideas* (Robert Graham, *Anarchism: A Documentary History of Libertarian Ideas* (Montreal: Black Rose Books, 2005, 2009), provides documents from all over the globe, attesting to the global nature of the history of anarchism, before and beyond its European story, and thereby questioning the Eurocentric bias that so much knowledge produced in the West still carries within it. Marshall also begins the history of anarchism with Taoism and Buddhism (Peter Marshall, *Demanding the Impossible: A History of Anarchism* (Oakland: AK Press, 1992), 53. Shannon, who provides a very useful historical perspective on anarchafeminism and rightly emphasized the need to question Western epistemologies in formulating a contemporary anarchafeminist perspective (Deric Shannon, "Articulating a Contemporary Anarcha-Feminism," 65), still provides a completely Eurocentric historical account of it, one that erases all contributions coming from outside Europe or the US (Shannon, 60–4), so the section of their work called "Anarcha-feminisms of the past" should have been more properly entitled "American and European anarchafeminisms of the Past." Among those explicitly taking up the task of decolonizing the anarchist canon, see Craib and Maxwell, and Ramnath: whereas Maia Ramnath's *Decolonizing Anarchism* (Oakland: AK Press, 2011) proposes an alternative history of India's liberation struggle, emphasizing the anarchist elements in them, Raymond Craib and Barry Maxwell set up the ambitious task of providing the contours of a global anarchism, significantly entitling their anthology, *No Gods, No Masters, No Peripheries* (Oakland: PM Press, 2015), thus signaling that the above-mentioned *Ni Dieu, ni Maître* had unfortunately focused only on the theory produced in the center of the global capitalist world system.

without formal governments for a great part of its existence.[29] It is a truism that is nevertheless worth repeating because we are now so used to living in a globe divided into sovereign states, that we have lost that long-term perspective. This certainly does not mean that all premodern societies lacked formal political institutions, as empires and other forms of political hierarchies existed for a very long time, too. But we tend to forget that, even after their appearance in the history of the human species, they were not the rule worldwide. According to Robert Graham, it was only around 6,000 years ago, at the beginning of the so-called "dawn of civilization" that the first societies with formal structures of hierarchy, command, and control began to develop.[30] At the beginning they were relatively rare and located primarily in today's Asia and the Middle East, but they slowly increased in size and influence, at times conquering the surrounding anarchic tribal societies in which most of humanity continued to live. Significantly, Robert Graham begins *Anarchism: A Documentary History of Libertarian Ideas*, a two-volume anthology of anarchist ideals, with a work by the Daoist philosopher Bao Jingyan (300 CE), a text in which the memory of a time when there were neither lords nor subjects is still present:[31]

> When the world was in its original undifferentiated state, the Nameless (*wu-ming*, i.e., the Tao) was what was valued, and all creatures found happiness in self-fulfillment. Now when the cinnamon-tree has its bark stripped or the varnish-tree is cut, it is not done at the wish of the tree; when the pheasant's feathers are plucked or the kingfisher's torn out, it is not done by the desire of the bird. To be bitted and bridled is not in accordance with the nature of the horse; to be put under the yoke and bear burdens does not give pleasure to the ox. Cunning has its origins in the use of force that goes against the true nature of things, and the real reason for harming creatures is to provide useless

---

[29] For an exploration of stateless societies in the African continent, see Paul Bohannan, *Social Anthropology* (New York: Holt, Rinehart & Winston, 1963) 282–3; and Walter Rodney, *How Europe Underdeveloped Africa* (Enugu, Nigeria: Ikenga Publishers 1984) 56–7. According to Mbah and Igariwey, stateless societies were the norm in Africa rather than the exception, at least until class stratification started to emerge (Sam Mbah and I. E. Igariwey, *African Anarchism: The History of a Movement* (Tucson: See Sharp Press, 1997), 32.

[30] Robert Graham, *Anarchism: A Documentary History of Libertarian Ideas*, xi.

[31] See also Marshall, who also begins their account of the history of anarchism with Taoism (Peter Marshall, *Demanding the Impossible*, 53–60).

adornments. [...] And so the people are compelled to labour so that those in office may be nourished; and while their superiors enjoy fat salaries, they are reduced to the direst poverty. [...] In the earliest times, there was neither lord nor subject. Wells were dug for drinking water, the fields were ploughed for food, work began at sunrise and ceased at sunset; everyone was free and at ease, neither competing with each other nor scheming against each other, and no one was either glorified or humiliated.[32]

We can see in this passage how a poetic account of the earliest times is infused with Bao Jingyan's Daoist philosophy. The reference to a time with neither lords nor subjects becomes thus an invitation to follow the Way, i.e. the *tao*, understood as a form of unity of all things and to consequently abstain both from the desire to rule and to be ruled.[33] Jingyan's anarchist ideals are based on a mixture between the memory traces of the earlier anarchical societies and on the insights of Daoist philosophy, so that it becomes hard to understand where one ends and the other begins. Although there are often said to be anarchist elements in the *Daode Jing*, one of the foundational texts of Daoism, going as back as to the sixth century BC, particularly in its "philosophy of nongovernment," advising rulers that the best way of governing is "non-rule," an explicitly developed anarchist ideal can only be found in Bao Jingyan.[34] We could say that the unity of the Dao lies at the basis of what other anarchists called the "indivisibility of freedom,"[35] and thus the idea that one cannot be free alone, because even if they are in the position of rulers instead of that of those being ruled, they are still part of a society based on a politics of domination, which oppresses all of its inhabitants, although some of

---

[32] Bao Jingyan, "Neither Lord Nor Subject," in *Anarchism: A Documentary History of Libertarian Ideas. Volume One: From Anarchy to Anarchism (300 CE to 1939)*, ed. Robert Graham (Montreal: Black Rose Books, 2005). We will come back later on to this idea that the domination of nature by Man, as an ethno-class, stems from the domination of human by human (see in particular Chapter 9).

[33] Bao Jingyan, "Neither Lord Nor Subject," 2.

[34] On the controversy, see John A. Rapp, "Daoism and Anarchism Reconsidered," in *Daoism and Anarchism: Critiques of State Autonomy in Ancient and Modern China* (London: Continuum, 2012), 19–50.

[35] McLaughlin uses the expression "indivisibility of freedom" to denote Mikhail Bakunin's conception of freedom as intrinsically dependent on that of equality (Paul McLaughlin, *Mikhail Bakunin: The Philosophical Basis of His Anarchism* (New York: Alogra Publishing, 2002), 86.

them pay a higher price than others. Hence the emphasis on abstaining from the desire of being ruled, but also from that of ruling.

Although one cannot speak of a proper anarchist political movement at that time, Bao Jingyan's work can certainly count as an example of anarchist text, and is therefore properly included in any non-Eurocentric genealogy of the history of anarchism.[36] We will tackle the question of the Eurocentrism of knowledge later on, but for now notice how it infiltrates even non-European accounts of the history of anarchism. For instance, Sam Mbah and I. E. Igariwey begin their *African Anarchism: The History of a Movement*, by stating that "anarchism as a social philosophy, theory of social organization, and social movement is remote to Africa—indeed, almost unknown" and did not start to spread until the arrival of texts and ideals developed by modern Western anarchist thinkers such as Pierre-Joseph Proudhon and Mikhail Bakunin.[37] But, in the course of their work, after providing an account of the arrival of those Western theories, they explore in detail what they call "anarchist precedents in Africa," that is, the incredibly rich history of anarchist ideals rooted in African communalism, the Igbo's oral philosophical tradition, the Niger delta, and the Tallensi peoples and ideas, to name only a few—all of which were well developed before European colonization.[38]

Thus, what appears as absent if looked at from the point of view of a theory or social movement resembling those typical of the European history of anarchism, can turn out to be very present from the point of view of the African traditions themselves. As they write in a significant passage:

The territory that lies between the Sahara Desert and the tropical rain forest is home to a variety of peoples. Between Senegal and Gambia live the Wolor and Tukulor, while between Gambia and the River Niger valley live the Soninke, Mandigo, Kharan, Tuareg, Ashanti, Banbara, and Djula. The Songhai dominate the middle Niger area, and the Masai inhabit the Upper Volta basin. Across the river in what is presently

---

[36] Robert Graham, *Anarchism*, 1–4.
[37] The very label "African anarchism" should be used as a ladder that we are ready to abandon once we have reached the top. To unify such a variety of peoples and cultures under the label of "African" is only a tool to make visible what has so far remained invisible (the history of anarchist ideals in a significant portion of the planet), but should not be taken as a homogenous and unifying whole. Sam Mbah and I. E. Igariwey, *African Anarchism*, 2.
[38] Ibid, 27, 28–34, 35–6, 37, and 38, respectively.

northwestern and north-central Nigeria live the Hausa-Fulani, while the Kanuri live in the northeast. Further south and spreading toward the east one finds the Igbo, Yoruba, Gikuyu, Luo, Shona, Ndebele, Xhosa, Bantu, Zulu, etc. To the north of Sahara lies Egypt and the Maghreb region, which are peopled by African Arabs and Berbers. To a greater or lesser extent, all of these traditional African societies manifested 'anarchic elements' which, upon closer examination, lend credence to the historical truism that governments have not always existed. They are but a recent phenomenon and are, therefore, not inevitable in human society. While some anarchic features of traditional societies existed largely in past stages of development, some of them persists and remain pronounced to this day.[39]

Thus, pointing towards the anarchist elements in African historical societies does not mean to state that all precolonial African societies were anarchical, as significant differences existed between them. Anthropologists usually distinguish between two categories of African societies.[40] On the one hand, those that possessed centralized authorities, an administrative machinery, and judicial institutions, the three pillars of a formal government, and in which, consequently, cleavages of wealth and privilege corresponded to distribution of authorities. Examples include the Zulu, the Zguato, and the Kede. On the other hand, there are acephalous societies, which lacked centralized authorities, administrative machinery and constituted judicial institutions, and where there were no sharp divisions of rank, wealth, and status. Examples of the latter are the Tallensi, the Nuer, and the Logoli.[41] Although both types of societies were impacted by the colonial rule, they were affected to different extents.

In the above-quoted passage Mbah and Igariwey seem to confirm these insights of anthropological literature, but it is a passage that therefore stands in even greater contrast to their opening statement about a lack of a proper anarchist tradition in the African continent. The book indeed persuasively shows, against its own opening statement, that the presence of these anarchist elements is rooted in what is commonly called "communalism," a mode of production based on the family and the village as the main unit for the production and reproduction of life, which

---

[39] Ibid, 27.
[40] H. S. Daannaa, "The Acephalous Society," 61.
[41] Ibid, 61.

remained the rule rather than the exception in innumerable African societies. As they argue, until the fifteenth century, when many African societies started to transition to a class-based system, most of them were characterized by the absence of hierarchical structures, of a governmental apparatus, and of the commodification of labor.[42] Furthermore, Mbah and Igariwey even contend that although some of these elements have been destroyed by the inequalities created by a class-based society, colonial rule, and the neo-colonial economy centered around the alliance between the local elites and foreign capital, some of those communalist elements survive even to this day in institutions such as village assemblies and the philosophy of *Ujamaa*.[43] In particular, they insist on the fact that in Africa the land was thought of as belonging to the community, so that each individual could be said to possess a right to use the land as part of their right to life. For instance, in the *Ujamaa*, which literally means "villagization," basic goods were to be held in common and shared among the members of the village, without any of them being able to claim a right to private property over them and thereby ensuring that social inequalities were not permitted to emerge.[44] In sum, it is only through a Eurocentric bias, which implicitly leads to privilege one particular story to the detriment of others, that traditions such as that of African anarchism can be left out of the history of anarchism.

At this point one may wonder why it is so important for us to insist on this critique of Eurocentrism. Although we will develop this point more later on, it should already be evident that such a critique should be an intrinsic component of any anarchafeminist theory: If one cannot fight a certain source of oppression without fighting all others, then there is a performative contradiction in putting forward an anarchist theory while encapsulating it into a Eurocentric view of the world. Eurocentrism, as we will see, is a particular view of the world, one that literally organizes space and time by using Europe as its focal point, and thus as its *archē*. It is a view that originated with European imperialism and that still reverberates today in much social and political philosophy in the form of methodological Eurocentrism, that is as a tendency to use European and Western developments and conditions as the global norm and yardstick. As Ina Kerner argued, methodological Eurocentrism implies not only a form of ethnocentric universalism, that is, a

---

[42] Sam Mbah and I. E. Igariwey, *African Anarchism*, 32.
[43] Ibid, 48–52.
[44] Ibid, 50.

presentation of a particular *ethnos* perspective as a universal, but also a division of the globe according to essentializing group differentiations along with their explicit, or implicit, hierarchical organization.[45] As a consequence, Eurocentrism is not a matter of where a certain body of knowledge is produced, since there can be works produced in Europe that do not reproduce Eurocentrism, while one can have works produced outside of the West that may be tainted by Eurocentric tropes, not least through the epistemic legacy of centuries of European colonialism.[46]

Moving beyond Eurocentrism is particularly crucial as one reconstructs not simply a history of anarchism, which goes beyond the scope of the present work, but a genealogy of it, that is, a history which is also at the same time a critique: The task of creating a genealogy of anarchism is not to present a linear account of its development, but rather to ask ourselves what we mean by "anarchy" and "anarchism" and why we have come to conceive of it in this way, and not another.[47] When approached from this point of view, we cannot but notice a tendency to think of anarchism and its history through a Eurocentric prism, and emphasize the need to move beyond it by provincializing Europe.[48] We have to be aware of our own peculiar place within such a genealogy, one that is made up of multifaceted, innumerable histories.

Eurocentrism emerges not only as an implicit lens through which to look at particular histories, but also, and most importantly, as implicitly presenting a single individual story as History without further qualification. Even philosophical usages of a single term can thus implicitly carry Eurocentric biases. A case in point is Giorgio Agamben's recent work *Creazione ed anarchia*.[49] In this collection of essays, Agamben emphasized that in

---

[45] Ina Kerner, "Postcolonial Theories as Global Critical Theories," *Constellations* 25, no. 4 (2018), 615–16.

[46] Ibid, 616.

[47] Following Nietzsche's definition of the genealogical method, a genealogy must address the question of "what is x?" by asking, simultaneously, "why we conceive of it in this way". As Nietzsche pointed out, a genealogy faces the problem of *meaning* by looking at the *circumstances* in which it was created and thus at the *values* that were at stake in its creation. See: Friedrich Nietzsche, *On the Genealogy of Morals*, trans. Carol Diethe (New York: Cambridge University Press, 1994), 3.

[48] We borrow this expression from the influential title of Dipesh Chakrabarty's *Provincializing Europe: Postcolonial Thought and Historical Difference* (Princeton: Princeton University Press, 2000).

[49] Giorgio Agamben, *Creazione ed Anarchia. L'opera nell'età della religione capitalista* (Vicenza: Neri Pozza Editore, 2017).

philosophy the *archē* is also the rule, because every creation is at the same a principle and thus also the "prince" (*principe*) who rules and governs.[50] This identification between origin=principle=command, however, only holds for a particular story, that of the Christian theology and philosophy: it is here alone that they coincide because, in the West, the monotheistic God of Christianity is said to have created the world *ex nihilo* and thereby also imprinted to the world a certain rule or government of things from the beginning.[51] If there was nothing before God created the world, and if God is said to be omnipotent, and to have created the world though his word (*logos*), then the beginning is also by definition the government of the world. As we read in the Gospel according to Saint John: "In the beginning was the Word, and the Word was with God, and the Word was God" (John 1:1, "*En archē ēn ho Logos, kai ho Logos ēn pros ton Theon, kai Theos ēn ho Logos*"). Thus, the *logos*, or word of God, is at the beginning, because within a Christian worldview there was nothing before God created it: the Christian God creates by naming things into being, and thereby ordering them from the very beginning according to a certain principle and command—that of God's omnipotence. There is nothing except through God's act of naming things because, in this particular history, there is nothing before God's creation. It is literally, *ex nihilo*, out of nothing. On the contrary, as we have argued elsewhere, in other worldviews, such as that emerging in the pluralistic theogony of Greek mythology, where the beginning is not the *ex nihilo* creation of a single omnipotent god, but the division of an already existing world between a plurality of celestial beings, there is no space for such an identification of *archē* and command.[52] Similarly, in the Daoist philosophy of Bao Jingyan described above, there is something already there at the beginning the world, and what is valued within it is the *Wu-ming*, or the Nameless, and not the ordered-naming-of-things-into-being. To argue that every beginning is a rule, and every principle is a prince, in the way Agamben does, means to exchange one particular story and philosophy (that of Christianity) for history and philosophy as such.[53]

---

[50] Giorgio Agamben, *Creazione ed Anarchia*, 91.

[51] Ibid.

[52] Chiara Bottici, *A Philosophy of Political Myth,* 46.

[53] As Reiner Schürmann emphasizes in a work significantly entitled *Le Principe d'Anarchie* (1982, 1987) we can indeed separate origin and command, to make the space for thinking about a simple emergence separated from any command or rule. Schürmann insists on this separation in his interpretation of Heidegger, emphasizing that the latter is implicit in Heidegger's philosophy. Needless to say, it is only one of the many possible interpretations

Furthermore, to insist that *archē* means both beginning and command because this is what it meant in Ancient Greek, means committing the historicist fallacy according to which, since things have been in certain way in the past, they must also remain so in the future. The past may influence, but does not completely determine, the present. There is no *a priori* reason why "the one who begins" should also be "the one who rules," and indeed there are plenty of cases when that is not the case. The above-mentioned examples of beginnings without a command are a case in point. Thus, if in ancient Athens the *archōn* meant both "he who begins" and "the highest city magistrate," as Agamben reminds us, then all we can conclude is that in *that* specific context *archōn* meant both the first to begin and the one who commands.[54] There is, however, no reason to assume that this particular history should count for history written large, and even less so to turn it into philosophy without further clarifications, thereby erasing all alternative histories into a false universality. In order to provide a genealogy of anarchism beyond Eurocentrism, one must therefore provincialize those histories that automatically turn the specifically European story into History as such, and thereby open the path for a plurality of histories and genealogies. It is certainly true that the specifically European anarchist ideals have given an important impetus to anarchism and constitutes an important episode in its history. But they are not the entire history.

It is with this methodological provincialization of Europe that we should approach the contribution of European experiences to the genealogy of anarchism. The emergence of a capitalist economy in early modern Europe—that, is of an economy based on private property and the consequent enclosures of common resources, the affirmation of a mode of production that enabled a few to accumulate capital by extracting surplus value from the labor of the vast majority of workers, condemned to sell their toil for a minimal wage—exacerbated inequalities and thus turned European social movements into a hotbed for anarchist cries against the exploitation and the rule of the few over the many. Although Communism is today mainly associated with Marxism, within the first

---

of Heidegger. Agamben himself opposed Schürmann's anarchic interpretation to Jacques Derrida's democratic interpretation (Giorgio Agamben, *Creazione e Anarchia*, 95). For the English translation of Schürmann's text, see: Reiner Schürmann, *Heidegger on Being and Acting*.

[54] Giorgio Agamben, *Creazione e Anarchia*, 91.

International Working Men's Association[55] anarchism and Marxism were often intermingled in socialist and trade-union movements, and they remained so at least until the break between Karl Marx and Mikhail Bakunin which lead to the expulsion of the latter.[56] The bone of contention were two different views about the nature of the International itself: whereas Marx and his followers insisted that the creation of political parties with a central executive authority was a necessary step for social change, the anarchists favored an anti-authoritarian strategy based on the free federalism of the already existing trade-unions sections.[57] In particular, anarchists criticized all attempts to turn the International into a centralized bureaucratic apparatus similar to a state, with the argument that its internal organization had to be consistent with its ideals, lest it would replicate the authoritarian institutions it was seeking to overthrow. Hence the anarchist insistence on the congruence of means and ends, which is the point where they converged with other non-authoritarian socialist movements.[58]

---

[55] It is seldom noted that among the women who influenced Marx's philosophy were women such as Mary Wollstonecraft (on the class character of the English idea of liberty) and Flora Tristan, whose idea of an international union of all workers was narrowed by Marx to that of an International Workingmen's Association. See: Penny A. Weiss and Loretta Kesinger, eds., *Feminist Interpretations of Emma Goldman* (University Park: Pennsylvania State University Press, 2007), 5.

[56] Robert Graham, *Anarchism*, 93–101. One of the reasons why the contribution of anarchists to the development of communist philosophy is so often marginalized, particularly within academia, may be due to the fact that anarchism and Marxism generated two very different types of traditions, with Marxism being a much better fit for the academization of social movements, and anarchists being reluctant to recognize themselves as a single movement. As Graber observes, Marxism was after all the only great social movement ever invented by a PhD, and it tended to generate schools such as Leninism, Maoism, Trotskyism, or Althusserianism, that is, all schools named after one single mind (and featuring prominently heads of states and university professors). On the contrary, anarchist schools, such as the Anarcho-syndicalists, the Anarcho-communists, The Cooperativists, etc. are never named after a single "great thinker." And significantly, the Marxist schools that are not named after a single individual, such as Autonomism and Council Communism, are also the closest to anarchism. See: David Graeber, *Fragments of an Anarchist Anthropology*, 3, 5.

[57] Robert Graham, *Anarchism*, 93.

[58] The link between anarchism and socialism is so strict in the European tradition that Chomsky argues that anarchism should be placed under the label "Libertarian socialism" along with all other non-authoritarian forms of socialism and Marxism. See: Noam Chomsky, *Chomsky on Anarchism* (Oakland: AK Press, 2005). For a discussion of the convergence between different forms of libertarian socialism, from Council Communism to Anarchocommunism, see: Alex Prichard et al., *Libertarian Socialism: Politics in Black and Red* (Oakland: PM Press, 2017).

Anarchists were, and still are, united by their refusal of coercive forms of authority, be they political or religious, and their plea for voluntary and spontaneous forms of organizations that follow a bottom-up logic. Yet, there are many different and variegated forms of anarchism. We can, for instance, group them according to the different *ends* and *means* of their political proposals. With regards to the *ends*, we can broadly distinguish between individualist and socialist approaches. The often-quoted example of a strict individualist credo is the philosophy of Max Stirner, who argued that freedom can have no other principle and end than the ego and its egoism and consequently opposed all existing universal theories, including any metaphysics of freedom, as mere "spooks."[59] However, individualist anarchism remained an exception in Europe and even in the case of Stirner, there have been interpretations that read his alleged individualism as congruous with communism.[60]

On the opposite side stand those approaches that see the realization of the self as possible only within and through society.[61] Among them we can distinguish between communists, such as Pyotr Kropotkin, and collectivists, such as Mikhail Bakunin: whereas the former privileged a form of radical communism, the latter favored a form of communism of production that also left some space for the individual enjoyment of the fruits of labor.[62] Behind the different forms of anarchism stand different conceptions of freedom: the idea that freedom is to be realized individually *versus* the insight that freedom can only be a communal enterprise since,

---

[59] Max Stirner, *The Unique and Its Property* (Berkeley: Ardent Press, 2007)

[60] In 2017, there appeared a new English translation Stirner's work, which reflects a recent resurgence of interest in his work (Max Stirner, 2017). All previous scholarship was based on an old 1907 translation. The new current of interpretations of Stirner's work have questioned the completely individualistic interpretation of the work. See for instance: Jacob Blumenfeld, *All Things Are Nothing to Me: The Unique Philosophy of Max Stirner* (Winchester: Zero Books, 2018), who put forward a communist interpretation of Stirner. See also: Saul Newman, *Post-anarchism* (Cambridge: Polity Press, 2016), who reads Stirner through Foucault's notion of power.

[61] We are using here the distinction between individualist *versus* socialist approaches as a heuristic tool to group different forms of anarchism together but, as we will see in the next chapter, in the light of a philosophy of the transindividual, such a distinction must not be turned into a dichotomy, that is, into a distinction that is both reciprocally exclusive and mutually exhaustive of its field of application.

[62] For an overview of their anarchist thought, see the following anthologies: Pyotr Kropotkin, *Anarchism: A Collection of Revolutionary Writings*; Pyotr Kropotkin, *The Essential Kropotkin* (London: Macmillan, 1976); Mikhail Bakunin, *God and the State* (New York: Dover, 1970); and Mikhail Bakunin, *La libertà degli uguali* (Milan: Eleuthera, 2000) respectively.

as Bakunin put it, you cannot be free in a society of slaves because their own slavery prevents the full realization of your freedom. The latter is what I have elsewhere called "the freedom of equals."[63] Kropotkin's communist anarchism extends this view to all life forms, by arguing that mutual aid, rather than competition, is the key factor in evolution. This does not mean that there is no space in life for competition, but simply that competition is one of the forms in which life is given, and not even the decisive one from the point of view of evolution, since the life forms that have most developed cooperation are actually those that have had a best chance of surviving.[64] All life forms, human, animal, and even vegetal, show moments of antagonism, but it is through cooperation, according to Kropotkin, that they manage to solve challenges from external environments and threats.[65] Kropotkin's theory of mutual aid does not mean that humans help each other out of sympathy and good will, but rather that no life as such would be possible without cooperation. If we are unable to grasp this fact it is because since the emergence of a capitalist mode of production, we have become blinded by an ideology that values competition above anything else, and thus we project the social antagonism typical of a capitalist society onto all life forms.

With regards to the *means* through which anarchy is to be realized, most anarchists agree that they must be homogenous to the ends: if the aim is freedom, then it cannot but be realized through free means. Differences emerge as to the way in which they must be conceived: some favored forms of rebellion and revolution, others valued non-violent means such as education and civic disobedience, while others still, taking an intermediate route, looked for an alliance with workers' organizations such as trade unions which can both educate the masses and provide the infrastructures for the reorganization of society.[66] Among the first, we

---

[63] Jacob Blumenfeld, Chiara Bottici, Simon Critchley, eds., *The Anarchist Turn* (London: Pluto Press, 2013).

[64] Pyotr Kropotkin, *Mutual Aid: A Factor in Evolution* (London: William Heinemann, 1902).

[65] Ibid.

[66] See in particular French and Spanish anarcho-syndicalism, where anarchism had an impressive following. During the Spanish Civil War, approximately one million people were members of the anarchosyndacalist CNT (*Confederacio Nacional del Trabajo*), an immense following if one considers that the Spanish population of the time was around twenty-four million (Deric Shannon, "Articulating a Contemporary Anarcha-Feminism," 61). Among them, 20,000 women mobilized and developed an extensive network of activities designed to empower individual women while building a sense of community. See: Martha Ackelsberg, *The Free Women of Spain: Anarchism and The Struggle for the Emancipation of Women* (Oakland: AK Press, 2005), 21.

must further distinguish between those who trust the spontaneity of revolution and others who believe in the "propaganda by the deeds," that is local rebellions or single individual acts of violence meant to stimulate masses towards a general revolution. Whilst the recourse to violence is debated among anarchists, most of them agree on the importance of education as a necessary condition for the creation of an anarchical society.[67] Among those who emphasized education are anti-violence writers such as the Russian Lev Tolstoy or today's pacifist ecological movements.

Recent trends in Western anarchist philosophy argued for a new development in anarchist philosophy called "post-anarchism," understood as an attempt to revise nineteenth-century anarchism through the lens of poststructuralist French philosophers such as Michel Foucault and Gilles Deleuze.[68] Whereas authors such as Todd May emphasized the convergence between them and thus the fundamentally anarchist moments in post-structuralism itself, others, such as Saul Newman called for a form of postanarchism that insists on the "post" and thus on the need to leave behind classical anarchism's allegedly outdated views.[69] In his *Post-anarchism*, Newman criticized nineteenth-century anarchism such as that espoused by Bakunin and Kropotkin for relying on a metanarrative of revolution, thus portraying anarchy as something that is to be realized in the future, instead of insisting that anarchy is an intrinsic possibility of the here and now, and for their reliance on a naïve view of power as if the latter were something that could ever be completely abolished.[70] Instead of conceiving power as a monolithic force located in formal institutions such as the Church and the State, Newman emphasized, with Foucault, that power is pervasive, diffused in all social relations and thus most often reproduced even by those who try to fight against it. By drawing from Michel Foucault's insights that power largely works

---

[67] Robert Graham, *Anarchism*, 220–30.
[68] Among the authors in this tradition, see: Todd May, *The Political Philosophy of Poststructuralist Anarchism* (University Park: The Pennsylvania State University Press, 1994); Saul Newman, *Post-anarchism*. As we will see, the label "postanarchism" that Newman uses for his position cannot be applied to authors such as Todd May, since the latter does not claim that we are "post" anarchism, but rather that there is an important convergence and mutual benefit in combining French poststructuralist philosophy with classical anarchist thinkers. See: Ruth Kinna, "Anarchism," 37.
[69] Saul Newman, *Post-anarchism*.
[70] Ibid, xi.

through a process of subjectivization, where subjects willingly reproduce the very conditions of their oppression, Newman invited to what he names acts of "voluntary inservitude," that is, acts of insubordination that question the logic of power as subjectification, as the best means of achieving an anarchical society.[71] As he puts it in a significant passage: "If we have freely chosen servitude, if we willingly participate in our own domination without the need for coercion, then this means that all power, even if it appears to bear down upon us, is essentially an *illusion*, one of our own making. If, in other words, we have created the tyrant in our own act of submission to him, this means that the tyrant has no real power. The power he has is only our power in an alienated form; the chains that bind us are the chains we have ourselves forged."[72] If that is the case, then the road for liberation does not lie in following some revolutionary narrative, but simply in exercising a "voluntary inservitude" and thus a discipline of indiscipline here and now. In other words, it is only by cultivating such a habit of involuntary servitude that we can aspire, if not to freedom, at least to being less governed.

Besides the fact that Saul Newman does not take into account that there are situations where power, understood as the capacity to influence other people's actions, still operates through coercion, he does not depict an accurate picture of nineteenth-century anarchist thinkers either. As we will see, not only does his criticism of classical anarchism not apply to authors such as Mikhail Bakunin, whom he quotes in his work, but it certainly misses the contributions of anarchafeminists such as Emma Goldman, whom he never mentions. To begin with, Bakunin's view, whose understanding of freedom can be summarized with the concept of a "freedom of equals," certainly questions his reconstruction.[73] According to Bakunin, it is precisely because power is so diffused in society and human beings are so dependent on one another, that one cannot be free in isolation, no matter how much of a habit of "voluntary inservitude" one may cultivate. If freedom consists "in the right to obey nobody other than

---

[71] Ibid, 91–112.

[72] Ibid, 103. Emphasis in the original.

[73] Jacob Blumenfeld, Chiara Bottici, Simon Critchley, eds., *The Anarchist Turn*. For many years, the understanding of Bakunin as an activist has obfuscated the depth of his thinking. However, in the last few decades there have been numerous attempts to give a more balanced picture (see for instance: René Berthier, *Bakounine politique: Révolution et Contre-révolution En Europe Centrale* (Paris: Edition du Monde Libertaire, 1991).

myself and to determine my acts in conformity with my convictions," then I also need the mediation of the equally free consciousness of everybody as well as the material conditions for its realization.[74]

In a passage that echoes contemporary theorists of the technologies of the self, such as Foucault,[75] Bakunin observed that it is not individuals who create society, but society that, so to speak, "individualizes itself in every individual."[76] Bakunin was well aware that freedom as self-determination is empty, if there is no such thing as a "self" that can choose autonomously. The crucial point is not simply doing what I want, but to be sure that what I believe to be the fruit of my free choice actually is that. If I am led by the circumstances of my life to believe that my servitude is either immutable or even desirable, there is no way I can be free. It is the dilemma of voluntary servitude, and therefore of the techniques through which compliant subjects are created, that has been at the center of anarchist thinking for a long time.[77]

Bakunin insists that human beings are determined by both material and representational social factors. When still in their mother's womb, every human being is already determined by a high number of geographical, climatic, and economic factors that constitute the material nature of their social condition.[78] In addition to material factors, Bakunin also mentions a series of beliefs, ideas, and representations that are equally crucial. Again, in an extremely timely passage, Bakunin observes that every generation finds as already made a whole world of ideas, images, and sentiments that it inherits from previous epochs.[79] They do not present themselves to the newborn as a system of ideas, since children

---

[74] This is a view of freedom that clearly resonates with Hegelian themes. In particular, it is a view that resonates with the influence of the left young Hegelians that Bakunin met in Berlin, but it goes beyond Hegelianism because it includes a sharp critique of the state as a form of political theology. See: Mikhail Bakunin, *Selected Writings*, ed. Arthur Lehning (New York: Grove, 1974), 214–31. See also: Mikhail Bakunin, *Tre Conferenze Sull'Anarchia* (Roma: Manifestolibri, 1996), 81.

[75] See, for instance: Michel Foucault, *Technologies of the Self: A Seminar with Michel Foucault* (Amherst: University of Massachusetts Press, 1988). On the convergence between post-structuralism and anarchism, see: Todd May, *The Political Philosophy of Poststructuralist Anarchism*.

[76] Mikhail Bakunin, *La Libertà Degli Uguali*, 85.

[77] On voluntary servitude, a classical reference point is Étienne de La Boétie, *The Politics of Obedience: The Discourse of Voluntary Servitude* (Auburn: Mises Institute, 2015).

[78] Mikhail Bakunin, *La Libertà Degli Uguali*, 86.

[79] Ibid, 87.

would not be able to apprehend it in this form. Rather, such a world of ideas imposes itself as a world of "personified facts," made concrete in the persons and things that surround them, as a world that speaks to their senses through whatever they see and hear since their very early days.[80]

If individuals are nothing but the society that individualizes itself in them, then you cannot be free unless everybody else is free. No human can achieve their own emancipation without at the same time working for the emancipation of all other human around them.

As Bakunin put it in a famous speech:

> What other humans are is of the greatest importance to me. However independent I may imagine myself to be, however far removed I may appear from mundane considerations by my social status, I am enslaved to the misery of the meanest member of society. The outcast is my daily menace. Whether I am Pope, Czar, Emperor, or even Prime Minister, I remain always the product of what the humblest among them are: if they are ignorant, poor, slaves, my existence is determined by their slavery. I, enlightened or intelligent, am, for instance—in the event—rendered stupid by their stupidity; as a courageous being, I am enslaved by their slavery; as a rich person, I cannot but tremble before their poverty; as a privileged person, I blanch at their justice. I who want to be free cannot be because all the humans around me do not yet want to be free, and consequently they become tools of oppression against me.[81]

Although this view resembles some of the contemporary theories of recognition, Bakunin also distances himself from a mere politics of recognition because he insists that his view entails a "materialist conception of freedom."[82] If freedom is to be realized not just by a separate

---

[80] Ibid, 87.

[81] Errico Malatesta, *L'Anarchia* (Rome: Datanews, 2001), 23. Translation from Italian is mine. The speech is also quoted by Hillary Lazar, "Until All Are Free: Black Feminism, Anarchism, And Interlocking Oppression," in *Perspectives on Anarchist Theory* 29 (2016), 41.

[82] Recognition is an important element of Bakunin's view: "For the individual to be free means to be recognized, considered and treated as such by another individual, and by all the individuals that surrounds him" (Mikhail Bakunin, *La Libertà degli Uguali*, 92, trans. and emphasis mine.) The concept of recognition has recently been at the center of a very lively debate. See for instance: Axel Honneth, *The Struggle for Recognition* (Cambridge: Polity Press, 1995); Nancy Fraser and Axel Honneth, *Redistribution or Recognition? A Political-Philosophical*

self (which, we will see, does not exist) but through society itself, it follows that an entire reorganization of society along the principle of free association is necessary for its realization.[83] Free federalism follows from a view of freedom articulated in three moments. The first, Bakunin says, is the positive and social moment, and consists in the development of human potentialities through education and material wellbeing—all things that can only be acquired through the psychical and intellectual work of the whole society.[84] The second moment is instead more negative, and is "the moment of the revolt."[85] First it is a revolt against the Christian God, and the Church, because "as long as we have a master in the sky, we will not be free on earth."[86] At times Bakunin seems to attack only the God of the Christian Church, but we can extend his thought to other forms of transcendent authority. If we believe that we owe a divine authority unconditional obedience, we are necessarily slaves to it, as well as to its intermediaries, such as ministers, prophets, or messiahs.[87] This is the reason why Bakunin strongly criticized nationalism as a new form of "political theology": by presenting the "nation" as a transcendent being, to which unconditional obedience is due just because it is our supposed "fatherland," we are replacing a God in the sky with another one on earth.[88] The revolt against God and transcendent authority must indeed be combined with the revolt against specifically human authority. Here Bakunin introduces a distinction between the legal and formal authority

---

Exchange (London: Verso, 2003). On the difference between Bakunin and the Hegelians, see footnote 74. As to whether recognition alone is enough or a politics of redistribution is also needed, see in particular Fraser's response in *Redistribution or Recognition?*

[83] Mikhail Bakunin, *La Libertà degli Uguali*, 91, 96.

[84] Ibid., 82. Despite the rupture between the two, notice that it is a view very close to Marx's positive conception of freedom, according to which freedom does not consist in the negative capacity to avoid this or that, but in the positive power to develop our potentialities. See for instance *The Holy Family*, where Marx says that man is not free for the negative force to avoid this or that, but for the positive power to develop his own individuality. See: Karl Marx and Friedrich Engels, *The Holy Family, or Critique of Critical Criticism*, in *Karl Marx and Frederick Engels Collected Works*, Vol. 5 (London: Lawrence and Wishart, 1975), 131.

[85] Mikhail Bakunin, *La Libertà Degli Uguali*, 82.

[86] Ibid., 82.

[87] Ibid., 82.

[88] Mikhail Bakunin, *Selected Writings*, 214–31. We see why Bakunin's notion of freedom, despite its Hegelian origins, goes well beyond Hegel: far from celebrating the nation state as the culminating point of ethical life, Bakunin calls for its elimination as a new form of political theology.

of the state and what he calls the "tyranny of the society."[89] The revolt against the first is easier because the enemy can effortlessly be identified, but the revolt against the second is much more complicated because, to a large extent, we are its products.

Hence the importance of addressing how prejudices circulating in our societies can come to influence our theories not simply in what we say, but through the very terms in which our inquiry is set up. By entering into contact with different social imaginaries and expanding one's knowledge to different regimes of truth, it is possible to find a moment of friction where the tyranny of each society breaks down. This is the reason why any genealogy of anarchism should strive to break the boundaries of ignorance created by Eurocentrism and sexism. Works such as Saul Newman's *Postanarchism*, which ignore theories produced by non-white and gender other than the "first sex," not only implicitly contribute to sexism and Eurocentrism, but also remain caught in a sort of performative contradiction: if anarchy means absence of an *archē*, then encapsulating it into a body of knowledge produced *only* by European white males means arguing for a fight against domination by reinforcing one of the greatest source of domination of our times—white patriarchy. The point, indeed, is not stopping to read nineteenth-century European male anarchists, but that it is not enough to complement them with twentieth-century European male post-structuralists. That body of knowledge may be an important part of the story, but it is not the only history, and it should therefore be treated as such. We need a pluralist genealogy of anarchism, which breaks the barrier of silence created by accumulated layers of Eurocentrism, racism, and sexism.

That is all the more necessary if we need to question the tyranny of society, because, as nineteenth-century Lithuanian-born anarchist Emma Goldman reminds us, the worst tyrant is not outside but inside ourselves.[90] It is indeed significant that Goldman puts forward her theory of the internal tyrant in her essay on "The tragedy of women's emancipation."[91] This tragedy consisted precisely in the fact that even when women manage to get rid of external tyrants, and attain economic independence, they often remain prey of the internal ones. This is evident both in the case of what she calls "traditional women," who mostly marry on

---

[89] Ibid, 214–31.
[90] Emma Goldman, *Anarchism and Other Essays*, 221.
[91] Ibid, 214–25.

economic grounds, and in the case of "emancipated women," who assume that, since they are emancipated, they have to do exactly the opposite of what traditional women do and thus often turn themselves into "compulsive vestals."[92] To renounce love, sex, and all the values associated with womanhood in the name of emancipation means reinforcing the views of moral detectives, those jailers of the human spirit, who imprisoned women between the two opposite poles of angels and devils.

Emma Goldman emphasized the centrality of puritan morality and the patriarchal family as tools for the oppression of women, but she also refused to reduce the causes of their oppression to one single factor.[93] She did not identify with the feminist movement of the time, which, like many other socialists and anarchists, she perceived as mainly concerned with questions that did not address capitalism and the state as a pivotal source of women's oppression. Hence also her critique of the suffragette movement of the time, and of its insistence on political rights as the only tool for the liberation of women. For her, women's suffrage is useless at best, and deceitful at worst: by merely casting votes in a ballot box women are most of the times unable to change the deeply intertwined inequalities of the societies we live in, while at the same time reinforcing an institution (the state) that contributes to their oppression.[94] Whereas a significant part of the suffragette movement of the time was composed by conservative feminists who saw in the women's suffrage movement a tool to purify politics of its corruption, as well as to enhance the purity of women themselves, Emma Goldman opposed this discourse of "social purity" as one of the main tools for the subjection of women. As she put in her essay on *Women's Suffrage*, "to assume [of the woman] she would succeed in purifying something which is not susceptible of purification, is to credit her with supernatural power."[95] If women's suffrage means turning women into better Christians, better homemakers, and better citizens of the state, as some suffragettes argued, then this cannot but enslave them once again to the very gods woman has served since time immemorial.[96]

---

[92] Ibid, 217.

[93] Alix Kates Shulman, "Dancing in the Revolution: Emma Goldman's Feminism," in *Feminist Interpretations of Emma Goldman*, 245.

[94] Deric Shannon, "Articulating a Contemporary Anarcha-Feminism," 60.

[95] Emma Goldman, *Anarchism and other Essays*, 198.

[96] Quoted in: Alix Kates Shulman, "Dancing in the Revolution: Emma Goldman's Feminism," 246.

Goldman once described the suffrage bill as a "wretched little bill which will benefit a handful of propertied ladies with absolutely no provision for the vast mass of working women."[97] Unfortunately, her prediction of how little the vote would actually benefit the women's cause has turned out to be correct, even to this day. Besides the right to vote, there needs to be a deep change in both the external and internal tyrants inhabiting within and among different genders alike in order for there to be a true emancipation of women. Thus, if Goldman did not join the feminist suffragette movement of her time, that was not because she was not a feminist, but because she was the most radical among them: for her, feminism did not mean the liberation of some privileged women, but of all of them. This is what she devoted her entire life to and what made her known as "the most dangerous woman in the world."[98]

Yet, for Goldman, like for other anarchists, there is not, and there cannot be, one single strategy for the liberation of women that could work in every context.[99] That is the reason why anarchists devoted themselves to fighting specific sources of women's oppression: Mikhail Bakunin criticized the Russian *mir* as a harmful form of patriarchy, Pyotr Kropotkin attacked the practice of sterilization, Voltairine de Cleyre denounced marriage as a tool for the subjugation of women, while Emma Goldman condemned both marriage and women's trafficking.[100] For Goldman, fighting on such multiple fronts is necessary because life constantly produces different circumstances so one has to be able to look at all of them simultaneously, while focusing on those that need most attention in each single context. But this also means that women cannot pursue their liberation alone. As she openly stated: "My quarrel with the feminists was that most of them see their slavery apart from the rest of

---

[97] Ibid, 246.
[98] Ibid, 242.
[99] This is a point emphasized by most interpreters of Emma Goldman's distinctive feminism. See, for instance, Lori Jo Marso, "A Feminist Search For Love: Emma Goldman On The Politics Of Marriage, Love, Sexuality And The Feminine," in *Feminist Interpretations of Emma Goldman*, 71–89; Marsha Hewitt, "Emma Goldman: The Case For Anarcho-feminism," in same collection; Loretta Kesinger, "Speaking with Red Emma: The Feminist Theory of Emma Goldman," in the same collection, Kesinger compares Goldman's feminism to that of bell hooks.
[100] Mikhail Bakunin, "Against Patriarchal Authority (1873)", in Robert Graham, Anarchism, 236–7; Pyotr Kropotkin, *Anarchism*; Voltairine de Cleyre, "They Who Marry Do Ill," in *Anarchy! An Anthology of Emma Goldman's Mother Earth*, ed. Peter Glassgold (Washington: Counterpoint, 2001), 103–13; Emma Goldman, *Anarchism and Other Essays*.

the human family."[101] But no such insularity is possible, because there is no liberation for anyone without the liberation of all—women included.[102] Goldman explicitly insists that, regardless all of the fundamental class and race distinctions, regardless of all artificial boundary lines between different genders, "there is a point where these differentiations can meet and grow into a perfect whole."[103] To use a contemporary term, we can say she developed an intersectional methodology: women cannot be free unless they can live in a free society, where all forms of oppression are dismantled. Feminism does not mean a society where women are sovereign and rule over genders. Feminism means no sovereignty at all. This is what is distinctively anarchist in Goldman's feminism.

The merit of Goldman's philosophy is indeed that "she gave a feminist dimension to anarchism and a libertarian dimension to the concept of women's emancipation."[104] However, her overall anarchist philosophy did not prevent her from focusing on the specificity of women's condition, as it emerges in her critique of marriage as an insurance pact, in her relentless struggle for birth control, and in her analysis of prostitution. Other anarchists failed to address the tragedy of women's emancipation, because they did not consider the specific institutions that perpetrate women's oppression, but simply assumed that their liberation was secondary. For Emma Goldman, at the top of the institutions perpetrating the oppression of women stood the continuum between marriage and prostitution, and, as such, they both deserved separate attention. She sees in the marriage of her time primarily an economic arrangement, some sort of "insurance pact" that differed from the ordinary insurance pact only in that it was more binding and more exacting, since its returns were significantly small compared with the investment.[105] In taking out an insurance policy one pays for it in dollars and cents, but remains always at liberty to discontinue payments, and does not have to invest an entire life into it. Women, however, pay for it with their own life and independence, as symbolized by the loss of their names, since, at the time of Emma Goldman's writing, most women took their husband's family

---

[101] Alice Wexler, *Emma Goldman: An Intimate Life* (New York: Pantheon Books, 1984), 197.
[102] Marsha Hewitt, "Emma Goldman: The Case For Anarcho-feminism," 313.
[103] Emma Goldman, *Anarchism and Other Essays.*
[104] Alice Wexler, *Emma Goldman*, 277.
[105] Emma Goldman, *Anarchism and Other Essays*, 228.
[106] Ibid, 228.

name in exchange for their father's.[106] This does not mean that women should not love men, or build life-long relationships with them, if they so wish. It means to emphasize that there is no predetermined way to love properly because "love is free" and "it can dwell in no other atmosphere" than freedom; one should never imprison it within the suffocating boundaries of an economic arrangement.[107]

On the other side of the spectrum, the tragic proportions of the traffic in women further proved, for her, the degree to which women are reduced to their sex and treated as such by modern society.[108] Emma Goldman was deeply committed to the idea of sexual freedom so she did not oppose sex work because it was *sex*, but because it was exploited *work*: for her, prostitution did not differ much from the other types of economic arrangements women are forced into—such as marriage. As she wrote:

> Nowhere is woman treated according to the merit of her work, but rather as a sex. It is therefore almost inevitable that she should pay for her right to exist, to keep a position in whatever line, with sex favours. Thus, it is merely a question of degree whether she sells herself to one man, in or out of marriage, or to many men. Whether our reformers admit it or not, the economic and social inferiority of women is responsible for prostitution.[109]

Emma Goldman recognizes that prostitution has existed since time immemorial, but still underlined that it is since the dawn of capitalism that it has become a "gigantic institution" and thus extremely exploitative.[110] For her, it was precisely the development of industry with vast masses of people in the competitive market, the growth and congestion of large cities, the insecurity and uncertainty of employment, that gave prostitution an impetus never dreamed of at any other period in human history.[111]

Hence the impossibility of handling the question of women's emancipation as an insular experience, separated from the other vast

---

[107] In another significant passage, with reference both to romantic love but also filial love, Goldman observes: "Love needs no protection; it is its own protection" (Ibid, 236–7).
[108] Ibid, 177–221.
[109] Ibid, 179.
[110] Ibid, 181.
[111] Ibid, 181.

array of economic, social, psychological and political forms of oppression. Individual and societal struggles are two sides of the same coin because individual and social instincts are two sides of the same coin. With an interesting twist to the organicist metaphor of the body politics, our Lithuanian-born anarchist wrote that the individual is the heart of society, which conserves and reproduces life, but society are its lungs which distribute the elements to keep life, and thus the individual, alive.[112] Notice here that she did not see the individual and society according to the traditional category of the body and its parts: both the individual and the society are parts (the heart and the lungs) of a much wider body, which is life itself.

As we have already mentioned, for her, despite all differences between gender, race, class, and sex distinction, there is a point where all oppressions meet, and, we can now add, that point is precisely anarchism. Anarchism, she writes, is the "teacher of the unity of life."[113] The reminder that life is not the compartmentalized being we have become accustomed to conceive through modern specialization, but a unity that constantly pulsates through difference.[114] This is the reason why anarchism is not a blueprint for the future, the story of a revolution to come, or an "iron-clad program" to be carried out under all circumstances: anarchism is a "living force in the affairs of our life," a force "constantly creating new conditions."[115]

In this vitalistic philosophy, which emerges in different pages of Goldman's writings, we can see echoes of Bakunin, Kropotkin, and others, but none of these intellectual precursors takes away the originality of her insights, and particularly the way in which she managed to give feminism a clear anarchist lens, while providing it with the analytical tools needed for addressing the specificity of the oppression of women.[116] Emma Goldman was one of the

---

[112] Ibid, 52.

[113] Ibid, 52.

[114] We can detect here some of Nietzsche's influence, whom Goldman read as a vitalist, and of Kropotkin's mutual aid theory.

[115] Emma Goldman, *Anarchism and Other Essays*, 63. In *Post-anarchism*, Saul Newman speaks of post-anarchism as an ethical-political practice that *starts* with anarchy rather than having it as *final* blueprint (see, in particular, Saul Newman, *Post-anarchism*, 9–13), and considers this to be a critical difference from classical anarchism, but he never quotes Goldman in his work, so his analysis remains truncated.

[116] Examples of such passages can be found in Emma Goldman, *Anarchism and Other Essays*, 49–52, 236–7. For a reading of Goldman's philosophy through a Nietzschean lens, see: Kathy E. Ferguson, "Religion, Faith and Politics: Reading Goldman Through Nietzsche," in Penny A. Weiss and Loretta Kesinger, eds., *Feminist Interpretations of Emma Goldman*.

most radical feminists of her era, precisely because she did not hesitate to point to the limit of feminism itself in her relentless opposition to *all* forms of domination she could perceive. Considering the constraints of her time, it is quite astonishing that, despite the at time simplistic binary opposition men *versus* women recurring in her writings, she also defended same-sex unions in public, which was unheard of during that era.[117]

It is therefore all the more puzzling that her work has been so systematically marginalized by political theory and feminist theory alike, not to mention contemporary post-anarchists such as Saul Newman, who would benefit so much from her insights. As Penny A. Weiss and Loretta Kensinger observe in their introduction to the anthology *Feminist Interpretation of Emma Goldman*, the first anthology to ever bring together the scarce and scattered secondary literature on her philosophy, the neglect and depreciation of women's work is common in most fields of endeavor, so there is nothing new in this. But such a neglect has been particularly egregious in social and political philosophy, and especially remarkable in the case of Emma Goldman, who has been granted a mythical status as "the most dangerous woman in the world," but also thereby denied any serious engagement as a theorist.[118] Whereas most works devoted to her do focus on her biography, very few engage with her writings from the point of view of their contribution to political philosophy, so it does not appear an exaggeration to say that turning her into a myth has sanitized, decontextualized, and thus ultimately deradicalized her philosophy.[119] And yet, she is an integral part of the

---

[117] Alix Kates Shulman, "Dancing in the Revolution: Emma Goldman's Feminism," 246.

[118] Penny A. Weiss and Loretta Kesinger, eds., *Feminist Interpretations of Emma Goldman*, 4–5. Unfortunately, this is also the case within anarchist thought. For instance, George Crowder's investigation of what stands for "*Classical Anarchism*," limits the analysis to men such as Godwin, Proudhon, Bakunin, and Kropotkin, thereby completely erasing the contribution of all other genders to what is "classical" in anarchist thought. See: George Crowder, *Classical Anarchism: The Political Thought of Godwin, Proudhon, Bakunin, and Kropotkin* (Oxford: Clarendon Press, 1992). Thinkers such as Emma Goldman and Voltairine de Cleyre are marginalized or passed over, never apparently deserving a proper chapter in the history of 'classical anarchism.'

[119] On Emma Goldman's life, see Emma Goldman, *Living My Life* (New York: Knopf, 1931); Alice Wexler, *Emma Goldman: An Intimate Life*; and Jason Wehling, "Anarchy in Interpretation: The Life of Emma Goldman," in *Feminist Interpretations of Emma Goldman*. Lori Jo Marso insists on how much one can learn both from Goldman's theories and from her life, but since most of the works on her have remained confined to her biography, for the purpose of this work, we have decided to leave those aspects of her legacy on a side. See: Lori Jo Marso, "A Feminist Search For Love: Emma Goldman On The Politics Of Marriage, Love, Sexuality And The Feminine," in *Feminist Interpretations of Emma Goldman*.

multifaceted genealogy of both anarchism and feminism, and one that, as we will see in the course of this book, is more useful today than ever. As Marsha Hewitt concludes: "Goldman's feminist insights deepened and enriched anarchist thoughts because she tried to show the interdependence of collective social transformation and the inner psychological, mental, and spiritual liberation of individuals. It is this legacy that anarcha-feminists must develop further and build upon."[120] It is therefore with Emma Goldman's remark that anarchism is the teacher of the unity of life, and that one cannot abolish one form of domination without tackling all others, that we will approach feminism, and contribute building an "anarcha-feminist" philosophy.

In the last few decades, political and technological transformations have led to a resurgence of interest in anarchism, a process that has led some of us to speak about "an anarchist turn."[121] On the one hand, the collapse of the Soviet Union seemed to have shown that anarchists such as Emma Goldman were right in their critique of Marxism-Leninism: a workers' state cannot but reproduce the same logic of every other state, where a minority of bureaucrats rule over the majority of people, so unless economic and political inequalities are eradicated together, they will keep reproducing each other, because they are nothing but two sides of the same coin.[122]

On the other hand, the technological developments of the last few decades, which are usually referred to as "globalization," gave a new impetus to anarchist theorizing and organizing. The rise of network form of social, economic and political organizations, in particular through the World Wide Web and associated technologies, have somehow proved what modern political theory has always been reluctant to recognize: order is possible without an orderer. This renders anarchy as a method,

---

[120] Marsha Hewitt, "Emma Goldman: The Case For Anarcho-feminism," 316.

[121] Jacob Blumenfeld, Chiara Bottici, Simon Critchley, eds., *The Anarchist Turn*. Simon Critchley puts forward an anarchist philosophy as a remedy to the political disappointment that he sees at the basis of Western liberal democracies, and uses that to propose a new ethics of commitment. See, in particular: Simon Critchley, *Infinitely Demanding. Ethics of Commitment, Politics of Resistance* (London: Verso, 2007).

[122] "They were servants, though called comrades, and they felt keenly the inequality: the Revolution to them was not a mere theory to be realized in years to come . . . these working women were crude, even brutal, but their sense of justice was instinctive. The Revolution to them was something fundamentally vital. They saw the inequality at every step and bitterly resented it." See: Emma Goldman, *My Disillusionment in Russia* (Garden City: Doubleday, Page & Company, 1923), 23–4.

and not as a blueprint, particularly timely. And it is within an increasingly globalizing world that, as we will see, lies the potential of the anarchafeminist philosophy. But it also within such a global context that it is more vital than ever to rethink anarchism beyond Eurocentrism, because as Kuan-Hsing Chen reminds us: "Globalization without deimperialization is simply a disguised reproduction of imperialist conquest."[123] To avoid the performative contradiction of an anarchist theory that is put forward as yet another form of white, patriarchal imperialism, we need to move beyond both methodological racism and sexism.

---

[123] Kuan-Hsing Chen, *Asia as Method: Toward Deimperialization* (Durham: Duke University Press, 2010), 2.

3 Within and against feminism: queer encounters

At this point of the argument, one might well wonder: why anarchafeminism and not just anarchism? If all forms of oppression are supposed to meet in a single whole, why insist on feminism? The simple answer is that no matter which axes of oppression one looks at, women are always at the bottom, at least in the current configuration of world affairs. This is already implicit in Emma Goldman's analysis and in her insistence on the tragedy of *woman*'s emancipation. Although working-class people, racialized bodies, differently abled bodies are all oppressed, women are even more so, because on top of all other forms of oppressions, women and feminized bodies in general must also carry the burden of being reduced to the second sex. Hence also the need to focus on the "tragedy of *woman*'s emancipation" specifically because we still live in a world where men in general, and white men in particular, are the sovereign sex, so women and all other gender cannot be anything other than the second. Globally, cisgendered men still enjoy the privilege of counting as both a specific gender, and the neutral form: in comparison to them, women and all LGBTQI+ people are all part of the "second sex," i.e. one that needs to be specified because it is never accorded the privilege of counting as the neuter, and thus as a name for humanity in general, in the way "Man" does.[1]

So there still is a need for feminism, but, as we will argue in this chapter, for one that combines it with anarchist insights: anarchafeminism. When joined with feminism, the prefix *anarcha* qualifies the type of feminism at

---

[1] "The relation of the two sexes is not that of two electrical poles: the man represents both the positive and the neuter..." in Simone de Beauvoir, *The Second Sex* (New York: Vintage, 2011), 5.

stake by suggesting that there is no *archē* explaining the oppression of women. As the work done in the name of intersectionality also emphasized, neither sex, nor class or race, or heterosexism, nor whatever other single item we can pick from our gender studies bookshelves, can ever aspire to be the unique factor, the decisive origin, the *archē* that explains, and thus also potentially explains away, the pluralistic nature of the oppression of women.

Between the different expressions available to designate this position— anarcho-feminism, anarchist feminism, or anarchafeminism—we will use the latter.[2] The term "anarcha-feminism" was used in 1970s by anglophone feminist social movements who combined anarchism and feminism. Among them, some emphasized the important convergence between the two—a convergence perceived as so significant that some feminists argued that "feminism practices what anarchism preaches."[3] Indeed, many feminist organizations pursued typically anarchist aims such as fighting domination and exploitation, and, in contrast to other social movements, very often used techniques traditionally used by anarchists, such as consensus-building, consciousness-raising groups, along with the emphasis on "the personal is political" or what anarchist traditionally called "prefigurative politics."[4]

Lynn Farrow and Peggy Kornegger were among those who insisted most vigorously on this connection between feminism and anarchism.[5] Kornegger went as far as to argue that radical feminists were "unconscious anarchists."[6] The structure of some women's movements, particularly those based on consciousness-raising groups, with their emphasis on small groups as the basic organizational unit, on the personal as political,

---

[2] In the Anglophone context, an important collection of historical texts of the anarcha-feminist tradition is now available in the Dark Star Collective's anthology: *Quiet Rumors: An Anarchafeminist Reader* (Oakland: AK Press, 2012). For a collection of more recent texts, see the 2016 special issue of *Perspectives on Anarchist Theory* entitled *Anarchafeminisms*. See: Hillary Lazar, Lazara Messersmith-Glavin, Paul Messersmith-Glavin, Maia Ramnath, and Theresa Warburton, ed., *Anarchafeminisms, Perspectives on Anarchist Theory*, No. 29 (Oakland: AK Press, 2020).

[3] Lynne Farrow, "Feminism as Anarchism," in *Quiet Rumors* 19; Julia Tenenbaum, "To Destroy Domination In All Its Forms: Anarchafeminist Theory, Organization and Action, 1970–1978," *Perspectives on Anarchist Theory*, No. 29 (2016), 13.

[4] Julia Tenenbaum, "To Destroy Domination In All Its Forms," 13–14.

[5] Lynne Farrow, "Feminism as Anarchism," 18–24; Peggy Kornegger, "Anarchism: The Feminist Connection," in *Quiet Rumors*, 156–78.

[6] Peggy Kornegger, "Anarchism: The Feminist Connection," 159.

and on spontaneous direct action, bore a striking resemblance to typically anarchistic forms of organization. Yet, while it is true that there is such a resemblance, to claim that feminists are unconscious anarchists or that feminists practice what anarchists preach is a misleading simplification.

In this book, we will be using the term anarchafeminism both to denote the movements that adopted the term and a political philosophy inspired by a different array of authors such as Emma Goldman and He Zhen, who did not explicitly use the formulation. This is because rather than identifying a tradition, a school, or a canon, we are interested in building an "anarchafeminist philosophy" that can include a variety of voices. However, such an enterprise cannot prescind from an engagement with those who have explicitly embraced the term, and perceived themselves as part of an "anarchafeminist" tradition. Despite the fact that a distinctively anarchafeminist activist tradition began a long time ago, it has suffered from an undeserved erasure within public debates, in general, and within academia, in particular.[7] This, as we have already mentioned, is partly due to the more general ban on anarchism, most of the time unfairly represented as synonymous with chaos and disorder, but also to the difficulty of distinguishing between anarchism in general and anarchafeminism in particular. Such a neglect has created a theoretical gap in the field, which has been filled only very partially.[8]

Whereas the term "anarcha-feminism" was originally used interchangeably with "anarcho-feminist" and "anarchist-feminist," we

---

[7] Roxanne Dunbar-Ortiz, "Quiet Rumors: An Introduction to this Anthology," in *Quiet Rumors*.

[8] Many anarchafeminist writings take the form of militant pamphlets, focused on specific issues, so the literature addressing the general theory remains scarce. Mitchell Verter proposed a form of anarchism based on a feminist politics of care that opens important directions for further consideration. See Mitchell Verter, "Undoing Patriarchy, Subverting Politics: Anarchism as a Practice of Care," in *The Anarchist Turn*, edited by Jacob Blumenfeld, Chiara Bottici and Simon Critchley (London: Pluto Press, 2013), 101–11. Deric Shannon has more recently argued for the need to articulate an anarchafeminist theory from the point of view of our contemporary predicament and thus engaged more directly with developments such as post-structuralism, post-colonial theory, intersectionality, queer theory, and ecology, but a lot of work in that direction is still to be done. As a first step, see: Deric Shannon, "Articulating a Contemporary Anarcha-Feminism." The 2016 special issue of *Perspectives on Anarchist Theory* devoted to "Anarcha-feminism" is only a partial response to that, since the contributions engage with only a part of the above-mentioned developments (Hillary Lazar, et al. eds., *Anarchafeminisms, Perspectives on Anarchist Theory* 29). This book is a further response to their call.

think it is important to keep the term anarcha-feminism in order to feminize the concept.[9] The reasons for this will become clear in the course of this book, but we can provisionally say that it is a terminological choice that signals the intent to keep the notion of *"femina"* at the center of emancipatory struggles, as we convey by eliminating the hyphen. This is also the reason why, in the context of this work, we will not be using the term "anarchx-feministix," which has been particularly popular in social movements.[10] The term suggests an attempt to queer the concept, going beyond the alternative between "a" and "o," that is, to go beyond the gender binarism "male/female" inherent in languages such as Spanish and Italian. Queer theory is particularly interesting in that respect, because, like the term "anarchx-feministix," it has within itself a pluralistic aspiration. Not all works in queer theory are necessarily committed to keeping the notion of womanhood. Although we think that it is absolutely crucial to engage and continue to do work in queer theory, in order to point to the pitfalls of binary gender identifications, we also think that we need to address the condition of people who are oppressed because they are perceived as "women" and thus insist on the need for a combination of queer theory's questioning of gender identification and a specific feminist agenda. That is the space where we situate "anarcha-feminism," that is, a form of feminism aimed at the liberation of women from all forms of oppressions, including those deposited in the hetero- and cisnormative dichotomy of "men" *versus* "woman". A dichotomy is a binary conceptual couple that is both reciprocally exclusive and mutually exhaustive of a field, and in this sense the "men" *versus* "women" dichotomy can indeed be itself a source of oppression for those who do not identify with either side. Hence the need to question such a dichotomy, even while focusing on the specific

---

[9] Julia Tenenbaum, "To Destroy Domination In All Its Forms," 15.

[10] The term "anarchx-feminism" or "anarchx-feministx" has recently been proposed as an alternative to anarchafeminism, in order to further signal the need to abolish gender oppression (https://anarchistbookfair.net/anarchx-feminist-manifesto/) (accessed on June 15, 2020). The term is similar to the expression "Latinx", which has been used to replace Latina/Latino, and thus displace the gender binary that is so imbued in languages such as Spanish and Italian. Although we share many of the goals highlighted in their manifesto, we strategically disagree with their usage of the notion of "femme" as a replacement for "woman": Instead of just using a different term, and thus risk alienating all those who are not familiar with the nuances of the usage of the term "femme" as a term for whatever body occupies a "woman's" position, it is better to articulate a notion of womanhood that is open, and thus create a broader network of solidarity with movements using the term "woman."

oppression of those who are perceived *as*, and/or perceive themselves, *as* "women."

But if the purpose is to address the specific oppression of women, why not just feminism? As we will now see, feminism alone is not sufficient as there can be feminisms that are compatible with domination. For instance, there are radical feminists who argue that since patriarchy has done so much harm, it is now time to flip the coin, returning to women the fundamental responsibility for human affairs, and thereby replacing patriarchy with matriarchy.[11] Among them Sally Miller Gearhart went as far as devising a quite detailed plan, structured in three fundamental steps: 1) every culture should build an ideology of a female future and systematically argue for female superiority; 2) every country should return species responsibility to women; 3) the proportion of men must be reduced to and maintained at approximately 10 percent of the human race, because, even if conditions 1) and 2) were successfully applied, there is no guarantee that the culture of violence and war that men have diffused on the planet will disappear.[12] Besides the fact that such view mistakenly attributes sexism only to men, thereby forgetting that women can also be sexist (and violent), the problem with this view is that it simply replaces one domination with another. It is therefore certainly a form of feminism, but not one that is striving for an abolition of all forms of domination.[13]

Feminism itself can indeed be a tool for domination, even when it does not openly call for it. For instance, in 1963 the American author Betty Friedan published an extremely influential work, *The Feminine Mystique*, in which she denounced what she called the "the problem that has no name."[14] Partly chronicle and partly manifesto, Betty Friedan explores here the deep dissatisfaction of stay-at-home American women, who devote their entire life to their mission of wives and mothers on the basis of the illusionary mystical belief that they are fulfilling an inner feminine essence—a belief Friedan aptly called "the feminine mystique."

---

[11] Sally Miller Gearhart, "The Future—If There Is One—Is Female," in *Reweaving the Web of Life: Feminism and Nonviolence*, ed. Pam McAllister (Philadelphia: New Society Publisher, 1982), 270.

[12] Sally Miller Gearhart, "The Future—If There Is One—Is Female," 271.

[13] For a critique of this position from the point of view of anarchism, see: L. Susan Brown, "Beyond Feminism: Anarchism and Human Freedom," in *The Anarchist Papers 3*, ed. Demetrios I. Roussopoulos (New York: Black Rose Books, 1990), 206–07.

[14] Betty Friedan, *The Feminine Mystique* (New York: W. W. Norton, 1963), 1–22.

To escape this fate, Friedan called for women to leave their self-imposed ghettos and fight for full equality with men, competing with them in the attainment of positions of power.[15] In advocating this, Friedan has no problem with the fact that such a feminist struggle leaves intact—or may even exacerbate—economic inequalities, capitalist exploitation, and racial domination: she just champions a fight for women's equality that could bring women to occupy the same position of power as white, middle-class men and thus a form of feminism that does not disturb existing hierarchies such as that of the state or the capitalist economy. Furthermore, by not even mentioning the condition of Black women, for whom exiting their own home often means entering that of more privileged women to replace them in care work, Friedan implicitly turns feminism into a form of white privilege, that is, into the idea that women should liberate themselves by struggling to occupy the place reserved for economically successful men, which, in the US context, often means white men. Similarly, by ignoring the political relevance of lesbian, intersex, trans- and non-binary bodies, experiences, and demands, she implicitly portrayed all women as straight and heterosexual, thereby reinforcing the heterosexist biases of the societies we live in. If by "feminism" we mean that white heterosexual women should pursue their liberation at the expenses of all other women, or that matriarchy should replace patriarchy, then anarchafeminism is against feminist.

Clearly Betty Friedan has a view of feminism very different from that of bell hooks, Audre Lorde, and Emma Goldman, who defined feminism as struggle to end women oppression,[16] and from He Zhen, who, as we have seen, argues that the liberation of women means no more submissive women nor men.[17] This malleability of feminism, which can indeed go in very different directions when not accompanied by the qualification "*anarcha,*" also explains how, closer to us, is it possibly for women such as

---

[15] Betty Friedan, *The Feminine Mystique,* 407.
[16] Although this view recurs in all of these authors, an explicit discussion of this definition can be found in bell hooks' insightful essay "Feminism: A Movement to End Sexist Oppression," where she argues that defining feminism as simply equality with men is insufficient. See: bell hooks, *Feminist Theory: From Margin to Center* (Boston, MA: South End Press, 1999), 18–33. See also: Audre Lorde, "Age, Race, Class, and Sex: Women Redefining Difference," in *Sister Outsider: Essays and Speeches* (Berkeley: Crossing Press, 1984); Emma Goldman, *Anarchism and Other Essays* (New York: Dover Publications, 1969).
[17] He Zhen, "Women's Liberation," in *Anarchism. A Documentary History of Libertarian Ideas,* Vol. 1, ed. by Robert Graham (Montreal: Black Rose Books, 2005–12), 341.

Ivanka Trump to reclaim feminist battles of the past and use them as a tool for promoting a fashion brand. For Ivanka Trump, the key to all of women's problems is indeed "boosting one's own productivity" so as to be able to both occupy the caring role of a mother and be a successful venture capitalist.[18] According to the view espoused in her bestselling book, *Women Who Work*, liberating oneself comes to mean—quite literally—dominating others: as we read in the book's last chapter, significantly entitled "Lead with Purpose," the whole point is how to become "a leader of others," and thus how to be successful in "leading" companies, "leading" co-workers, "leading" families, and so on and so forth.[19]

The problem is not only that some women literally see their liberation in the domination of others. More generally, given how life is interconnected on our planet, even when women do not call for the domination of others, but simply focus on their own specific struggles without taking into account those of others, it may well be the case that their emancipation will happen at the expense of further oppression for less fortunate women, beginning with those who most often replace them in the reproductive labor within the household. As we will see later on, this risk is particularly evident when we adopt a global perspective, all the more necessary today because of the increased mobility of capital and labor forces, and the increasingly global nature of the chain linking gendered labor across the globe. We need a multifaceted approach to domination, in particular, one able to incorporate different factors as well as the different voices coming from all over the globe, because just competing with white middle class men for power will not do. As He Zhen wrote in the passage from her *Women's Liberation* quoted in the Introduction, when a few women in power dominate the majority of powerless women, unequal class differentiation proliferates and divides women from one another. But if the majority of women do not want to be controlled by men, why would do they want to be controlled by a few women? Not being controlled by men (nor by a few privileged women), also means that instead of competing with men for power, women should strive for overthrowing male rule, because once men are stripped of their privilege, they will become the equal of women, and there will be no

---

[18] Ivanka Trump, *Women Who Work: Rewriting the Rules for Success* (New York: Penguin, 2017), 113.
[19] Ivanka Trump, *Women Who Work* , 171–208.

submissive women or men. This is because, as we will see, for He Zhen being a "man" or a "woman" is not an identity, but a social relation.[20]

As early as 1907 He Zhen was very well aware that the best antidote against the possibility of feminism becoming simply (white and bourgeois) privilege and, thus, a tool in the hands of a few women who dominate the vast majority of them, was to call for the abolition of all exploitation and domination. In an epoch when new venture capitalists can claim feminist battles of the past as a tool to sell a fashion brand, the fundamental message of anarchafeminists of the past is therefore more urgent than ever. As Peggy Kornegger put it: "Feminism does not mean female corporate power or a woman president: it means no corporate power and no presidents."[21] More political or economic rights for women will not transform society; they will only give women the "right to plug into a hierarchical economy."[22] On the contrary, challenging sexism means challenging all hierarchies—economic, political, and personal. And that means an anarcha-feminist revolution."[23]

The anarchafeminist philosophy must thus be placed within the socialist tradition, which saw the liberation of women as necessarily involving a deep change of the social, political and economic structure of current capitalist societies. Yet, in contrast to other forms of socialist feminism, the anarchafeminism philosophy is by definition anti-authoritarian and is thus incompatible with any form of hierarchy, including that of the state and of vanguard political parties. There has been a tendency within the socialist movements to consider the oppression of women as a secondary issue, to be dealt with after the problem of class exploitation has been resolved, under the assumption that a classless society will also be a free society for everybody, women included. As some feminists have argued, by reducing the problem of women's oppression to the single factor of economic exploitation, certain forms of Marxism have all too often ended up dominating feminism precisely in the same way in which men in a patriarchal society dominate

---

[20] He Zhen, "Women's Liberation," 341. We will return later in this book to He Zhen's philosophy of gender as a social relation.

[21] Peggy Kornegger, "Anarchism: The Feminist Connection," in *Reinventing Anarchy: What Are Anarchists Thinking These Days*, Howard J. Ehrlich, et al. eds. (London: Routledge, 1979), 160.

[22] Peggy Kornegger, "Anarchism: The Feminist Connection," 160.

[23] Ibid.

women, through an alliance that could turn out to be a rather "unhappy marriage."[24] Although this has not always been the case, and there have been also much happier marriages between Marxism and feminism,[25] it is undeniable that there have been tensions between these two schools of thought, so much so that, as Cinzia Arruzza puts it, we can define that relationship as "dangerous liaisons."[26]

Any critical analysis of the oppression of women needs to take into account a multiplicity of factors, each with its own drivers, without attempting to reduce them to one all-explaining source or *archē*—be it the extraction of surplus value in the workplace or unpaid domestic labor in the household. There is something intrinsically multifaceted in the oppression of women and that is why a connubial between anarchism and feminism is particularly welcome. If anarchism does not mean a fixed blueprint for a future to come, but a method aimed at questioning any established *archē*, then it is a tool that can be happily combined with a form of feminism that is attentive to the specific configuration of oppression in the different contexts, but without losing track of the ultimate end to shatter the politics of domination at its foundation.[27]

Although not all forms of feminism are anarchist, because not all of them are anti-authoritarian, anarchism is by definition feminist. If anarchism is a philosophy that opposes all forms of domination, it has to oppose the subjection of women too, otherwise it is out of alignment with its own principles. Most anarchist thinkers work with a conception of freedom that emphasized the indivisibility of freedom; that is, the fact that I cannot be free unless everyone else is equally free. If I cannot be

---

[24] Lydia Sargent, ed., *Women and Revolution: A Discussion of the Unhappy Marriage of Marxism and Feminism* (Boston, MA: South End Press, 1981).

[25] Example of happier marriages include Nancy Fraser's multi-dimensional approach to gender (Nancy Fraser, *Fortunes of Feminism* [London: Verso, 2013]), Cinzia Arruzza's investigations of the dangerous liaisons between Marxism and feminism (Cinzia Arruzza, *Le relazioni pericolose: Matrimoni e divorzi tra marxismo e femminismo* [Roma: Alegre, 2010]); Silvia Federici's rethinking of reproduction theory (Silvia Federici, *Revolution at Point Zero: Housework, Reproduction, and Feminist Struggle* [Oakland, PM Press, 2012]), and the intersectionalist approaches collected in the recent anthology *Marxism and Feminism*, ed. Shahrzad Mojab (London: Zed Books, 2015) in particular, pp. 203–21, 287–305.

[26] Cinzia Arruzza, *Le relazioni pericolose*.

[27] This insight into the nature of anarchism as a methodology combines authors as different Errico Malatesta (2001) and Reiner Schürmann. See: Errico Malatesta, *L'Anarchia*; Reiner Schürmann, "On Constituting Oneself an Anarchist Subject," *Praxis International* 6, no. 3 (1986), 294–310.

free unless I live surrounded by people who are equally free—so, unless I live in a free society—then the subjection of women cannot be reduced to something that concerns only a part of the society: A patriarchal society is oppressive for everybody, despite harming some more than others, precisely because nobody can be free on their own. And this is something that we tend to forget: patriarchy is not just a women's issue. As He Zhen put it, liberation of women means no more submissive women and no more submissive men—and thus, we may add, no submission at all.

Otherwise stated, anarchafeminism does not mean that women should take the place occupied by privileged white men, but that they should fight to radically subvert the logic of patriarchal oppression where sexism, racism, classism, statism, heterosexism, and other systems of oppression reciprocally reinforce one another by purporting a politics of domination. This has never been more apparent than today, in a globalizing world where diverse forms of oppression and exploitation are increasingly bound up with global capitalism.[28]

To conclude on this point, maybe feminism has not always been anarchist, but it should become so now, because it should aim at combating all forms of domination. We can start to see what it means to develop an anarchafeminist philosophy at the methodological level too: It means developing a form of feminism without patronyms. In contrast to other forms of feminism, such as the Marxist or Foucauldian versions, the very term anarchafeminism gestures at an attempt to get rid of any patronym, because it is a critique of hierarchy and oppression in all of its multifaceted forms, including in theory-making.

In sum, feminism does not mean the liberation of some women, but of *all* of them.[29] Any "outcast" is a menace to freedom. Thus, for anarchafeminists, freedom cannot but be a freedom of equals, because, given the indivisibility of freedom, either it exists as such or not at all. But if that is the case, can there be feminism without a questioning of the

---

[28] On the problem raised by the so-called "global chain care" and the way it restructures global economy see: Nicola Yeates, *Globalizing Care Economies and Migrant Workers: Explorations in Global Care Chains* (New York: Palgrave Macmillan, 2009). While on the way in which it challenges traditional Marxist assumptions, see: Silvia Federici, *Revolution at Point Zero*, 115–25.
[29] Cinzia Arruzza, Tithi Bhattacharya, and Nancy Fraser called their manifesto *Feminism for the 99%*, thereby using a popular slogan during the Occupy Wall Street movement: "We are the 99%," See: Cinzia Arruzza, Tithi Bhattacharya, and Nancy Fraser, *Feminism for the 99%* (London: Verso, 2019). In this way, they do signal their distance from liberal feminism, but an anarchafeminist would go even further and argue for a liberation of 100 percent of us.

heteronormative and cisnormative biases that implicitly portray the category of women as straight, cisgendered bodies? An anarchafeminist philosophy must address not only the liberation *of* women, but also the liberation *from* "women," that is from a hetero- and cisnormative understanding of this category that may liberate some bodies while potentially reinforcing hierarchies that exclude others.

Queer theory has been pivotal in investigating how heteronormativity, with its gender binarism, fundamentally shapes not only gender, but also gender as a field.[30] By dividing people into heterosexual and homosexual, and propping up heterosexuality as the norm, heteronormativity shapes institutions and individuals' lives alike. "Heteronormativity" is a term created to denote the way in which heterosexuality dictates explicit or implicit norms to our daily life, thereby casting behaviors, identities, and situations that fall outside of it as deviation.[31] Since its creation in the 1990s, the term has been widely embraced to investigate the cluster of assumptions according to which there are only two genders, that they reflect the biological binary opposition between male and female, and that only sexual attraction between two opposite sexes is natural and thus acceptable.[32] This threefold cluster of assumptions structures social beliefs, organizations, policies, institutional practices, as well as gestures and behaviors, thereby perpetrating "heterosexism," that is the associated idea that "heterosexuality" is the sole, legitimate expression of eros, sexuality, and affection.[33]

---

[30] For an assessment of queer theory's contribution to gender studies, see the very insightful: David Eng, Jack Halberstam, and José E. Muñoz, "What's Queer About Queer Studies Now?," *Social Text* 23, no. 3–4 (2005), 1–17; and also: Michael Warner, "Queer And Then? The End Of Queer Theory," *The Chronicle for Higher Education* (2012); and the two volumes of reconstruction of a few decades of queer theory provided by Lorenzo Bernini. See Lorenzo Bernini, *Queer Apocalypses* (London: Palgrave, 2017); Lorenzo Bernini, *Queer Theories: An Introduction* (New York: Routledge, 2020).

[31] The term was coined by Michael Warner and has since replaced Adrienne Rich's fortunate expression "compulsory heterosexuality." See: Michael Warner, "Introduction: Fear of a Queer Planet," *Social Text* 29 (2001), 3–17; Adrienne Rich, "Compulsory Heterosexuality and Lesbian Existence," *Signs* 5, no. 4 (1980), 631–60.

[32] Panteá Farvid, "Heterosexuality," in *The Palgrave Book of the Psychology of Sexuality and Gender*, eds. Christina Richards and Meg John Barker (London: Palgrave Macmillan, 2015), 98.

[33] If we dig a little into the genealogy of the term "heterosexuality," however, we discover that at the beginning, it denotes something almost opposite of its current meaning as "normative sexuality." In a context where sex was so tightly bound up with reproduction, the term denoted a desire for sex with people of the opposite sex, thus a desire that did not necessarily have procreation as an end, but was instinctually driven by it (Farvid, "Heterosexuality," 93). It was only in the 1920s, when sex became associated with a general libido separate from procreation, that the term came to mean a "normal" sexuality.

Judith Butler is among the philosophers who most systematically emphasized how much heteronormativity has shaped also our understanding of feminism. Her path-breaking *Gender troubles* opens indeed with that daunting question: how to define feminism without presupposing that there exists a very stable and pregiven subject for it? In what ways are women the "subject" of feminism, the origins but also result of the very same movement that tries to liberate them? How is feminism entangled with the heterosexual matrix? "For the most part, Butler writes, feminist theory has assumed that there is some existing identity, understood through the category of women, who not only initiates feminist interests and goals within discourse, but constitutes the subject for whom political representation is pursued."[34] Is there such a subject of feminism pursuing representation, and if so, to what a degree is that *subject* also *subjected* to the discourse of feminism?

By questioning the concept of a pre-given identity, and emphasizing that there is no doer behind the deeds, Judith Butler further developed the Foucauldian analysis of power that some post-structural anarchists addressed: Whereas traditional theories of power conceived it as a force exercised between two already constituted subjects, so that A is said to have power over B, if it has the capacity to make B do things that B would otherwise not do, Butler strongly challenged that assumption and focused instead on how subjects themselves are created in the first place. As we have already mentioned in the analysis of post-structural anarchism, whereas traditional views of power see it as primarily located in certain institutions such as the state and army, Foucault insisted that "power isn't located in the State apparatus and that nothing in society will be changed if the mechanisms of power that function outside, below and alongside the state apparatuses, on a much more minute and everyday level, are not also challenged."[35] We could say that whereas the traditional model helps us understand how oppression work, that is how a course of events is prevented from happening because of an "external" influence, the Foucauldian understanding of power points to much deeper mechanisms "internal" to the subjects of power themselves, and thus, more than a theory of oppression, provides the building blocks for a theory of domination. Whereas the concept of oppression has indeed a physical connotation, and presupposes the pre-given existence of those whose

---

[34] Judith Butler, *Gender Trouble* (New York: Routledge, 1990), 2.
[35] Michel Foucault, *Power-Knowledge* (New York: The Harvester Press, 1980), 60.

suffer from it, the concept of domination points to how subjects themselves come into being through practices and an internalized discipline of obedience.[36]

Instead of focusing on sexual identity, Michel Foucault's analysis of the history of sexuality excavated the way in which sexuality itself has been created as a field by several techniques distinctive to modern societies, such as medicine, science, and biopolitical practices. Despite the fact that this analysis is located in the Western history of sexuality and thus deeply embedded in Western epistemologies, it has the merit of underlying a crucial paradigm shift in the understanding of power, as well as providing important tools for analyzing disciplinary practices that originated in Western epistemologies but which have also become hegemonic worldwide. In particular, with the expansion of the institution of the modern state from its origins in Europe to the rest of the world, the biopolitical practices that lead states to use modern science and statistics to map and discipline their subjects through their sex(ualities) is a worldwide phenomenon. There is indeed no state on the planet that that does not divide citizens according to their gender identity, which almost always is conceived in terms of the binary males/females, and that does not try to make sure such a gendered identity remains attached to them through their identity papers. Along with the state apparatus, there is however an entire apparatus of secular knowledge experts that carry out the work of gender, and which includes disciplines such as medicine, psychology, and demography.[37]

We tend to forget that states do not a priori need to map and discipline the gender of their inhabitants and that the biological life of its citizens has not always been a primary concern of political power: before the emergence of what Michel Foucault termed "biopower," the primary aim of the state was to discipline citizens through the power of the sword, and thus through the threat of coercion, and not through a governmental apparatus aimed at

---

[36] See: Thomas Hippler, "Spinoza's Politics of Imagination and the Origins Of Critical Theory," in *The Politics of Imagination*, eds. Chiara Bottici and Benoît Challand (London: Routledge, 2011), 55–73. This insight about the nature of domination recurs in different exponents of critical theory broadly understood, from Spinoza to Foucault. What queer theory adds to this is a further questioning of the inside/outside dichotomy.

[37] This is what leads Foucault to introduce the notion of "biopolitics" precisely during his investigations into the history of sexuality. See in particular: Michel Foucault, *The History of Sexuality*, Vol. 1 (New York: Vintage Books, 1990).

making its citizens live.[38] By developing Foucauldian themes, Butler emphasized how the construction of the category of sexuality as a field helped to construct identities such as that of the homosexual and the heterosexual, which did not even exist before European sexologists and psychiatrists started to investigate sexuality as a separate field of enquiry. By turning erotic gestures and behaviors into the effect of a supposed "homosexual identity," perceived as an inversion of the natural sexual drive, the "heterosexual matrix" is established and, through biopolitical apparatuses, progressively developed as the implicit norm of our social life.[39]

This heterosexual matrix is thus not only imposed so to speak from above, but also reproduced by those who seek a deliverance from it. For instance, the apparently liberatory language of "coming *out,*" which is widely employed within anglophone LGBTQI+ communities, implicitly reinforces the heterosexual matrix because it presupposes the idea that if somebody's sexual desires do not conform with the heterosexual paradigm, then they must have remained in the "closet."[40] To insist that there is no doer behind the deeds, that there is no performer before the performance, the way Butler does, means emphasizing that there is no already constituted subject before the process of subjectification that turns bodies into subjects.[41] If that is the case, then the question is not only how to liberate sexuality and women from external authorities oppressing them, but also how to liberate ourselves from sexuality and womanhood as fields of operation of power that are constitutive of our own identity: there is an important shift here from a politics of external institutions to "a politics of ourselves."[42] In other words, the problem is

---

[38] According to Foucault, while classical sovereignty was a power aimed at controlling life by threatening it with the possibility of death, the new form of power that emerges in the mid-nineteenth century is that of a power aimed at inciting and preserving life. As he put it, while the sovereign power—crucially symbolized by the sword—was essentially a power to kill, a power to take life, the new biopower manifests itself as "a power to make live and let die." Hence the increased significance of biological life, as the medium where political power displays itself. See: Michel Foucault, *"Society Must be Defended:" Lectures at the Collège de France, 1975–1976,* trans. David Macey (New York: Picador, 2003), 241.

[39] Judith Butler, *Gender Trouble,* 47–106.

[40] Judith Butler, "Imitation and Gender Insubordination," in *The Lesbian and Gay Studies Reader,* David M. Halperin, Henry Abelove, and Michele Aina Barale, eds. (New York: Routledge, 1993), 309. For a critique of the "closet epistemologies," see also: Eve Kosofsky Sedgwick, *Epistemology of the Closet* (Berkeley: University of California Press, 2008).

[41] Judith Butler, "Imitation and Gender Insubordination," 315.

[42] Amy Allen, *The Politics of Our Selves: Power, Autonomy, and Gender in Contemporary Critical Theory* (New York: Columbia University Press, 2008).

no longer just how to liberate sex and gender, but also how to liberate ourselves *from* sex and gender a field of operation of power-knowledge.

Consider for instance the role of medicine and knowledge experts in classifying certain behaviors and deeds into identities both in Europe and in the US. In the 1930s homosexuality was considered as a perversion, as a shift away from the normal order of the libido or sexual drive, which deviates from its natural aim, being the union with a body of the opposite sex.[43] Even in 1960s, at the peak of the so called "sexual liberation" movement, "homosexuality" was still officially considered a "psychosocial disorder" within the second edition of the *Diagnostic Statistical Manual of Mental Disorders* (DSM), the official handbook for the classification of mental disorders issued by the American Psychiatric Association—a manual used by innumerable researchers, pharmaceutical and insurance companies, lawyers, and policy-makers, not to mention the countless clinicians who applied it to their everyday treatment of patients.[44] Thanks to the work done by social activists in general, and by homosexual psychologists and psychiatrists in particular, the 1974 edition of the *DSM* removed "homosexuality" from the list of "psychosexual disorders," but it added "transsexuality" (which had been treated a just a specific case of homosexuality until then). So while homosexuality was now left to psychologists, transsexuality kept being treated as a mental disorder, at least until the fourth edition of the *DSM* published in 1994, when it was also finally expunged from the list (probably also as a consequence of the proliferation of work by queer theorists and activists in the 1990s). Yet, at the time of writing, the category of "transsexualism" has been replaced by that of "gender dysphoria," which is arguably a very similar category, since the term means that there is an ongoing discrepancy between the gender assigned at birth and the person's current feelings about it. Rather than being viewed as the result of an oppressive gender system, it is actually classified as a "mental disorder." As a "disorder" within the order implemented by medical and state gender systems, "gender dysphoria," the

---

[43] On the history of heterosexuality as an institution and its origin in the work of European sexologists and psychiatrists, see: Farvid, "Heterosexuality."

[44] Stephen Thomas Whittle, "Gender Fucking or Fucking Gender?" in *Queer Theory*, eds. Iain Morland, and Dino Willo (London: Palgrave, 2005), 116.

etymology of which means "carrying the wrong gender,"[45] has come to play exactly the same disciplining role exercised previously by its predecessor categories of "homosexuality" and "transsexualism."[46] There does not seem an easy way out of the biopower of the modern gender system.

Hence the importance of the drag experiences and performances because, as Judith Butler rightly emphasized, they imitate a masculine or a feminine for which there is no original and in doing so they reveal the fundamentally imitative structure of gender.[47] Drag does not mean putting on a gender that belongs to another group—that is, an act of appropriation presupposing that gender is the rightful property of a certain sex, on the binary assumption that masculine belongs to the male and feminine belongs to female. It means revealing that sex is as socially constructed as gender, or, as Butler's felicitous expression puts it, "that gender is a kind of imitation for which there is no original."[48] Through the illumination of drag-queen performances then we can perceive that any gender has a performative dimension to it. It is not only the case that drag performances are imitative, but so are, and to a greater extent, heteronormative ones: Whereas the drag queens performances assembled in movies such *Paris is Burning* suggest that there is no pregiven performer before the performance itself, gender imitations such a Beyoncé's *Crazy in Love* video, which are a performance of femininity, add to the performance the illusion that it correspond to a true, deeper identity that precedes the performance itself.[49] The naturalistic effect of heterosexualixed

---

[45] The word dysphoria comes from two ancient Greek roots "*dys*" meaning "bad, wrong" (like in terms such as "dystopias") and "*phoria*" from the verb *phero*, meaning "to carry, to bring." As such, it has been subversively reappropriated by activists who opposed it to the term "gender eu-phoria," meaning a condition yet to come (*ou*) where everybody is given the possibility to feel "happy" (*eu*) about their gender.

[46] Stephen Thomas Whittle, "Gender Fucking or Fucking Gender?" 117.

[47] Judith Butler, *Gender Trouble*, 186–9. See also: Judith Butler, *Bodies That Matter: On the Discursive Limits of "Sex"* (New York: Routledge, 2011).

[48] Judith Butler, "Imitation and Gender Insubordination," 313.

[49] See Judith Butler's brilliant analysis of the movie *Paris is Burning* in *Bodies That Matter*, in particular pp. 88–95. On the notion of the feminine as a masquerade, see Jacqueline Rose, "Introduction II" in *Feminine Sexuality. Jacques Lacan and the école freudienne*, edited by Juliet Mitchell and Jacqueline Rose, New York/London: Norton, 42–4. Rose 1982: 43 and the translated passages, ibid.: 84 (cf. Jacques Lacan, *Écrits*, trans. Bruce Fink (New York: W. W. Norton, 583). See also Lacan's extended engagement with Joan Riviere's "Womanliness as a masquerade," *International Journal of Psychoanalysis* 10 (1929), 303–13: "To go further into my formulas, I will say that in man's realm there is always the presence of some imposture. In the woman's, if something corresponds to this, then it's the masquerade. . . ." Jacques Lacan, "*The Seminar of Jacques Lacan, Book X: Anxiety*," trans. Adrian R. Price (Cambridge: Polity Press, 2014), 191, 266.

genders are produced through imitative strategies, not less than any other gender: "What they imitate is a phantasmatic ideal of heterosexual identity, one that is produced by the imitation as its effect."[50]

The specific contribution of queer theory within this field of operation lies in its questioning of the boundaries of such sexual and gender identities, and thus inviting us to resist the process of subjectification that they produce. What is specifically queer about queer theory, therefore, is that it is itself an open-ended process aimed at critiquing those hegemonic social structures by which certain subjects are rendered "normal" and "natural," through the production of "perverse" and "pathological" others.[51] As such, queer critique is directed at questioning all boundaries and processes of normalization via naturalization, and should remain an open-ended process that does not stop at sexual and gender identities, but also looks at their intersections with other normativizing processes such as racial, class, and imperial epistemologies. Butler emphasized this from the very beginning in her essay "Critically queer," according to which "it is necessary to insist on the contingency of the term, to let it be vanquished by those who are excluded by the term but who justifiably expect representation by it, to let it take on meanings that cannot now be anticipated by a younger generation whose political vocabulary may well carry a very different set of investments."[52]

Despite this early call not to turn queerness into yet another identity to assume, queer culture itself has gone through a process of commercialization and commodification that turned queerness into just a synonym for gay identity.[53] As such, it has often been turned into a politics of recognition, aimed at recognizing the legitimacy of certain (queer) identities, for the critique of which it had emerged in the first place. Even more, as an identity for the protection of which certain political regimes can boost themselves, it has given support to a homonationalist politics, that is, of a form of patriotism and attachment to certain regimes, that can pink-wash their imperial politics in the name of protection of this new form of queer liberalism. According to critics such a Jasbir Puar, there is something intrinsically problematic in queer

---

[50] Judith Butler, "Imitation and Gender Insubordination," 313.
[51] David Eng, Jack Halberstam, and José Esteban Muñoz, "What's Queer About Queer Studies Now?," 3.
[52] Judith Butler, *Bodies That Matter*, 230.
[53] Michael Warner, "Queer And Then? The End Of Queer Theory."

theory's assumption that one can always potentially question one's own identity: if all of our identities must constantly be challenged, then there must be some sort of "an impossible transcendent subject who is always already conscious of the normativizing forces of power and always ready and able to subvert, resist, or transgress them."[54] In this sense, queer theory itself, not just its reappropriation by imperial governments for the purpose of pink-washing, would be imbued with a liberal imperial imagination centered on the idea of a disembodied transcendent subject.[55]

Although Jasbir Puar's analysis points to an undesirable union between queer liberalism and homonationalism that has been a recurrent problem in the geopolitics of the last thirty years, it also does not do justice to the multifaceted cacophonies of queer theory, that is, to the multiplicity of queer voices that very often speak in contrast with one another, let alone to many queer theorists' invitation to let the queer proliferate. There have certainly been attempts to turn queerness into yet another identity to be recognized by state authorities, or as a commodity to sell on "Gay Pride" days, which can lend themselves to homonationalist politics. But there have also been voices against this tendency and reclaiming queerness as a futurity. For José Esteban Muñoz, for instance, queerness is not an identity to choose in the present, but rather that thing that makes us feel that this present is not enough, that something is missing. As a consequence, "queerness is not yet here. Queerness is an ideality. Put another way, we are not yet queer. We may never touch queerness, but we can feel it as the warm illumination of a horizon imbued with potentiality."[56]

Muñoz's perspective on queerness as a futurity, and not as an already given identity one can claim, is very close to the spirit of Butler's fundamental insight on the performativity of gender. Queerness is performative because it is not a being, but a doing for and towards a future. Despite all misunderstanding around the notion of the performativity of gender, Butler pointed out from the very beginning that

---

[54] Jasbir Puar, *Terrorist Assemblages: Homonationalism in Queer Times* (Durham: Duke University Press, 2007), 24.

[55] Jasbir Puar, *Terrorist Assemblages*, 206.

[56] José Esteban Muñoz, *Cruising Utopia: The Then and There of Queer Futurity* (New York: New York University Press, 2009), 8.

this does not mean that gender is a role that one can choose at will, as if humans were transcendent subjects choosing from a menu restaurant. As we read in their *Imitation and Gender Insubordination*, "there is no volitional subject behind the mime who decides as it were, which gender it will be today. On the contrary, the very possibility of becoming a viable subject requires that a certain gender mime be already underway [...] In this sense, gender is not a performance that a priori subject elects to do, but gender is *performative* in the sense that it constitutes as an effect the very subject it appears to express. It is *compulsory* performance in the sense that acting out of line with heterosexual norms brings with it ostracism, punishment, and violence, not to mention the transgressive pleasure produced by those very prohibitions".[57]

We can therefore see where the convergence between anarchism and queer theory potentially lies: They both work with a manifold understanding of domination and with a commitment to critically engage with it. For both anarchafeminism and queer theory holds Bakunin's admonition "the outcast is my daily menace": each time there is somebody who is labeled as deviant, abnormal, there must be a process of normalization going on, and that is the space where the politics of domination thrives, because it implicitly cast people into superior and inferior.

By questioning boundaries and identities, queer theory gestures at a critique of all forms of hierarchies because there cannot be hierarchies without boundaries; in this sense, its spirit, if not its letter, is anarchafeminist. As we will see in the course of this book, this is particularly evident in queer ecology. If it is true that queer theory aims to question boundaries, why not also include those that affect the categorization of living being into human and animal, social and natural, animal and vegetal, and perhaps even animate and inanimate? If we push queer theory to its logical extension, we cannot avoid meeting ecology.[58] But similarly, if we push Emma Goldman's insight that anarchism is the teacher of the unity of life, we cannot help but meet queer ecology, and thus question the boundaries that have for centuries separated and regulated lives, beginning with the hierarchy of man>woman>slave>animal>plant>stones. It is perhaps not by chance that many anarchists, from Kropotkin to Élisée Reclus, were geographers, and thus people who

---

[57] Judith Butler, "Imitation and Gender Insubordination," 314–15.
[58] Timothy Morton, "Queer ecology," *PMLA* 125, No. 2 (2010), 273–82.

developed anarchist ideals by observing and studying the unity of life in all of its various forms. As Goldman, who named her anarchist newspaper *Mother Earth*, underlined, anarchism is not so much a theory about a future to be realized by divine inspiration, but "a living force in the affairs of our life, constantly creating new conditions."[59] It is because of this unity in plurality that freedom is indivisible and we cannot therefore oppose one form of domination without equally questioning all others, including those that have not yet been created, but may constantly appear on the horizon under yet another opposition between the normal and the deviant.

How to speak about feminism, though, without some form of unity in a constantly changing plurality? Not all queer theory is by definition feminist, and the worries about the exclusionary mechanisms triggered by naturalized understanding of womanhood may actually lead some queer theorists to distance themselves from it.[60] On the other hand, a lack of engagement with the subjection of bodies that are oppressed here and now because they are perceived as "women" can lead to the unhappy circumstance that the queer theory potential flight from feminism can contribute to the perpetration of misogyny and patriarchy. A question then emerges for an anarchafeminist project to investigate further: how can we speak about the oppression of "women", without turning the latter into yet another tool for domination?

If it is true that even within queer theory, transgender studies remained queer theory's "evil twin," because by privileging issues of sexual orientation as the primary means for differing from heteronormativity, queer theory relegated trans-experiences to simply another genre of sexual identity, can we formulate a definition of womanhood that is both queer and trans-inclusive? As Susan Stryker emphasized, transgender experience is a question of an atypical form of embodiment, and not just yet another sexual orientation to be added to the list of LGBTQI+ sexual

---

[59] Emma Goldman, *Anarchism and Other Essays*, 62. It is perhaps not by chance that she decided to name the anarchist newspaper to which she devoted most of her editorial energies *The Mother Earth*: she had initially thought of the title *The Open Road*, but had to abandon it because it was already in use. During a buggy ride in the countryside, she noticed the early signs of spring, "indicating life was germinating in the womb of mother earth" and ever since she is said to have known very clearly how to name her anarchist newspaper. See: Peter Glassgold, ed., *Anarchy! An Anthology of Emma Goldman's Mother Earth*, xviii.

[60] One recent attempt to bring together queer and feminist theory through a truly intersectional and transnational scope, is Saraswati's and Shaw's anthology of feminist and queer theory. See: Ayu Sarawasti and Barbara L. Shaw, eds., *Feminist and Queer Theory: An Intersectional and Transnational Reader* (Oxford: Oxford University Press, 2020).

orientations.[61] Can we take this critique into account and define womanhood away from hetero- and cisnormativity, that is, from the view that assume cis-bodies are the norm and that transbodies are a deviation from it? Can we speak about individualities without turning the latter into identities or, even worst, hierarchies? If it is true that gender is an imitation for which there is no original, what is the original individuality created by each performance and how can we put them together to speak of "womanhood"?

---

[61] Susan Stryker, "Transgender Studies: Queer Theory's Evil Twin," in *Feminist and Queer Theory* 10, no. 2 (2004), 71.

Intermezzo

In nomine matris

breast cancer, liver cancer, colon cancer, chills, high fever, swelling of the lower legs, continuing nervousness, cough, dizziness, fainting, fast heartbeat, increased sweating, nausea, severe and sudden, unexplained shortness of breath, severe and sudden, unexplained headache, slurred speech, sudden loss of coordination, severe and sudden, unexplained weakness or numbness in the arms, vaginal bleeding, vision changes, blurred vision, burning, crawling, itching, numbness, prickling and tingling feelings, dilated neck veins, extreme fatigue, increased need to urinate, irregular breathing, irregular heartbeat, irregular painful and difficult urination, sore throat, white spots on the lips, swollen glands, unusual bleeding, weakness, joint pain, muscle pain, confusion, diarrhea, dry mouth, metallic taste, skin rash, sleepiness, spinning sensation causing loss of balance, vomiting, anxiety, forgetfulness, dry skin, hair loss, irritability, nervousness, red, sore eyes—and a broken foot

Filiae

in the name of the mother, my pious catholic mother, i get to her house, i am happy, for the first time i am, and i feel like i can enjoy it, i can enjoy it without sinking, everything is very light, walking to the beach, walking in the street, i want to lick the whole path, instead of walking over it, so that i can retain its taste in my mouth, my sister gets here, announces she has a new girlfriend, who is going to leave her wife to be with her, and my mother falls down the stairs, cries, starts saying my sister is ruining a family because she is going to leave a husband, i tell her it is a wife, she cries even more, she say there are three children in the family, i say it is a wife and there are no children, my mother herself, three children, but the foot is swollen, visibly broken, and i try to bring her to the hospital, she does not want to go, all she wants is that my father gives her a shot of pain-killer in her belly, i tell her you are supposed to do that kind of shot in your butt cheeks, she replies that my father does it better in the belly, what are those shots in the belly doing to her, but she spends a week like this, with a swollen foot, visibly broken, bringing my sister's daughter into her bed, because, so she says, she has no father, and my father, the only father in the house, is sleeping downstairs, and required to give her shots, shots in the belly, they must be painful those shots, and all of this until her sicilian friend calls her, she calls and tells her the tarots say she should go to the hospital, and then she goes, she really goes to the hospital, and she comes back, with her foot in a cast, and now she is in bed, in bed with her foot in a cast, triple fracture, the foot, i look at her foot, a swollen foot, a swollen foot in a cast: this is what OEDIPUS means, the swollen foot. which is now in a cast.

Et corporis sancti

flesh, i felt beautifully dressed, i wanted to wear those virtual images, i felt like i could wear them whenever i wanted, the image, the digital image, inexhaustible, inextinguishable, the copy that had become more authentic than the original itself, you had brought life to it, to it and to me, but i felt naked when you stopped sending images, naked, naked in my bare skin, but can anyone ever be naked, naked, like the naked body, which is always and necessarily dressed, always a portrait, there is nothing more caught in the image than the naked body, image of itself, essence of bourgeois individualism, the naked body, the classical body, the sculpture, the painting, the bronze, there is no nakedness, there is just being, being and not being, plenitude and lack, a being that is for itself, flesh, fullness, and overabundance, and a being that is for an-other, a being in others, and for others, to be looked at, with no smell, and no touch, and thus no flesh, so perhaps you are right, my image is too intellectual, too cerebral, an image caught in seeing itself from the outside, and we should try to make an image from the inside, so the skin will leave its flatness and become flesh again, flesh and tissue, flesh and meat, flesh and viscera, flesh and fruit, flesh and taste, flesh and health, flesh and death, flesh and decay, flesh and living

in the name of the mother, the daughter, and the whole body

PART TWO

The philosophy of transindividuality

One of the most powerful ideas recurring in the Western philosophical tradition is that of a *scala naturae*, of a great chain where beings could be ordered hierarchically according to their respective degree of perfection. The basic building blocks of this view were originally formulated by Greek philosophers such as Plato and Aristotle, but it is only through their adoption and reinterpretation in scholastic philosophy that they acquired the hegemonic power they subsequently enjoyed in the West.[1] The Aristotelian philosophy, where all living things are placed according to their different degree of perfection, and thus proximity to man, was indeed re-interpreted through a Christian lens and transformed into the very influential idea of a *scala naturae*, which was not only sealed by Aristotle's metaphysics, but, also—and much more powerfully—by the subsequent decree of the Christian God.

Aristotle is often thought to be at the origin of the idea that "man is the most excellent of all living things" since he identified in man's capacity for rational and political deliberation the source of his

---

[1] Arthur O. Lovejoy, *The Great Chain of Being. A Study of the History of an Idea* (Cambridge, MA: Harvard University Press, 1936); William Hodos and C. B. G. Campbell, "Scala Naturae: Why There is no Theory in Comparative Psychology," *Psychological Review* 76, no. 4 (1969), 337–50.

excellence.[2] Being an animal endowed with rationality and a political animal (*zoon politikon*),[3] man, according to Aristotle, is superior not only to other animals, but also to women and to slaves. For Aristotle, man is by nature superior to woman, and thus rightfully rules over her,[4] but the woman is in her turn superior to slaves: "the slave is wholly lacking the deliberative element, the female has it but lacks authority [...]."[5] Being deprived of both the deliberative element and authority, the slave is thus placed in an intermediate place between the human and the animal.

According to Aristotle's *De Anima*, human, animals, and plants differ according to the different degree of excellence of their animating principle, or *psyche:* humans are endowed with the *nous*, and thus capable of both thinking and reflection, whereas animals only possess a "sensitive soul," that is a capacity for sensing and appetite.[6] Plants occupy the bottom of the scale, because they are only capable of growing and reproducing themselves, thanks to their "vegetative soul," but they are necessarily rooted, and thus incapable of the degree of mobility and sensing that we observe in animals. And yet, since they are endowed with life, defined as the capacity for self-sustenance, growth, and decay,[7] they are said to be superior to dead matter such as stones.

This idea of a well-ordered cosmos, where beings are placed in a hierarchy according to their different degrees of perfection, was a very good fit with the Christian creation myth, by which it was re-appropriated. According to the Bible, God creates man (Adam) in his own image, then creates the woman out of Adam's rib, so as to keep him company (Gen. 2:19–21), and then gives Adam the power to name all of the natural things around him, thus symbolizing his dominion over the rest of nature (Gen. 2:19–20). Thus, whereas for Aristotle animals are endowed with a

---

[2] For instance, this is the view that Kelly Oliver attributes to Aristotle. See: Kelly Oliver, "Animality," in *Encyclopedia of Political Theory*, Vol 1, ed. Mark Bevir (Thousand Oaks, CA: Sage, 2010), 50. This view may be more the result of subsequent Christian reinterpretation of Aristotle than of his own view, which seems to be more refined. For instance, Aristotle states that "for just as man is the best of the animals when completed, when separated from law and adjudication, he is the worst of all" (1253a30). I am grateful to Austin Burke for pointing me to this passage. Note that we will be using the standard academic reference system for Aristotle's works, the Bekker numbering system, throughout.

[3] Aristotle, *Politics* I.2 1253a1–18.

[4] Aristotle, *Politics* I.3 1254b13–14.

[5] Aristotle, *Politics* I.13.

[6] Aristotle, *De Anima* II.3. 414a28–414b23.

[7] Aristotle, *De Anima* II.1. 412a18–412b24.

"sensitive soul," an animating principle, according to Thomas Aquinas, the philosopher who largely systematized Aristotle's philosophy and made it compatible with Christian faith, man has absolute dominion over animals because they were given to him by God, so he can kill and dispose of them as he pleases, without any recognition for whatever animating principle they may have.[8]

The idea of a great chain of being became thus the basis not only for theological speculations but also for the conventional cosmology, that is, for the representations of the world that accompanied image-making and the care of the soul. This cosmology was based on the combination of the Christian faith with Greek astronomy, which was in itself largely an ethno-astronomy, that is as an astronomy that justified the principle of organization of the Greek ethnos.[9] As Sylvia Wynter noted:

Their projected premise of a value distinction and principle of ontological distinction between heaven and earth had functioned to analogically replicate and absolutize the central order-organizing principle and genre-of-the-human distinction at the level of the sociopolitical order, between the non-dependent masters, who were Greek-born citizens and their totally dependent slaves classified as barbarian Others. With this value distinction (sociogenic principle or master code of symbolic life/death) then being replicated at the level of the intra-Greek society in gender terms (correlatedly), as between males, who were citizens, and women, who were their dependents.[10]

It is this notion of a fundamental principle of the "nonhomogeneity of substance,"[11] of a fundamental dualism between the heavens and the earth, the soul and the body, that helped to justify a political order that dominated some bodies in the name of the ontological superiority of others.

Towards the end of the Middle Ages, philosophers engaged in the creation of a new scientific approach to the world often encountered persecution precisely because questioning this idea of a great chain of

---

[8] Kelly Oliver, "Animality," 50.
[9] Sylvia Wynter, "Unsettling the Coloniality of Being/Power/Truth/Freedom: Towards the Human, After Man, Its Overrepresentation—An Argument," *CR: The New Centennial Review* 3, No. 3 (2003), 272.
[10] Ibid, 272.
[11] Ibid, 274.

being meant questioning both established dogmas and the political order they supported. We may remember here that in 1600 Giordano Bruno was burnt at stake as a heretic for holding that the universe is infinite, while in 1633 Galilei was incarcerated and made to repent for holding the Copernican view of the world (heliocentrism), while women, as we will see later on, were persecuted as witches. Why did the Church struggle so much against the idea that the earth is not at the center of the universe, and that the world is infinite?

Whereas in the Aristotelian-scholastic image of the world, the universe is closed, qualitatively and teleologically ordered, in the modern scientific view the universe is infinite, quantitative, and composed by matter and movement. In the former, the earth is at the center of the universe, and surrounded by the different skies, thus culminating in the immobile motor that is God himself. Aristotle conceived of the world in purely qualitative terms: he divided the universe into several parts constituted by different qualities and corresponding to different degrees of perfection. In this universe there is, on the one hand, the sub-lunar world, whose elements—earth, water, air, and fire—move according to a linear movement, which is imperfect. On the other hand, beyond the moon are the skies, conceived as spheres, of the sun and the other planets, which are made by an incorruptible substance (ether) and which move according to a circular movement, which is perfect. Beyond the sphere of the fixed stars, which is the limit of the Aristotelian universe, there is the first immovable motor, the first principle of everything, which is non-material (because matter is subject to corruption), pure thought of thought. With imperfection on the one hand, and all the perfection culminating in an immovable motor on the other, one can easily see why the Church adopted this view. And its agreement with the dogmas of faith certainly helps to explain its persistence.

It is the contention of this book that, in order to rethink the roles of sexed and gendered bodies, we need to rethink the role of bodies in general, and that we need to do so by rethinking not only the Aristotelian-scholastic idea of a great chain of being, or *scala naturae*, but also their very metaphysical and ontological presuppositions. The European Enlightenment, along with the advent of modern science, has largely questioned this image of the world by substituting the idea of a hierarchical cosmos with that of a mechanical world composed of matter and movement, but many of the ontological assumptions underlying the idea of the great chain of being survived under other names.

In particular, two of the underlying assumptions of the idea of a *scala naturae* have proved to be particularly persistent: the body–mind dualism and what we can call its underlying methodological individualism. The image of man as the most excellent of the living creatures was based for Aristotle in the fact that he is endowed with full rationality and capacity for deliberation; for Aquinas and other Christian theologians, this excellence came to be perceived as a result of the fact that man was created in the image of God, who placed him above all the other living creatures (Gen. 1:26). The Christian worldview thus reinforced the Aristotelian body–mind dualism, or what, following Sylvia Winter we can call the Western dogma of the "nonhomogeneity of substance," which worked, in its many different guises, as a tool to purport what she called the overrepresentation of Man.[12] This idea of the heterogeneity of substance, of a fundamental opposition between the celestial realm of perfection *versus* the imperfect realm of the terrestrial, still reverberates in many different forms in Western culture: from the Christian opposition between soul and the flesh to the various form of secular body–mind dualisms.

Along with such a presupposition, which is crucial in order to justify the dominant position of man, there is an even more fundamental one: the idea that beings can be arranged within such a scale, presupposes that their individuality is given, and that we can arrange man>woman>slave>animal>plant>stones on a scale because they are discrete individuals. In this Part, we will question both such assumptions and argue that a monist philosophy of transindividuality is the best way to do so. There are many different philosophical traditions that have questioned such assumptions and emphasized in their stead the idea of the unity of being and homogeneity of substance. From the already mentioned Taoist idea of the *wu ming* to the Buddhist's concept of co-origination of all beings (*pratītyasamutpāda*) or the African philosophy of the Ubuntu, we can find plenty of philosophical perspectives outside of the West that question both the body–mind dualism and the methodological individualism described above. But even inside of the West, there are philosophers who have provided the tools for doing so. In the following chapter, we will focus on the contribution provided by Baruch Spinoza, a Jewish philosopher born in Amsterdam in 1632 to a family of Marrano origins, and whose philosophy can rightly be defined as a "savage

---

[12] Ibid.

anomaly."[13] There were many reasons for this, beginning with the fact that, positioned as it is between the Jewish mystical tradition and the European modern scientific view of the world, it largely escapes the easy ideological divide between Eastern and Western philosophical traditions. Not by chance, Spinoza's philosophical career began with his excommunication: whereas it is not uncommon for philosophers to question the authorities of a given time and thus end up being persecuted, what is striking in Spinoza's life is indeed the fact that he was excommunicated from the Jewish community for his heretical views even before becoming a philosopher, when he was just twenty-four years old. And yet, despite the excommunication, he went on to develop one of the most original and subversive philosophical systems of the Western philosophical tradition, one that is systematically laid out in his major work, the *Ethics*, and to which we will now turn our attention.

---

[13] Antonio Negri, *The Savage Anomaly: The Power of Spinoza's Metaphysic and Politics* (Minneapolis: University of Minnesota Press, 1991).

4 From individuality to transindividuality

With the help Étienne Balibar's insight that Spinoza's concept of individuality is best understood as transindividuality, and of the feminist readings of Spinoza, we will now argue that the most monist of all ontologies can also be the most pluralist.[1] The implicit starting point of Spinoza's philosophy, as well as of the philosophy of transindividuality inspired by him, is that there is being rather than nothing. This starting point must not be understood as an *archē* in the sense of an ordering principle or, even less so, as a government of being, but as a mere beginning. That there is being does not yet say anything as to its ordering, and even less so about its government. Why being, then? Because, as we read in the *Ethics*, it is self-evident that to be able not to exist is to lack power, and to be able to exist is to have power (EI P11, 2 alternative proof).[2] Thus, if what necessarily exists are only finite beings, then finite beings are more powerful than an

---

[1] Étienne Balibar, "Spinoza: From Individuality to Transindividuality," in *Medelingen vanwege het Spinozahauis*. (Delft: Heburon, 1997), 3–36. In this project of combining Spinozism with feminism, we are also indebted to Moira Gatens' feminist reading. See, in particular, her *Imaginary Bodies: Ethics, Power and Corporeality* (London: Routledge, 1996). On the idea that the most monist of the ontologies can also be the most pluralist, see also the influential *Spinoza et le problème de l'expression* (Paris: Éditions de Minuit, 1985) by Gilles Deleuze, who argues the same point by focusing on the often-neglected notion of expression. See also its English translation: Gilles Deleuze's *Expressionism in Philosophy: Spinoza* (New York: Zone Books, 1992).

[2] The standard critical edition of Spinoza's Latin works is: Benedict de Spinoza, *Opera*, 4 Vol., ed. Carl Gebhardt (Heidelberg: Winter, 1925). For the English translations, we use the following text and standard abbreviations: E = *Ethics*, translated by Edwin Curley in *The Collected Works of Spinoza* (Princeton: Princeton University Press, 1985) followed by the indication of the part in roman numeral (I, II, III, IV, V) and by the number of the Proposition (P 1, 2, 3, etc.).

absolutely infinite being, which is absurd. So, either nothing exists or an absolutely infinite being also exists. But we exist, either in ourselves or in something else, which necessarily exists. Therefore, an absolutely infinite being necessarily exists (EI P11, 2 alternative proof). This is, in our view, the most beautiful lesson of Spinozism: If there are twenty persons in this room, then an absolutely infinite being necessarily exists.[3]

In order to prevent this being from being classified as different substances, regardless of their number, Spinoza identifies this infinite being with the substance itself. The latter is defined as "what is in itself and is conceived through itself, that is, that whose concept does not require the concept of another thing, from which it must be formed" (EI D3). This happens in the course of Part I of the *Ethics*, appropriately called *Of God* (*De Deo*), where the concept of substance is identified with that of God, defined from the beginning as "a being absolutely infinite" (*ens absolute infinitum*), consisting of an infinity of attributes (EI D6). The concept of God is for Spinoza defined by infinity, and the bulk of the argument consists in showing that, since there is one unique substance, then it must also be infinite because it would otherwise the limited by another substance, which, as we have seen, is absurd. By recovering the old ontological proof of the existence of God, Spinoza argues that God is *causa sui*, cause of itself, "i.e. that whose essence involves existence, or that whose nature cannot be conceived except as existing" (EI D1). Precisely because God is by definition an absolutely infinite being, and one and the same thing with the unique substance (EI P14), then God must also be the cause of itself.

Spinoza's *a priori* demonstration of the existence of God (EI P1–P7) is very similar to that developed by the Christian theologian Anselm of Aosta, who defined God as the most perfect being (*ens realissimum*) and then concluded that it must also exist because it would otherwise be lacking one of its perfections.[4] Although there is much talk about God in Spinoza's *Ethics*, it should not be identified with the Christian God of Anselm nor with any other monotheistic gods. We can see here a specific

---

[3] The argument of the twenty persons is used in the scholium 2 to Proposition 7 EI, where Spinoza starts adding some *a posteriori* elements to the *a priori* proof for the existence of an infinite substance developed in EI P1–P7.

[4] See, in particular, the third chapter of Anselm's *Proslogion*, significantly entitled "That he cannot be thought not to exist." See, Anselm, *Basic Writings* (Indianapolis: Hackett, 2007), 82–3.

trait of Spinoza's philosophy, who has rightly been called a "Marrano of reason": Like the persecuted Marranos who had to keep up the appearance of religious observance, while not believing in it, Spinoza uses traditional philosophical and theological terms but by inserting them into a system where they completely change their meaning so that they come to work against that very orthodoxy from which they derive.[5] Spinoza uses the term God but his philosophical system deeply questions the concept of God as a person, arguing it is a prejudice derived from our tendency to imagine that everything acts according to an end, in the way humans do, and thus to project onto God specifically human features (EI, appendix). In the course of the *Ethics*, it becomes clear that this God that Spinoza identifies with the unique infinite substance is nothing but nature itself: *Deus sive natura*, God or nature (EIV Praef, E IV P4D). The concept of substance, identified with God as infinite being, is the opposite to that of modes, defined as "the affections of a substance, or that which is in another through which it is also conceived" (EI D5). Whereas everything that is therefore necessarily is in the substance, the latter does not function as an ordering principle, but rather as an antidote against any Christian *archē*, precisely because, properly speaking, only modes—and thus, *res singulares*—exist.[6] To put it bluntly, Spinoza's invocation of *deus sive natura*, of god as the infinite unique substance is the best possible way for getting rid of any God.

According to Spinoza, all we know is that such a substance expresses itself through infinite modes and in infinite attributes. Among the infinite attributes that pertain to substance, only two, according to Spinoza, are accessible to us: thought and extension. If we consider that an attribute is what the intellect perceives of the substance as constituting its essence (EI D4), and that substance is what is through itself and conceived through itself, it is easy to understand why such attributes are by definition infinite. If there were a limit to them, there would then be another substance. On the contrary, we know that substance can express itself in

---

[5] We take the expression "Marrano of reason" from Yovel's masterful work on Spinoza and the influence of the heretical tradition on his philosophy. See: Yirmiyahu Yovel, *Spinoza and Other Heretics: The Marrano of Reason* (Princeton: Princeton University Press, 1989).
[6] Note here that the concept of mode does not exactly coincide with that of finite beings, since, as Spinoza argues in EI P21-23, there are also infinite modes: God's idea in thought is for instance a mode, a single idea in the attribute of thinking, but is also infinite (EI P21, Dem).

infinite ways but also that most humans can only perceive thought and extension. Within this ontology, a single thought is therefore a mode in the attribute of thinking, whereas a single body is a mode in the attribute of extension.

However, this does not mean that thought and extension, ideas and things, are parallel to one another. As Spinoza clearly put it, "The order and connection of ideas is the same (*idem*) as the order and connection of things" (EII P7): thought and extension are the same (*idem*), not parallel to one another. We need to underline this, because whenever we speak about mind and body, or ideas and things, our long inherited dualistic metaphysical framework tends to surreptitiously creep in. The first step in order to get to a truly pluralistic conception of the body is to get rid of this framework, and thus of the idea that a body is something different, parallel, or even opposite to a mind. Body and mind are just two modes that express two different attributes of an infinite substance expressing itself in an infinity of attributes.[7] One may even say that these were the two attributes of substance that Spinoza, writing in the Amsterdam of the seventeenth century, deemed the only two accessible to us. Coming from a Marrano family, and having thus been exposed to Jewish and Christian theology along with the Cartesian philosophy in fashion at the time, Spinoza lived in a world where thinking and extension were considered the default attributes of modal existence. But there is nothing in the ontological framework here described that prevent us from imagining a possible expansion of such a list of attributes accessible to us.

For example, one could argue that discoveries of contemporary astrophysics could lead us to expand such a list. On the one hand, most accredited contemporary astrophysical theories, with their emphasis on the infinity of the universe, do confirm Spinoza's fundamental intuition of a unique infinite substance, accessible to us as extension and thinking.[8] But, on the other hand, they also emphasize that we ultimately know very little about the nature of such attributes. New and unexpected attributes

---

[7] Although Spinoza never defines the concept of expression in his *Ethics*, the latter concept is crucial to understanding the relationship between substance and modes as well as those between substance and attributes, as persuasively shown in Gilles Deleuze's *Expressionism in Philosophy*. It is not by chance that the last demonstration of the first part of the *Ethics* concludes by saying: "Whatever exists expresses the nature, or essence of God in a certain and determinate way" (EI P36).

[8] See Pekka Teerikorpi et al., *The Evolving Universe and the Origin of Life: The Search for Our Cosmic Roots* (New York: Springer, 2009), 109–12, 317–50.

of substance could be revealed by contemporary investigations into the nature of materiality. In particular, discoveries about the nature of dark matter and of dark energy can open new paths in that direction. For instance, although we know very little, or almost nothing about it, dark energy is currently thought to compose the vast majority the our universe, reducing the existing visible matter, i.e. the ordinary matter made of atoms, to a only a small part of it.[9] Despite being a "savage anomaly" within modernity, Spinoza lived and thought in his own time, so we can think that new discoveries, or insights from different but similar philosophical systems, could lead to a revised list of attributes.[10]

We should not therefore fall into the temptation of interpreting thought and extension as a return to a dualistic metaphysic, but rather as first approximation to a list of attributes that, as Spinoza explicitly says, are infinite. The English language, as all other Western philosophical languages, is imbued with dualistic assumptions, so much so that whenever we say "idea" we immediately assume we are dealing with a "mental content,"[11] whenever we say "body," we immediately assume that

---

[9] For a general discussion of the possible new paths opened by the concept of a dark matter, and dark energy respectively, see: Sabino Matarrese et al., *Dark Matter and Dark Energy: A Challenge for Modern Cosmology* (Dordrecht: Springer, 2011).

[10] Antonio Negri, *The Savage Anomaly*. For instance, there seem to be striking similarities between this philosophy of transindividuality and the Buddhist notion of "*pratītyasamutpāda*." While one may be tempted to translate that word as interdependence, the latter term may misleadingly suggest that beings are already constituted before such dependence from each other emerges, so a better translation would be "mutual origination." I am grateful to Austin Burke for illuminating insights on this point. For a general survey of this notion, see: Peter D. Hershock, *Valuing Diversity: Buddhist Reflection on Realizing a More Equitable Global Future* (Albany: SUNY Press, 2012); Goran Kardas, "From Etymology to Ontology: Vasubandhu and Candrakīrti on various interpretations of pratītyasamutpāda," *Asian Philosophy* 25, no. 3 (2015), 293–317. A discussion of different African perspectives on the concept of interdependence is contained in: David Oladipupo Kuranga, *The Power of Interdependence: Lessons from Africa* (London: Palgrave, 2012).

[11] This understanding of ideas as mental contents, which prevails in most Western modern languages, is however one that is historically and geographically situated, being rooted in the philosophy of René Descartes and Western empiricist philosophers. See: Nicola Abbagnano, *Dizionario di Filosofia* (Turin: UTET, 1971), 450. Along with this definition, even in the Western history of philosophy, we can find alternative definitions that defy such body–mind dualism. For instance, it is often forgotten that the very word "idea" derives from the Ancient Greek term *orao*, to see, and thus originally denoted the object of an intellectual vision or intuition able to capture the essence of things within the multiplicity and becoming of them. See: Sergio Landucci, "Idea," in *Enciclopedia di filosofia*, eds. Gianni Vattimo, Maurizio Ferraris, Diego Marconi (Milan: Garzanti, 1993), 515.

this must be something distinguished, or even opposed, to the "mind" or the "soul." But this is because of the influence of a few millennia of Christian and metaphysical dualism that still reverberates in our language. To paraphrase Friedrich Nietzsche, we could say that we have not yet got rid of the Christian God, because we still have language.[12] In order to enter into Spinoza's ontology, we need to move God out via the front door and constantly be on alert to make sure language itself does not bring him back through the rear window.[13]

Even the label "materialism," which has often been used to define Spinoza's ontology, must be used with an important qualification. If thought and extension are just two of the *infinite* attributes of the unique substance, then we cannot speak of a simply materialist ontology, without immediately adding that it is not the brute, inanimate, static matter that is at stake here.[14] By using an oxymoron, one could argue that Spinoza's materialism is more akin to a form of "mental materialism" than to what we tend to associate with "materialism" as a label, precisely because extension and thought are just two of the infinite attributes of the same substance. We can even push the argument further, and argue that Spinoza's monist philosophy escapes

---

[12] The original sentence states: "We have not yet got rid of God because we still have faith in grammar." See: Friedrich Nietzsche, *Twilight of the Idols; or, How to Philosophize With a Hammer*, trans. Duncan Large (Oxford: Oxford University Press, 1998), 19.

[13] Whereas Nietzsche famously defined Christianity as Platonism for the people (See: Friedrich Nietzsche, *Beyond Good and Evil: Prelude to a Philosophy of the* Future, trans. Walter Kaufmann (New York: Vintage Books, 1966), 3), we define Cartesianism and Kantianism as Christendom for philosophers, since both Descartes and Kant have salvaged metaphysical dualism from the potentially deadly attack of modern science (and of Spinoza). If one adopts the early modern scientific view of the universe as made by matter and movement, there is no space there for the three pillars of Christian dogmatism: the existence of God as a person, the immortality of the soul, and freedom of the will. Whereas both Descartes and Kant managed to defend them though their dualism, Spinoza radically questioned them. The distinction between Spinoza and Kant can thus be described as that between a radical and a moderate Enlightenment. On this, see: Jonathan Israel, *Radical Enlightenment: Philosophy and the Making of Modernity* 1650–1750 (Oxford: Oxford University Press, 2001). On Kant's critical philosophy as a response to Spinoza, see: Omri Boehm, *Kant's Critique of Spinoza* (Oxford: Oxford University Press, 2014).

[14] For a useful overview of the philosophical usages of the term "materialism" in Western philosophy, see: Nicola Abbagnano, *Dizionario di Filosofia*, 564–5. On Spinoza's materialism, see the influential interpretation by Pierre Macherey (in particular: Pierre Macherey, *In a Materialist Way*, ed. Warren Montag (London: Verso, 1998), 117–58; Antonio Negri, *The Savage Anomaly*; Étienne Balibar, *Spinoza and Politics* (London: Verso, 1998); Vittorio Morfino, *Plural Temporality: Transindividuality and the Aleatory Between Spinoza and Althusser* (Leiden: Brill, 2014); and Dimitris Vardoulakis, *Spinoza, the Epicurean: Authority and Utility in Materialism* (Edinburgh: Edinburgh University Press, 2020).

the opposition of materialism *versus* idealism, precisely because ideas and material conditions are not opposed in the first place. In this philosophical framework, when we speak about an individual body, we are always also speaking about an individual mind, because we are speaking of a mode that expresses an infinite substance whose infinite attributes also include thinking. More than a "vibrant matter," as some have recently suggested, we should speak here of a "thinking matter," but then also add that by "thinking" Spinoza clearly does not mean merely propositional thinking, but some form of mental activity considered as inherent to every materiality.[15]

With that warning in mind, we can now move to exploring the concept of individuality that Spinoza develops in his *Ethics* and in particular from the sort of compendium of his physics that he put forward in Part II (EII P13–P15). From the very beginning, Spinoza states that "by singular things," he understands "things that are finite and have a determinate existence" (EII D7). But then he immediately adds that "if a number of individuals so concur in one action that together they are the cause of one effect, I consider them all, to that extent, one singular thing" (EII D7). From the very beginning we have a conception of the individual that emphasizes action and thus the possibility of joining more individuals into a singular one. Later, during the course of the argument, Spinoza differentiates between "simple bodies," which are distinguished only by ratio of motion and rest, so that if the latter remains the same, all individuals participating in it remain the same individual (EII A2"D), and more "complex ones," where the criteria for continuity in individuality is whether or not the individuals replacing those that have left are of the same nature (EII L4). An example of the former are simple bodies such as a musket ball, whereas an example of the latter are more composite bodies such as a human being. In contemporary terms, we can say "simple bodies" remain the same if their chemical components hold together, whereas "complex bodies" remain the same if, for example, the water exiting a human body in the form of sweat or excrement is being replenished with individuals of the same nature, that is with the same H_2O atoms.

---

[15] Jane Bennett looks at the life of a metal as an example of her Spinozist understanding of vibrant matter, but we could think about any chemical compound, with the energy thereby stored, as a minimal form of mental activity that pertains to all kind of matter, and thus confirming Spinoza's intuition that every form of extension is to some degree "animate" (*animatus*) (EII P13 Scholium). See: Jane Bennett, *Vibrant Matter: A Political Ecology of Things* (Durham: Duke University Press, 2010), 52–62.

The picture that Spinoza provides here is that of a continual process of individuation that constantly joins together simpler and more complex individuals. In this ontology, every individual, even the simplest ones, are never just brute inert matter. Spinoza explicitly says that these mechanisms of association are common (*communis*) to both human beings and other individuals, which are all to a different degree animate (*animatus*) (EII P13 Scholium).[16] The affirmation that all bodies are to some extent animate, which is a consequence of his monism, directly contrasts the influential Aristotelian-scholastic hierarchy of being according to which humans, animals, and vegetables are to some degree animate, but stones are not, because the latter are mere dead matter.[17] It is not, however, a form of "animism", if by the latter we mean the doctrine according to which all beings are animated by spirits similar to the human soul.[18] Spinoza is very critical of those forms of animism and considers them a type of anthropomorphic projection that derive from the fact that human beings are conscious of their desire, but unaware of their causes, and thus act in view of a certain end, and consequently tend to project such teleological thinking all around themselves.

Spinoza's position, according to which all beings are to some extent animate, is more akin to that contemporary panpsychists philosophers,

---

[16] *Animatus* is the Latin adjective, and *anima/animus* is the substantive. Notice that whereas *anima* means also the soul of dead people, the term *animus* denotes the mind, the spirit in the sense of an animating principle and thus does not imply the immortality of the soul. Spinoza explicitly argues there is something eternal in the mind, but also denies the immortality of the soul. On Spinoza' theory of the eternity of the mind and why that does not imply any immortality of the soul see EV, P23, and Yirmiyahu Yovel, *Spinoza and Other Heretics*, 20.

[17] This is implicit in the definition of life provided in *De Anima* II.1 412a: "Matter is potentiality, while form is realization or actuality, and the word actuality is used in two senses, illustrated by the possession of knowledge and the exercise of it. Bodies seem to be pre-eminently substances, and most particularly those which are of natural origin; for these are the sources from which the rest are derived. But of natural bodies some have life and some have not; by life we mean the capacity for self-sustenance, growth, and decay. Every natural body, then, which possesses life must be substance, and a substance of the compound type. But since it is a body of a definite kind, viz., having life, the body cannot be soul." This dichotomy between bodies that have life and those that do not have life is currently under debate. In particular, the concept of "animacy" is at the center of a contemporary lively debate that questions the traditional ordering of being, thanks to, among others, the insightful work of Mel Y. Chen. See, in particular, Mel Y. Chen, *Animacies: Biopolitics, Racial Mattering, and Queer Affect* (Durham: Duke University Press, 2012).

[18] See for instance the entry "animism" in *Enciclopedia di filosofia* (Milano: Garzanti, 1999), 37.

who think that some form of mental activity is ubiquitous and inherent to any form of materiality, but do not project human features onto it. Panpsychism is a view that goes far back in the history of philosophy both within and beyond the West, but has recently gained particular attention because of the failure of both metaphysical dualism and the physicalism of natural sciences in providing a convincing view of the world: Whereas metaphysical dualism leaves us with a highly dichotomic view of nature and endless problems in explaining how brains and bodies interact, the opposite physicalist position incurs the difficulty of being unable to explain how and why consciousness suddenly appears from non-conscious matter in animals and humans.[19]

It may seem counterintuitive to believe, with Spinoza, that wherever there is extension there is thinking. That is not the way we immediately experience things. We think that we want to read a book, and then we read it. We experience wanting a glass of water, and then drink it. But this, according to Spinoza, is because human beings are conscious of their desire, but unaware of the causes behind it, so we think that it is our thinking that has the power to move our body (EI Appendix), instead of the order and connection of ideas just being the same thing (*idem*) as the order and connection of things. However, in this, as well as in many other cases, our common perceptions can prove to be misleading. In the past, very often they did. Scientific theories that are now commonly accepted, such as heliocentrism, the idea that the Earth rotates around the sun, clearly do not conform with how we immediately perceive things. We can see the sun on its trajectory through the sky and it took a few millennia

---

[19] David Chalmers emphasized the impasse encountered by all attempts at of deriving consciousness from non-conscious matter and declared it "the hard problem of consciousness." Despite all discoveries made by neuroscience in mapping the mechanisms for explaining how the brain works, there is not yet a satisfying explanation of how consciousness emerges in terms of having a subjective experience. Neuroscience can lead us to depict a creature that is empirically indiscernible from a human being in terms of its physical brain processes and the behavior they give rise to, but which has no subjective experience whatsoever, meaning that it could scream and reach if you stick a knife in their body, but it doesn't actually feel pain. See: David Chalmers, "Facing up to the problem of consciousness," *Journal of Consciousness Studies* 2, no. 3 (1995) 200–19; David Chalmers, *The Conscious Mind: Towards a Fundamental Theory* (New York: Oxford University Press, 1996). See also: Philip Goff, William Seager, and Sean Allen-Hermanson, "Panpsychism," *The Stanford Encyclopedia of Philosophy.* Stanford University, 1997–. Article published May 23, 2001; last substantive revision July 18, 2017. https://plato.stanford.edu/archives/sum2020/entries/panpsychism/

to persuade human beings to abandon a view that seemed to be so well supported by our common experience.

We walk on the Earth and we do not fall. At the time in which Spinoza was writing, scientists like Galileo Galilei were imprisoned for thinking that the Earth is not flat and that it is not the center of the universe. His views went not only against the dogma of the church of the time, but also against commonsense: We do not fall if we walk on the Earth, so how can it be round? We see all the planets around us, so how could we not be the center of the universe? We have now adopted those very counterintuitive views, so there is no a priori reason to discard monism because it seems counterintuitive. We assume today that Galilei was right and that, for reasons that were unknown in the Middle Ages, it is possible to walk on the earth with the impression that it is flat, even if it is actually round. Thus, is it possible that a lot of today's common sense is also equally wrong? How much do we know about extension and thinking to prove one case or the other, if it is true that, for instance, the "dark energy" that is said to compose the majority of the universe really exists, although we know almost nothing about it? Should the awareness of how little we actually know not lead us to be at least suspicious of common experience?

Recent developments in physics and neuroscience do come close to a Spinozist monism, and they probably explain the recent revival of interest in panpsychism.[20] Philip Goff summarizes such developments in a very useful way: Common sense tells us that only living things have something close to a mind and an inner life, because cats and dogs respond to us, appear to have feelings, sensations, and experiences, but plants and tables and molecules do not seem to. These do not respond to us; they are not able to return a ball to us if we throw it at them. Panpsychists deny this datum of common sense. According to panpsychism, the smallest bits of matter—things such as electrons and quarks—have a very basic kind of mental life; even an electron has one. This may seem crazy and counterintuitive, but

---

[20] On the recovery of Spinoza's philosophy from the point of view of contemporary neuroscience, see Antonio Damasio's path-breaking monograph, *Looking for Spinoza: Joy, Sorrow, and the Feeling Brain* (Orlando: Harcourt, 2003). On panpsychism, besides the already quoted Philip Goff, William Seager, and Sean Allen-Hermanson, "Panpsychism," see: Nicola Abbagnano, *Dizionario di Filosofia*, 746; Jiri Benovsky, *Mind and Matter: Panpsychism, Dual-Aspect Monism, and the Combination Problem* (Cham, CH: Springer, 2018); and Ludwig Jaskolla and Godehard Brüntrup, *Panpsychism: Contemporary Perspectives* (Oxford: Oxford University Press, 2017).

actually provides the most elegant and simple solution to the impasse generated by opposite views.[21] Furthermore, as we will see, this view is also able to provide the best support for a form of "ecocentric egalitarianism" that is our best ally in times of ecological crises and climate change.[22]

The image of the world that comes out of Spinoza's version of panpsychism is an eccentric one. It distances itself from previous forms of pantheism, because of its emphasis on individualities conceived as transindividualities. Whereas for pantheist thinkers, every individual in nature is God, for Spinoza every mode is *in* God, or the unique infinite substance, but it is not itself God.[23] In this picture, we begin with the

---

[21] In his recent *Galilei's Error*, Philip Goff explicitly argues that panpsychism may seem crazy, but it is also most probably true, and that part of the reluctance in accepting it is due to the fact that it has that "New Age" feel that people have a hard time accepting, but it is in no way less crazy than Einstein's relativity, which argues that time slows down at high speeds, or of quantum mechanics according to which particles have a determined position only when observed. See: Philip Goff, *Galileo's Error: Foundations for a New Science of Consciousness* (New York: Pantheon, 2019); Philip Goff, William Seager, and Sean Allen-Hermanson, "Panpsychism," 108). The most Spinozist of the only apparently crazy theories of contemporary physics that Goff mentions is that of quantum entanglement, according to which "particles can act as one even when light-years apart": As a result of the experiments performed in 1970s, quantum entanglement is one of the "one of the best supported facts of modern science" (ibid, 144).

[22] Spinoza's philosophy has indeed been inspiring for ecological movements since their very inception. Arne Naess, for instance, one of the founders of the "deep ecology" movement, refers to Spinoza's ontology as providing the basis for a form of "biocentric or ecocentric egalitarianism." See: Arne Naess, "Spinoza and the Deep Ecology Movement," in *The Selected Works of Arne Naess*, ed. Alan Drengson (New York: Springer, 2005), 407. Although we would argue against the label "biocentric" because, as we have seen, for Spinoza all bodies are to some degree "animate," we think that Naess is correct in identifying what is so attractive in Spinoza's philosophy for ecological movements. Naess also identifies in Spinoza's argument for an *Amor intellectualis dei* (EV P36) the source of a form of love directed towards all individual finite beings (Ibid, 401). More recent examples of ecological thinking inspired by Spinoza's philosophy are Bennett's notion of a vibrant matter, Rawes' ecological ratios or Braidotti's posthuman philosophy. Respectively: Jane Bennett, *Vibrant Matter: A Political Ecology of Things*; Peg Rawes, "Spinoza's geometric and ecological ratios," in *Politics of Parametricism*, eds. Manuel Shvartzberg and Matthew Poole (London: Bloomsbury, 2015), 213–30; Rosi Braidotti, *The Posthuman* (Cambridge: Polity, 2013).

[23] Although the term "pantheism" has been used in a variety of ways to denote the identification of "all things" (*pan*) with God (*theism*), we should broadly distinguish between forms of acosmic pantheism, that dissolves all individualities into god, and the atheistic pantheism, which dissolves the notion of God into the individual things (Gianni Vattimo, Maurizio Ferraris, Diego Marconi, eds., *Enciclopedia di filosofia* (Milan: Garzanti, 1993), 828). Despite having been accused of a form of acosmic pantheism, Spinoza's views are very distant from it, so much so that a more appropriate term would be "panenthesim," that is the idea that "all things" (*pan*) are in (*en*) God (*theism*). For a definition of panentheism, see: Nicola Abbagnano, *Dizionario di Filosofia* (Turin: UTET, 1971), 674.

simplest individuals, and then progressively follow complex processes of association and dissociation that create other individualities. As we read in an important passage from the second part of the *Ethics*:

> We have conceived an individual which is composed only by bodies which are distinguished from one another only by motion and rest, speed and slowness, i.e., which is composed of the simplest bodies. But if we should now conceive of another, composed of a number of individuals of a different nature, we shall find that it can be affected in a great many other ways, and still preserve its nature. For since each part of it is composed of a number of bodies, each part will therefore (by L7) be able, without any change of its nature, to move now more slowly, now more quickly, and consequently communicate its motion more quickly or more slowly to the others. But if we should further conceive a third kind of individual composed of this second kind, we shall find that it can be affected in many other ways, without any change of its forms. And if we proceed in this way to infinity, we shall easily conceive that the whole of nature is one individual, whose parts, i.e. all bodies, vary in infinite ways without any change of the whole individual.[24]

This passage summarizes Spinoza's view on individuality within nature. In such a picture, the human body is not a kingdom within a kingdom ("*imperium in imperio*," EIII, pref), but just a particularly complex body which is made by a number of other bodies, which are inserted into a network of bodies that affect each other in multiple ways. As Moira Gatens observed while commenting on this passage, this also means that the human body can never be viewed as a final or finished product: It is in a constant interchange with its environment and other bodies that can also compose and decompose it.[25] This porosity of the human body is a condition of both its life, because the human body, being a particularly complex one, "requires a great many other bodies, by which

---

[24] E II, LEMMA 7, Scholium. Notice here the striking convergence with contemporary quantum mechanics, which shows that when it comes to the smallest particles of matter, particles can act as one, even when light-years apart: this is the quantum entanglement theory, one of the currently best supported theories of contemporary science (Philip Goff, William Seager, and Sean Allen-Hermanson, "Panpsychism," 144).

[25] Moira Gatens. *Imaginary Bodies: Ethics, Power and Corporeality*, 110.

it is, as it were, continually regenerated," and its eventual death, because it can encounter bodies that are more powerful than it is and can thus eventually destroy its integrity.[26]

The human body does not therefore occupy any a priori special position in this ontology, but it is just one individuality that is mutually originated with all other individualities. Properly speaking, it exists only in these relations. All individual things (*res singulares*) exist only as a consequence of the existence of other individual things (EI P28), with which they participate in an infinite network of connections.[27] Notice here this also implies that causality must not be understood in the sense of a linear succession of events, but rather as a multiplicity of connections between individuals, which are made up of simpler and more complex individuals all causally related. Every individual is thus constantly composed and decomposed by other individuals with which it individualizes through a process that involves both the *infra*-individual and the *supra*-individual levels.[28]

Despite some similarities, this trans-individual approach is different from inter-subjective theories that focus on the way in which individuals interact with each other (*inter*-individual level) and within a given social context (*supra*-individual level). The important cognitive shift is here the focus on the *infra*-individual level. Whereas intersubjective approaches can still endorse some form of methodological individualism, this transindividual ontology questions the traditional notion of individual, etymologically understood as what cannot be divided within itself, and pushes us to either abandon the notion of individuality altogether or to reframe it on radically different terms. And it is in order to render this novelty as well as the complexity of the mechanisms that come to make up any individuality, that, Balibar argued, Spinoza's individuality must be understood as a transindividuality.[29]

---

[26] Ibid, 110.

[27] Étienne Balibar, "Spinoza: From Individuality to Transindividuality," 27.

[28] Ibid. There are some clear affinities between this transindividual philosophy and Deleuze and Guattari's notion of assemblage (*agencement*), as developed in *A Thousand Plateaus*. However, the notion of assemblage has a more mechanic connotation than the philosophy of transindividuality developed here. See: Gilles Deleuze and Félix Guattari, *A Thousand Plateaus: Capitalism and Schizophrenia*, trans. Brian Massumi (Minneapolis: University of Minnesota Press, 1987).

[29] Spinoza does not use this term. It is Balibar who borrows it from Gilbert Simondon's *L'individuation psychique et collective* (Paris: Aubier, 1989). Since the appearance of Balibar's seminal essay (1997), the topic of the transindividual has been object of an intense

This does not mean that individuals disappear: The notion of individuality is indeed central to Spinoza's monist philosophy, because it is the very form of actual existence. As Balibar notes, in the strong sense of the term, only individuals really exist. If we consider that for Spinoza the substance is not something that transcends or underlines the multiplicity of singular things, but an infinite process of production of multiple individuals, whereas individuals, being all different and all causally dependent, are the necessary existence of the substance, we come to the striking conclusion that substance is nothing other than individuals themselves.[30] It is not by chance that, as Antonio Negri observed, after the beginning of Part II of the *Ethics*, the term substance is no longer used by Spinoza, while the focus is moved to the modes (*modi*) and their multiplicity.[31]

Just as what Spinoza calls *natura naturata*, which could be described as the set of all individuals, is second to the *natura naturans* (EI P29), which could be translated as the "*naturing nature*," every individual is an effect of, or a moment in, a more general and perpetual process of individuation and individualization.[32] Balibar distinguishes the concept of individuation, as the moment when individuals become separated

---

philosophical debate. Besides Balibar's 1997 essay, explored below, recent influential views include: Étienne Balibar and Vittorio Morfino, eds., *Il transindividuale* (Milan: Mimesis, 2014); Étienne Balibar, "Philosophies of the transindividual: Spinoza, Marx, Freud," *Australasian Philosophical Review* 2, No. 1 (2018), 5–25; Jason Read, *The Politics of Transindividuality* (Chicago: Haymarket Books, 2016); Daniela Voss, "Immanence, Transindividuality and the Free Multitude," *Philosophy and Social Criticism* 44, no. 8 (2018). Voss expands on Simondon's *L'individuation psychique et collective*, by comparing it with Balibar's view, while Muriel Combes' *Gilbert Simondon and the Philosophy of the Transindividual* (Cambridge, MA: MIT Press, 2013) was the first monograph fully devoted to Simondon and his philosophy of the transindividual.

[30] Étienne Balibar, "Spinoza: From Individuality to Transindividuality," 8.

[31] Antonio Negri, *The Savage Anomaly*, 72. On the centrality and solidity of every existential emergence, see also the following passage: "The Spinozian horizon knows nothing of the hypothesis of emptiness, of the abstract possibility, of formalism; it is a philosophy of fullness, of the material stability of the assumptions, of determinateness, of passion. Making an ideology out of the Spinozian utopia, transforming it in accordance with bourgeois thought, is possible only if the fullness of the Spinozian conception of the thing, of things, of modality and substance is limited, diluted until it is reduced to a shadow, a duplication of reality—and not the true and immediate reality. Precisely in Proposition 13 of Book II, which we have just studied, this materiality of the thing is expressed so radically that only a paradoxical form of argumentation can make sense of it. Fullness: in other words, solidity, determinacy, the ineradicability of every existential emergence" (ibid, 11)

[32] Étienne Balibar, "Spinoza: From Individuality to Transindividuality," 9.

from the environment, from that of individualization, which is the process that makes every individual unique, so much so that no such thing as "indiscernible" individuals can exist.[33] But it is a distinction that does not exist in Spinoza, and which is potentially misleading, if by "environment" one understands something that is outside of the transindividuality itself. In a philosophy of transindividuality, there is no space for conceiving the environment as something separated, because properly speaking the environment is us. It is important, however, to mention this distinction because it rightly points to the fact that Spinoza's philosophy combines its emphasis on the trans-individual nature of individuality with an emphasis on the uniqueness of each individuality. We are transindividual bodies not because we are all the *same*, but precisely because of the *unique* nature of the relations that make each process of individualization possible.

There are individuals for Spinoza, except that they are never atoms, let alone subjects. They are processes, the result of constant movements of association and dissociation that connect more simple individuals with other simple individuals, but also with more complex ones that constantly do and undo a body. To get a crude but hopefully efficient sense of what we mean here, think of how our bodies are composed and decomposed by the food that traverses it: We are constantly processing solids and liquids by which in turn we are being processed. Similarly, we are constantly composed and decomposed by the molecules that we breathe in and out of our bodies, which connect us with an infinite network of other individualities, including the rain forest on the other side of the globe, or the oceans that store carbon dioxide. But also at the infra-individual level: When we eat a salad, it is actually processed by the bacterial microbes in our digestive ecosystem, and it is thus properly described as an encounter between two sets of infra-individuals inside the more general transindividual body of a human being.

We mentioned food and molecules, but keep in mind that the same holds for thoughts: As individuals, we are the result of all the modes in the attribute of thinking that we constantly encounter, be they the book you are reading or the phone conversation you had this morning. As we have seen, this is because the order and connection of ideas is the same as the order and connection of things, since ideas are nothing but

---

[33] Ibid, footnote 8.

affirmations of the body.[34] Thinking ceases here to be the privilege of the human species. This processual nature of bodily composition is not a peculiarity of human bodies, although the latter do exhibit a particularly complex nature and thus require many other individuals for their own survival. As Hasana Sharp emphasized in her reading of Spinoza's *Ethics*, all bodies are created by encounters between bodies that modify both the body that encounters and the body encountered, such as their affects, that is, their capacity to act or being acted upon, and thus to increase or lose power.[35] As a consequence, such encounters are good or bad for a body according to whether they increase or diminish their characteristic constitution, or what Spinoza called their *conatus*.

According to Spinoza, every being endeavors to persist in its being (E III P6: "*Unaquaeque res, quantum in se est, in suo esse perseverare conatur*"). The *conatus* is this "striving" or "endeavoring" to persist in our being that at times Spinoza also calls *potentia* (EIII P7Dem). This striving to persist in its being must not be understood as a defense against others in a sort of Hobbesian war of all against all, where every being is struggling to accumulate as much power as possible in order to defend themselves against others.[36] Within a transindividual perspective, such a view does not make any sense. To begin with, the *conatus* applies to all and every being (*unaquaeque res*), including the simplest individual such as a rock, which strives to persist in its being through the energy stored in the chemical links between its atoms. While every individual, even a stone, is endowed with *conatus*, what is typical of human beings is their being constituted through a more complex series of movements of attraction, repulsion, and imitation generated by their affects (EIII P14–16; P21–34, EIV P6–P19), where an "affect" indicates, at the same time, an affection

---

[34] Spinoza defines an idea as "a concept of the mind which the mind forms because it is a thinking thing" (EII D3), but then he immediately adds an explanation, that emphasizes their affirmative side: "I say concept rather than perception, because the word perception seems to indicate that the mind is acted on by the object, but concept seems to express an action of the mind" (EII, D3 EXPL).

[35] Hasana Sharp, *Spinoza and the Politics of Renaturalization* (Chicago: Chicago University Press, 2011).

[36] Hobbes uses this expression in *De Cive*, but the same conceptual apparatus also recurs in the *Leviathan*: see in particular: Thomas Hobbes, *Malmesburiensis Opera Philosophica Quæ Latine Scripsit Omnia in Unum Corpus Nunc Primum Collecta*, Vol. 2, ed. Gulielmi Molesworth (London: Joannem Bohn, 1939), 148.

of the body and the idea of that affection.[37] Second, Spinoza is very clear in stating that by joining two individuals of the same nature, one obtains an individual which is twice as powerful as those joined (E IV P18 S cholium), so rather than striving for depriving others of their power, individuals strive to persist in their being by forming associations that enable them to maintain a certain form of equilibrium. It is a paradoxical form of altruistic egoism, or egoistic altruism if you prefer, where striving to persevere in its being does not mean defending *against* other individuals, but keeping an equilibrium—literally—*through* them.

At this point the question may emerge of how we know what is increasing our *conatus* and what does not, and thus more generally, how knowledge is possible. Within this monist perspective, we need to conceptualize knowledge in radically different terms. To begin with, if individuals are always transindividual and if the body and the mind are nothing but modes within different attributes of the unique substance, then no radical separation between a subject of knowledge and its object can subsist. As a consequence, for this perspective, the central epistemological question is no longer how knowledge is possible, but rather how mistakes can occur. And Spinoza's answer is quite persuasive: Mistakes occur because, as complex individuals, we are affected in multiple ways, from which confusion often result. Our "Marrano of reason" explicitly says that nothing can happen in the body which is not perceived by the mind (EII P12) but he also emphasized that the way a body is affected depends on both the affecting body and the affected body (EII A11), so the confusion can well be the result of a condition in the affected body and not simply in the affecting one. This happens quite regularly because human beings possess consciousness,[38] and are thus most of the time conscious of their appetites, but they remain unaware of their causes, and can thus hardly grasp all the infinite network of causes and effects affecting their bodies.

---

[37] Spinoza defines affects (*affectus*) as "the affections of the body, by which the body's power of acting (*potentia agendi*) is increased or diminished, aided or restrained, and at the same time the idea of these affections" (E3 D3). Notice here that, as a consequence of Spinoza's ontology and radical monism, affects are both bodily and mental at the same time.

[38] Although, quite interestingly, Spinoza never defines consciousness in the *Ethics*, we find an implicit definition in part III of the *Ethics* where he explains that the difference between appetite and desire is that desire is an appetite of which we are conscious (EIII Aff. D 1). As Balibar also observes, for Spinoza, "*consciousness is nothing else but the (modal) difference between Appetite and Desire*, which is typically human" (Étienne Balibar, "Spinoza: From Individuality to Transindividuality," 4, italics his).

Spinoza is very clear in stating that each being strives to persist in their being *quantum in se est,* that is for the quantum that they are; and human beings are complex finite modes—nothing less, but also nothing more.[39]

For instance, if we were to perceive a unicorn in front of us, this is probably because there is a physiological process happening in our body that alters our perception in that specific way, but, if we are not aware of its causes and remain simply at the level of vague experience, we will attribute it to the fact that there is a unicorn before us. The mistake is thus the result of incomplete knowledge: If we were able to follow all the intricate network of causes and effects affecting our body, then we would have adequate knowledge, and thus add to the perception of the unicorn knowledge about its causes, for instance the fact that the molecules of my nervous system are being affected by a hallucinogenic substance. And this would address the mistake.

When we perceive something, for Spinoza, we immediately tend to form "universal notions," because we tend to follow certain patterns of association, but "universal notions," despite their name, contain only the universality of habits, of what we are accustomed to feign. As such, they are opposed to what Spinoza calls "common notions," those properties that are common to all things and can therefore be conceived adequately (EII P38). For Spinoza, the transformation of our perceptions into so called "universal notions" happens in two ways. The first is "from particular things that are represented to us through the senses in a way that is mutilated, confused and without intellectual order," which results in "knowledge from a vague experience" (*ab experientia vaga*), and the second is from signs (*ab signis*), for example, from the fact that on hearing or reading certain words we recollect things, and form certain ideas about them that are similar to those through which we imagine the things (E II P40 Scholium 2). This is the level of imagination, which for Spinoza is the sole source of error, although imagination does not err in itself. When we reach a particular degree of clarity and distinctness, we reach the second kind of knowledge, that is reason.

In Spinoza's view, imagination is therefore not a separate faculty, but a certain type of knowledge that is distinguished from other kinds of

---

[39] This also explains why, even though Spinoza denies the existence of contingency, because everything happens necessarily, we still experience encounters as if they happened by chance. On Spinoza's materialism as a form of aleatory materialism, see "Chapter 3 'The World by Chance': On Lucretius and Spinoza," trans. Ted Stolze, pp. 72–88 in Vittorio Morfino, *Plural Temporality*.

knowledge only in terms of degree.[40] In the first place, this means that there is no dichotomy of "imagination" vs "reason," but a threefold scheme: imagination, reason, and what Spinoza calls "intuitive science" (EII P40 Scholium 2). The first, imagination, which includes perception, memory, and induction, is at times also called "opinion" (it is thus quite a broad understanding of imagination that includes processes such as induction that many would rather associate with reason or the intellect). The second kind of knowledge is reason, and is generated by the fact that we have common notions (*notiones communes*) and adequate ideas of the property of things. The third is finally "intuitive science," which "proceeds from an adequate idea of the formal essence of some of the attributes of God to an adequate knowledge of the essence of things"; to characterize this type of knowledge Spinoza furnishes the example of a mathematical intuition (EII P40 Scholium 2).

Whereas reason and intuitive science always produce adequate ideas, imagination, as we have mentioned, is the sole cause of falsity. Yet, as Spinoza explicitly says, it is not necessarily false (EII P17 Scholium). The imaginations of the mind, regarded in themselves, contain no error (EII P17 Scholium). "For if the mind, while it imagines non existent things as present to it, knew at the same time that those things do not really exist, it would ascribe this power of imagining to a *virtue* of its own nature and not to a defect—especially if this faculty of imagining depended on its own nature alone, that is (by EI D7 I) if this faculty of imagining that the mind has were free" (EII P17 Scholium).

This eccentric understanding of knowledge derives from the fact that the very notion of a self-enclosed subject—of a Cartesian ego, to which we are so accustomed—does not make any sense in a philosophy of transindividuality. Human beings are nothing but particularly complex individuals resulting from movements of attraction and repulsion between more or less complex individuals.[41] In other words, they are not given entities, but rather processes,

---

[40] Chiara Bottici, "Another Enlightenment: Spinoza on Myth and Imagination," *Constellations* 9, no. 4 (2012), 1–19.

[41] As Hippler observes, developing insights from Balibar, Spinoza reverses the perspective of social contract theorists who begin with individuals bearers of rights in order to justify a certain social contract: for Spinoza, the individual is not the given first matter of politics, but is conceived as a process that is coextensive with politics itself (Thomas Hippler, "Spinoza's Politics of Imagination and the Origins of Critical Theory," in *The Politics of Imagination*, eds. Chiara Bottici and Benoît Challand (London: Routledge, 2011). The third part of the *Ethics* emphasizes the affective mechanisms of association and transfer (EIII P14–16), in addition

webs of affective relations, which are never given once and for all. This is the sense in which Spinoza's radical statement that desire is the very essence of the human must be interpreted (*cupiditas est ipsa hominis essentia*: EIII, Definition of the Emotions, D1). Desire, defined as an appetite of which we are conscious, is not just a feature of human beings. It is, much more radically, what creates them, and what does so through a process of constant of individuation that is transindividual in nature.[42]

This means also that, as Moira Gatens underlined, in the process of individuation that generates human beings, complex dynamics of imaginary identification become particularly crucial:[43] We constantly meet and recognize or misrecognize ourselves in certain body images, which include images that we have of our bodies and of other bodies, as well as images that others have of them and which become constitutive of our own being. For Spinoza, the key term for keeping together the mental and the material side of this process is "imagination." The latter, as we have seen, in his theory of knowledge, denotes a set of ideas produced on the basis of present or past bodily affections (EII P26D, P40 Scholium2). But, in order to avoid misunderstandings, we should immediately recall that, within this monist ontology, an idea is not only a mental content. An idea is for Spinoza "a conception of the mind" (EII D3) and imagination is thus a form of bodily grounding, because the mind is just the body that is felt and thought (EII P11). Following Gatens and Lloyd, we can

---

to mimesis and imitation (EIII P21–34), and thus helps us understand how individuals literally comes into being. In the TTP, Spinoza explores instead how compliant subjects can also be created through rituals and disciplines of obedience. See: Chiara Bottici and Miguel de Beistegui, "Spinoza and the Hydraulic Discipline of Affects: From the Theologico-Political to the Economic Regime of Desire," in *Spinoza's Authority*, Volume II, eds. A. Kiarina Kordela and Dimitris Vardoulakis (London: Bloomsbury, 2018), 167–92.

[42] Note that desire is for Spinoza clearly distinguished from will, because will is the name that we give to man's effort to preserve himself when, by a fiction, we think of the soul in isolation from the body, whereas desire is the same effort as it relates inseparably to the soul and the body (EIII P9, Scholium). On the relationship between the two, see: Étienne Balibar, *Spinoza and Politics*, 105.

[43] One of the first commentators to point to this constitutive role of imagination in Spinoza has been Negri (see in particular Antonio Negri, *The Savage Anomaly*, 86–97). According to Williams, what is new in Étienne Balibar's "Spinoza: from individuality to transindividuality," and *Spinoza and Politics*, and Moira Gatens and Genevieve Lloyd, *Collective Imaginings: Spinoza, Past and Present* (London: Routledge, 1999) is that they draw attention to Spinoza's novel, materialist rendering of the imagination, without simply dismissing it as a source of errors. See: Caroline Williams, "Thinking the Political in the Wake of Spinoza," *Contemporary Political Theory* 6 (2007), 350.

summarize Spinoza's view of imagination by saying that it is a form of bodily awareness, which means awareness of both our body and the other bodies with which we come into contact and that, as such, it is always, properly speaking, a form of "collective imagining."[44]

Whereas Spinoza and Gatens focus on the role that imagination plays in these dynamics of attraction and repulsion that are constitutive of our being, we propose to re-conceptualize them in terms of what has recently been called the imaginal.[45] Despite the fact that feminists such as Gatens and Lloyd have brought Spinoza's concept of imagination much further, the concept of imagination remains too imbued with the presuppositions of methodological individualism, with its alternative between "imagination" as an individual faculty and the "social imaginary" as a social context.[46] On the contrary, imaginal is that which is made by images in the most radical sense of the term, that is images as (re)presentations that are also presences in themselves.[47] As such, the notion of imaginal does not make any epistemological assumption as to whether such images are the result of an individual or a collective process and is therefore a better theoretical companion for the transindividual than either imagination or the social imaginary. Indeed, like the transindividual, the concept of the imaginal points to the need of getting rid of the social *versus* individual dichotomy.[48] The further advantage of the concept of imaginal is that it does not make any ontological assumptions as to the real or unreal status of images: whereas the concept of imaginary is associated with the idea of unreality, as in the expression "this is purely imaginary," the term imaginal does not carry any such strong ontological presupposition.[49] Despite the fact that the "imaginal" is not a very common word, the *Oxford English Dictionary* includes this peculiar aspect of it in its definition, by stating that "imaginal"

---

[44] Moira Gatens and Genevieve Lloyd, *Collective Imaginings*, 12.

[45] Cynthia Fleury, *Imagination, imaginaire, imaginal* (Paris: PUF, 2006); Chiara Bottici, *Imaginal Politics: Images beyond the Imagination and beyond the Imaginary* (Columbia University Press: New York, 2014).

[46] Moira Gatens and Genevieve Lloyd, *Collective Imaginings*.

[47] Chiara Bottici, *Imaginal Politics*, 54–63.

[48] Chiara Bottici, "Bodies in Plural: Towards an Anarcha-feminist Manifesto," *Thesis Eleven* 142, no. 1 (2017), 91–111.

[49] In this sense, it is also a better companion to a Spinozist ontology of the transindividual, given that for Spinoza reality is a synonym of perfection (EII D6). I have explored more in details the link between Spinoza's theory of knowledge and this eccentric definition of reality as synonym with perfection in Chiara Bottici, "Another Enlightenment."

primarily means what pertains to imagination or to images.[50] There is no mention here of how real or not such images or imaginations are. In contrast, the same dictionary's definition of "imaginary" clearly points to the ontological bias of this term insofar as the "imaginary" is said to denote what exists only in fancy, that which has no real existence and is therefore opposed to what is "real" or "actual" (ibid.). Finally, the term imaginal also has the advantage to include both conscious and unconscious images. This is important to note not only because the term "imaginal" has been explicitly used by psychoanalysts to denote the space of a therapy where conscious and unconscious images meet,[51] but also because the unconscious itself escapes the alternative between individual and collective and is therefore at best characterized as transindividual.[52] As we will see, this "transindividual unconscious" dimension is particularly crucial to understand how domination works, and how images circulating in societies can become an unconscious lens through which we perceive and act within the world.

It is in terms of what Moira Gatens calls "imaginary bodies," and that we would like to call "imaginal bodies," that we can understand the psychological side of the process of individuation described above.[53] Whenever our body encounters another body, which can be a simple one, like a glass of water, or a more complex one, like another human being, a change in its own constitution will occur. It is in this sense, and in order to keep together what happens both at the infra-individual level and at

---

[50] John Simpson and Edmund Weiner, *The Oxford English Dictionary*, Vol. 2 (Oxford: Oxford University Press, 1989), 668.

[51] James Hillman, *Healing Fictions* (Putnam: Spring Publications 2005), 56.

[52] It is revealing that one of the first occurrences of the term transindividual in contemporary debate is in a passage where Jacques Lacan explicitly says that the unconscious is transindividual (Étienne Balibar and Vittorio Morfino, eds., *Il transindividuale*, 9). In our previous work, we have used the expression "social unconscious" to point out to a third alternative between conception of the individual unconscious *versus* those of the collective unconscious (Chiara Bottici, *Imaginal Politics*, Chap 3), but it would be more appropriate to speak of the "transindividual unconscious". See: Jacques Lacan, *Écrits*, trans. Bruce Fink (New York: W. W. Norton, 2006), 214.

[53] Notice the similarity between this process and what Drucilla Cornell described in her *The Imaginary Domain: Abortion, Pornography and Sexual Harassment* (London: Routledge, 1995). Although Cornell phrases her theory in Lacanian terms, the fundamental insight that the imaginal is a crucial battleground where sexualized bodies negotiate their own being is the same.

the supra-individual level, that the notion of transindividuality becomes particular helpful. Our bodies are always necessarily bodies in plural, because their individuality is always and inevitably a form of transindividuality. We are all born from other bodies and, since birth, we are being constantly transformed by encountering other bodies, while continuously affecting them in our turn. The concept of transindividuality is meant to signal that we exist as a complex network of relations as well as our processual nature.

5 The philosophy of the transindividual as transindividual philosophy

Before we return to the woman question, let us further investigate what it means to speak about bodies in plural and how this understanding can lead us beyond some of the impasses that have plagued feminist philosophy in the past few decades. With those insights, we will be able to go back to the ontology of the transindividual elucidated in the previous chapter and present it as part of a more general movement towards a transindividual philosophy.

First, the expression "bodies in plural" underscores the transindividual nature of the process of individuation, that is, of a process that unfolds by connecting the *infra-*, *inter-*, and the *supra*-individual levels. This leads us beyond the opposition between individualistic approaches, focusing on the rights, needs, and constitution of single persons, and the various forms of social organicism, focusing instead on the social and collective selves. If every body is transindividual by definition, then we can no longer conceive of the relationship between individuals and society according to usual categories, such as the part and the whole, as in Aristotelian models, or the founders and the founded, as in European social-contract theories. What these two very different models have in common is that they take individuals, whether single societies or single persons, as the starting point for philosophizing, and not as effects of it. Philosophies of the transindividual are attempts to move beyond this false alternative by asking the question of how individuals themselves come into being in the first instance.

Second, by placing the body within an ontology of the unique substance, we can also bypass the opposition between nature and culture that has accompanied feminist debates from the very beginning: Is the subjection of women the result of their biology (nature) or of their upbringing (culture)? Behind this opposition, as well as behind the opposition between sex and gender, there is indeed the typical Western metaphysical dualism centered around the dichotomy of body and mind.[1] If we understand thinking and extension as just two different ways of perceiving the same substance, then no opposition between the two can hold: and it is within such an ontological framework that it also becomes possible to raise the question "what is a woman?" by avoiding the false alternatives between "essentialism" and "culturalism." Once the body is no longer understood as an inert, fixed entity, there is no more need—but also no more space—to raise the charge of "essentialism," nor to invoke "culture" as the site for malleability and change.

Through a philosophy of transindividuality, as we have seen, we can leave behind any form of body–mind dualism, in all of their different ramifications: from the Christian form to their more secular versions. In such a philosophical approach, we can also find the resources to go beyond the methodological individualism that lies at the basis of the Aristotelian-scholastic idea of a *scala naturae*. The term "transindividuality" does not come from Spinoza, but from the French philosopher Gilbert Simondon. It is therefore to his philosophy that we must now turn, in order to elucidate how the notion of transindividuality tackles the question of methodological individualism.

Simondon's philosophical project was indeed motivated by the desire to question the opposition of nature *versus* culture, a desire that lies at the basis of his systematic exploration of the concept of the transindividual.[2] Pursued across physical, biological, psychosocial, and technological domains, Simondon's work can be read as a call for a transmutation in how we

---

[1] Moira Gatens, *Imaginary Bodies: Ethics, Power and Corporeality* (London: Routledge, 1996), 3–20.

[2] As we have mentioned, Balibar takes the expression directly from Simondon. The term had already been used by philosophers before, but not extensively nor in any systematic form. See: Étienne Balibar, "Spinoza: From Individuality to Transindividuality," in *Medelingen vanwege het Spinozahauis*. (Delft: Heburon, 1997); Étienne Balibar and Vittorio Morfino, eds., *Il transindividuale* (Milano: Mimesis, 2014), 9–10.

approach being.[3] In his monumental *L'individuation à la lumière des notions de forme et d'information*,[4] he begins by noticing that being is used in two senses: on the one hand, "being is being as such," which is to say there is being, about which we can only confirm its "givenness," and, on the other hand, "being is being insofar as it is individuated."[5] These two meanings are most often confused because the latter sense of being, in which being appears as a multiplicity of individual beings, is "always superimposed upon the former sense within the theory of logic," which is, in turn, what is used to approach being.[6] Although this criticism seems to be specific to logic, it actually applies to most of the Western philosophical traditions which perpetuates this confusion. As Muriel Combes rightly underlines in reading this passage, "just as logic deals with statements that are relative to being after individuation, so philosophy focuses on being as individuated, thus conflating being with individuated being."[7] Consequently, for Simondon the (Western) philosophical canon can be divided into two types of traditions, atomism and hylomorphism: both of them indeed deal with the problem of the one and many, but thereby think of the problem of individuation *already on the basis of the individual*.[8] On the contrary, we should distinguish between being as such and being as individual, thus making space for thinking also about what Simondon call the "pre-individual," that is, the being as being which precedes any individual.[9]

For the French philosopher, therefore, the crucial philosophical problem is precisely that of individuation: That is, not so much how to think of the problem of the relationship between the one and the many,

---

[3] Muriel Combes' *Gilbert Simondon and the Philosophy of the Transindividual* (Cambridge, MA: MIT Press, 2013), 1.

[4] This work corresponds to the doctoral thesis that Simondon defended in 1950s. The first part entitled *L'individu et sa genèse physico-biologique* was published in 1960s (Gilbert Simondon, *L'individu et sa genèse physico-biologique* (Paris: Presses Universitaires de France, 1964)). The second part was published posthumously with the title *Individuation psychique et collective* (Paris: Aubier, 1989). Both parts are now published together in *L'individuation à la lumière des notions de forme et d'information*, which has become the standard reference for his work (Grenoble: Edition Million, 2005).

[5] Gilbert Simondon, *L'individuation à la lumière des notions de forme and d'information psychique et collective*, 23–36. Translations from French are mine.

[6] Ibid, 34.

[7] Muriel Combes, *Gilbert Simondon and the Philosophy of the Transindividual*, 1.

[8] Gilbert Simondon, *L'individuation à la lumière des notions de forme and d'information psychique et collective*, 23.

[9] Muriel Combes, *Gilbert Simondon and the Philosophy of the Transindividual*, 2.

but rather how to think about the operation constituting the individual, and thus "seek to know the individual through individuation rather than individuation through the individual."[10] The fundamental philosophical problem should therefore no longer be that of ontology, that is of the *logos* of the *being* (to *on*), which already presupposes the existence of individuals, but rather than of the *ontogenesis*, that is of how to think the genesis of individuated being. It is in this ontogenetical perspective that we propose to understand the concept of transivididuality.

The Western philosophical tradition, with its classical dualism of interior and exterior, "psychologism" and "sociologism," has always subordinated the understanding of individuation to the definition of the individual as (an ideally stable) form. All language of interior/exterior, internal/external, already presupposes individuals as constituted. By drawing inspiration from modern thermodynamics and, in particular, from the study of crystalline structures, Simondon attempted to construct an alternative understanding of ontogeny by arguing that stable forms, which reduce the potential energy to a minimum, are less important than *metastable* equilibria, requiring an elevation of potential energy which has to be preserved.[11]

The notion of metastability is crucial to this understanding of the process of individuation. A physical system is said to be in a metastable equilibrium when the least modification of systems parameters (pressure, temperature, etc) suffices to break the equilibrium. For instance, in super-cooled water—that is, in water remaining liquid at a temperature below its freezing point—the least impurity with a structure isomorphic to that of ice plays the role of a seed for crystallization and is enough to turn water into ice. Following this model, Simondon underlines that, before all individuation, being can be understood as a system containing potential energy, whereas the emergence of an individual within the preindividual being must be understood in terms of the resolution of a tension between potentials belonging to previously separated orders of magnitude.[12]

---

[10] Gilbert Simondon, *L'individuation à la lumière des notions de forme and d'information psychique et collective*, 24.

[11] Étienne Balibar, "Spinoza: From Individuality to Transindividuality," 11.

[12] A plant, for instance, Combes observes, establishes communication between a cosmic order, to which the energy of light belongs, and an infra-molecular order, to which mineral salts, oxygen, carbon dioxide, etc, belong. See: Muriel Combes, *Gilbert Simondon and the Philosophy of the Transindividual*, 3–4.

Within this philosophy, then, "the individual is the reality of a constituting relation, not the interiority of a constituted term."[13] Instead of moving from the assumption that a relation consists in piecing together two (existing) terms, Simondon tries to reverse it by considering any true relation as itself being.[14] There is a postulate of the reality of the relations at the basis of this philosophical enterprise, one that is very close to our reading of Spinoza's *Ethics*. Such a postulate sums up Simondon's method on its own: "The method consists in trying not to piece together the essence of a reality by means of a conceptual relation between two final terms, and in considering any true relation as having a rank of being."[15] Thus, in this philosophical perspective, we do not have first the given individual and then the relations between them, but relations as the only reality.

This shift, for Simondon not less than Spinoza, also implies reconceptualizing knowledge itself. The latter cannot be conceived as a relation between two already constituted individuals, the knowing subject and the known object. On the contrary, for Simondon, knowledge is a "relation of two relations of which one is in the domain of the object and the other in the domain of the subject."[16] If relation is not something that links together two preexisting terms but is something that arises by constituting the terms themselves as relation, then we understand how knowledge can only be a relation of relations.[17] This, in turn, means that the distinct operation that constitute the knowing subject and the known object are unified in, but also constituted by, the act of relation that is called knowledge.[18] As a consequence, similarly to Spinoza's eccentric theory of knowledge, the problem of the conditions of the possibility of knowledge is recast into that of the ontogenesis of knowing. As Simondon writes: "we cannot, in the habitual sense of the terms, know individuation; we can only individuate, individuating ourselves, and individuating

[13] Gilbert Simondon, *L'individuation à la lumière des notions de forme and d'information psychique et collective*, 62.

[14] Ibid, 32.

[15] Muriel Combes, *Gilbert Simondon and the Philosophy of the Transindividual*, 16; Gilbert Simondon, *L'individuation à la lumière des notions de forme and d'information psychique et collective*, 32.

[16] Gilbert Simondon, *L'individuation à la lumière des notions de forme and d'information psychique et collective*, 83.

[17] Muriel Combes, *Gilbert Simondon and the Philosophy of the Transindividual*, 17.

[18] Ibid.

within ourselves."[19] If we combine these insights with the philosophy of the transindividual described above, we come to the conclusion that a philosophy of the transindividual is also by definition a "transindivdual philosophy," that is, one where we individuate along with it, individuating ourselves and within ourselves. In other words, we can never philosophize alone, because we can only individuate with others and through others.

Although Simondon openly distances himself from Spinoza's philosophy, mistakenly interpreting it as a form of pantheism and denial of the reality of the individual, it is not hard to perceive the deep affinity between the two approaches.[20] Yet, some differences remain. In the first place, Simondon is not as clear as Spinoza on the question of monism and the project of rethinking the relationship between thinking and being leads him to rely on the notion of analogy, which is a form of parallelism.[21] But, as we have argued, parallelism is misleading because it reintroduces a form of dualism, whereas Spinoza is quite clear in stating that the order and connection of ideas is the same (*idem*) as the order and connection of things. Yet, the two philosophies converge in important points, so much so that, as Balibar noticed, one can justifiably use Simondon's notion of transindividuality in order to argue that, within Spinoza's philosophy, individuality must always be understood in terms of transindividuality.[22]

When putting forwards this interpretation, Balibar did not mention that Simondon also restricts the concept of transindividuality to the psychic and collective individuation, whereas, in Spinoza's philosophy, it applies to all bodies. And this is, in our view, a crucial difference, which makes Spinoza's philosophy of transindividuality a much better companion for our age than Simondon's. The latter separates the physical from the biological domain: the former is the domain wherein the individual, by appearing, causes the metastable state to disappear, by suppressing the tensions within the system in which it appears, while the domain of the living is defined by the fact that the individual maintains the metastability of the system in which it arose.[23] Living beings spring from a first biological individuation, but in order to

---

[19] Gilbert Simondon, *L'individuation à la lumière des notions de forme and d'information psychique et collective*, 36.
[20] Étienne Balibar, "Spinoza: From Individuality to Transindividuality," 10; Muriel Combes, *Gilbert Simondon and the Philosophy of the Transindividual*, 9.
[21] Muriel Combes, *Gilbert Simondon and the Philosophy of the Transindividual*, 17.
[22] Étienne Balibar, "Spinoza: From Individuality to Transindividuality."
[23] Muriel Combes, *Gilbert Simondon and the Philosophy of the Transindividual*, 28.

maintain their existence they have to keep this initial individuation through another series of individuations, that is, through what Simondon calls "individualization."[24] A living being "in order to exist, needs to be able to continue individualizing by resolving problems in the *milieu* surrounding it, which is its *milieu*."[25]

This creates an opposition between living and non-living matter, to which Simondon adds a further level of distinction, which is the sphere of the properly human or what he calls the "psychic-collective individuation." Indeed, Simondon does not apply the concept of transindividuality before reaching the stage of psychological individuality, thereby reproducing the idea of a hierarchy of being.[26] For Simondon, transindividuation is indeed the specific way in which psychic individuation happens in humans, that is the process through which a character, a personality or psyche is formed. He is very clear in stating, for instance, that psychological individuality appears as that which is formed in elaborating transindividuality.[27] The latter is understood as an impersonal zone of subjects that is simultaneously a molecular or intimate dimension of the collective.[28] The novelty of this approach is supposed to consist in stating that psychic individuation is not opposed to the collective one but rather an integral part of it (but, as we have seen, this may not be as novel as it appears). Since individuation is an ongoing process, the pre-individual sensations and affects which form the basis of our individuation never cohere, so the psychic individuation tries to resolve itself in collective structures: hence the reason why Simondon speaks of a "psychic-collective individuation."[29]

---

[24] Ibid, 27.

[25] Gilbert Simondon, *L'individuation à la lumière des notions de forme and d'information psychique et collective*, 264.

[26] Ibid, 229.

[27] Ibid, 281.

[28] Muriel Combes, *Gilbert Simondon and the Philosophy of the Transindividual*, 52.

[29] *Individuation psychique et collective* is the title of the last two chapters of the second part of the doctoral thesis. As Combes noticed, he does not speak of a "psychic and collective individuation" but rather of one individuation in the singular, thereby making it clear that they are reciprocal and thus two poles of a single constituting relations, one interior (psychic) and one exterior (collective) (Muriel Combes, *Gilbert Simondon and the Philosophy of the Transindividual*, 25). From a Spinozist perspective, though, this move could be seen as a reintroduction of a dualism: that between the domain of the transindividual (or psychic-collective individuation) *versus* the biological individuation, whereas our usage of the concept of transindividuality rather aims at overcoming any type of dualism.

Consequently, whereas in the Spinozist philosophy of the transindividual sketched above nothing prevents us from conceiving that animals think, Simondon recast the traditional opposition between humans and animals in terms of a distinction between somatic and psychic, between feeling and thinking: For Simondon, "in contrast with the human who perceives, the animal appears perpetually to feel without being able to raise itself to the level of representing the object separate from its contact with the object."[30] Thus, whereas in Simondon the term "transindividual" signals the co-presence of the psychic and collective individuation for human beings alone, the Spinozist transindividual philosophy includes all types of individuation, of which the specifically human is only one. Whereas Simondon's usage of the term can therefore still be interpreted in a dualistic framework, as reproducing a hierarchy between physical individuation *and* the psychic-collective-human individuation, we emphasize, with Spinoza, that human beings are not a separate kingdom in the kingdom of nature (*imperium in imperio*), but just bodies with different degree of complexity of the same transindividual process.

Balibar's 1997 essay, with its attempt to use the notion of transindividuality to interpret Spinoza's philosophy sparked indeed a new interest in both this notion and in Simondon's philosophy—an interest which is likely to continue for some time to come.[31] Whereas Simondon's usage of the term only refers to a certain type of individuation, the Spinozist interpretation enables us to use it in a sense that is at the same time broader but also less vague. If by transindividual we mean just that, for human beings, psychic individuation is inseparable from the collective individuation, then a vast

---

[30] Ibid, 29.
[31] Examples of the works that followed the publication of that essay, include: Nicola Marcucci and Luca Pinzolo, eds., *Strategie della relazione. Riconoscimento, transindividuale, alterità* (Rome: Meltemi, 2010); Étienne Balibar and Vittorio Morfino, eds., *Il transindividuale* (Milano: Mimesis, 2014); Jason Read, *The Politics of Transindividuality* (Chicago: Haymarket Books, 2016); and Balibar's own continuation of his attempt to develop a philosophy of the transindividual by pairing Spinoza with Marx and Freud (Étienne Balibar, "Philosophies of the Transindividual: Spinoza, Marx, Freud," *Australasian Philosophical Review* 2, no. 1 (2018). The latter has been the object of a special issue of the *Australasian Philosophical Review*, edited by Dimitris Vardoulakis and Mark Kelly, with contributions by the two editors, Ingrid Diran, Yannik Thiem, Daniela Voss, Andrea Bardin & Pablo Rodriguez, Jason Read, Christopher Davidson, Vittorio Morfino, Spyridon Tegos, James Martel, and myself. See: Mark G. E. Kelly and Dimitris Vardoulakis, "Balibar and Transindividuality," *Australasian Philosophical Review* 2, no. 1 (2018). Among the works devoted only to Simondon's philosophy, Muriel Combes' *Gilbert Simondon and the Philosophy of the Transindividual* remains to date the most important monographic commentary to his work.

array of philosophers, from Averroes to Hegel, from Marx to Freud, all come to be part of the philosophy of the transindividual.[32] But if that is the case, then it becomes hard to exclude even philosophers such as Jean-Jacques Rousseau or even Adam Smith, and the list could keep growing.[33] This enabled thinkers of the transindividual such as Balibar to join together authors as different as Spinoza and Freud, but, in this enlarging of the field, we risk losing track of the difference between monist and dualist approaches and thus also to recast the philosophy of the transindividual in a philosophical tradition imbued with the humanist hubris, which assign a special place to human beings instead of conceiving them as primarily just complex modes along with other more or less complex ones.[34] What one risks losing in such an enlargement of the field of the philosophies of transindividuality is the *ecocentric egalitarianism* inspired by Spinoza's *Ethics*, i.e. the view that considers all bodies as modes of the same infinite substance, and thus, to some extent animate.

Notice also how, within a Spinozist prospective, it does not even make sense to distinguish between an ontological *versus* an historical philosophy of the transindividual. Jason Read, in an important work on *The Politics of Transindividuality*, provides a useful map of the different philosophies of transindividuality that can be mobilized from an historical materialist perspective, but, in doing so, Read begins precisely with that separation.[35] In this interpretation, the orientation of Simondon's philosophy of the transindividual is more that of a general ontology than a historical-critical philosophy, and this is the reason why Read feels the need to supplement it with thinkers in the Marxist tradition, pointing to the socio-historical transformation of individuation under capitalism.[36] For Read, one needs to supplement the ontological perspective of Simondon with that of Marx himself, as well as Balibar and other Marxist theorists of post-Fordist capitalism such as Paolo Virno and Maurizio

---

[32] Étienne Balibar and Vittorio Morfino, eds., *Il transindividuale*.
[33] Spyridon Tegos, "Identification with Authority and the Transindividual in Rousseau: Critical Comments on Balibar's Concept of the Transindividual," *Australasian Philosophical Review* 2, no. 1 (2018); Mike Hill and Warren Montag, *The Other Adam Smith* (Stanford: Stanford University Press, 2014).
[34] Chiara Bottici, "From the Transindividual to the Imaginal: A Response to Balibar's 'Philosophies of the Transindividual: Spinoza, Marx, Freud'", in *Australasian Philosophy Review* 2, no. 1 (2018), 69–76.
[35] Jason Read, *The Politics of Transindividuality*.
[36] Ibid, 6.

Lazzarato, which are considered the driving force for a political interpretation of the concept.

But if the problem of a philosophy of transindividuality is explaining how individuation is possible, and if the latter is always thought of as a process, then there is no reason to oppose ontological approaches *versus* historical ones: As we emphasized in the previous chapter, once we get rid of the two twin assumptions that being is always individuated being and that individuals are the stable entities presupposed by classical logic and metaphysics, then the very opposition between ontology, a discipline devoted to reflect on the *logos* of being, and history, the discipline of the becoming, disappears. Both become part of a more general series of reflections on the process of individuation, which Simondon, usefully labels "ontogenesis." With a shift from onto-logy to onto-genesis, we want to underline that there cannot be any *logos* of being that is not at the same time a *genesis* of being. As we will now see, the ontogenetic reflections on the physics of liquids can therefore go hand in hand with Marxist reflections on how individuals are created by the capitalist mode of production in different contexts, but also with the insights of contemporary biology, queer ecology, and even with those of quantum physics—all being part of the same individuating process of a transindividual philosophy.

As Hasana Sharp (among others) has emphasized, Spinoza's eccentric philosophy can indeed be the basis for a politics or re-naturalization, but one, we should add, where the nature that is brought back into the center of feminist politics is no longer the same thing that left it a while ago.[37] Among others, it is a nature deeply transformed by the insights of contemporary materialist feminism and queer ecology. In recent years, a number of feminists have indeed been calling for a new "materialist turn" in feminism.[38] The main rationale for such a project is that feminist theory, in its attempt to fight the oppression of women, all too often has been neglecting or bracketing the role of the body. Since women have historically been treated as "naturally" inferior to men, and thus excluded from domains of human rationality, subjectivity, and transcendence on the basis of their biology, most feminist theory has worked to disentangle woman from nature in a variety of ways and thus tended to shy away

---

[37] Hasana Sharp, *Spinoza and the Politics of Renaturalization* (Chicago: Chicago University Press, 2011).
[38] Stacy Alaimo, *Bodily Natures: Science, Environment, and the Material Self* (Bloomington, IN: Indiana University Press, 2010), 6.

from biology.[39] This was not without success. The introduction of the pivotal distinction between sex and gender has indeed been liberating for women precisely because it has enabled them to argue that their inferior position was not the result of their supposed immutable nature but rather of a social and cultural upbringing that could be modified.[40] This led to an emphasis on the cultural, psychological, and linguistic modalities that justified women's oppression. Yet, in doing so, according to the sustainers of a "new materialist turn," feminist theory has neglected the role that nature and materiality play in women's lives as well as in their oppression. Hence the need to recast nature as a feminist space and to call for a more general materialist turn that could compensate for the pitfalls of post-"linguistic turn" feminisms.[41]

In light of our previous discussion, we can now argue that if we remain at the level of the alternative between cultural *versus* natural, or linguistic *versus* materialist approaches to feminist theorizing, we are just inverting the agenda but not really questioning the dualistic ontological assumption that cast them as opposite in the first place: Saying that we need to focus on the body to compensate for the excessive concentration on culture and language means implicitly assuming that the body is not cultural, and that culture is not bodily.[42] Through a monist approach instead—and, in particular, through the ontology of the transindividual described above—the very opposition between materialist and non-materialist approaches no longer holds, because the order and connection of things is the same as the order and connections of ideas. The label "materialism" may have

---

[39] Ibid, 4–14.

[40] Simone de Beauvoir's claim that one is not born but becomes a woman aptly summarizes this position. As she observes, "no biological, psychic or economic destiny defines the figure that the human females take on in society; it is civilization as a whole that elaborates this intermediary product between the male and the eunuch that is called feminine," Simone de Beauvoir, *The Second Sex* (New York: Vintage, 2011), 283.

[41] Stacy Alaimo, *Bodily Natures. Science, Environment, and the Material Self.*

[42] This is something that we have always implicitly questioned in our previous work, where we tackled questions of imagination and cultural productions as tools of oppression, but always did so by reading them, implicitly or explicitly, as just one side of the material conditions of their production. See for instance: Chiara Bottici and Benoît Challand, *The Myth of the Clash of Civilizations* (New York: Routledge, 2010), for an analysis of Islamophobia as rooted in the long shadow of European colonialism, or Chiara Bottici, *Imaginal Politics: Images beyond the Imagination and beyond the Imaginary* (Columbia University Press: New York, 2014), for an analysis of the rise of a global society of the spectacle through the emergence of cognitive turn in contemporary capitalism.

been necessary for projects such as Marx's historical materialism, because in a context such as nineteenth-century Germany, philosophy was indeed dominated by idealist approaches, thereby justifying the need to turn them upside down, and thus put material conditions and relations of production where the idealists had enthroned ideas and their realization. But repeating such a move today risks leaving underlining dualist assumptions turned on their head too. In order to question them one needs to unpack the underlying ontological assumptions, which also explains why so many thinkers in the Marxist tradition of historical materialism have found in Spinoza a vital pair to Marx.[43] If, along with Alaimo, we simply call for a "new materialism" without questioning such assumptions, ideas, and things, thinking and extension, ideality and materiality are still presupposed to be separated, if not opposed, because that is what is implicitly conveyed by our language.

Materialist feminists are, however, right in saying that a flight from nature and biology can be detrimental to the feminist cause. To begin with, it presupposes the assumption that nature, and thus, biology is fixed, whereas culture, and thus social upbringing, are changeable.[44] This reflects a very limited, and inadequate, view of biology as there are a number of biological approaches that purport nature as a constantly changing series of processes and thus as opposed to just fixed objects given once and for all. Even biological approaches, as we will see, can therefore be themselves part of a transindividual philosophy. The idea that "anatomy is destiny" has haunted feminism for too long, and it is now the time to abandon that ghost, because there is no reason to assume that anatomy is fixed whereas culture is malleable at will.

Transgender studies have questioned such an assumption in a variety of ways, so much so that the very dichotomy of sex and gender appears now as outdated, while alternative approaches to biology increasingly challenge the sexual dimorphism that relegated women to the status of the second sex.[45] For instance, in the illuminating essay "Naturally queer," Myra Hird shows how non-linear biology defies static notions of sexual difference. To begin with, Hird reminds us that the vast majority of cells in

---

[43] See for instance the already quoted Étienne Balibar, "Spinoza: From Individuality to Transindividuality"; Étienne Balibar, *Spinoza and Politics* (London: Verso, 1998); and Vittorio Morfino, *Plural Temporality: Transindividuality and the Aleatory Between Spinoza and Althusser* (Leiden: Brill, 2014), both of whom have been largely influenced by Althusser.

[44] Stacy Alaimo, *Bodily Natures. Science, Environment, and the Material Self*, 5.

[45] Tina Chanter, *Gender: Key Concepts in Philosophy* (London: Continuum, 2006), 1–7.

the human body are intersex—a category that itself makes sense only if we maintain the division between "female" and "male" chromosomes, and which therefore does not adequately convey the fact that most cells in our body are actually both.[46] The only cells that are sexually dimorphic are eggs and sperm: In terms of the transindividual philosophy highlighted above, we could say that sexual dimorphism is a striking exception rather than the rule among the infra-individuals that make human bodies, and there is no reason why the exception should be perceived as the rule in terms of the basic constituent of human life. Most cells in our bodies reproduce indeed through recombination (cutting and patching of DNA strands), merging (fertilization of cells), meiosis (cell division by halving chromosomes number), and mitosis (cell division with maintenance of cell number).[47] Thus, as a rule, reproduction does not happen between discrete selves, as we tend to assume: "indeed, only by taking our skin as a definitive impenetrable boundary are we able to see our bodies as discrete selves."[48] Our bodies are rather more accurately described as a mass of interacting selves, a mass that also includes a variety of bacteria, viruses and countless genetic fragments that come from outside the boundaries of our skin. And yet, we keep considering the skin cells as the definitive boundaries. From a Spinozist perspective, this may well be due to the fact that human consciousness is a figment of imagination, a necessary illusion deriving from the fact that human beings are conscious of their appetites but unaware of theirs causes, and so they think in terms of final ends and attribute the same type of thinking to all creatures around themselves without realizing how much of that picture is inadequate.[49]

If we adopt a transindividual philosophy, there is no reason for looking only, or primarily, at the individuals defined by the boundaries of the skin. If we look at the process of production and reproduction of life from the point of view of the unique substance and the infinity of modes expressing it, we have to conclude that most reproduction takes place in non-sexual form and that there is no linear relationship even between sexual reproduction and sexual dimorphism. Hird points this out by observing that a number of male animals such as male sea horse and hares can get pregnant, whereas many types of fish change sex back and

---

[46] Myra J. Hird, "Naturally Queer," *Feminist Theory* 5, No. 1 (2004), 85.
[47] Ibid.
[48] Ibid.
[49] Étienne Balibar and Vittorio Morfino, eds., *Il transindividuale*, 16.

forth depending on the environmental conditions:[50] they are truly transindividual beings. And this is nothing if we consider that many species have multiple sexes[51] and that most of the organisms in four out of the five kingdoms of life do not require sex for reproduction.[52] Thus, Hird concludes, the sexual difference that seems so culturally significant to us, obscures the much more prevalent sex diversity among other life forms on Earth. As a consequence, the flight from biology for fear of falling into any type of dimorphic essentialism seems to miss the point: If we ponder the insights of non-linear biological research, "we may no longer be certain that it is nature that remains static and culture that evinces limitless malleability."[53] Even more so, we may conclude, with Myra Hird, that the living matter is also naturally queer.[54]

To sum up this point, new materialist feminisms (along with queer ecology) have deeply transformed the concept of nature, and thereby contributed to a questioning of not just the hierarchy but also the very boundary between man and woman that lay at the top of the old *scala naturae*. Along with them, we have assisted to a deep change in perspective in biological approaches that have questioned other boundaries, such as that between (wo)man and the animal, the animal and the vegetal. For instance, new insights in symbiotic biology have interrogated the very notion of individuality that lies at the basis of the concept of a *scala* between different individuals, a concept that has been extremely influential not only within Western metaphysics, but also in modern taxonomy.[55] In their 2012 article, aptly entitled "A Symbiotic View of Life: We Have Never Been Individuals," Scott Gilbert, Jan Sapp, and Alfred Tauber make precisely this point.[56] The authors begin by noticing that,

---

[50] Myra J. Hird, "Naturally Queer," 85.

[51] For instance, the Schizophyllum has more than 20,000 sexes, meaning that this fungus can mate with nearly every individual of their species they meet (Ibid, 85).

[52] Ibid, 86.

[53] Ibid, 88.

[54] Ibid.

[55] William Hodos and C. B. G. Campbell, "Scala Naturae: Why There is No Theory in Comparative Psychology," *Psychological Review* 76, No. 4 (1969), 337–50.

[56] Scott F. Gilbert, Jan Sapp, and Alfred I. Tauber, "A Symbiotic View of Life: We Have Never Been Individuals," *The Quarterly Review of Biology* 87, No. 4 (2012), 326. For a more general survey of the role of the transindividual in contemporary life sciences, see: Andrea Cavazzini, "Cellule, Organismi, Comunità: Il transindividuale nelle scienze della vita contemporanee," in *Il transindividuale*, eds. Étienne Balibar and Vittorio Morfino (Milan: Mimesis, 2014), 231–52.

whereas in the past, the rising hegemony of the notion of individual in life sciences mirrored that of the individual citizens and subjects of right of the Early Modern period, since the emergence of the ecological movements, a new shift and attention to systems has started to appear within biology itself.[57] Today, they argue, we have reached a new critical threshold within that process, namely one from which we can state that, even from the point of view of genetics, immunology, evolution, anatomy, and physiology, it is now clear that we are not, and we have never been, individuals: Rather, we are all more like lichens, that is beings whose life is strictly dependent on the symbiosis with their environment and with the bodies that inhabits our bodies.[58]

Studies made possible by the new technologies have not only revealed a microbial world of much deeper diversity than previously imagined, but also depicted a world of complex and intertwined relationships—not only among microbes, but also between microscopic and macroscopic life. And, as they remind us from the very beginning of their study, "in the microbial world, 'you are what you eat' can be taken literally."[59] These discoveries have deeply transformed the traditional view of "individuals," while "symbiosis," literally meaning "life in common,"[60] is becoming a core principle of contemporary biology.[61] As they make clear in the course of their argument, during the past decade, nucleic acid analysis, especially genomic sequencing and high-throughput RNA techniques, have challenged genetical, immunological, anatomical, and physiological conceptions of individuals, by showing significant interactions of animals and plants with symbiotic microorganisms that disrupt the boundaries that heretofore had characterized the biological individual. Animals cannot be considered individuals by anatomical or physiological criteria because a diversity of symbionts are both present and functional in completing metabolic pathways and serving other physiological

---

[57] Scott F. Gilbert, Jan Sapp, and Alfred I. Tauber, "A Symbiotic View of Life," 326.
[58] Ibid.
[59] Ibid.
[60] A powerful call for a shift of paradigm, and a seminal work in symbiotic studies, was Lynn Margulis' *Symbiotic Planet*, a work that explores the way in which members of different species living in physical contact with one another reach individuation through the incorporation of others, and how the planet earth itself can be considered as such a symbiotic system. See: Lynn Margulis, *Symbiotic Planet: A New Look at Evolution* (New York: Basic Books, 1998).
[61] Scott F. Gilbert, Jan Sapp, and Alfred I. Tauber, "A Symbiotic View of Life," 326.

functions. For instance, the entity we call a cow is more properly described as an organism whose complex ecosystem of gut symbionts—that is, a diverse community of cellulose-digesting bacteria, ciliated protists, and anaerobic fungi—gives shape to its specialized anatomy, defines its plant-digesting physiology, regulates its behaviors, and ultimately determines also its evolution.[62] The boundaries between animal and vegetal life are thus questioned at their very basis.

Such a symbiotic view is equally poignant when it comes to the notion of anatomical individuality in humans, where thousands of bacterial species, which are themselves genetic composites, live with our own eukaryotic cells.[63] According to recent studies, 90 percent of the cells that comprise our bodies are indeed bacterial: "this data alone belie any simple anatomical understanding of individual identity."[64] For example, recent metagenomic sequencing has shown that for every human gut there is a persistent partnership with over 150 species of bacteria, and that the human species maintains about 1,000 major bacteria groups in our gut microbiome, where the gene set contained by this symbiotic metagenome is about 150 times larger than that of the human eukaryotic genome.[65] And this only concerns our gut, and does not include the symbionts of the respiratory apparatus, skin, mouth, or reproductive orifices. If one considers that bacteria are unicellular microorganism without an organized nucleus, and thus able to share their DNA, we understand why symbionts constitute a second mode of genetic inheritance, which shatters the traditional notion of individuality based on genetic inheritance. The individual that transmits its genes is literally, like the Spinozist individual, a trans-individual made by many individuals.

Not even immunology, which was once called "the science of self/non-self discrimination," can any longer provide a viable definition of the individual. Indeed, the immune system itself also develops in dialogue with symbionts and thereby functions as a mechanism for integrating

---

[62] Ibid, 327. Notice how this view of evolution confirms Kropotkin's critique of Darwinism and his argument that mutual aid, and not competition, is the key factor in evolution (Pyotr Kropotkin, *Mutual Aid: A Factor in Evolution* (London: William Heinemann, 1902). The concept of mutual aid remains however misleading because it may suggest that the individuals engaging in it are already constituted, whereas the symbiotic view questions the notion of individuality altogether.

[63] Scott F. Gilbert, Jan Sapp, and Alfred I. Tauber, "A Symbiotic View of Life," 327.

[64] Ibid.

[65] Ibid.

microbes into the animal-cell community.[66] This, in turns, throws a different light on theories of natural selection. Immunity does not simply guard the body against other hostile organisms in the environment, but it also mediates the body's participation in a community of "others" that contribute to its welfare. The immune system has learned through evolution itself which organisms to exclude and kill, and which organisms to encourage, allow entry, and support. Once accepted, the symbiont can mutually participate in development and physiological processes and thus help mediate the organism response to other organisms.[67] This confirms Spinoza's intuition that every being strives to persist in its being not despite others, but *through* others.

Biological organisms are thus "holobionts," a term introduced to denote the multicellular eukaryote plus its colonies of persistent symbionts. Just taking this into account as a critically important unit of anatomy, development, physiology, immunology, and evolution conceptually challenges the ways in which biological disciplines and philosophy have heretofore characterized living entities. As Gilbert, Sapp, and Tauber conclude: "animals can no longer be considered individuals in any sense of classical biology: anatomical, developmental, physiological, immunological, genetic, or evolutionary. Our bodies must be understood as holobionts whose anatomical, immunological, and developmental functions evolved in shared relationships of different species. Thus, the holobiont, with its integrated community of species, becomes a unit of natural selection whose evolutionary mechanisms suggest complexity hitherto largely unexplored."[68]

While Gilbert, Sapp, and Tauber operate within the field of biology and are thus concerned with questioning the notion of individuality within the hierarchy of (wo)man>slaves>animals>plants, the transindividual philosophy derived from Spinoza's *Ethics* leads us to also question the very boundary between life and non-life, animate and inanimate matter, and thus the very last and perhaps most persistent boundary in the *scala naturae*. Contemporary approaches such as that of Stacy Alaimo, focused as they are on the notion of transcorporeality, point indeed to the way in which every body is constituted through incorporation and interaction with the environment. As Alaimo writes: "The environment as we now

---

[66] Ibid, 330.
[67] Ibid, 333.
[68] Ibid, 334.

apprehend it, runs right through us in endless waves, and if we were to watch ourselves via some ideal microscopic time-lapse video, we could see water, air, food, microbes, toxins entering our bodies as we shed, excrete, and exhale our processed materials back out."[69] If the environment, with its substances, toxins, viruses, etc, is not something that is around us, but rather something that is constitutive of human transindividuality, then the very boundary between life and non-life is also called into question.

Notice how this new perspective leads us to rethinking the very concept of disability and the fundamental insights of disability studies according to which we transform constantly in response to our surroundings and register that history on our bodies. If disability is a change that occurs when a body encounters the world, then it is not an anomaly or sickness intrinsic to *some-bodies*, but something that happens to *all-bodies* all the time, with the exception that for some bodies such encounters are more harmful than for others.[70] Indeed, in a philosophy of transindividuality, there is no a priori distinction between able and disabled bodies, because we are all differently able, according to whether the encounters between our bodies and the other bodies that determine our individuality increase our conatus, and thus our capacity to strive to persist in our being, or decrease it, leading to our impairment.

By pushing the argument further, we can argue that precisely because the relation comes before the *relata*, all bodies are to some degree animate. This Spinozist insight is also confirmed by recent interpretations of quantum physics, such as that put forward by another materialist feminist, Karen Barad. In Barad's philosophy, it is not only the boundary between animal and vegetal that is questioned, but even that between animate and inanimate matter. By discussing Niels Bohr's quantum physics, Barad points out that even at the levels of the most elementary particles constituting matter, individuals do not pre-exist their interactions.[71] Matter and meaning are not just "intertwined" with one another, but they are "entangled," meaning that neither of them has any self-contained existence. As we read in *Meeting the Universe Halfway*: "mattering is simultaneously a matter of substance and significance, most evidently perhaps when it is the

---

[69] Stacy Alaimo, *Bodily Natures*, 2.

[70] Although Alaimo does not quote Spinoza, the notion of trans-corporeality presented in *Bodily Natures* has significant overlaps with the ontology of trans-individuality developed here (Ibid, 2; 102–05).

[71] Karen Barad, *Meeting the Universe Halfway: Quantum Physics and the Entanglement of Matter and Meaning* (Durham, NC: Duke University Press, 2007).

nature of matter that is in question, when the smallest parts of matter are found capable of exploding deeply entrenched ideas and large cities. Perhaps this is why contemporary physics makes the inescapable entanglements of matters of being, knowing, and doing, of ontology, epistemology, and ethics, of fact and value, so tangible, so poignant."[72]

If we assume indeed such a monist perspective, the very dichotomy of fact *versus* values is questioned, being rooted in an outdated early modern mechanistic view of the world, which opposed the brute matter, populating the world of phenomena, to a noumenal world of norms, from which human reason could dictate its principles. Spinoza was very critical of such a dualism, when he declared that human beings are not an *imperium in imperio* and when he stated his intention to consider human actions as if they were a question of "lines, planes and bodies" (EIII Pref). Given the influence of body-mind dualism in Western philosophy, such a fact *versus* value dichotomy remained extremely influential, as signaled by the recurring language of "normativity," which, by itself, presupposes an opposition to what is merely "factual," thus obscuring the fact that even our eminently empirical descriptions of the world are never pure, but always imbued with values.[73]

Instead of opposing a world of given facts to which we could dictate norms formulated by reason, Barad draws inspiration from contemporary physics to develop an "agential realism," that is a view which underlines that all entities literally do not precede their "intra-actions" and are thus, to some extent, real because of their agency.[74] The shift from the notion of interaction to that of "intra-action" has also the function of stressing this point, because whereas inter-action presupposes the existence of already independent entities, that of "intra-action" emphasizes exactly the opposite point: There is no individual being pre-existing the inter-action, that is, the action between things. More than "individual things," we should understand bodies as "relata," that is, as beings that exist only because the relation exist.[75] By criticizing human-centered notions of agency, Barad emphasize that "intra-actions" entails the complex co-productions of human and non-human matter, time, space and their significations.

---

[72] Ibid, 3.

[73] On the need to get rid of the dichotomy between facts and values, see the very persuasive arguments put forward by Hilary Putnam in *The Collapse of the Fact/Value Dichotomy* (Cambridge: Harvard University Press, 2002).

[74] Karen Barad, *Meeting the Universe*, 132.

[75] Ibid, 139–40.

Whereas Barad never mentions Spinoza nor Simondon in their approach, Carlo Rovelli has recently emphasized how the image of the universe that comes out of quantum physics, particularly when combined with the theory of relativity, strikingly resembles that of Spinoza's philosophy.[76] As Rovelli points out, the complex mathematical equations of quantum physics do not describe what happens to a physical system, but rather how a physical system is perceived by another physical system, thus pushing us to accept the idea that reality is *inter*, or as we could say with Karen Barad, *intra*-action.[77] In quantum physics no object has any position whatsoever until it encounters another object, so much so that, Rovelli concludes, not only is the relation real, but "only the relation is real," because the world is literally made of relations well before being made of objects.[78] This also explains why Spinoza could say that the entirety of being is an expression of the one infinite substance: When seen through the paradigm of quantum entanglements, particles really can act as one even when light-years apart from each other.[79]

One may be tempted to dismiss the complexity of such approaches as too abstract to make sense for our purposes. For instance, Stacy Alaimo, in her development of the concept of trans-corporeality, criticizes Karen Barad's theory, labeling it as a "timeless onto-epistemology."[80] Besides the fact that in the world depicted by the theory of relativity, there cannot be any such thing as a "timeless" theory, note how, in the perspective of the transindividual philosophy developed here, such a charge does not make any sense, because all ontologies must be understood as *ontogeneses*. And yet, as we will see, whether it is through the abstract equation of quantum physics or through the geometrical prose of a seventeenth-century philosopher, shifting our perspective from methodological individualism to a philosophy of transindividuality is a crucial step for rethinking feminism today.

Part of the resistance to such a shift towards a philosophy of transindividuality is that we are still attached to the humanist view that led us to consider humans as a kingdom within a kingdom. With a

---

[76] Carlo Rovelli, *Sette brevi lezioni di fisica* (Milan: Adelphi, 2014), 79
[77] Ibid, 29.
[78] Ibid, 51.
[79] Philip Goff, *Galileo's Error: Foundations for a New Science of Consciousness* (New York: Pantheon, 2019), 144.
[80] Stacy Alaimo, *Bodily Natures*, 21.

philosophy of transindividuality, the fear is that by questioning all boundaries we may end up in a night where the cows all equally look gray. Against this fear, we can respond that questioning boundaries does not amount to eliminating them, and thus to eradicate distinctions. Within a philosophy of transindividuality, there is space to add enough determinations to each transindividuality in order to be able to distinguish between them. However, they will be determinations and distinctions within an ecocentric egualitarianism that does not allow any being ontological superiority over others.

Humans have enjoyed such a special place in the great chain of being for too long, and they will not easily accept any view that questions that supremacy. Among the philosophical assumption that guaranteed their enthronement on the top of the *scala naturae,* the body–mind dualism has been particularly effective. Humanism thrives on body–mind dualism because the latter justifies a hierarchy of being where those endowed with a soul/mind/psyche can be said to be ontologically superior to the bodies that are considered to lack them. Spinoza's radical monism shatters that humanist hubris at its very foundations, while still being able to articulate a transindividual philosophy that can distinguish between different individualities. Spinoza used the expression humans are not a kingdom within a kingdom (*imperium in imperio*) (EIII Preface), but a more appropriate expression could be: Humans are not the sovereign among the sovereign beings, because no being is accorded any ontological sovereignty as such. The problem with the humanist view of the world is not only that humans are turned into a kingdom separate from the rest of nature, but also that they are implicitly situated in a hierarchy of beings, where humans occupy the top, and then all other beings follow according to a scale of how much they resemble humans: Animals come before plants, and plants before rocks, because the latter are dead matter. Thus, quite often, philosophical perspectives on animal ethics that appear anti-humanist, because they argue for extending ethical treatment to animals, very often end up reinforcing that very humanism that they are trying to combat: If we should treat animals in an ethical way because they resemble us humans, then we are once again confirming that humans remain the yardstick for what is valuable, and stay at the very top of the great chain of being. On the contrary, the philosophy of the transindividuality here proposed radically questions such a hierarchical order of being and emphasize that all bodies are to some extent animate.

The transindividual philosophy is therefore a "posthuman philosophy," because it emphasizes the self-organizing structure of *all* matter and thus contests the conceptual apparatus that sustains the nature *versus* culture dichotomy.[81] But it also differs from vitalistic forms of post-humanism in that it argues that *all* bodies are to some extent animate, not just the humans, animals, and plants that have traditionally been considered as part of Earth's living matter.[82] It is therefore a more radical form of "ecocentric egalitarianism," one that questions any hierarchical order of being at its very foundation.

We can summarize these insights from quantum physics, holobiont biology, and the philosophy of transindividuality sketched above, by stating that they depict a form of "somatic communism," where bodies exist only through other bodies in a constant process of individuation that involves the *inter-* the *supra* but also the *infra*-individual level. It is not by chance that so many philosophers of transindividuality come from the Marxist tradition, with its interest in how life is produced and reproduced through the common circuits of production but is then hijacked by the institution of private property and the market. The philosophy of transindividuality enables us to identify a form of somatic communism that can be the starting point for thinking about political communism. But it is perhaps also not by chance that we borrow the term "somatic communism" from Paul B. Preciado, who argues that, given the failure of the Left to redefine emancipation in terms other than in relation to the Western, white, male, patriarchal body, the only way to a global change today is to construct a "planetary somatic communism, a communism of (all) living bodies within and together with the earth."[83] To this call, we should add, following the philosophy of transindividuality sketched above, that such a somatic communism is not only an ideal we should strive towards, but also, to a large extent, a reality that has always been there, rooted as it is in the very transindividual nature of all bodies, which are all to some degree, animate.

---

[81] Rosi Braidotti, *The Posthuman* (Cambridge: Polity, 2013), 3.
[82] Although Braidotti's posthuman philosophy, which is inspired more by Deleuze and Guattari than by Spinoza, converges in important points with the transindividual philosophy, important differences remain. Like Deleuze and Guattari's philosophy, her view is a form of vitalism, which focuses on becoming animal as a way to decenter humanism (see, in particular, Rosi Braidotti, *The Posthuman*, 67–76).
[83] Paul B. Preciado, *Counter-sexual Manifesto* (New York: Columbia University Press, 2018), 13.

6 Women in process, women as processes

We can now move to the question of what it means to be a woman within this transindividual philosophy. In particular, if women's bodies, like all other bodies, are transindividual, how can we identify enough continuity and stability to speak about a specific individual? How do we account for the fact that we experience ourselves not simply as individuals, but also as unique? Last, but not least, how can we perceive ourselves as "women"? Drawing inspiration from a philosophy of transindividuality combined with a feminist philosophy of narration, we answer by saying that we do it through narratives. The concept of woman is a universal term, and, as we have seen, such universals are beings of the imagination, that is, ideas that we produce and reproduce on the basis of certain patterns of association we became accustomed to. Every context presents its own patterns of imagination, which are also suggested patterns of recollection. It is indeed through a story of the encounters past and present which make up a single individuality that we can find the thread enabling us to speak about a single "woman" at some point in time. The self that speaks womanhood is a narrating self.[1] What is a woman, indeed, if not a story?

As feminist philosopher Adriana Cavarero argued, our selves are "narratable selves" not only because we engage in the active process of telling stories about ourselves (although some of us do, and then we become "narrated selves"), but because the very modality of our being in the world is intrinsically linked to the narrative impulse of involuntary

---

[1] We have dealt more extensively with this issue in Chiara Bottici, *A Feminist Mythology*, where the question "what does it mean to be a woman?" is discussed through a process of re-elaboration of the myths of femininity. See, in particular the Introduction to: Chiara Bottici, *A Feminist Mythology* (London: Bloomsbury, 2022).

memory.[2] We perceive ourselves as that unique person, with that unique life story, whether we actively engage in recollecting that story or not. Each life story is unique: From birth, our very first appearance in the world, we are marked by that uniqueness, which is not only the uniqueness of our bodies, but also of our appearance. Every life is an unrepeatable existence, so no matter how much one could try to imitate somebody else's life, nobody could ever leave behind exactly the same story.[3] From the moment we are born, then, we are indeed unique, because the story that we can tell about it is unique.

This also explains why life stories are narrated and listened to with so much pleasure: They can be similar, even monotonous, but each one exhibits its own peculiar features. A life story is unique not despite the others, but because of the others: From the youngest age, we are constantly exposed to encounters with, and the gaze of, others and thus are immersed in this constantly ongoing reciprocal exhibition. This is also, in its turn, a process of reciprocal story-telling.[4] There is an exhibitionistic character in our being in the world: birth, acting in the world, and story-telling are all scenes of an identity that always postulates the presence of an *other*.[5] Indeed, being in the world means being exposed to the possibility of being seen, smelled, touched, heard, and sensed by other humans—but also by other bodies in general. Using the words of Maria Zambrano, Cavarero speaks of a "cosmic fest of reciprocity" to describe what appearing in the world means.[6] Within that cosmic fest, we are that precise (trans)individuality[7] that can say: "I was born in . . ." and therefore tell a story about it.

The fact that, along with Spinoza, we emphasize that consciousness mainly operates in the realm of imagination, because we are conscious of our desire but not aware of its causes, does not imply that it does not exist.

---

[2] Adriana Cavarero, *Relating Narratives: Storytelling and Selfhood*, trans. Paul Kottman (London: Routledge, 1997).

[3] Ibid, 2.

[4] Ibid, 20.

[5] Cavarero builds on the philosophy of Hannah Arendt, but, as we will see, she develops it in an original and feminist direction (Ibid). In particular, she combines her theory of action with an original theory of narration.

[6] Ibid, 20.

[7] Adriana Cavarero does not use the term (trans)individuality, but we use that expression to mean that such individuality can only come into being through a cosmic fest of reciprocity, which, in our view, is also a cosmic fest of co-origination.

It simply means that it is not the whole story, and that if we were able to reconstruct all of the infinite networks of causes and effects that lead to our actions, we would not think that we are telling a certain story just because we want to tell that story. And yet, each time we perceive ourselves, each time we turn our gaze inwards asking: "who am I?," we recognize a certain narrative, that particular series of more or less coherent events and fragments that make our (trans)individuality so unique. This happens all the time, whether we intentionally set out to tell a story or not.

As Adriana Cavarero observes: "We are all familiar with the narrative work of memory, which, in a totally involuntary way, continues to tell us our own personal story. Every human being, without even wanting to know it, is aware of being a narratable self—immersed in the spontaneous auto-narration of memory. Indeed, it is not necessary that the personal memory be explicitly solicited in the autobiographical exercise; that is, memory need not make of itself an 'active remembering'. The narratable self finds its home, not simply in a conscious exercise of remembering, but in the spontaneous narrating structure of memory itself."[8] Thus, whether we consciously engage with it or not, we are narrating-selves not only because we have the imaginal capacity to tell stories, but also because the self unfolds through the stories that we tell about ourself, which, in its turn, transindividually depend on those that we are told.

Indeed, independently of how aware we are of this narrating structure of memory, we constantly approach not only our selves, but also others as vehicles of storytelling. To begin with, ever since we appear in the world through birth, we are exposed to the gaze of others, and it is through that exposure that we are assigned a sex. In this sense, sex or gender is not something that we can give to ourselves, but something that, at best, we can ask others to give us.[9] Indeed, as Cavarero makes clear in the course of her argument, every life story is always the story of a sexed being, because none of us can escape being assigned a sex at birth and carrying

---

[8] Ibid, 33–4. On the distinction between memory and recollection, see also: Dmitri Nikulin, *Memory: A History* (Oxford: Oxford University Press, 2015), 7–10. Following Plato and Aristotle, Nikulin distinguishes between memory, as the act of immediate access to what is remembered (mainly as picture-like internal images) from recollection, as the process of searching for something that has to be remembered and that is reconstructed in a step-by-step process, which mainly happens through a discursive process (ibid, 7).

[9] On this point, see also Andrea Long Chu, *Females* (London: Verso, 2019), 38.

it throughout our lives.[10] As we will see, identity papers and official documents are one of the tools which guarantee that we retain a sexed identity for all of our life: Like other institutions, with their rituals and repetitions, they provide a bedrock upon which the flow of storytelling happens, and which requires questioning if we want to tell a different story.

There is a story behind each of us, a unique story, depending on the fragile, always incomplete, work of memory, but also necessarily reflecting all the stories that others, including institutions, have told, and may potentially tell, about ourselves. Thus, we are a unique story not despite, but precisely because of this *plurality* over which we have no absolute control.[11] Otherwise we may just tell one story about ourselves and then lead an entire life to fulfill it. One may indeed be tempted to do so (and, again, some of us do that), but we will inevitably fail because we are always suspended in this fest of reciprocity and relationality where one never gets to tell the entire story. In our own terms, we can say we are always individual through our transindividuality.

This is also the reason why myths and other narratives circulating in the social imaginary are so important. Lives can be lived according to a story, but they are not themselves models, narrative plots. Myths, understood as a process of elaboration of a narrative core that always responds to a need for significance, are a particularly powerful type of plot, because they live in the unconscious and are thus able to influence the involuntary work of memory in a subtle way.[12] Myths are not objects, but processes that involve both the production and the reception of a certain narrative core. In the reception of myths, narrative cores are re-appropriated by the needs of each specific and unique context, thereby leading to a process of elaboration of a mythologem that expresses itself through the continuous generation of variants. In sum, myths are processes of elaboration that express themselves through variants because they need to respond to a constantly changing need for significance. As such, they provide imaginal patterns according to which we perceive connection between events, and thus influence not only how we see the world but also how we act within it. They are particularly powerful

---

[10] Adriana Cavarero, *Relating Narratives*, 49–77.
[11] Ibid, 43; emphasis ours.
[12] Chiara Bottici, *A Philosophy of Political Myth* (Cambridge: Cambridge University Press, 2007).

because of their condensational capacity, whereby a single image or icon can come to summarize the entire work that came before.

A case in point is the influential role exercised by the icon of the Madonna and the myth of femininity it conveys within Christian cultures. Icons work as synecdoche, that is, as images that can symbolize and thus recall the whole process of story-telling that lies behind them. As such, icons blur the distinction between myth and reason and can appear as much in story-telling as in philosophy or theology. The icon of the Madonna points to what is left out of a trinity that takes place "In the Name of the Father": The sacred trinity is composed of the Father, the Son and the Holy Ghost—*In nomine patris et filii et spiritus sancti*. There is no space here for the "second sex," so the "Madonna" is first and foremost the result of an exclusion. The Madonna, the *Mea-donna*, or the "my-woman" of Christianity, is the mother of God, but one who has conceived it immaculately. As Simone de Beauvoir writes:

> Christianity's repugnance for the feminine body is such that it consents to doom its God to an ignominious death, but saves him the stain of birth: the Council of Ephesus in the Eastern Church and the Lateran Council in the West affirm the virgin birth of Christ. The first Church Fathers—Origen, Tertullian, and Jerome—thought that Mary had given birth in blood and filth like other women; but the opinions of Saint Ambrose and Saint Augustine prevail. The Virgin's womb remained closed.[13]

Thus, despite no clear indication in that sense from the Gospels, the re-elaboration of the Madonna mythologem produced the double icon of an immaculate conception and an immaculate birth: through the sanction of the Church, the myth becomes dogma. The Madonna conceived the God who has become flesh, but her body remained immaculate. Thus, she is not only excluded from the parental trinity "father, child, mother," where she is replaced by the Holy Ghost, but she is even excluded *from her own body*: Thanks to his immaculate conception, paired with his immaculate birth, the Christian (male) God appears so omnipotent that he can be born through the female body but without touching it. This creation myth, which replaces the maternal body with an immaculate

---

[13] Simone de Beauvoir, *The Second Sex* (New York: Vintage, 2011), 186.

conception, and the mother-goddess with an ineffable sacred spirit, consequently also "defines maternity as an impossible elsewhere, a sacred beyond, a vessel of divinity, a spiritual tie with the ineffable godhead, and a transcendence's ultimate support—necessarily virginal and committed to assumption."[14] The iconic representation of the Madonna is the result of this "impossible elsewhere," a maternity that expresses itself through tears, milk, and pain: the *Mater dolorosa*. As we read in first lines of the very influential medieval hymn *Stabat mater*:

Stabat Mater dolorosa,
iuxta Crucem lacrimosa,
dum pendebat Filius.
Cuius animam gementem,
contristatam et dolentem
pertransivit gladius.
O quam tristis et afflicta
fuit illa benedicta,
mater Unigeniti!
Quae maerebat et dolebat,
pia Mater, dum videbat
nati poenas inclyti.
Quis est homo qui non fleret,
matrem Christi si videret
in tanto supplicio?
Quis non posset contristari
Christi Matrem contemplari
dolentem cum Filio. [. . .][15]

This mother "*dolorosa,*" full of pain, and "*lacrimosa,*" full of tears, is the other side of the Christian trinity of "Father, Son, and Holy Ghost," in its

---

[14] Julia Kristeva, "Motherhood According to Giovanni Bellini," in *The Portable Kristeva* (New York: Columbia University Press, 2002), 303.
[15] "At the Cross her station keeping,/stood the mournful Mother weeping,/ close to Jesus to the last./Through her heart, His sorrow sharing,/ all His bitter anguish bearing,/ now at length the sword has passed./ O how sad and sore distressed/ was that Mother, highly blest,/ of the sole-begotten One./ Christ above in torment hangs,/ she beneath beholds the pangs/ of her dying glorious Son./ Is there one who would not weep,/ whelmed in miseries so deep,/ Christ's dear Mother to behold?/ Can the human heart refrain/ from partaking in her pain,/ in that Mother's pain untold?". English translation from http://www.preces-latinae. org/thesaurus/BVM/SMDolorosa.html (accessed on March 25, 2021).

conspicuous denial of any godly status to "the second sex." The Holy Spirit is thus a ghost, that of a concomitant denial of full divinity and full maternity, and thus the icon of a "second god" that is nothing but the mythical representation of the "second sex." As Julia Kristeva observes in her beautiful attempt at retelling this myth, milk and tears are the privileged signs of the *Mater Dolorosa* who became so prevalent in the West as of the eleventh century. What milk and tears have in common is that they are metaphor of nonspeech, a semiotics that linguistic communication cannot account for.[16] When speech is interrupted, the body itself speaks through its symptoms.[17] And those symptoms are milk, tears, and blood. Why is it the case that in so many Catholic countries, miracles attributed to the Virgin concern Madonna statues that cry blood? Are these statues menstruating from their eyes? Are they reclaiming their capacity for a *maculate* conception? And why this systematic association between motherhood and suffering? If the Madonna is the mother of the Christian God, then she must also know that Christ will be resurrected, but in the hymn quoted above—and in the many representations of the *Mater Dolorosa*—she continues to shed tears over his dead body.

Consider Figure 6.1, with a canonical representation of the Weeping Virgin.[18] The image is taken from the Santuario Madonna delle Lacrime di Siracusa, a church built to celebrate one of the most famous cases of the miracle of the Weeping Madonna. On August 29, 1953, a woman who had been confined to bed due to a difficult pregnancy, experienced a sudden loss of sight. She quickly regained it, only to realize that the terracotta bust of the Madonna next to her bed was weeping. In contrast to other miracles or Marian apparitions, such as that of Lourdes or Guadalupe, this event was studied by a scientific commission, which even had the opportunity to collect the uncanny tears falling down the immaculate face of the Madonna statue.[19] Despite the proliferation of

---

[16] Julia Kristeva, "Stabat Mater," in *The Portable Kristeva* (New York: Columbia University Press, 2002), 322.

[17] On this point, see Jamieson Webster, *Conversion Disorder: Listening to the Body in Psychoanalysis* (New York: Columbia University Press, 2019), 61–85.

[18] From Wikimedia Commons (https://commons.wikimedia.org/wiki/File:Santuario_ Madonna_delle_Lacrime-Syracuse.JPG, accessed on March 25, 2021). Creative Commons Attribution-ShareAlike 2.0 Generic.

[19] https://www.catholicculture.org/culture/library/view.cfm?recnum=3196 (accessed on March 25, 2021).

FIGURE 6.1 Madonna delle Lacrime di Siracusa (The Weeping Madonna of Syracuse). Author: Hein56didden. Title: The crying Virgin Mary, Santuario Madonna delle Lacrime, Syracuse (Beeld van huilende Maagd Maria-Santuario Madonna delle Lacrime, Syracuse). Date: September 24, 2009. Source: WikiCommons (under the Creative Commons Attribution-Share Alike 3.0 Unported, 2.5 Generic, 2.0 Generic and 1.0 Generic license): https://commons.wikimedia.org/wiki/File:Santuario_Madonna_delle_Lacrime-Syracuse.JPG

miracles of weeping Madonnas in Catholic countries, from Ireland to Croatia, this remains the only one recognized by the Church.[20]

As Kristeva points out, the *Mater Dolorosa*, and her symbols evoking a sorrowful humanity, are the representative of a "return of the repressed" in monotheism: They re-establish what is non-verbal and become the necessary complement of the otherwise too empty Holy Ghost. Hence their recurrence in the arts, particularly painting and music, of which the Virgin Mother became both the patron and the object, as well as in the many popular variants of the cult of the Virgin.[21] Retelling the myth

---

[20] Among the attempt to explain the miracle, see this 2015 study, which finally claimed to have found a scientific explanation (https://www.independent.co.uk/news/science-debunks-miracle-weeping-madonna-1590530.html, accessed March 25, 2021).
[21] Ibid, 322–3.

of the Madonna, as Kristeva does in her book by retelling the story of her own maternity, along with that of the Madonna mythologem, becomes thus a way for negotiating models of maternity and thus possible "tales of love."[22] In Kristeva's retelling, the *Stabat Mater* begins with a "FLASH—instant of time or of dream without time; inordinately swollen atoms of a bond, a vision, a shiver, a yet formless, unnamable embryo. Epiphanies. Photos of what is not yet visible and that language necessarily skims over from afar, allusively. Words that are always too distant, too abstract for this underground swarming of seconds, folding in unimageable spaces. Writing them down is an ordeal of discourse, like love. What is loving, for a woman, the same thing as writing. Laugh. Impossible." Not only women are processes, but, like any other subject, they are also in process.[23]

Naming is a crucial moment in any narrative. The monotheistic God of the Old Testament creates the world by naming it: "And God said, Let there be light: and there was light" (Genesis 1: 3), and, subsequently transfers this power to Adam, the first man he created, by giving shape to the dust of the ground: "And the LORD God said, *It is* not good that man should be alone; I will make him an help meet for him. And out of the ground the LORD God formed every beast of the field, and every fowl of the air, and brought *them* onto Adam to see what he would call them: and whatsoever Adam called every living creature, that was their name thereof. And Adam gave names to all cattle, and to the fowl of the air, and to every beast of the field; but for Adam there was not found an help to meet for him" (Genesis 2: 18–20). Thus, it is in order to give man company that all the living creatures are created and Adam, consequently, accorded the sovereign right *par excellence*, which is the right to name them: all of this, including the creation of woman, happens, literally, *in nomine patris*: in the name of the father. As the following verse explains: "And the Lord cause a deep sleep to fall upon Adam, and he slept: and he took one of his ribs, and closes up the flesh instead thereof. And the rib, which the LORD God had taken from man, made he a woman, and brought her unto the man. And Adam said, This is now bone of my bones, and flesh of my flesh: she shall be called

---

[22] It is not by chance that the "Stabat Mater" piece was first published in a book with that title. See: Julia Kristeva, *Tales of Love* (New York: Columbia University Press, 1987).

[23] We have reworked the myths of "womanhood" from our own specific position, which also includes a re-elaboration of the maternal, in Chiara Bottici, *A Feminist Mythology* (London: Bloomsbury, 2022).

Woman, because she was taken out of Man" (Genesis 2: 21–3). With an extraordinary reversal of the typical human birth, whereby babies generally come out of women's bodies, in the Genesis' creation myth it is the LORD God that creates man out of dust, and woman out of man, who is then consequently also given the right to name her. This explains why in most Western countries, most newborns still carry the name of the father, as well as why those who may want to question the sexual identity that they have been assigned, usually have to engage in a process of retelling their own story and renaming themselves. To displace that logic, which privileges the "family name," so that Julia Kristeva, for instance, becomes Kristeva, in this book, we refer to authors by alternating between their "family" and their "first name." This should be taken as in invitation to question the often-unacknowledged but relentless perpetration of "the name of the father."

In sum, life stories imply an entire transindividual process of storytelling, which must also be the result of the encounters between the stories that we tell ourselves and those that we are told, between the stories we recognize ourselves in and those we do not, between the narrative plots that we consciously fabricate and those mythologems that we unconsciously reproduce, and over which we have little mastery.[24] And it is by putting together all the stories that we can associate with the term "woman" that we respond to the question "what does it mean to be a woman"? Hence the importance, as María Pía Lara underlined, of the role of narratives for the critique and expansion of the public sphere.[25] Narratives circulating in that sphere and deposited in our social unconscious are not just stories: They are constitutive of what we are in general and as a sexed being in particular.

A recurrent objection raised against feminism, and in general against all theories that hold on to the notion of womanhood, is that one risks

---

[24] On how to combine a theory of recognition with a theory of the trans-individual, see the volume edited by Nicola Marcucci and Luca Pinzolo, *Strategie della relazione* (Rome: Meltemi, 2010), and in particular Vittorio Morfino's essay within it ("Transindividuale e/o riconoscimento: ancora sull'alternativa Hegel/Spinoza"). By drawing insights from the work of sociologist Alessandro Pizzorno, we have further elaborated the relationship between identity and story-telling, by insisting on the plural nature of such a process, in Chiara Bottici, *A Philosophy of Political Myth*, 227–45.

[25] María Pía Lara, *Moral Textures: Feminist Narratives in the Public Sphere* (Cambridge: Polity Press, 1998). More recently, see her *Beyond The Public Sphere. Film and the Feminist Imaginary* (Evanston/Illinois: Northwestern University Press, 2021), which focuses on the way in which movies can work as a way to question the patriarchal imaginary.

falling into a form of essentialism or, what is even worse, into a form of cis- or heteronormativity that freezes gender potentialities within the binary woman/man. As should be evident at this point, within a monist ontology of the transindividual, no such objection can hold. The body is not an inert matter, or an essence, to which we can attribute fixed immutable properties (such as certain types of genitalia or hormones). Rather, the body in general, and women's bodies in particular, are relational processes.[26]

For those who reject the sex they are assigned at birth, and transition into a different gender, re-telling their own story becomes therefore the tool for renegotiating their selves. To begin with, there is the story given to them by the sex assigned at birth, and, in order to change that story, one has to necessarily enter a personal process of re-elaboration of that given narrative. Furthermore, within the current medical apparatus of many Western countries, where, as we have seen, "gender dysphoria" is a clinical condition, those who want the assistance of such apparatus in their transition have to produce stories that are credible and that will be accepted as valid by the system—the same system that has assigned them either "female" or "male," as that is the binary way in which most gender systems across the globe currently work. The problem then becomes how to turn what is diagnosed as a "pathology," the "gender dysphoria" (literally: "carrying the wrong body"), into a process that can be appropriated—that is, how to turn "dysphoria" into a "gender euphoria" (that is, literally, "carrying the good body").

Revisiting and subversively re-appropriating old mythologems can also be a way to renegotiate one's own sense of the self. McKenzie Wark, for instance, following others who went before her, tells her own story of traversing the gender dysphoria through a re-appropriation and re-telling of the myth of Orpheus and Eurydice, the myth of the poet-singer who had to go back to Hades, the world of the dead, to bring back his beloved Eurydice.[27]

---

[26] This is different from Gatens' remark that the body is an historical product (Moira Gatens, *Imaginary Bodies: Ethics, Power and Corporeality*, London: Routledge, 1996), because an individual body can change over time, but still be conceived within a methodological individualism. Among those gender theorists who have more recently put forward a view of the body that, in our reading, is in the spirit, if not in the letter, inspired by a transindividual philosophy, see: Beatriz Preciado, *Testo Junkie: Sex, Drugs, and Biopolitics in the Pharmacopornographic Era* (New York: The Feminist Press at CUNY, 2013), 99–130.

[27] In particular, McKenzie Wark follows in the footsteps of Jean Cocteau and Kathy Acker, both of whom produced modern variants of the Orpheus and Eurydice mythologems. McKenzie Wark, *Reverse Cowgirl* (Cambridge, MA: Semiotext(e), 2020), 182–3.

In McKenzie's *Reverse Cowgirl*, "Orpheus" is the voice that speaks of years of not knowing why he did not feel at home in his body, except in highs induced by drugs and sex, the story of all the failed attempts at being straight, as well as at being gay, within the shifting political landscapes of the late twentieth century. In this memoir, Eurydice starts speaking only towards the end of the book, as a "myth to live by,"[28] as the figure that, one day, suddenly appears in the mirror when Orpheus looks at himself. But for this to happen, Orpheus had to go down, "down from the heights, down even further, under the waters, where non-existence does not live."[29] After finally seeing Eurydice, it is not the woman who dies, as in the old mainstream variant of this tale, but Orpheus himself. In the chapter following the retelling of this myth—and significantly entitled "Gender euphoria"—McKenzie Wark writes:

> The mushrooms were humming and thrumming away. Or maybe that was insects. Bug, cloud, drug, bird: all joined in a chorus in which all the parts resonate together. Augmented reality production. All the theories came out to play. I made a story that made it all connect. I wrote it in my head, not like linear writing, but in three dimensions—as you can when you're high. [...]
>
> It's decided. I'm giddy with resolve, adventure, logistics, epidermal charms, demigod blessings. I will transition. I am going to make my exit from masculinity. I don't know how far I can get away from it. I don't know who this I is or who she will have been or become. And I know I have left it too late. But it doesn't matter. I'm out. Out as trans. Out as trans to the trees and the hawk up in the tree and the lake and the fish down in the lake and the beaver downstream in the river. Out to the sun, out to the sky. Hello world, I'm trans! Am I binary or non-binary? Am I trans-femme or a trans woman? No idea. Well, some ideas, some steep inclinations. But the decision that's made is to jump off the edge of masculinity and hope to float.[30]

Telling the story of transitioning is a floating device, something that enables her, as we learn from the following page, to jump into the icy lake and, indeed, swim. No more going down "under the waters, where non-existence does not live," in an exponential accumulation of negations.

---

[28] McKenzie Wark, *Reverse Cowgirl*, 181.
[29] Ibid, 182.
[30] Ibid, 185–7.

Writing a memoir, retelling the myth of Eurydice, is the floating device that links the story of the recurrent feeling of a hole, the stories of not knowing why he did not really feel at home in his body, the story of all the unsuccessful attempts at being something identifiable, in sum, all the stories of all the futile efforts to come to terms with the opacity of the self. Telling such a story is literally a way of telling oneself, and thus not sink "under the waters." In her Eurydice voice, McKenzie goes on:

> After a while, I dismount the hammock, shell out all of my clothes, sprint across the dock and plunge into the lake, with a foam noodle under my arms. Not enough fat to be buoyant, the noodle is a handy prosthesis. I tell myself that a layer of psychic man-skin is cleansed from me at the moment the shock of cold water hits.[31]

This work, like many others before it, thus contributes retelling the myth of womanhood. The word "woman," a space that is inhabited, retold, and thus constituted both by women who were assigned female at birth and those who were not, is indeed nothing but the shortcut for a storytelling process that keeps together a series of processes and potentialities that we can associate with individuals instituted as and instituting themselves as "women." Writing from the position of author of this book, for instance, stories about "womanhood" can include potentialities such as all those we have witnessed: being assigned the female sex at birth, being assigned male sex at birth, wearing feminine clothes, wearing androgynous clothes, using women's restrooms, using gender neutral restrooms, menstruating, not menstruating, giving birth, not giving birth, transitioning, cisgendering, being paid less than your colleagues who are perceived as men, walking in the street as a self-identified woman, walking in the street while challenging the assigned identification of a woman, and so on, and so forth. The list is obviously as open as the process or series of processes that one can potentially associate with being a woman. Within such a transindividual plurality, the word "woman" can then come to include all types of women: AFAB women, AMAB women, feminine women, masculine women, intersex women, trans-women, and so on. To those who argue that another world is possible, we should reply that another world is always in the making, in

---

[31] Ibid, 188.

as much as different ways of being a woman are constantly being disclosed to us.

That said, challenging established patterns takes time and it is particularly hard to accept ways of individualizing as woman when they question long-established views of what a woman should look like. State institutions provide a crucial stabilizing factor, in as far as most of them implement and police gender according to the male/female binary. That is not the whole story, though, because the worst tyrant, as Emma Goldman reminds us, is not outside but inside ourselves.[32] Artistic practices can be particularly useful in addressing both tyrants. By providing challenges to hegemonic views in ways that connect critique with emotional attachment, they are often a particularly effective space for renegotiating our imaginal beings. In the words of José Esteban Muñoz, artistic illuminations provide a surplus of both affect and meaning—a surplus that is generated by the specifically anticipatory illumination of art, thus opening a space for disclosing what is not yet there.[33] We use "art" here in a very broad sense, to denote all sort of encounters or objects that can work as such an illumination. "The anticipatory illumination of certain objects is a kind of potentiality that is open, indeterminate, like the affective contours of hope itself."[34] So if it is true that being a woman, in our capitalist societies, increasingly involves the "imaginary domain"[35] and the register of commoditized spectacle,[36] then we can look at artistic practices as a possible site for the enactment of counter-spectacles, and thus for disclosing alternative narrative plots.[37]

---

[32] Emma Goldman, *Anarchism and Other Essays* (New York: Dover, 1969), 221.

[33] José Esteban Muñoz, *Cruising Utopia: The Then and There of Queer Futurity* (New York: New York University Press, 2009), 3.

[34] Ibid, 7.

[35] Drucilla Cornell develops this notion in *The Imaginary Domain* (New York: Routledge, 1995).

[36] Carol Ehrlich, "Anarchism, Feminism and Situationism," in R. Graham (ed.), *Anarchism: A Documentary History of Libertarian Ideas*, Vol II (Montreal: Black Rose Books, 2005), 499–506.

[37] We have developed the notion of counter-spectacles in: Chiara Bottici, *Imaginal Politics: Images Beyond the Imagination and Beyond the Imaginary* (Columbia University Press: New York, 2014), 106–24. Although we have developed it within the framework of a theory of the imaginal, we are also indebted to the seminal work of María Pía Lara, who has shown how feminist narratives can exercise their critical impact in the public sphere, thereby disclosing us alternative ways of being a woman (Lara, *Moral Textures*).

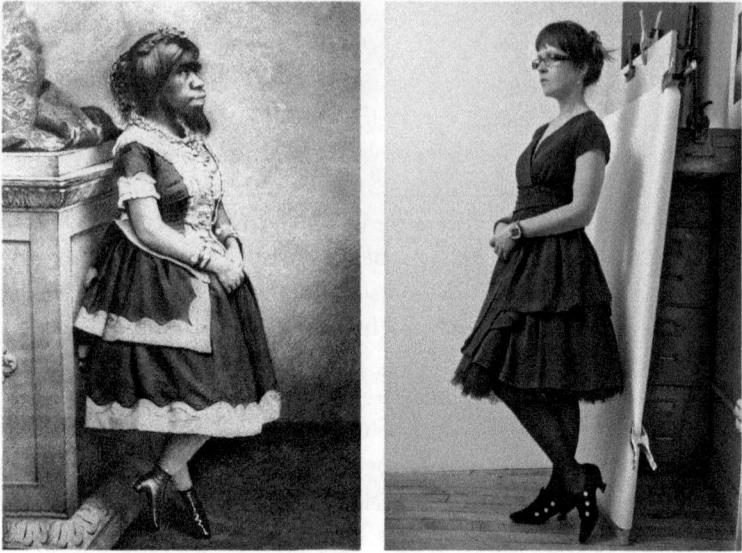

FIGURE 6.2 Laura Anderson Barbata. "Julia y Laura" (2013). Reproduced courtesy of the artist.

Let us consider the series of works on Julia Pastrana created and performed by the New York-based Mexican artist Laura Anderson Barbata. The artwork "Julia y Laura" beautifully captures one of those moments.[38] You can see in the picture a woman-artist (the canvas on her back) who is projecting herself as a mirror of another woman, standing next to a statue, and wearing a black beard. The two women have similar purple dresses, the same sort of pose, similar shoes and hairstyles, but one is wearing glasses and the other a thick, long beard. Laura Anderson Barbata is the artist without a beard, and interestingly, her last name is very close to *barbuta*, which literally means a bearded woman in Italian and Spanish. Is this suggesting that the woman on the left of the image is the truth of the patronym of the woman on the right? Is the artist standing in front of the canvas the truth of the bearded woman on the left? Or is the break in the middle of the image suggesting a process of simultaneous identification and dis-identification? We argue that it is both, and

---

[38] See Laura Anderson Barbata's website for a description of the series of works on Julia Pastrana, which includes visual art and performances: http://www.lauraandersonbarbata. com/ (accessed on June 9, 2020).

precisely by doing so, this image works as a means of interrogation and renegotiation of hegemonic views of womanhood.

In the "Julia y Laura" story that Laura Anderson Barbata has been telling in her performances, we learn that Julia Pastrana was born in 1834 in a small Mexican village in the state of Sinaloa.[39] Very little is known about the first twenty years of her life, except that at some point she was living in the house of the Governor of Sinaloa, where she was trained as a dancer and mezzo-soprano, and where she learned French and English. In 1854 she was sold to an American businessman, who brought her to the US where she was exhibited for money. The same year she married Theodore Lent in New York City. From then on, her manager and husband showcased her as: "The Ugliest Woman in the World," "The Nondescript," "The Hirsute," "The Ape Woman," "The Female Hybrid," "the Bear-woman," "Baboon Lady," and the "Monkey Woman"—among others. As a contemporary newspaper put it, after the incredible economic success of her first exhibitions: "The eyes of this *lusus natura* beam with intelligence, while its jaws, jagged fangs and ears are terrifically hideous [...] Nearly its whole frame is coated with long glossy hair. Its voice is harmonious, for this semi-human being is perfectly docile, and speaks Spanish language."[40]

Given the ensuing economic success, the husband impresario kept exhibiting her in the US and in Europe. He would show her both to the curious general public and to scientists, who considered her often as a hybrid between woman and orangutans, and even speculated that all other indigenous people of Pastrana's tribe must have been as hairy and apelike as she was, and thus belonged to such a hybrid species.[41] After tremendous success in London, in 1857, the couple moved to Berlin, where Lent exhibited her as a dancer and singer until the German police declared the performances obscene and closed them down. A significant role was played by German obstetricians, who objected very strongly to Pastrana appearing in public, arguing that pregnant ladies might miscarry at the sight of her, or even have children exactly like her, as a consequence of such an unfortunate "maternal impression."[42]

---

[39] For a full chronology of Julia Pastrana's life, see *The Eye of the Beholder: Julia Pastrana's Long Journey Home*, eds. Laura Anderson Barbata and Donna Wingate (Seattle: Lucia Marquard, 2017), 181–7.

[40] Jan Bondeson, "The Strange Story of Julia Pastrana," in Laura Anderson Barbata and Donna Wingate (eds), *The Eye of the Beholder*, 11.

[41] Ibid, 12.

[42] Ibid, 15.

In 1860 Julia Pastrana, who was herself pregnant with her husband's child, travelled to Moscow where she gave birth to a baby diagnosed with the same condition as hers (that is, covered with extensive amounts of black body hair and having an overdeveloped jaw). Both mother and child died soon after the baby's birth. After their death, Theodor Lent sold their bodies to Dr. Sokolov of the University of Moscow, who had developed a special embalming technique and wanted to use them for further scientific investigations. Two years after, however, Lent went back to Moscow to reclaim them and, with the support of the US embassy, managed to obtain their bodies. He placed them inside a glass case and began exhibiting them all over Europe, with a certain commercial success.[43]

For some time, the corpses of Julia Pastrana and her baby kept on being exhibited, researched, stolen, and damaged. The fascination they exercised did not end with their death. In 1976, thieves broke into a warehouse in Oslo where the bodies were kept and threw the body of the infant in a field where it was eaten by rodents. While Julia's arm was ripped from her body and found only much later, the rest of the mummy disappeared. In 1988, the mummified body emerged again, albeit briefly. Historical records show that, in 1994, the body was in the custody of the department of Anatomy Forensic Studies of Oslo for research purposes. Articles and publications describing her case appeared worldwide. Julia Pastrana, whose fame continued even after her death, was at the time still virtually unknown in her native Mexico.

In 2003, Laura Anderson Barbata encountered the story of Julia Pastrana through a play devoted to her life. From that point, Laura became very active in an international campaign attempting to reclaim Julia's body and have it returned to Mexico.[44] After ten years of struggles, the body was finally transported to Sinaloa, Mexico, where it was buried with a picture of her child on her chest. The artist-activist Laura was very active in making sure that her tomb would be completely covered in concrete and enclosed in walls more than one meter thick to guarantee

---

[43] For a more extensive analysis of how this exhibitionistic logic is increased by death and how it converges with the logic of museumification, see: Bess Lovejoy, "Lives on Show, Bodies behind Glass: Julia Pastrana's Parallels in Museum Collections," in *The Eye of the Beholder*.

[44] Laura Anderson Barbata and Donna Wingate, eds., *The Eye of the Beholder*.

FIGURE 6.3 "Opate Indian!" Advertisement for a Pastrana performance in Worcester, Massachusetts, 1855. Special Collections, University of Virginia, Charlottesville.

that she will never be disturbed again.[45] Yet, at the same time she kept performing that story and exposing it through her work.

In order to understand the artistic operation displayed here we have to take a step back and explore the sort of exhibitionistic logic that is displayed in the life-story of Julia Pastrana. Consider Figure 6.3, which reproduces the advertisement for a Pastrana performance in Worcester, Massachusetts (1855).[46] The capture immediately tells us that we have an "Opate Indian!," while the picture assembles two features (Woman, Bear) that are usually perceived as separate, if not as incompatible. The picture emphasizes both the quantity of hair on Pastrana's body and her masculine traits, which then stand in even stronger contrast to her womanhood: It is the eccentric combination of elements that the hegemonic view of femininity of the time did not allow to go together that makes of her "the Misnomered," the creature that is impossible to name.

However, such alleged "monstrosity" also explains the fascination for her body and thus the reasons for turning her into a spectacle. The beautiful voice of a trained mezzo-soprano, the fancy clothes, and the composed posture, invoking values of adornment and submissiveness associated with modern Western femininity, was perceived to be at odd with the thickness of her beard and the excessiveness of her hair, which recalled instead the attributes of modern Western masculinity. The fascination for Pastrana was part of a general fascination of the time for the freak shows, the exhibitions of those monstrosity that by (ex)posing some bodies as "deviant" implicitly marked the boundary between the "normal" and the "abnormal." Whereas the fascination for monsters always played that role of reinforcing the boundaries of any given social order, what was typical of the freak shows of the second half of the nineteenth and the early twentieth centuries was the impetus given to them by the capitalist economy: The secularizing, mobile, rapidly changing social order dominated increasingly by a market economy, individualism, and a developing mass culture engendered both a trust in

---

[45] The complex story of the repatriation of the body of Julia Pastrana is beautifully reconstructed in ibid. For a discussion of the scientific and ethical dilemmas of the repatriation, see: Nicholas Marquez-Grant, "The Repatriation of Julia Pastrana: scientific and ethical dilemmas," in *The Eye of the Beholder*.

[46] Special Collections, University of Virginia, Charlottesville. For additional information on this image: https://v4.lib.virginia.edu/sources/books/items/u2032021 (accessed July 25, 2021).

and an anxiety about how things looked, which explains why grand exhibitions, circuses, museums, parades, and department-store displays flourished[47]. Within this phantasmagoria of commodities, the exhibition of monsters functioned as the deviation necessary in order to establish the boundaries of the normal, as the abject that is rejected at the very same time that the subject is created.[48]

As Preciado has noted, the displacement of body hair is a crucial site for the production of gendered and racialized bodies in modernity.[49] In the techno-gender system of the nineteenth century, the exhibition of "bearded ladies" as monstrosity went hand in hand with the invention of "hirsutism" as a clinical condition, making normal women potential clients of the normalizing medical and cosmetic system. (They still are.) Notice here how gender is sealed with race, since "hirsutism" has become a clinical condition that helped to identify both abnormal femininity and inferior races, thereby propping up white femininity as the implicit norm for womanhood.[50] Not by chance then, the advertisement presents Julia Pastrana's combination of femininity and masculinity traits as an "Opate Indian," thus relegating it to an allegedly inferior race. If we consider that the advertisement was for a show taking place in Worcester in 1855, and thus at a time when the settler colonial process of creation and consolidation of United States of America was already well advanced, we can imagine the impact that this show had on both the local settlers and on the Native Americans who had been pushed onto reservations, exterminated, and/or forced into adopting the settlers' way of life.[51]

It is not difficult to recognize in this advertisement the typical exhibitionistic logic of colonialism, and how the latter capitalized on the

---

[47] Rosemarie Garland-Thomson, "Julia Pastrana, 'The extraordinary Lady'" in *The Eye of the Beholder*, 33.

[48] See, Julia Kristeva, *Powers of Horror: An Essay on Abjection* (New York: Columbia University Press, 1982). As Kristeva points out in this seminal work, in order to have "subjects" there needs to be "abjects" to execrate and vomit: the two mutually constitute each other.

[49] Beatriz Preciado, *Testo Junkie*, 114.

[50] For instance, since 1961, hirsutism started to be measured through the so-called Ferriman-Gallway scale, according to which a Caucasian woman with a score of eight is indicative of androgen excess, whereas in East Asian women a much lower score reveals hirsutism. See: Beatriz Preciado, *Testo Junkie*, 115.

[51] For a reconstruction of the history of the United States, from a perspective that centers on the relations between Indigenous people and settlers, as perceived through the eyes of the former rather than the latter, see Roxanne Dunbar-Ortiz's *An Indigenous Peoples' History of the United States* (London: Beacon Press, 2014).

emergent commodification of social life. The fascination of and for the "Opate Indian" is precisely that of the colonial fetish that needs to be exhibited in the heart of the colonizers' territories in order to reinforce the hegemonic views of femininity at home, but thus also to foreclose alternative images of womanhood and make sure they remained relegated to the sphere of the "less than human." It is therefore not by chance that Julia Pastrana is advertised as *both* "Opate Indian" and "Bear Woman," with the first appearing above her head, and the words "Bear" and "Woman" appearing on either side of her body. The label "Bear Woman" indeed symbolically relegates Pastrana's body to a liminal space between superior (human) and inferior (animal) species, thereby reinforcing the boundaries between normal humanity and a bestiality sealed with racial inferiority. In so doing, the entire hierarchy of man>woman>slave>animal> plants is reproduced and reinforced.

With regards to this colonial exhibitionist logic, the work of Anderson Barbata operates a therapeutic counter-spectacle, a homeopathic therapy: The artist takes small pieces of the past spectacle in order to turn it against itself, thereby using the evil against the evil, performing a different spectacle of womanhood against the inherited spectacular logic of womanhood.[52] Instead of simply inviting us to identify with the story of Pastrana, the juxtaposing of the two images, and the white break in the middle, invites us to a questioning of the established dichotomies they represent: the bearded *versus* the depilated woman, the masculine *versus* the feminine, the less-than-human *versus* the fully human. As such, it interrogates the past spectacle of womanhood and opens the door for thinking about a different future. This counter-spectacle enacts what Muñoz defined as "disidentification," that is, a creative act of transgression, by which racial and social minorities articulate the truth about cultural hegemony.[53] The disidentificatory subject does not assimilate (identify)

---

[52] We develop this concept of a "homeopathic strategy" at more length in Chiara Bottici, *Imaginal Politics*, 106–24. Drucilla Cornell proposes a similar strategy in her work on pornography, inviting feminists not to simply dismiss pornography but to rather engage from within in order to generate a different imaginary. See: Drucilla Cornell, *The Imaginary Domain: Abortion, Pornography & Sexual Harassment* (London: Routledge, 1995), 95–167.

[53] "Disidentification is about recycling and rethinking encoded meaning. The process of disidentification scrambles and reconstructs the encoded message of a cultural text in a fashion that both exposes the encoded message's universalizing and exclusionary machinations and recircuits its workings to account for, include, and empower minority identities and identifications." See: José Esteban Muñoz, *Cruising Utopia: The Then and There of Queer Futurity* (New York: New York University Press, 2009), 31.

nor reject (counter-identity) dominant ideology. By simply rejecting the position of the "other than," one risks reinforcing precisely the binary between the normal and the deviant that one wanted to question in the first place. On the contrary, disidentificatory performances "tactically and simultaneously work on, with, and against a cultural form."[54] As such they are crucial vehicle for the creation of "queer counterpublics," that is, communities and relational chains of resistance that question the dominant public sphere from the inside.[55]

In sum, the story of Julia Pastrana powerfully illustrates the fascination that the plurality of her body exercised but also how ambivalent our responses to it can be. Renegotiating the stories that have been told about her through the spectacle of the "monster" is both a way to negotiate her story and the story of "womanhood" more generally. We are all bodies in plural, but people are not usually open to accept such a plurality (because it also implies accepting one's ambivalences) and therefore the fascination comes back in the form of the abject, the ugliness, as a strict boundary between the normal and the abnormal. In the story of Julia Pastrana, the ambivalent fascination culminated into the adoration, but also the tearing apart of an embalmed body. Her husband-impresario, who was clearly not reticent in exploiting her for financial ends, was, however, probably interested in more than making money out of her. After her death, he married another woman, Marie Bartel, whose body also exhibited a great amount of hair, but his life ended alone and insane in a Russian asylum. His problem, but also perhaps ours, lay in the difficulty of maintaining a truly pluralist openness, which also implies the capacity of navigating ambivalences. To rephrase Friedrich Nietzsche, the formula of happiness is here, more than ever, a Yes, a No, a straight line, and—why not?—a beard.[56]

---

[54] Ibid, 12.
[55] Ibid, 146.
[56] The original aphorism states: "a Yes, a No, a straight line, a goal." See: Friedrich Nietzsche, *The Portable Nietzsche*, trans. Walter Kaufmann (New York: Penguin Books, 1976: 570).

Intermezzo

Itinerarium in semen

un nuovo continente, la terra, la mia terra, la tua terra, la loro terra, i nativi, quelli che erano qui all'origine, ma quale origine, la mia origine, la tua origine, la loro origine, tutti si muovono e persino le piante, persino le più sedentarie tra tutti i viventi, si muovono, si muovono e viaggiano, viaggiano e volano, volano e si spostano, si spostano col vento, con gli animali, anche con quelli che non vogliono e non volevano viaggiare, tonnellate e tonnellate, di semi, portati involontariamente, nelle zavorre, nelle sacche, nelle suole, nelle piume, ed adesso lì, strato dopo strato, proprio sulla terra dove camminiamo ogni giorno, ignari della vita che dorme sotto i nostri piedi, ogni corpo, ogni merce, ogni creatura che ha attraversato i continenti, inconsapevole zattera, sordi migranti, che dormono sottoterra, a tratti fanno pure capolino, tra un mattone e l'altro, per dire che ci sono ancora, che stanno lì, addormentati forse, ma viventi, nell'anonimato della terra, in attesa di un solco, di una mano, di un evento che li liberi dal peso della clandestinità, mentre noi ce ne andiamo sicuri, certi di camminare su una terra che ci appartiene, e che invece appartiene sempre ad un altro, un altro che non sappiamo, un altro che non conosciamo, fino a che un giorno, forse, incontreremo un fiore che parla e saremo in grado di udirne il grido

Itinerarium in semen

a new continent, the land, my land, your land, their land, those who were here at the origin, but which origin, my origin, your origin, their origin, all move and even plants, even the most sedentary of all living beings, move, move and travel, travel and fly, fly and flow, flow with the elements, flow with the beasts, even with those who do not want and did not want to travel, tons and tons, and even more seeds, carried involuntarily, in the ballast, in the bags, in the soles, in the furs, and in the feathers, and now there, layer after layer, right on the earth where we walk every day, unaware of the life sleeping under our feet, every body, every being, every creature that has crossed continents, unconscious raft, deaf migrants, dormant underground, at times they even peek out, between one brick and another, to say that they are still there, that they are there, perhaps asleep, but still living, in the anonymity of the earth, waiting for a hand, for an event that could free them from the burden of clandestinity, while we carry on, certain that we are walking on a land that belongs to us, and which instead always belongs to another, another that does not know us, another we do not know, until one day, perhaps, we will meet a speaking flower and we will be able to hear its cry

PART THREE

The globe first

At the beginning was movement—not the word (*logos*), nor any other already given individuality. Instead of beginning with a world already divided into discrete individuals, the following reflections will focus on how individuals themselves come into being. Pursuing the monist ontology of transindividuality previously elucidated, these reflections will be both a theory about ontogenesis and a process of ontogenesis. We will proceed along three axes: First, adopting a gaze that starts with the *supra*-individual level, and then progressively focusing on the inter- and infra-. Second, we will continue with the *inter*-individual level, and from that point of view look at how it connects with the supra- and infra-individual level. Finally, we will focus on the *infra*-individual and look at the inter- and supra- levels from that point of view.

Beginning with the supra-individual level means adopting the globe as our framework. The reason for this is easy to perceive: if we want to avoid both methodological individualism (single discrete people as starting point) and methodological nationalism (single societies and states as the starting point), we need to take at least the globe as our minimum horizon. But can we adopt such a global perspective without falling into yet another form of Western imperialism and/or Eurocentrism? We need to remember Kuan-Hsing Chen's words: "globalization without deimperialization is simply a disguised reproduction of imperialist conquest."[1] Similarly, global

---

[1] Kuan-Hsing Chen, *Asia as Method: Toward Deimperialization* (Durham: Duke University Press, 2010), 2.

theory without deimperialization risks being a disguised reproduction of theoretical imperialism. Otherwise stated, adopting a global framework without having done the work of deimperialization means falling again into an *archē*, and thus the performative contradiction of putting forward an anarchafeminist theory by reproducing the imperialist order of knowledge, or what Boaventura de Sousa Santos called "the cognitive empire."[2]

By "globalization," we mean a series of capital-driven forces which seek to penetrate and colonize all spaces of the earth and have thus a tendency to erode national frontiers. As Marx and Engels observed in their *Communist Manifesto*, and as Malatesta echoed in his writing: "*Oggi lo sviluppo immenso che ha preso la produzione, il crescere di quei bisogni che non possono soddisfarsi se non col concorso di gran numero di uomini di tutti i paesi, i mezzi di comunicazione, l'abitudine dei viaggi, la scienza, la letteratura, i commerci, le guerre stesse, hanno stretto e vanno sempre più stringendo l'umanità in un corpo solo, le cui parti, solidali tra loro, possono solo trovare pienezza e libertà di sviluppo nella salute delle altre parti e del tutto*".[3] There are thus drives towards globalization, that is, towards an intensification of the communication between different locations around the globe, but they must not be mistaken for an overcoming of colonialism and imperialism, as they may well work towards their deepening.

While adopting the globe as a framework is thus all the more necessary, it must be accompanied by a call for deimperialization and decolonization.[4] When considering the knowledge produced globally in the field of social and political theory, we cannot but notice how deeply Eurocentric and

---

[2] Boaventura de Sousa Santos, *The End of the Cognitive Empire: The Coming of Age of Epistemologies of the South* (Durham: Duke University Press, 2018).

[3] "Today the immense development of production, the growth of those requirements which can only be satisfied by the participation of large numbers of people in all countries, the means of communication, with travel becoming a commonplace, science, literature, businesses and even wars, all have drawn mankind into an ever tighter single body whose constituent parts, united among themselves, can only find fulfilment and freedom to develop through the wellbeing of the other constituent parts as well as of the whole" (Errico Malatesta, "L'anarchia," trans. ours [Roma: Datanews, 2001], 24).

[4] Following Kuan-Hsing Chen (*Asia as Method*), we understand colonialism as a deepening of imperialism: whereas the latter can be exercised by means other than the direct occupation of the land and the material resources of a country, colonialism usually implied some form of material occupation. In "Towards the African Revolution," Fanon wrote: "Colonialism is the organization of the domination of a nation after military conquest" (Frantz Fanon, *Toward the African Revolution: Political Essays*, trans. Haakon Chevalier [New York: Grove Press, 1967], 83). We could say that imperialism is the organization of the domination of a nation even if there has never been any military conquest.

androcentric that process is. Both, as we will see, find their origin in the "historical fact of European political and cultural domination from the fifteenth century onwards":[5] although Europe may no longer be the center of the world, the legacy of its five centuries of imperialism are still with us in the form of a coloniality of power that goes hand in hand with a coloniality of gender. We will begin by exploring these processes on the supra-individual level and thus call for a form of decolonial and deimperial anarchafeminism (Chapter 7). Subsequently, we move to the inter-individual level and focus on how individuals come into being through a capitalist mode of production that structures relations both at the material and psychological level, calling for a critique of the heteronormative mononuclear family, and arguing that Western psychoanalysis itself needs a sex change (Chapter 8). Finally, we look at the process of ontogenesis beginning with the infra-individual level and argue for a form of ecofeminism as transindividual and queer ecology (Chapter 9).

---

[5] Syed Farid Alatas and Vineeta Sinha, *Sociological Theory Beyond the Canon* (London: Palgrave Macmillan, 2017), 4.

7 The coloniality of gender: for a decolonial and deimperial feminism

If we take the globe as our framework to think about gender both as a materiality and as a concept, the first major issue to come to the fore is that not all people around the globe are or have been doing gender, and—even when they did so, it was on very different terms. And yet, as we will see, this historical truism is all too often neglected, if not foreclosed, in much of the gender theory work undertaken in the West. One of the main reasons for this is that the canon of social and political theory is still largely characterized by the dual product of global modernity: Eurocentrism and androcentrism. It is striking how, despite all talk about globalization, social theory still exhibits a lack of awareness of the "historical fact of European political and cultural domination from the fifteenth century onwards and thus of the need to have a non-Eurocentric and non-androcentric canon in social sciences."[1] It is indeed this historical fact that has shaped not only the materiality of global relations of economic production, but also those of intellectual (re)production. Both Eurocentrism and androcentrism are a way of seeing as well as a way of not seeing,[2] so they cannot be addressed by simply adding non-Westerners and non-males to the dinner table. One has to be ready to change the topics that are addressed, by creating the conditions for possible changes in the dinner plans.[3] And this can be done

---

[1] Syed Farid Alatas and Vineeta Sinha, *Sociological Theory Beyond the Canon*, 4.
[2] Ibid, 5.
[3] In his *Ten Theses on Decoloniality*, Maldonado-Torres insisted that we need to decolonize every building block of what gets to count as knowledge (Nelson Maldonado-Torres, "Outline of ten theses on coloniality and decoloniality," [available at http://fondation-frantzfanon.com/outline-of-ten-theses-on-coloniality-and-decoloniality/ : 2016], 4).

only if one follows a "bottom-up epistemology" and thus not only invites a plurality of voices but also allows them to suggest a different menu.[4]

By "Eurocentrism" we mean here, very generally, the attitude to consider Europe as the center and observational point for looking at the entire globe. Eurocentrism envisions the world from a single privileged point of view, mapping a cartography that, literally, centralizes Europe and its perspective on the world. Those countries west of Europe are assimilated to Europe itself (although Latin America is generally excluded), while the east is divided into "Near," "Middle," and "Far." All this makes of Europe the arbiter of spatial order, just as the establishment of Greenwich Mean Time makes England the regulating center of temporal measurement.[5]

Well beyond cartography, Eurocentrism permeates our thinking in a way that we are often unable to recognize. People keep repeating phrases such as "the West" or "Western civilization" or "Western culture" without realizing that, properly speaking, they are nonsense, because in a globe there is no "east" and "west" without qualification. West of what? How diverse or diffuse is this West? What is the center of this West, which now comes to include, in certain understandings, Australia and Japan? How can there be an absolute West in a world that is spherical? The West only exists in its capitalization because by speaking about "The West," we are implicitly transforming a globe into a bidimensional map, placing Europe at its center, and assuming that this is the only way of looking at it. As Naoki Sakai has observed, the West, as the cartographic area where modernity originates, has become a mythical locus that "prescribes and presages, as a sort of regulative machinery, what the world must look like."[6]

The notion of the West, and the imaginal cartography it presupposes, is inseparable from the notion of modernity, and its corresponding organization of time. In Eduardo Mendieta's words, it is an entire

---

[4] We take the notion of bottom-up epistemology from Boaventura de Sousa Santos, who writes: "The epistemologies of the South thus affirm and valorize the differences that remain after the hierarchies have been eliminated. They aim at a bottom-up subaltern cosmopolitanism. Rather than abstract universality, they promote pluriversality. A kind of thinking that promotes decolonization, creolization, or mestizaje through intercultural translation" (Boaventura de Sousa Santos, *The End of the Cognitive Empire*, 8–9).
[5] Ella Shohat and Robert Stam, *Unthinking Eurocentrism: Multiculturalism and the Media* (London: Routledge, 1994), 2.
[6] Naoki Sakai, "'You Asians': On the Historical Role of the West and Asia Binary," *South Atlantic Quarterly* 99, no. 4 (2000), 794.

"chronotopology," a process of mapping time and temporalizing space.[7] Europe is placed at the center of this imaginal organization of space because modernity is fantasized as "emanating" from the center and then reaching the hinterlands of the world.[8] The notion of modernity presupposes many different places and polities being in contact with one another, in as much as it presupposes a certain ordering of time. It is the yardstick according to which the rest of the world can be organized in different developmental stages, going from "Ancient" to "Modern" times and passing by the "Middle" Ages. Again, in the "Middle" of what? How, if not by the modern-colonial system of knowledge that implicitly makes European history the universal History,[9] do we classify all histories? Speaking about "Ancient" or "Medieval history" without further qualification means reproducing the narrative created and sustained by European Enlightenment intellectuals, according to which European modernity was the destination of history—the *Neuzeit*, literally the "new time," as the German term for modernity clearly states. Within this narrative of modernity as the *telos* of history, Ancient Greece and Rome were taken as its natural beginning, while quite a few centuries of Christendom were placed in the "Middle." The narrative of Greece as the cradle of European civilization was invented by those European intellectuals who rejected Christendom and proposed Ancient Greece as the true beginning of the European spirit, thereby paving the way for an alternative, secularist origin myth. The myth of a "classical Europe," of a European identity rooted in the Greek civilization, is one of the most powerful founding narratives of the concept of Europe.[10] We tend to

---

[7] Eduardo Mendieta, *Global Fragments: Globalizations, Latinamericanisms, and Critical Theory* (Albany: SUNY Press, 2007), 5 and 71.

[8] Naoki Sakai, "'You Asians,'" 798.

[9] Cf. Walter D. Mignolo, *Local Histories/Global Designs: Coloniality, Subaltern Knowledges, and Border Thinking* (Princeton: Princeton University Press, 2000). To reject this teleological understanding of history does not mean rejecting history altogether. For an example of the recent attempts to conceptualize history outside of its modern teleological understanding, see Dmitri Nikulin's *The Concept of History*. By criticizing the modern understanding of history, Nikulin argues that it does not have a unique purpose. However, this does not mean that it does not have any meaning; it simply means that there are many histories and not just one universal history with a single *telos* (Dmitri Nikulin, *The Concept of History* [London: Bloomsbury, 2017], 173–4).

[10] During the Enlightenment, European travelers on their Grand Tours, in their pursuit of the ruins of ancient civilizations, contributed to the discovery as well as the invention of a specific European civilization. In a way, they were modernity's secular pilgrims, engaged in a ritual of passage, embarking upon journeys to pay their respects to the Holy Land of

forget that "Europe" has not always been there, since for most of its history it was conceptualized through the much broader category of *Latin Christianitas*, but it has now been imagined for quite some time through narratives such as that of the "classical" or the "modern" Europe.[11] Besides the irony of naming more than a millennium of European history simply as a "middle," notice how this teleological understanding also explains the special position consistently accorded to the so-called "Classical Age": As the "ancient" roots of a history that, after the Middle period, was destined to flourish into the European modernity, Greek and Roman history is thereby transformed into the necessary mythical "pedestal" for modernity.[12]

The concept of modernity is inseparable from a "chronology of maturity,"[13] one that ranks social formations into the chronological hierarchy of advancement and retardation. It is the racialization of space that enables the teleological organization of time, and vice versa. The imaginal organization of space according to the West/East dichotomy reproduces the Eurocentric "emanating" fantasy, according to which European modernity is the yardstick for a global "chronotopology,"[14] thus fulfilling the narcissistic wishes of those still arrested in the "missionary positionality"[15] that justified European colonialism.

---

civilization rather than to the Holy Land of the Bible. See Robert Wokler, "Rites of Passage and the Grand Tour: Discovering, Imagining, and Inventing European Civilization in the Age of Enlightenment," in *Finding Europe: Discourses on Margins, Communities, Images; ca. 13th–ca 18th Centuries*, eds. Anthony Molho, Diogo Ramada Curto, and Niki Koniordos (New York: Berghahn Books, 2007), 207.

[11] For instance, the myth of a European identity born out of "classical civilization" is constantly being reproduced by rituals, school curricula, and even buildings, in the US settler-colonial mythology. The "classical Europe" narrative was imported by European settlers and adapted to the American context through the mythical projection of an American Arcadia, of a *terra nullius*, that, like the corresponding Greek Arcadia, was simply there waiting for culture and knowledge to be brought by the settlers, thereby erasing the indigenous history of the Americas. We have developed this point more at length in Chiara Bottici, "Philosophy, Coloniality and the Politics of Remembrance," in *Graduate Faculty Philosophy Journal, Philosophy and Coloniality* special issue, 41, n. 1, (2020), 87–127).

[12] Nelson Maldonado-Torres, "What is Decolonial Critique?," (*Graduate Faculty Philosophy Journal*, in *Philosophy and Coloniality* special issue,Vol. 41, n.1 (2020). It is often forgotten that "classical" is strictly associated with "class," and that taking a course in Classical Studies is thus a way to obtain both intellectual and class status. See Chiara Bottici, "Philosophy, Coloniality, and the Politics of Remembrance."

[13] Naoki Sakai, "'You Asians,'" 800.

[14] Eduardo Mendieta, *Global Fragments*, 71.

[15] Naoki Sakai, "'You Asians,'" 815.

Notice that Eurocentrism first emerged as a discursive rationale for European colonialism, the process by which European powers reached positions of hegemony in much of the world. In this sense, it is the "colonizer's model of the world," as the title of James Morris Blaut's book reminds us.[16] Yet Eurocentrism does not immediately mean colonialism or racism.[17] Although colonialist and Eurocentric discourses are intimately intertwined, the terms point to two different concepts. While the former explicitly justifies colonialist practices, the latter embeds, takes for granted, and thus normalizes, the hierarchical power relations generated by colonialism and imperialism, without necessarily even thematizing those issues directly. As a consequence, although generated by the colonizing process, Eurocentrism' links to that process are obscured in a "buried epistemology."[18]

This is why it is important to distinguish between decolonization and deimperialization: Whereas colonialism implies the expropriation of land and resources, imperialism is a form of domination that does not necessarily imply material occupation of land. The pervasiveness of Eurocentrism is therefore more an example of the latter. And yet, as Ella Shohat and Robert Stam remind us, the two are linked in a sort of buried epistemology that is pivotal to debunk if we want to avoid turning our global gaze into yet another form of imperialism.[19] The legacy of European colonialism and imperialism is so deep-seated that decolonization and deimperialization must be conceived as an "attitude" to be cultivated over time rather than a gesture done once and for all.[20]

As Aníbal Quijano, among others, observed, Eurocentrism is pervasive because it is the cognitive perspective not only of Europeans, but of all people educated in the Eurocentric world, and thus of all people educated under the hegemony of world capitalism. "This is the cognitive perspective produced over time in the colonial/modern eurocentric capitalist ensemble and that naturalizes people's experiences in accordance to that pattern of power"[21] and, through this naturalization, forecloses the possibility of perceiving its own historical connection with racism and colonialism.

---

[16] James Morris Blaut, *The Colonizer's Model of the World: Geographical Diffusionism and Eurocentric History* (New York: Guilford Press, 1993).
[17] Ella Shohat and Robert Stam, *Unthinking Eurocentrism*, 2–4.
[18] Ibid.
[19] Ella Shohat and Robert Stam, *Unthinking Eurocentrism*.
[20] Nelson Maldonado-Torres, "Outline of ten theses . . .," 22.
[21] Aníbal Quijano, "Colonialidad del Poder y Clasificacion Social," *Festschrift for Immanuel Wallerstein Part 1, Jornal of World System Research, V*, xi, no. 2 (2000), 343.

Whenever we divide history into "ancient," "modern," and "medieval," we implicitly reproduce not only that physical image of the world that literally has Europe as its center but also its imaginal past, and the ordering of space and time according to a chronology of maturity. Notice the same Eurocentric map that Google retrieves when we search for a "political map of the world." One could argue that the "Google" result for "political map of the world" has become a gigantic and all too powerful—perhaps even *the* most powerful—site for the reproduction of this imaginal cartography. Although political maps of the world can be done from the point of view of infinite centers, the Eurocentric map has become so hegemonic worldwide, that, when situated in the Americas, one ends up paradoxically ascribing the heading of "Western civilization" to a whole series of texts, buildings, and traditions that have actually been produced in its geographic "East."

This standard political map of the world is imbued with what Quijano called "the coloniality of power," being an organization of space that presupposes Eurocentrism and its accompanying racial classification of people around the globe as more or less worthy.[22] Hence the importance of focusing on "coloniality," and not simply "colonialism," as decolonial theorists have emphasized.[23] Whereas the latter may be perceived as an item of the past, coloniality denotes the relations of power that continue to exist even when the formal process of colonization is over.[24]

---

[22] Aníbal Quijano, "Coloniality of Power, Eurocentrism, and Latin America," *Nepantla: Views from the South* 1, no. 3 (2000), 551–2.

[23] In an important footnote of his seminal essay, Quijano clarifies this point: "Coloniality is a concept that is different from colonialism, although it is linked to it. The latter concept refers strictly to a structure of domination and exploitation, where the control of political authority, of the resources of production and the labor of a determined population is held by another one of a different identity, and whose headquarters are, furthermore, in a different territorial jurisdiction. But it does not always, nor necessarily, imply racist relations of power. Colonialism is obviously more ancient, while coloniality has proven to be, in the last five hundred years, more profound and lasting than colonialism. But without a doubt, coloniality was engendered within colonialism and, furthermore, without it, it would not have been able to impose itself on the world's intersubjectivity, in such an in-depth and prolonged fashion" (Aníbal Quijano, "Colonialidad del Poder," 381, trans. ours).

[24] For an argument in favor of this distinction see Aníbal Quijano, "Coloniality of Power," esp. 551–3; and Nelson Maldonado-Torres, "Outline of Ten Theses…," 10. Among those who prefer to keep the notion of colonialism is Ann Laura Stoler. She is reluctant to use the term "post-colonialism" and prefers to speak of (post)colonialism to show that colonialism is still with us (Ann Laura Stoler, *Duress: Imperial Durabilities in Our Times* [Durham: Duke University Press, 2017], ix). We should also distinguish "coloniality of power" from imperialism: whereas the former implies the historical legacy of colonialism, imperialism can be exercised in areas that have never been formally colonized.

Eurocentrism must therefore not be considered as a kind of prejudice, as some sort of poor judgment affecting some people but not others. It propagates an unconscious image of the world that is constantly reproduced through language and the practices of exploitation and exclusion that began with European colonialism. The physical map of the world with Europe at its center may or may not be present to our minds when we use expressions such as "Middle East," "Western civilization," or, another case in point, "Continental Philosophy." When we utter terms such as the latter, we presuppose a "Continent" that does not even have to be qualified or further identified because it is the continent through which we look at all others. Eurocentrism is the transformation of a specific continent (Europe) into a meta-continent through which we locate all other continents—Asia, Africa, the Americas—the histories of which are all imbricated with European colonialism and Europe's own definition of itself as a space distinguished from its colonies. As Frantz Fanon very aptly put it, "Europe is literally the creation of the Third World,"[25] that is, a geopolitical space whose existence and self-definition came into being through colonialism.

As Aníbal Quijano showed in his seminal essay "Coloniality of Power, Eurocentrism and Latin America," to understand the scope and depth of Eurocentrism as a system of knowledge, we have to keep in mind that since the beginning of modernity, the affirmation of a capitalist world system went hand in hand with the emergence of the concept of race, understood as a tool to classify people according to their labor.[26] This does not mean that racism and discrimination did not exist before. Rather, it means that it is only with the emergence of a world capitalist system, based on an international division of labor that separated the center from its periphery (and semi-peripheries), that the modern concept of race, with its specific biological and hierarchical connotation, became hegemonic worldwide. 1492 is a crucial threshold, not only because of the immense cultural turmoil its events created, but also

---

[25] Frantz Fanon, *The Wretched of the Earth*, trans. R. Philcox (New York: Grove Press, 2004), 58. On the way in which the definition of the European space went had in hand with the inventions of the Americas, see Enrique Dussel, *The Invention of the Americas: Eclipse of "the Other" and the Myth of Modernity*, trans. Michael D. Barber (New York: Continuum, 1995). On the concept of Asia as a result of European imperialism, see Naoki Sakai, "'You Asians';" and on the geopolitics of knowledge of all these terms, see Walter D, Mignolo, *Local Histories/Global Designs*.

[26] Aníbal Quijano, "Coloniality of Power," 536–7.

because previously established trade routes for the accumulation of capital were not truly global. As Aníbal wrote:

> [Coloniality] originates and is globalized departing from America. With the constitution of (Latin) America, in that very historical moment and movement, the emergent capitalist power is made global, its hegemonic centers settle themselves on the Atlantic – which will later identify themselves as Europe – and coloniality and modernity are established as central axes of its new pattern of domination. In brief: with (Latin) America, capitalism becomes global, Eurocentric, and coloniality and modernity have installed themselves as the constitutive axes of its specific pattern of power. In the course of the deployment of the characteristics of this current power, new social identities of coloniality (Indigenous, Black, brown, yellow, white, *mestizo*), and the geocultures of colonialism such as America, Africa, Far East, Near East, (both become Asia later on) and West or Europe, were configured. And the corresponding intersubjective relations, in which the experiences of colonialism and coloniality slowly fused themselves with the needs of capitalism, gradually configured themselves as a new universe of intersubjective relations of domination under Eurocentric hegemony. This particular universe is the one that later come to be called modernity.[27]

The history of how we have come to perceive people as classified according to race still needs to be written in all of its details, some arguing that it originated in the discussion about whether the Native Americans were human, while others point to later developments such as the Atlantic slave trade.[28] In all of the different accounts of this history, it is clear that the concept of race was fully in place when eighteenth- and nineteenth-century European intellectuals and natural historians systematically elaborated the notion of "race," based on information that was largely supplied by travelers involved in missionary activity, colonial enterprises, and slave trading.[29]

---

[27] Aníbal Quijano, "Colonialidad del Poder," 342–43, trans. ours.
[28] Robert Bernasconi and Tommy Lee Lott, *The Idea of Race* (Indianapolis: Hackett Publishing, 2000), viii.
[29] Ibid, vii.

Quijano, among others, explored the way in which racial classification was understood during the "invention of the Americas," and how this understanding developed.[30] The classification was initially framed mainly in terms of the *conquistadores'* Christian identity and then increasingly assumed other, specifically biological, connotations.[31] Initially, the main driving force behind these identitarian classifications was the dichotomy between "Christians" and the "Indians," between the "civilized" and "savages," with its inbuilt allochronism.[32] As an aside, notice here how allochronism, i.e. the placing of others into "another time," works as a tool to justify genocide and elimination. Even when the "savages" were recognized as human beings, their placement in the infant or pre-civilizational stage of humanity meant they were implicitly presented as pre-Christians and thus as immature Europeans, to be assimilated either through physical elimination or by cultural transformation.

With the expansion of the colonization of the Americas, skin color increasingly became the phenotype that signified race and so came to replace the "Christians *versus* savages" distinction as the tool for labor control. In Latin America, for instance, where waged labor was largely reserved for white people, other races (and skin colors) became signifiers for different sorts of unwaged labor, ranging from serfdom, reserved mainly for *Indios*, to slave labor, mostly performed by Black people.[33] In Anglo America, Native Americans were occasionally reduced to serfdom, and were instead mainly exterminated, assimilated, or pushed into reservations.[34] Blackness remained the signifier for bodies whose labor could be extorted for free, while waged labor was largely performed by white settlers, who progressively arrived in great numbers.[35]

By systematically showing the intertwinement of racism and capitalism, Quijano's "coloniality of power" thesis connects the critique of Eurocentrism with Marx's concept of world capitalism and Immanuel Wallerstein's world system theory.[36] In this view, since 1492, when

---

[30] See Enrique Dussel, *The Invention of the Americas.*
[31] Aníbal Quijano, "Coloniality of Power," 554–6.
[32] Fabian Johannes, *Time and the Other: How Anthropology Makes its Object* (New York: Columbia University Press, 1983), 32.
[33] See esp. Aníbal Quijano, "Coloniality of Power," 560, 565.
[34] See esp. ibid, 560.
[35] Ibid, 536, 539.
[36] Ibid, 540.

European colonialism reached the entire globe, the capitalist division of labor on a world scale has been linked to race, despite differences depending on context and epoch.[37] The motivation for this is easy to understand: As a system predicated on the endless expansion of profit, capitalism needs both the extraction of surplus value from waged labor and the extortion of free labor and resources from unwaged relations of production. The concept of race provided the perfect justification for such a process. Without the slaves and Indigenous people whose labor was extorted through colonialism, there would not have been any original accumulation of wealth and thus no capitalism and no modernity. The plantations in the colonies are as central as the spinning machines of Lancashire to the development of modernity, so instead of speaking about "European modernity" or even "multiple modernities," we should speak of a global modernity. Or, as Quijano proposes, of the "colonial/modern Eurocentred capitalism."[38] There is no "Asian Modernity" to be situated next to the European one, for just as there was no "America" without the European gaze, so too there was no "Asia" nor "Africa." Until the nineteenth century, no subject ever represented itself as "Asian," since Asia is a term coined by the Europeans in order to distinguish Europe from its eastern "others," and is thereby imbued with the process of European colonialism and self-identification.[39] The rhetoric of an "Asian modernity" or of "Asian values" is nothing but the reversal of Eurocentric culturalism.[40]

This explains why Quijano insists on the notion of an intrinsic "coloniality" of modern power and its global scope. His theoretical move implies a distinction between colonialism—as a system of colonial rule that does not, by definition, imply racism—and the coloniality of the modern system of power, which is inconceivable without taking race and racism into account. It is this centrality of racism to the capitalist world system that explains why Eurocentrism is so pervasive. Eurocentrism, and its map of the world, is inseparable from a system of knowledge that distinguishes between different skin colors only in order to prop up whiteness as the (elevated) norm. There is no Black (or any other color) skin without a white gaze in the same way that there is no "Middle East"

---

[37] Ibid, 540–2.
[38] Ibid.
[39] Naoki Sakai, "'You Asians,'" 800.
[40] Ibid, 801.

without the Eurocentric gaze that assumes Europe as its two-dimensional middle and Greenwich as the point from which time moves forward or back.

That white and black are the two colors that serve to classify all other colors is something built into racial thinking from its very inception. In his 1777 text "Of Different Human Races," the influential Prussian philosopher Immanuel Kant stated that "Negroes and whites [*Neger und Weiße*] are the base races," while all the other colors are the result of their combination and the influence of climate.[41] This is a crucial text in the history of racial thinking because it is one of the first to assign full humanity to all humans, but at the price of further dividing them into different races. While Kant considers all human beings as part of the same species (human), he nevertheless reproduces a hierarchy by classifying them into superior and inferior races.[42] Kant defines race as "deviations that are constantly preserved over many generations and come about as a consequence of migration (dislocation to other regions) or through interbreeding with other deviations of the same line of descent."[43] "Deviations" are, in turn, defined as "hereditary dissimilarities that we find in animals that belong to a single line of descent" (ibid), thereby inscribing the concept of race into the realm of hereditary traits and biology. Skin colors became the traits that literally name the different races, the level of iron in the blood identified as the main cause of the different colors. As Immanuel writes:

We now justifiably account for the different colors of plants by noting that the iron content of certain identifiably distinct plant juices varies. Similarly, since the blood of all animals contains iron, there is nothing to prevent us from accounting for the different colors of the human races by referring to exactly the same causes. Perhaps the hydrochloric

---

[41] Immanuel Kant, "On the different human races," in *The Idea of Race*, eds. Robert Bernasconi and Tommy Lee Lott (Indianapolis: Hackett Publishing, 2000), 12, 19–20.
[42] For a detailed discussion of the role of race in Kant's geography, see the essay collection, *Reading Kant's Geography* (eds. Stuart Elden and Eduardo Mendieta, [Albany: SUNY Press, 2011]), and in particular the critical essays: David Harvey, "Cosmopolitanism in the *Anthropology* and *Geography*," (267–84); Eduardo Mendieta, "Geography Is to History as Woman Is to Man: Kant on Sex, Race, and Geography," 345–68; Robert Bernasconi, "Kant's Third Thoughts on Race," 291–318; and Walter D. Mignolo, "The Darker Side of the Enlightenment: A De-Colonial Reading of Kant's *Geography*," 319–44.
[43] Immanuel Kant, "On the different human races," 9.

acid, or the phosphoric acid, or the volatile alkaline content of the exporting vessels of the skin, were, in this way, reflected red, or black, or yellow, in the iron particles in the reticulum. Among whites, however, these acids and the volatile alkaline content are not reflected at all because the iron in the bodily juices has been dissolved, thereby demonstrating both the perfect mixing of these juices and the strength of this human stock in comparison to the others.[44]

The Prussian philosopher does not provide any other explanation of why those acids and alkaline content would not be reflected at all in white-skinned people, and even admits that his opinions on the question of blood composition are only "preliminary."[45] Nevertheless, he sets up whiteness as the norm from which all other colors are derived. He argues that since the part of the Earth that has "the most fortunate combination" of cold and hot regions lies between the northern latitudes of 31 degrees and 52 degrees, which is where the "old world" is located, this must also be the place of "the greatest riches" of the earth, including the human beings who "diverge the least from their original form," humans who must therefore have been "well prepared to be transplanted into every other region of the earth."[46] The term "old world" reveals its racist implication here, as it denotes the place where allegedly the oldest people lived. Given that, according to the Prussian philosopher, this is where we find "white" and "brunette inhabitants," they are said to be the first lineal root genus of human beings, and the "nearest northern deviation to develop from this original form appears to be the noble blond."[47] Beginning with this lineal root genus, Immanuel develops a full classification into four fundamental human races based on skin color as well as those natural causes that, owing to their presumed influence on bodily juices, initiate skin color variation: "First race: Noble blond (northern Europe), from humid cold; Second Race: Copper red (America) from dry cold; Third race: Black (Senegambia) from humid heat; Fourth race: Olive-yellow (Asian-Indians) from dry heat."[48]

---

[44] Ibid, 19.
[45] Ibid.
[46] Ibid, 19–20.
[47] Ibid, 20.
[48] Ibid.

Notice here that Kant, who notoriously never left his native Königsberg, based his racial theory on biology and accounts provided by travelers, missionaries, and European merchants who were involved in world trade, including the very profitable slave trade. It is thanks to Enlightenment texts such as this one that skin color and other visible physical traits became crucial ingredients of the modern concept of race, which is still largely defined in terms of fixed biological differences between groups of humans.[49] But notice also that labor capacity, which must have been of crucial interest for the European merchants writing such reports, is explicitly invoked in these pages. For instance, when speaking about Native Americans, he observes that they reveal a "half-extinguished life power," which is probably the effect of the cold weather of that region, which stands in sharp contrast to the humid warm weather of Africa.[50] Accordingly, Kant remarks that "the Negro . . . is well-suited to his climate, namely, strong, fleshy, and agile" and only made "lazy, indolent, and dawdling" because "so amply supplied by his motherland."[51] As an indication of this difference in strength, Kant supplies the following example: "red slaves (Native Americans) are used only for domestic work in Surinam, because they are too weak to work in the fields. Negroes are thus needed for fieldwork. The difficulties in this case are not the result of a lack of coercive measures, but the natives in this part of the world lack ability and durability."[52]

Immanuel provides no source for this example, but it is not hard to imagine it must have come from somebody who had a vested interest in labor needs. As Brian Van Norden, among others, points out, Kant also used the ability for abstract thought as a further criterion to arrange races in a hierarchical order, thus distinguishing between those who are fit and those who are unfit for intellectual labor. According to Kant:

---

[49] This summary of the definition of race is by Lentin (Alana Lentin, *Racism: A Beginner's Guide* [Oxford: Oneworld, 2008], 37–8, 47–8), who also distinguishes between racial naturalism and racial historicism, thereby making it clear that even after abandoning the biological connotation of the very first elaborations, the concept of race survived (ibid, 23–31). Elaborating on Lentin's definition, and incorporating racial historicism into it, we can provisionally define race in terms of fixed hereditary differences between groups, no matter whether such "hereditary" transmission happens through biology, history, or a mix of both.

[50] Immanuel Kant, "On the different human races," 17.

[51] Ibid.

[52] Ibid.

(1) "The race of the whites contains all talents and motives in itself."

(2) "The Hindus . . . have a strong degree of calm, and all look like philosophers. That notwithstanding, they are much inclined to anger and love. They thus are educable in the highest degree, but only to the arts and not to the sciences. They will never achieve abstract concepts."

(3) "The race of Negroes . . . [is] full of affect and passion, very lively, chatty and vain. It can be educated, but only to the education of servants, i.e., they can be trained.[. . .]"

(4) "The [Indigenous] American people are uneducable; for they lack affect and passion. They are not amorous, and so are not fertile. They speak hardly at all, . . . care for nothing and are lazy."[53]

If we add to this that, according to Kant, "Philosophy is not to be found in the whole Orient," the strikingly inevitable conclusion is that the Chinese, Indians, and Africans, as well as the Indigenous[54] peoples of the Americas, are congenitally incapable of philosophy, whereas white people are naturally—and uniquely—suited to it.[55] In sum, it does not appear to be an exaggeration to say that races were largely set up as job descriptions.

This insight that the international division of labor and racial classification are a twin product of European colonialism has also been at the center of Frantz Fanon's heterodox historical materialism.[56] Elaborating on classical Marxism, Fanon explicitly stated that "what divides this world is first and foremost what species, what race, one belongs to."[57] As he goes on to explain, in the colonies, "you are rich because you are white, you are

[53] This list is compiled in Bryan W. Van Norden, *Taking Back Philosophy: A Multicultural Manifesto* (New York: Columbia University Press, 2017), 21–2.

[54] In this book, we use "Indigenous" in the technical sense of the term, as linked to claims to land by people who have been dispossessed through colonization. Kim TallBear argues there has been too much emphasis on DNA and diaspora in the definition of indigeneity, which should, on the contrary, be understood in term of land dispossession, connection to ancestors and networks of tribal belonging. See Kim TallBear, "Genomic Articulations of Indigeneity," *Social Studies of Science*, 43, no, 4 (2013a), 509–33.

[55] Julia Ching, "Chinese Ethics and Kant," *Philosophy East and West*, 28, no. 2 (1978), 169.

[56] In his oft-forgotten seminal *Capitalism and Slavery*, Trinidadian historian Eric Williams extensively argued that racism emerged as a justification to the increasing use of slaves in the Atlantic commerce (Eric Williams, *Slavery and Capitalism*, [Chapel Hill: University of North Carolina Press, 1944]). According to this reading, it is capitalism that breeds racism (see esp. ibid, 7).

[57] Frantz Fanon, *The Wretched of the Earth*, trans. Richard Philcox (New York: Grove Press, 2004), 5.

white because you are rich."[58] Therefore, while it makes sense in the center of capitalist production to distinguish between structure and superstructure, in the colonies we have to emphasize that the superstructure is also the economic infrastructure, and thus "the cause is effect."[59]

In contrast to Quijano, we find in Fanon not only an analysis of the intertwinement between racial schemes and world capitalism but also an investigation of how the unconscious reproduces both aspects. Like Quijano, Frantz Fanon calls for decolonization, but he operates with a combination of Marxist and psychoanalytic insights in order to point out how even those who are oppressed can come to internalize the worldviews and ideological formations of their oppressors. Psychoanalysis helps us unpack some of those mechanisms, but needs to be decolonized in turn: Early European psychoanalysts like Sigmund Freud and Carl Gustav Jung thought they were reaching the depths of the infancy of humanity through their conceptual apparatus, but what they reached was only the depth of the European bourgeois mind,[60] as shown, for instance, by their emphasis on the universality of the Oedipus complex. Fanon, by comparison, was one of the first psychoanalysts to point out that the Oedipus complex does not exist in contexts such as the Antilles, thereby inviting reconsideration of the historically situated nature of a pillar of European psychoanalysis.

By adopting a truly global framework, Frantz Fanon thus pushes us to decolonize both the racial scheme and psychoanalysis itself. Since the capitalist division of labor is global, the unconscious patterns that sustain it must also be global. As early as 1963, Frantz observed that "the colonized, underdeveloped man is today a political creature in the most global sense of the term."[61] We must understand "global" in the dual sense of both the pervasiveness of the oppression and its scope. When we take the perspective of the colonized, of the entire international division of labor that the concept of race came to signify, we cannot but assume the entire globe as a framework of analysis. This does not mean that there exists a global racist unconscious that works in the same way and in the same manner all around the world. Despite the fact that Fanon used the notion of "collective unconscious" when analyzing the psychological effects of

---

[58] Ibid.

[59] Ibid.

[60] Frantz Fanon, *Black Skin, White Masks,* trans. Richard Philcox (New York: Grove Press, 2008), 165.

[61] Frantz Fanon, *The Wretched of the Earth*, 40.

the complex of the colonized, he also emphasized that the latter changed considerably from one context to the other,[62] including, for instance, the fact that for the Antilleans the complex of the colonized is much more important than the so-called Oedipus complex. Following Franz, we can therefore conclude that, in order to analyze the structures that perpetuate racism, we need both a potentially global framework, but also careful consideration of the specificity of each context. Thus, more than a "collective unconscious," we should speak of a transindividual unconscious that is intrinsically social in scope.

By combining Fanon's remarks about the pervasive nature of unconscious racial schemes and Quijano's thesis of a coloniality of power, Sylvia Wynter proposed the notion of a "coloniality of being."[63] By coloniality of being, we can understand the coloniality of the language we use to articulate being: if it is true that the unconscious is, as Fanon suggests, God gone astray in the flesh,[64] then we have to conclude that the unconscious cannot but speak about being through the coloniality of power. In Wynter's view, the struggle of our time is precisely the struggle against such a coloniality of being, centered as it is on what she calls the "overrepresentation of Man." As she writes: "the struggle of our new millennium will be one between the ongoing imperative of securing the well-being of our present ethnoclass (i.e., Western bourgeois) conception of the human, Man, which overrepresents itself as if it were the human itself, and that of securing the well-being and therefore the full cognitive and behavioral autonomy of the human species itself/ourselves."[65] Any attempt at unsettling the coloniality of power must call for the unsettling of this over-representation. It is this same over-representation that, as we have seen, has placed Man at the top of the *scala naturae*, according to the hierarchy man>woman>slave>animal>plant>inanimate life. Although

---

[62] Frantz Fanon, *Black Skin, White Masks,* 164–9.

[63] Sylvia Wynter, "Unsettling the Coloniality of Being / Power / Truth / Freedom: Towards the Human, After Man, Its Overrepresentation—An Argument," *CR: The New Centennial Review* 3(3).

[64] In a significant chapter on "'The Black Man and Language," Frantz Fanon observes that the more the black Antillean assimilates the French language, the whiter s/he gets, because though a language an entire world is acquired, and then he notes that "there is an extraordinary power in the possession of a language. Paul Valéry knew this, and described language as "'The god gone stray in the flesh" (Frantz Fanon, *Black Skin, White Masks,* 2). In light of the consequent argument in the rest of the book, we interpret this statement as referring to the power of unconscious racial schemes.

[65] Sylvia Wynter, "Unsettling the Coloniality of Being," 260.

Wynter does not explicitly refer to the idea of the *scala naturae*, she explores how Greco-western epistemology, with its emphasis on the opposition between the celestial realm of perfection (object of true knowledge) and the imperfect realm of the terrestrial (object of doxa) generated a conception of being centered on the idea of the "nonhomogeneity of substance."[66] It is the ontological dualism between the celestial and the terrestrial, skies and earth, that guaranteed such a hierarchy and in particular assured the privileged position of Man, as the only being endowed with immortal soul and thus able to participate in both realms. The Christian theory of the fall from paradise, and its language of "original sin" and "fallen flesh", reproposed in Christianized form the same idea of a "non-homogeneity of substance" that enabled Greek philosophers to first formulate the idea of *scala naturae*. And so, while woman is deemed inferior to Man, both are superior to the slave. In the Christian racial scheme, Black people are considered to be descendants of Noah's son Ham, whom he had cursed, condemning his progeny to be the servants to the descendants of the children of his other sons. In this Christian mythology, Black people's sin consists in being entrapped in the Adamic original sin, whereas in the secularized version of this story, what Wynter calls "Man 2," the superiority of Man over them is justified in terms of their irrationality.[67] With the shift from the *Christian civitas dei* to the *civitas secularis*, there is a permutation of the understanding of slaves and their place in the *scala naturae*: imprisoned in their original sin, as non-Christian, and imprisoned in their irrationality, as non-(or less than) human. The over-representation of Man went in tandem with the invention, labeling, and institutionalization of the inhabitants of Americas and Africa as physical referents of the irrational or sub-rational human other to be opposed to the civic-humanistic self-understanding of the (European) man.[68] Thus, whereas the "overrepresentation of Man 1" was ratio-centric, and still hybridly religio-secular, that of Man 2, as we see in Kant, becomes purely secular and biocentric.[69] In both cases, the over-representation of Man is strictly dependent on the de-humanization of slaves and people of color,

---

[66] Ibid, 274.
[67] Ibid, 307.
[68] Ibid, 282.
[69] Ibid.

who could at best aspire to the role of "*homunculi,*" the "less than human," to use the expression that Ginés de Sepúlveda employed to classify the Indigenous people of the Americas.[70]

In a significant passage from a fictitious dialogue, Sepúlveda wrote:

> Leopoldo is asked to compare the Spaniards with the Indians, who in prudence, wisdom (*ingenium*), every virtue and humanity are as inferior to the Spaniards as *children are to adults, women are to men, the savage and ferocious to the gentle, the grossly intemperate to the continent and temperate and finally, I shall say, almost as monkeys are to men.* [...] 'Compare the gifts of magnanimity, temperance, humanity and religion of these men', continues Democrates, 'with those *homunculi* [i.e., the Indians] in whom hardly a vestige of humanity remains.[71]

The passage illustrates how the idea of a *scala naturae* is reproduced through an ontological hierarchy based on the different level of "maturity" that places Man at the top, followed by "children," "women," "savages," and finally animals. The Indigenous people are described as *homunculi* because they are perceived as less than human, as inferior as "monkeys to men," and so placed somewhere between human and animals.

Note that the construction of the dichotomy between "civilized" *versus* "savages" also went hand in hand with the inferiorization of both women and animals, which explains why, according to Maria Lugones, the rise of the coloniality of power is inseparable from the coloniality of gender, that is from the emergence of the "modern/colonial gender system."[72] The separation of race, class, gender, and sexuality is a creation of colonial modernity itself, with its categorial and hierarchical logic.[73] In focusing on the novelty represented by the modern/colonial gender system, Lugones did not simply propose adding a gendered reading to colonial modernity, but rather emphasized how the "colonial imposition of gender cuts across questions of ecology, economics, government, relations with the spirit world, and knowledge, as well as across everyday practices that either habituate us to take care of the world or to destroy it."[74] Gender is

---

[70] Ibid, 283. Translation from Latin ours.
[71] (Quoted, emphasis ours) ibid.
[72] Maria Lugones, "Towards a Decolonial Feminism," *Hypatia* 25(4).
[73] Ibid, 742.
[74] Ibid.

not something to be added to an analysis of the modern/colonial system, but is a category that is constitutive of the system from its beginning.

Not all cultures "do" gender, nor do they do it in the familiar binary that opposes male to female. If we analyze the literature exploring pre-colonial gender systems in areas such as Africa, Asia, and the Americas, the first striking datum that emerges is indeed that, from the point of view of many of those cultures, gender was a colonial imposition.[75] This does not mean that those cultures did not have any way to articulate sexual differences, nor that there was no patriarchy before colonialism. It simply means that a binary gender system was not as hegemonic as it is today. The three features that, in Maria Lugones' analysis, characterize this system are: 1) the reduction of sexes to biological dimorphism; 2) compulsory heterosexuality; and 3) patriarchy. All three could be interpreted as different faces of the same coin: The reason gender is understood in binary terms is because it maps gender onto reproduction, thereby also making heterosexuality not just a possible sexual orientation among others, but the norm, one in which men are literally "on top." The feminine, weak, sexually passive woman is thus opposed to the masculine, strong, sexually aggressive man.

This does not mean that such gender norms are imposed throughout the spectrum: Maria distinguishes between the "light" and the "dark" side of the "modern/colonial" gender system, where the terms "light" and "dark," in our reading, hints at skin color, and thus at the intersection of racial and gender axes of oppression. Whereas the "light" side is the one that is structured around gender dimorphism and is hegemonic, those on the "dark side" escape this dichotomy. For instance, Black women in the US are not perceived as "weak" and "sexually passive": As the pervasiveness of the stereotypes inherited from slavery shows, Black women are more often perceived as strong, apt to hard work, and viewed as either sexually aggressive or as wet nurses.[76] The two stereotypes of the "mammy," agent of care work in white homes, and the "jezebel," the sexually insatiable Black woman, represent two sides of a spectrum of controlling images that circulate in the North American imaginary and which place Black women firmly on the dark side of the "modern/colonial gender system." These two

---

[75] Maria Lugones, "The Coloniality of Gender," in *The Palgrave Handbook of Gender and Development*, ed. Wendy Harcourt (New York: Palgrave Macmillan, 2016).
[76] Patricia Hill Collins, *Black Feminist Thought: Knowledge, Consciousness, and the Politics of Empowerment* (New York: Routledge, 2000), 83–4.

imaginaries, albeit apparently opposed, actually reinforce each other, as we have seen in the story of Julia Pastrana: The exhibition of the "Bear Woman," "the Nondescript," with her thick hair, strength, and aggressivity, works as the colonial fetish, as the abject that structures and unconsciously reproduces the white hegemonic understanding of femininity: hairless, weak, docile.

The reason why capitalism needs gender is easy to see. As Marxist feminists have been pointing out for quite some time, besides a racialized division of labor, capitalism also needs a *gendered* division of labor. To put it bluntly, capitalism needs women to believe that they are fulfilling their very nature when they cook dinner or wash their children's clothes. Along with the extraction of surplus value from waged productive labor, capitalism also relies on the extraction of free reproductive labor, that is, on the performance of care work which is excluded from the wage system because it is denied the status of proper work.[77] For the Black women working in white households, the coloniality of power is the "coloniality of gender." With this term, Lugones emphasizes that the binary division "man/woman" and the classification of bodies according to their racial belonging were fused in the practices of colonial domination of Indigenous territories and cannot be separated.[78] Again, this does not mean that sexual difference did not exist before colonialism. It simply means that the dimorphic gender organization was not as hegemonic as it became with colonialism and has continued to be into the twenty-first century. Lugones' work is in line with a quite substantial amount of scholarly work devoted to showing that gender roles among Indigenous nations were more flexible and variegated before the advent of European settlers. Very often, sexualities that escaped the gender dimorphism were valued and, in some contexts, even highly praised, while a number of Native American tribes adopted matrilineal inheritance and matrilocal culture as their norm, rather than as the exception.[79] The point here is not to romanticize the past, and certainly not to retrieve the old colonial myth of a

---

[77] For instance, Maria Mies speaks of a form of "superexploitation" because, in contrast with the exploitation of waged labor, women's work very often takes place through the denial of the status of work to their labor (Maria Mies, *Patriarchy and Accumulation on a World Scale: Women in the International Division of Labour* [London: Zed Books, 1986], 48).

[78] Maria Lugones, "The Coloniality of Gender," 31.

[79] Besides Lugones' "The Coloniality of Gender," which relies on scholarly historical accounts, we find it also illuminating to see that many political texts and petitions were produced by Native American women early on, proving that they did not need to ask for the permission to intervene in political affairs, but simply voiced their political concerns. See Cherokee Women's Councils, "'Petitions to the Cherokee National Council'", in Feminist Manifestos: A Global Documentary Reader, ed. Penny A. Weiss (New York: New York University Press, 2018), 47–50.

supposed state of nature, where sex and gender fluidity flourished, but to emphasize the historically situated nature of the contemporary modern/colonial gender system and the fact that we cannot understand the coloniality of power without taking into account the coloniality of gender. As Maria Lugones puts it, while reflecting the modern biological and thus binary understanding of gender roles, Aníbal Quijano paradoxically followed the Eurocentric understanding of gender when he reduced it to sex, and thus overlooked the fact that the naturalizing of "sexual differences" is yet another product of the modern use of science that Quijano points out in the case of "race."[80] It is important to remember that not all different traditions correct and normalize intersex people, and thus it is as crucial to ask how sexual dimorphism served, and serves, Eurocentric global capitalist domination/exploitation.[81]

Following Lugones, we argue that it is pivotal to revisit Quijano's thesis on the coloniality of power in order to analyze what she calls "the modern/colonial gender system."[82] In doing so, Lugone combines Quijano's reading of global capitalism with an intersectional feminist's emphasis on the impossibility of separating gender from race, because it is only at this intersection that the specific position of women of color emerges. As we read in *Towards a Decolonial Feminism*:

> The gender system is not just hierarchical but racially differentiated, and the racial differentiation denies humanity and thus gender to the colonized. Irene Silverblatt, Carolyn Dean, Maria Esther Pozo, Pamela Calla and Nina Laurie, Sylvia Marcos, Paula Gunn Allen, Leslie Marmon Silko, Felipe Guaman Poma de Ayala, and Oyèrónkẹ́ Oyěwùmí,[83] among others, enable me to affirm that gender is a colonial

---

[80] Maria Lugones, "The Coloniality of Gender," 21.

[81] Ibid.

[82] Ibid, 14. To further prove Lugones' point, we could observe that François Bernier's "A New Division of the Earth" (in Robert Bernasconi and Tommy Lee Lott, *The Idea of Race*) 1–4, which was originally published in 1684 and which is often referred to as the first text that proposes classifying people according to the concept of race (see the editors' note on 1), is also constructed according to the gender binary of men versus women. After classifying different human groups according to their skin color and other physical traits such as eye shape or hair texture, Bernier suddenly moves on to women, presenting them as a separate category, and, significantly enough, one according to which the consideration of beauty and desirability trump all other criteria for classification (ibid, 3–4).

[83] Irene Silverblatt, *Taller de historia oral Andina: La Mujer Andina en la historia* (Chukiyawu: Ediciones del THOA, 1990), and *Moon, Sun, and Witches* (Princeton: Princeton University

imposition, not just as it imposes itself on life as lived in tune with cosmologies incompatible with the modern logic of dichotomies, but also that inhabitations of worlds understood, constructed, and in accordance with such cosmologies animated the self-among-others in resistance from and at the extreme tension of the colonial difference. The long process of subjectification of the colonized toward adoption/ internalization of the men/women dichotomy as a normative construction of the social—a mark of civilization, citizenship, and membership in civil society—was and is constantly renewed. It is met in the flesh over and over by oppositional responses and lived as sensical in alternative, resistant socialities at the colonial difference.[84]

Although the unconscious internalization and (re)production of the modern/colonial gender system is an ongoing process, resistance is also equally present. For instance, in her groundbreaking *The Invention of Women*, Oyèrónké Oyěwùmí, explores the Yoruba African pre-colonial cultures in which gender was not a criteria for the ordering of social life, so much so that translating terms such as *obinrin* and *okunrin* as "female/ woman" and "male/man" is not just a mistranslation, but also an act of cultural imperialism since those two categories were neither binarily opposed nor hierarchical.[85] After colonization, "women" came to mean bodies who do not have a penis, who do not have power, and whose role is defined in relation to men, but none of these features applied to Yoruba *obinrin* prior to colonization.[86] Consequently, whereas the in the West the

Press, 1998); Carolyn Dean, "Andean Androgyny and the Making of Men," in *Gender in Pre-Hispanic America*, ed. Cecilia Klein (Washington D.C.: Dumbarton Oaks Publications, 2001); Pamela Calla and Nina Laurie, "Desarrollo, poscolonialismo y teoría geográfica política," in *Las displicencias de genera en los cruces del siglo pasado al nuevo milenio en los Andes*, eds. Nina Laurie and Maria Esther Pozo (Cochabamba, Bolivia: CESU-UMSS, 2006); Sylvia Marcos, *Taken From the Lips: Gender and Eras in Mesoamerican Religions* (Leiden and Boston: Brill, 2006); Paula Gunn Allen, *The Sacred Hoop: Recovering the Feminine in American Indian Traditions* (Boston: Beacon Press, 1992); Leslie Marmon Silko, *Ceremony* (New York: Penguin Books, 2006); Felipe Guaman Poma de Ayala, *The First New Chronicle and Good Government: On the History of the World and the Incas Up to 1615* (Austin: University of Texas Press, 2009); Oyèrónké Oyěwùmí, *The Invention of Women: Making an African Sense of Western Gender Discourses* (Minneapolis: University of Minnesota Press, 1997).
[84] Maria Lugones, "Towards a Decolonial Feminism," 748.
[85] Oyèrónké Oyěwùmí, *The Invention of Women*, 32–3.
[86] Ibid, 34.

challenge of feminism is how to question gender stereotypes and move towards an unsexed humanity, for the Yoruba *obinrin*, the challenge is obviously different because, at certain levels and in some areas, the notion of an "unsexed humanity" is a lived experience, a space of resistance that exists next to the reality of separated and hierarchical sexes imposed during the colonial times.[87]

Lugoness's Oyěwùmí's analysis not to idealize the past, but rather to point to sites of resistance to the modern/colonial gender system, and thus also to the different agendas that different types of feminisms across the globe may have. For the Yoruba *obinrin*, or "anafemales," as Oyěwùmí translates it into English, colonization meant a threefold process of inferiorization: as colonized, as women and, most of the time, also as workers excluded from the waged labor circuit created by the colonizers. Whereas men were often employed as waged workers, women remained most of the time in charge of the reproductive labour, including the subsistence work, which provides food for the family, but not value for the market economy. This, in turn, contributes to their relegation to an inferior status.

Thus, for Oyèrónkẹ, the coloniality of power is inseparable from the coloniality of gender: "The last five centuries, described as the age of modernity, have been defined by a number of historical processes including the Atlantic Slave Trade and attendant institutions of slavery, and European colonization of Africa, Asia, and Latin America. The idea of modernity evokes the development of capitalism and industrialization, as well as the establishment of nation states and the growth of regional disparities in the World system. The period has witnessed a host of social and cultural transformations. Significantly, gender and racial categories emerged during this epoch as two fundamental axes along which people were exploited and societies stratified."[88]

The development of the modern/colonial gender system, from the point of view of the Yoruba cultures, happened through a multifaceted process, in which race was tied to gender. Among the institutions mentioned by Oyěwùmí, three are crucial for our analysis: 1) the imposition of the European state system; 2) the bio-logic that sustains

---

[87] Ibid, 156.
[88] Oyèrónkẹ Oyěwùmí, "Conceptualizing Gender: Eurocentric Foundations of Feminist Concepts and the Challenge of African Epistemologies," *Jenda: A Journal of Culture and African Women Studies* 2, no. 1, 1.

both race and gender in the West; and 3) oculocentrism. The state, understood as a firm dominion over a territory and characterized by the monopoly of legitimate coercion, implied, among other things, a process of mapping and controlling of the gender of its subjects. And since gender, according to the Western bio-logic, is reduced to biological sex, the imposition of the state system on the African continent also meant the introduction of a form of biopolitics that was unprecedented in pre-colonial times. It is the state that enables the mapping, monitoring, and regulating its subjects' gender in a systematic and thorough way, through a formidable apparatus of identity papers, hospitals, schools, and police records, as well as statistics. Once gender is assigned—and most of the time this happens on the basis of genitals (and a combination of genitals and chromosomes)—a person carries this denomination with them for their entire life. But this emphasis on sight reflects a form of somatocentrism and oculocentrism that, for Oyèrónkẹ, is another Western import of colonization.[89] Before the advent of the European colonizers, the Yoruba cultures had a different system of social organization that valued age as the major criterion for social hierarchy, not skin color or gender.

To understand how colonization worked for Yoruba *obinrin*, it is necessary to embark on a critique of the Eurocentric foundations of feminist concepts. To begin with, there is the idea of gender as an autonomous concept and sphere of oppression. This view, and even the very possibility of conceiving gender as separate from other sources of oppression, is for Oyèwùmí rooted in a Eurocentric approach that projects worldwide concepts and assumptions that are only valid for the (European) gendered mononuclear family.[90] First, there is the assumption that the family is an institution necessarily gendered. That is a typical Eurocentric move, because in the African continent not all families are gendered, and marriage, as a social institution, is not always about gender.[91] Second, there is the idea that one can separate gender from race and class: "Because race and class are not normally variable in the family, it makes sense that white feminism, which is trapped in the family, does not see race or class."[92] And, we can add, even when it sees race and class,

---

[89] Oyèrónkẹ Oyèwùmí, *The Invention of Women*, 3.
[90] Oyèrónkẹ Oyèwùmí, "Conceptualizing Gender," 8.
[91] Ifi Amadiume's *Male Daughters, Female Husbands: Gender and Sex in an African Society* (London: Zed Books, 1987) also emphasizes that, in Africa, marriage as a social institution is not always about gender, as white feminist theory presupposes.
[92] Oyèrónkẹ Oyèwùmí, "Conceptualizing Gender," 3.

white feminism often conceives them as separate from gender, as a racial perspective to be added to gender, and that is where the Eurocentric bias comes in, again projecting the nuclear gendered family worldwide, implicitly turning it into an universal mode of female oppression. As Oyèrónkẹ writes: "The nuclear family, however, is a specifically Euro/American form; it is not universal. More specifically, the nuclear family remains an alien form in Africa despite its promotion by both the colonial and neocolonial state, international (under)development agencies, feminist organizations, contemporary nongovernmental organizations (NGOs) among others."[93]

The degree to which the mononuclear family still remains alien to Africa changes from one location to another, both spatially and temporally, given that Africa itself is not a unified whole, but rather an extremely varied space. But Oyěwùmí's general point about how much white feminism is bound up in the concept of the nuclear family is still valid. Mainstream feminism generally presupposes that the family is gendered, that it is centered on the sexual division of labor according to the binary "male/female," and that it is inseparable from the institution of private property, with its "spatial configuration of the nuclear family household as an isolated space."[94] But none of these assumptions is universally applicable to the African continent. For Oyěwùmí, even common expressions such as "single mother" remain alien to an African perspective, centered as they are on co-belonging and the clan structure: For her, a mother is never, by definition, single. A mother can only be said to be "single" if we presuppose that maternity needs the complement of a heterosexual relationship. It is only by implicitly presupposing that the nuclear family is a universal that a woman with her children can be said to be "single." In sum, as Oyèrónkẹ puts it with a very useful metaphor, the woman at the heart of much white feminist theory is like a snail, who carries the household wherever she goes.[95]

It is because when we say "woman" we mean not just the creature inside the shell, but also the whole apparatus around her, that there have been forms of feminism unable to perceive those factors that usually do not vary in the (European) family, that is race and class. Both Lugones

---

[93] Ibid, 2.
[94] Ibid.
[95] Ibid.

and Oyěwùmí wrote in the last few decades, but the same intuition can be found in other feminist thinkers from earlier generations. Among these, we should remember the already mentioned He Zhen, an anarchafeminist writer of Chinese origin, who flew to Tokyo at the beginning of the twentieth century, where she worked relentlessly on the circulation of anarchist, socialist, and feminist ideals until her death. As a side remark, notice that whereas He Zhen is mainly known by this name that combines her first name with the patrilinear family name, in her published works, she preferred to sign her name as He-Yin Zhen, so as to include her mother's maiden name: From this point on, that is how we will refer to her.[96] For He-Yin Zhen, who changed her name as a political gesture, it is very clear that the liberation of women can only be achieved by the abolition of all social hierarchies, and thus that gender is inseparable from race and class. As mentioned in previous chapters, in her seminal essay *On the Question of Women's Liberation* (1907),[97] she criticized Western feminists who saw the emancipation of women as simply the attainment of positions of wealth and power that would put them on par with men. As she wrote:

My understanding of gender equality (*nannü pingdeng*) implies equality among all human beings, which refers to the prospect of not only men no longer oppressing women but also men no longer oppressed by other men and women no longer oppressed by other women. [...] As for the idea of equal division of power between men and women, most people seem to believe that since there are power holders among men, there should be among women as well. But did such powerful female sovereigns as Queen Victoria of the British Empire or Empress Lu Zhi and Empress Wu Zeitan in the dynastic history of China ever bring the slightest benefits to the majority of women? A minority of women holding power is hardly sufficient to save the majority of them.[98]

---

[96] Lydia H. Liu, Rebecca E. Karl, and Dorothy Ko (eds.), *The Birth of Chinese Feminism: Essential Texts in Transnational Feminism* (New York: Columbia University Press, 2013), 10.
[97] He Zhen (also known as He-Yin Zhen), "On the Question of Women's Liberation," in *The Birth of Chinese Feminism: Essential Texts in Transnational Theory*, eds. Lydia H. Liu, Rebecca E. Karl, and Dorothy Ko (New York: Columbia University Press, 2013).
[98] Ibid, 66.

For He-Yin Zhen, thus, being a woman (*nüxing*) or a men (*nanxing*) is not a question of nature, of a pregiven identity, but is rather a series of social relations stratified over time.[99] In order to understand the operation she is doing here, we need to consider the linguistic innovation and operation she did with the concept of *nannü*. Although the concept of *nannü* is now usually translated as indicating the difference between male/man (*nan*) and female/woman (*nü*), and thus as "gender," for He-Yin the term *nannü* had a much broader meaning, indicating all hierarchies included in social relations: *nannü* is a "mostly untranslatable conceptual totality" that signifies not only gendered social relations between men and women, but also, much more broadly, "the relationship of past to the present, of China to the rest of the world, of politics to justice, of law and ritual to gendered forms of knowledge, interaction and social organization."[100] In sum, we could say that *nannü* is far from meaning the woman-snail in her household of white feminism and is used instead by He-Yin Zhen to mean the foundation of all patriarchal abstractions and marking of differences, which include much more than what we tend to associate with the concept of gender.[101] Because she conceives of *nannü* in such broad terms, far removed from the biological reductionism we are so used to, she can argue that the liberation of women means no more oppressed women and no more oppressed me. As we read in her *The Feminist Manifesto* (1907):

By 'men' (*nanxing*) and 'women' (*nüxing*) we are not speaking of 'nature', as each is but the outcome of differing social customs and education. If sons and daughters are treated equally, raised and educated in the same manner, then the responsibilities assumed by men and women will surely be equal. When that happens, the nouns 'men' and 'women' would no longer be necessary. This is ultimately 'the equality of men and women' of which we speak.[102]

---

[99] On this point, see in particular her "The Feminist Manifesto," in *The Birth of Chinese Feminism: Essential Texts in Transnational Theory*, eds. Lydia H. Liu, Rebecca E. Karl, and Dorothy Ko (New York: Columbia University Press, 2013), 184.
[100] *The Birth of Chinese Feminism: Essential Texts in Transnational Theory*, eds. Lydia H. Liu, Rebecca E. Karl, and Dorothy Ko (New York: Columbia University Press, 2013), 10.
[101] Ibid, 11.
[102] He Zhen, "The Feminist Manifesto," 184.

We have quoted He-Yin Zhen's understanding of *nannü* not only because it shows how Western understanding of gender tends to segregate what in other traditions goes together, but also because she develops her thesis in a clear anarchafeminist direction. The liberation of women cannot mean the liberation of a few bodies which have been assigned the "female sex" at birth: it means the liberation of all human beings from hierarchical relationship of domination and exploitation. Far from meaning that women should come to occupy the place reserved to men, liberation of women means reaching a society in which nouns like "men" and "women" are no longer necessary, because the asymmetries of power and the oppressive social relations that they denote would no longer exist. While Lugones does not quote He-Yin, we believe they fundamentally agree on what feminism means: A society in which the very words "men" and "women" are no longer necessary, and thus a society that has overcome the "coloniality of gender."[103] From the point of view of each, the separation of gender, race, and class is a creation of Western modernity itself, and one that must be resisted and overcome.

It may seem strange to add the case of a Chinese feminist writer, given that Chinese patriarchal relations certainly pre-dated European colonialism. And yet, it is important to hear her voice, because although the coloniality of gender does not mean in this instance the introduction of patriarchy, colonialism re-signified that institution in light of the new "coloniality of power" inaugurated by global, Eurocentric capitalism. As we will see in the following chapter, the coloniality of gender still reverberates in places like China today, as is attested by the many examples of processes of subjectification that merge race and gender, and whereby individual "women" come into being. For instance, Western ideals of beauty and femininity are being reproduced in China through practices such as plastic surgery and the adoption of Western fashions and lifestyles. There is also a class dimension to this process, as not everybody can afford the costs of a double eyelid operation (blepharoplasty) that makes one's face look more Western,[104] thereby confirming once again that

---

[103] Maria Lugones, "Towards a Decolonial Feminism," 745–7.
[104] According to *Glamour* magazine, millions of Chinese girls born after 1990 have undergone double eyelid surgery to enhance their career chances. See: https://www.glamourmagazine.co.uk/article/double-eyelid-surgery-china (accessed on March 25, 2021). According to a report, in 2018 alone 22 million Chinese citizens underwent cosmetic procedures, over half of them (54 percent) were under the age of twenty-eight. One of the

nannü is not just an issue concerning bodies that have been assigned "female" at birth, but a much wider social relation that is inseparable from all other social hierarchies.

We will come back to this issue in the following chapter. For now, notice how adopting the lens of the "coloniality of gender" does not mean affirming that a European-precolonial understanding of gender has been exported worldwide. Affirming this would mean falling into a form of cultural imperialism that does not recognize the disparities that existed between different traditions, histories, and social arrangements before the advent of European colonization, and which, we should not forget, produced both the colonizers and the colonized, and cannot therefore be reduced to a sheer imposition of the colonizers' views worldwide. It rather means emphasizing how the "light" and the "dark" sides of the modern/colonial gender system have constituted themselves reciprocally, thereby reinforcing each other. To begin with, the mononuclear family, is a specifically modern institution even in Europe, where, as we will see, its emergence is inseparable from a capitalist mode of (re)production centered on market economy and private property.

Far from falling into a form of nativism, or romanticization of the past, Maria Lugones invites us to a collaborative research and educational project aimed at unpacking the different configurations of the colonial/modern gender system, an invitation "to uncover collaboration, and to call each other to reject it in its various guises as we recommit to communal integrity in a liberatory direction."[105] For Lugones, this is the direction we need for a "decolonial feminism," defined here as "the possibility of overcoming the coloniality of gender."[106]

Decolonial feminism calls for engaging with epistemologies and traditions different from the West not as a form of particularism to embrace and idealize, but rather as a liminal space from which one can perceive the processes of subjectification enacted by the coloniality of gender.[107] Lugones' referents include Native American traditions in both

---

reasons most often reported for this is the desire of looking like their own doctored social media images: As social media provide more and more filters to enhance one's appearance, some people feel compelled to keep up the pretense with make-up; when that is not enough, surgery follows. See https://asiamedia.lmu.edu/2019/08/01/china-plastic-surgery-industry-booms-as-millions-of-gen-zs-go-under-the-knife/ (accessed March 25, 2021).

[105] Maria Lugones, "The Coloniality of Gender," 32.

[106] Maria Lugones, "Towards a Decolonial Feminism," 747.

[107] Ibid, 753.

anglophone and Latin America, a particularly vital consideration for US scholars. Mainstream critical theory tends to marginalize Native American voices, presenting their knowledge as example of "Indigenous" knowledge perhaps to be admired, but rarely to be included in our theoretical apparatuses.[108] Although the creation of "Ethnic Studies Departments" in the United States has helped gather scholarship produced by the different Native American tribes, the very categorization of that body of knowledge as "Ethnic Studies" reinforces their exclusion from the circuit of "knowledge," such as produced in, say, "Politics" or "Philosophy Departments," where Native American theories are hardly ever represented and discussed. By comparison, knowledge produced by other specific groups, such as French philosophers of the seventeenth or twentieth centuries, is never labeled "Ethnic" but simply presented as (philosophical) knowledge itself. This epistemic genocide of Native Americans instills and perpetrates the idea that white people of Caucasian descent are not an "ethnic group," but merely the norm of knowledge production, and so we see here how much the "coloniality of power" impacts the coloniality of knowledge production. Hence the importance, particularly from our perspective, to engage with Native American gender theories not as examples of native studies, but as sources of gender theory and philosophy.

To begin with, a cautionary remark is needed: Native American tribes are so many and so diverse that speaking about their way to approach gender and sexualities, as if this was a discrete entity, would mean adopting another form of colonial gaze. However, there is agreement in the literature that most Native American tribes had a more fluid gender organization, as attested by the proliferation of gender terms in the different languages. In pre-contact Indigenous communities in North America, gender played an important role in defining social structures and sociocultural responsibilities. For instance, responsibilities for land, water, plants, and animals were traditionally gendered: In some

---

[108] The construction of the category of "indigenous" is inseparable from the colonial gaze, so rather than understanding "indigeneity" as synonymous of a given individuality, we will use this term as connected to land dispossession. As we have seen, Kim TallBear invited us to understand indigeneity in terms of dispossession, connection to ancestors, and networks of tribal belonging (Kim TallBear, "Genomic Articulations of Indigeneity," 510;). For a more general discussion, see also Kim TallBear, *Native American DNA: Tribal Belonging and the False Promise of Genetic Science*, Minneapolis: University of Minnesota Press, 2013.

Indigenous communities, women were responsible for managing and harvesting plants and engaging in agricultural activities, and men responsible for hunting and/or fishing activities.[109] These roles, however, were not assigned according to a bio-logic. In contrast to the modern/colonial gender system, gender in these communities was not understood primarily in biological terms and tribal gender roles were assigned "on the basis of proclivity, inclination, and temperament."[110] For instance, "the Yuma had a tradition of gender designation based on dreams; a female who dreamed of weapons became a male for all practical purposes."[111]

The fact that gender was not strictly mapped on biological dimorphism also led to a much more flexible attitude towards different sexual orientations and gender embodiments than the general compulsory heterosexuality that Lugones identifies as a crucial ingredient of the "coloniality of gender." Among the eighty-eight tribes that recognized homosexuality, many did so in positive terms, including the Apache, Navajo, Winnebago, Cheyenne, Pima, Crow, Shoshoni, Paiute, Osage, Acoma, Zuni, Sioux, Pawnee, Choctaw, Creek, Seminole, Illinois, Mohave, Shasta, Aleut, Sac and Fox, Iowa, Kansa, Yuma, Aztec, Tlingit, Maya, Naskapi, Ponca, Maricopa, Lamath, Quinault, Yuki, Chilula, and Kamia.[112] Gender-variant individuals were also regarded positively. Every nation had its own specific term, but in the last few decades the term "third gender"[113] has become a widespread umbrella term to denote what in the West are called LGBTQI+ people. The term has been introduced to replace the old term "berdache," which derived from the colonial times, when used by European colonizers to denote individuals who did not fit the gender binary.[114] "Third gender" must not be understood in strictly numerical terms, as if denoting a third gender after the first two, but rather as an open possibility, suggesting combinations other than the men *versus* women dichotomy.

---

[109] Kirsten Vinyeta, Kyle P. Whyte, and Kathy Lynn, "Indigenous Masculinities in a Changing Climate: Vulnerability and Resilience in the United States," in *Men, Masculinities and Disaster*, eds. Eliane Enarson and Bob Pease (London: Routledge, 2016), 140.

[110] Paula Gunn Allen, *The Sacred Hoop*, 196.

[111] Ibid.

[112] Maria Lugones, "The Coloniality of Gender," 26.

[113] Michael J. Horswell, "Toward an Andean Theory of Ritual Same-Sex Sexuality and Third-gender Subjectivity," in *Infamous Desire: Male Homosexuality in Colonial Latina America*, ed. Pete Sigal (Chicago: University of Chicago Press, 2003), 27.

[114] Robert Cremins, "Is there a political myth of settler homosexuality?", MA Thesis Submitted to the Philosophy Department of the New School (2019).

Although the settler-colonial myth of "the vanishing Indian" often suggests the idea that those subjectivities have been erased and/or completely assimilated to the modern/colonial gender system,[115] that is far from true. Harlan Pruden and Se-ah-dom Edmo, in their presentation at the National Congress of American Indians (NCAI), helpfully provided a map of terms still in use to describe "two-spirited people": Among them, the Aleut terms *Ayagigux'* and *Tayagigux'* denote what can be translated as a "man transformed into a woman" and a "woman transformed into a man"; the Cherokee *nudale asgaya* and *nudale agehya* denote a "different man" and a "different woman," whereas the term *asegi* is a gender-variant person and can be assigned to both male and females. The Cree language has six different terms to mean respectively "a man dressed as a woman" (*napêw iskwêwisêhot*), "a woman dressed like a man" (*iskwêw ka napêwayat*), "a man dressed/living/accepted as a woman" (*ayahkwêw*), "a woman dressed/living/accepted as a man" (*înahpîkasoht*), "a fake woman" (*iskwêhkân*) and a "fake man" (*napêhkân*). (The last two terms are literal translations from Cree language but not considered as negatively as the translations may suggest.) The Ojibwa *agokwa* literally means a "man-woman," *Okitcitakwe* means "warrior woman"; and finally the Otoe and Kansa word *mixo'ge*, "instructed by the moon," points to the notion that the moon itself can be a source of gender-fluid identifications.[116] These are only some of the examples of tribe-specific names still used to denote subjectivities other than those captured by the male/female binary, thus attesting to the ongoing resistance to the coloniality of gender, and the flexibility and openness of other possible languages of gender.

Furthermore, many tribes have been—and some still are—gynecratic, granting much more power to women than is found in Western patriarchy. Among these were the Susquehanna, Hurons, Iroquois, Cherokee, Pueblo, Navajo, Narragansett, Coastal Algonkians, and Montagnais.[117] Quoting these examples is not meant to provide simply a "multicultural add-on" to our gender inventory, let alone be mere celebration of diversity. Rather, these communities provide a lens through which we can examine and provincialize our Eurocentric toolboxes and thus more aptly perceive

[115] Paula Gunn Allen, *The Sacred Hoop,* 199.
[116] For a much longer list of "two-spirit" names, see https://www.ncai.org/policy-research-center/initiatives/Pruden-Edmo_TwoSpiritPeople.pdf (accessed on February 10, 2021)
[117] Maria Lugones, "The Coloniality of Gender," 26.

how individualities are shaped by the supra-individual coloniality of gender.

Taking as her starting point the Keres Indians of the Laguna Pueblo, Paula Gunn Allen asks how a tendentially egalitarian gynecratic system can be progressively transformed into a hierarchical and patriarchal one. Gunn Allen notes the centrality of the spiritual in all aspects of Indian life and how creation myths shape different types of subjectivity through their ritual re-enactment. A comparison between gynecratic creation myths and patriarchal ones can be illuminating: Gynecratic tribes shared the belief that "the primary potency in the universe was female," and that precept authorized and shaped tribal activities.[118] Old Spider Woman, Serpent Woman, Corn Woman, and Thought Woman are examples of iconic female creators recurring, most often in the plural, within Keres creation myths.[119] By replacing powerful and multiple female symbols with one supreme male creator, as the colonizers did through the imposition of Christianity, not only did they destroy the spiritual autonomy of those tribes, but they also forcibly introduced patriarchal values and an individualistic worldview. The process of transforming an egalitarian and gynecratic system into a hierarchical and patriarchal one involves replacing female-centered myths with male-centered ones and also destroying the gynecratic institutions within each tribe, in particular the replacement of the clan structure with the mononuclear family: Female clan heads were replaced by male officials, eradicating the psychic and spiritual net of gynecratic institutions.[120]

An example of the progressive internalization of patriarchal values and the settler mentality can be found in a comparative reading of a series of nineteenth-century petitions by the Cherokee Women's Council. Cherokee women had their own gynecratic institutions and were at the time more empowered than their European counterparts, as shown by the way they simply used their authority to voice their political ideals rather than asking for them to be recognized. However, a comparative reading of texts of March 2, 1817, June 30, 1818, and October 17, 1821, shows how Cherokee women increasingly internalized the "civilizational" narrative, along with the Christian language of the Great Father.[121] Having

---

[118] Paula Gunn Allen, *The Sacred Hoop*, 24.

[119] Ibid, 14–18.

[120] Ibid, 41.

[121] Cherokee Women's Councils, "'Petitions to the Cherokee National Council.' Cherokee Lands; May 2, 1817, June 30, 1818, and October 17, 1821," 47–50.

had to adopt the customs and social habits of the Europeans, they started to speak of the pre-colonial period as a time in which they still lived in a state of nature,[122] thereby implicitly recasting themselves as savages. The question of the land and of land-based feminine authority is also central to these documents. The process of destruction of gynecratic institutions and imposition of patriarchy was made possible by the land dispossession, as Native Americans found themselves pushed off their lands, and thus deprived of their economic livelihood; they were forced to curtail or end altogether pursuits on which their ritual system, philosophy, and subsistence had depended hitherto. Now dependent on white institutions for their survival, tribal systems could ill afford gynocracy when patriarchy—that is, survival—requires male dominance.[123] Thus, it is not just creation myths that were at stake here, but an entire philosophy based on a different material relationship to the land and the elements: And so, again, from the perspective of a transindividual philosophy, the two cannot be separated.

For the Keres gynecratic creation myth, "in the beginning was thought and her name was woman."[124] This is very different from the Christian creation myth, where, as we have seen, "at the beginning was the word (*logos*), and the word (*logos*) was God." In the Keres creation myth, there is thinking and womanhood, and thus endless creativity, to be transmitted orally, whereas in the Christian creation myth we have a *word* by a male God that is already written, and, as such, can be transmitted as a set canon: We tend to forget that as a word, the "Bible" literally means the "book." Hence, as we have seen, in the Christian monotheism, the beginning (*archē*) is also the principle (*logos*) and the command (*archein*). Thus, an orally transmitted spirituality of the thought-woman *versus* the written word of a male God, who, even when manifested as a trinity, does not allow any space for fully divine femininity, as it unfolds "In the name of the Father, the Son and the Holy Ghost."

These two alternative creation myths also ground two different understandings of temporality: the cyclical time of the Keres mythology *versus* the linear time of Christianity, in which the becoming human of (the male) God is the referent point of human history. We live in this Christian linear understanding of time, and thus literally in the time

---

[122] Ibid, 49.
[123] Paula Gunn Allen, *The Sacred Hoop*, 42.
[124] Ibid, 42.

inaugurated by the immaculate birth of Christ, which is very different from the gynecratic temporality described by Gunn Allen. This alternative understanding of time is the result of a different relationship to the land as, for most Native American tribes, land was considered part of the collective livelihood, not as private property to be occupied and exploited. The linear understanding of time, projected towards an infinite future, is well adapted to an economic system predicated upon the endless expansion of profit, which explains why capitalism absorbed and re-signified Christian linear time, but did not fit well with the lives of tribes following seasonal migration patterns, and cyclically regenerating ecosystems.[125] This is also why most gynecratic tribes had a much more egalitarian economic system than the Europeans, largely based on reciprocity.

Although we have plenty of accounts of European travelers who marveled at the impression of classlessness, and propertylessness of Native American tribes,[126] it is also useful to take the other perspective: that of Native Americans who traveled to Europe. As Paula Gunn Allen observes, when Iroquois travelers visited France during the colonial period, they were shocked at the great gap between the lifestyles of the wealthy and the poor, a select few "full gorged" with wealth and the vast majority starving in poverty.[127] These reports show the disparity between the Iroquois' gynecratic and tendentially egalitarian societies and France's patriarchal and economically hierarchical social organization, the first modeled on the cycles of the land, the second on the perpetually expanding artifice of capital.

Whereas the settler-mythology of the "vanishing Indian" may lead us to believe that such ideals and organization have completely been overcome by patriarchy, Gunn Allen invites us to look at the sites where they actually survive. As she points out, many of the values, institutions, and philosophies elaborated during a multi-secular history by Native Americans still exist in what is today called the Unites States.[128] Paula remarks that while the white settlers of European descent are eager to forget those ties, presenting the history of the United States as beginning

---

[125] Kyle Whyte, "Settler Colonialism, Ecology and Environmental Injustice," *Environment & Society* 9, no. 1 (2018), 125-144.
[126] Paula Gunn Allen, *The Sacred Hoop*, 215.
[127] Ibid, 219.
[128] Ibid, 2, 209–21.

only when their forebears arrived, Native American have a different perspective in which "the red roots of white feminism" are quite evident.[129] Not only have the gynecratic traditions of certain tribes never been eradicated completely, but they also meet with other liberation movements, cementing centuries of common struggles. Nor does the legacy of Native American history stop at feminism: "America does not want to remember that it derived its wealth, its values, its food, much of its medicine, and a large part of its 'dream' from Native America."[130] For instance, according to Gunn Allen, the Native American tribal federation system clearly influenced American federalism, just as many of the ideals of social justice and equality circulating in the US partake of the legacy of gynecratic egalitarianism. Among traditional Indian values and social styles that Gunn Allen sees as characterizing American life are 1) a "permissive childrearing practice," and the concomitant belief that imprisoning, torturing, caning, starving, or verbally abusing children is unacceptable (whereas the Christian idea that children are also marked by an original sin often led to the justification of all of the above); 2) "sexual openness" and "scant clothing" (whereas Christianity generated a very puritan attitude towards both); 3) female symbols seen as equal of or, in some cases, of greater value than their male equivalents (whereas Christianity embodied so much misogyny in its symbolism that, as we have seen, its God was spared the shame of being born by touching a feminine body). Although this certainly does not mean that contemporary Americans have become Indians, given that this Native American heritage coexists with a settler culture that has systematically tried to erase it, it would also be absurd to deny their presence. "Tribal systems have been operating in the 'new world' for several hundred thousand years. It is unlikely that a few hundred years of colonization will see their undoing."[131]

While Native American perspectives on gender are a crucial component of a discussion of the coloniality of gender, as they emphasize the link between heteropatriarchy and the settler colonial history of the United States, we should also be aware of the risk of an "ethnographic entrapment,"[132] of an appropriation of Native American voices as mere

---

129 Ibid, 209.
130 Ibid, 211.
131 Ibid, 2.
132 Andrea Smith, "Queer Theory and Native Studies: The Heteronormativity of Settler Colonialism," *GLQ: A Journal of Lesbian and Gay Studies* 16, nos. 1–2 (2010), 44.

"multicultural add-ons" to traditional disciplines.[133] Instead of an extractivist logic that freezes Indigenous people into the role of an object of analysis, sealed into an immutable past, Native American voices should be included as producers of knowledge. In particular, native studies must be part of any critical theory of society because, as it has been observed, "the logic of settler-colonialism structures all of society, not just those who are indigenous."[134]

Going beyond the coloniality of gender also means going beyond the binary logic of colonialism that opposes a Western universal subject, producer of theory without further qualification, to the native particular other, producer of indigenous theories: "Within this colonial logic, native particularity cannot achieve universal humanity without fundamentally becoming 'inauthentic' because Nativeness is fundamentally constructed already as the 'other' of Western subjectivity."[135] This colonial trope places native peoples on the horizon of death, reproducing the logic of "genocidal appropriation" which holds that Indigenous people must disappear, either physically, through elimination, or psychically, through assimilation.[136] The practice of playing Indian by non-Indians, for instance, reproduces this myth, even when done by liberatory gay movements.[137]

As a way of questioning this colonial logic, Andrea Smith proposes an encounter between queer theory and native studies. In this view, such a convergence can produce both a new series of tools to explore the normalizing effect of settler colonialism, with its heteronormativity, but also a productive turn towards a more critical attitude vis-à-vis identity politics, as it emerges in queer theory's call for a "subjectless critique."[138] As the coeditors of the *Social Text* special issue on "What's Queer about Queer Studies" write: "What might be called the 'subjectless' critique of queer studies disallows any positing of a proper subject *of* or object *for* the field by insisting that queer has no fixed political referent [...]. A subjectless critique establishes, in Michael Warner's phrase, a focus on 'a wide field of normalization' as the site of social violence."[139]

---

[133] Ibid, 45.
[134] Ibid, 46.
[135] Ibid, 44.
[136] Ibid, 50.
[137] See Robert Cremins, "Is there a political myth of settler homosexuality?."
[138] Andrea Smith, "Queer Theory and Native Studies," 46.
[139] David L. Eng, Judith Halberstam, and José Esteban Muñoz, "What's Queer About Queer Studies Now?," *Social Text* 23, nos, 3–4 (2005), 3.

In this book, developing a "subjectless critique" means avoiding the colonial logic that reduces native people to the dichotomy between the universal subject, trapped in his transparency, and the particular one, trapped in its ethnicity. It means adopting a transindividual philosophy which, instead of taking already given individualities as the starting point of analysis, explores the process of ontogenesis that creates them at the supra, inter- and infra-individual level. A "subjectless critique" is thus a critique without a pregiven subject(ification). As such, it is not simply post-identity: Identities can at times be useful in political struggles, so we need to develop a non-binary attitude towards binaries themselves, beginning with the binary of "colonizers" and "colonized."[140] There are contexts in which adopting a colonizer/colonized lens can help illuminate the colonial conditions that still operate, but we should refuse a colonial logic that would like to perpetually trap us into them. To refuse identifying with the dominant (settler) culture is indeed a necessary step for many indigenous movements, but such struggles should not be frozen into an identity politics that places indigeneity itself on the horizon of death.

Along with counter-identification processes, a "subjectless critique" also pushes us to recognize the possibly shifting terrain of resistance, and opens the path for what José Esteban Muñoz called processes of "dis-identification."[141] As already mentioned in previous chapters, whereas assimilationism produces individualities that identify with dominant society, and counter-identification seeks to reject this completely, disidentification "is the third mode of dealing with dominant ideology, one that neither opts to assimilate within such a structure nor strictly opposes it; rather, disidentification is a strategy that works on and against dominant ideology."[142] Disidentification, as conceptualized by Muñoz and invoked by Smith, is not a middle ground between assimilation and counter-identification, but a strategy that neither fully accepts nor outright rejects the dominant ideology, rather working on the inside towards its subversion. It thereby enables us to exercise a critique by escaping the "ethnographic entrapment," while also allowing us to be non-binary about the binaries. As Andrea Smith concludes:

---

[140] Andrea Smith, "Queer Theory and Native Studies," 54–5.
[141] José Esteban Muñoz, *Disidentifications: Queers of Color and the Performance of Politics* (Minneapolis: Minnesota University Press, 1999).
[142] Ibid, 11–12.

Thus, a politics of counteridentification can be helpful to the project of decolonization, it provides a theoretical apparatus that can allow colonized people to engage in multiple strategies to build a base of support sufficient to dismantle the settler state. Disidentification forces us to admit that we cannot organize from a space of political purity, that we have been invariably marked by the processes of colonization. When we no longer have to carry the burden of political and cultural purity, we can be more flexible and creative in engaging multiple strategies and creating a plethora of alliances that can enable us to use the logic of settler colonialism against itself.[143]

Beyond gesturing towards a "post-identity" politics, Smith invokes a form of "identity-plus politics,"[144] a politics that can make recourse to identities strategically, without being caught in the colonial logic/demand of either identify or counter-identify. This is a particularly helpful strategy which acknowledges how individualities are constantly shaped by processes of affective relations situated at the supra, but also inter-, and infra-individual level. More than calling for an anti-colonial feminism trapped in the logic of what it opposes, we therefore follow Maria Lugones' call for a "decolonial feminism," understood as the possibility of overcoming the coloniality of gender.[145] A decolonial feminism must certainly take note of Eve Tuck and K. Wayne Yang's powerful reminder that decolonization is not a metaphor and implies reparation for the land dispossession.[146] Decolonization is not a metaphor, but neither is slavery nor heteropatriarchy. It is a work that takes time and we must be constantly vigilant towards conscious and unconscious biases, and those material and immaterial structures of coloniality that have stratified throughout the centuries and that can "speak" through our own tongue without us realizing it.

Following the philosophy of transindividuality highlighted above, we prefer to speak about "de-colonial," as opposed to "anti-colonial" feminism: while the latter is caught in the opposition between two conceptual blocks and thus into the logic of counteridentification, the notion of "de-colonial" emphasizes turning away from the colonial, a turn that can take the form

---

[143] Andrea Smith, "Queer Theory and Native Studies," 56.
[144] Ibid, 61.
[145] Maria Lugones, "Towards a Decolonial Feminism," 747.
[146] Eve Tuck and K. Wayne Yang, "Decolonization is not a metaphor," *Decolonization: Indigeneity, Education and Society* 1, no. 1.

of "counteridentification" but also of "disidentification". Given that decolonizing cannot be done all at once, but is a long-term process, we follow Nelson Maldonado-Torres' invitation to conceptualize decolonizing as an "attitude."[147] The decolonial attitude is one that express itself as a constant exercise of "epistemic insubordination," an insubordination "that challenges the epistemic privilege that has been accorded and delegated to certain knowledge producers and withdrawn from and refused to other knowledge producers."[148] Therefore evidenced as a constant questioning of epistemic hierarchies and forms of erasures: more than definitive answers, the decolonial attitude constantly asks "Who is allowed to speak and to be heard?"[149]

Whereas a decolonial attitude unpacks the different layers of oppression generated by colonialism, a deimperial attitude also calls attention to the risk of forms of cultural imperialism, beginning by recognizing the cognitive empire we inherited from more than five centuries of Western imperialism. Following the metaphor of the snail invoked earlier, a deimperial attitude invites us to look at our shoulders, be aware of the shell that we may be carrying, and, when needed, be ready to break out and break free.

To summarize the content of this chapter, we could say the globe comes first, but differences are not secondary. To assume that, when the globe comes first, then differences only follow, means mapping the global *versus* local distinction onto the universal *versus* particular dichotomy, simply reversing but not questioning the colonial logic. Not all distinctions and differences imply dichotomous thinking, i.e., the assumption that the conceptual pair is both reciprocally exclusive and jointly exhaustive of our possibilities. Imperialism thrives on this split, because it presents itself as universal, pretending that where there is a universal claim there cannot be a specific one, and vice versa. Instead of adopting this logic of splitting, which, as Maria Lugones argues, is a logic of purity, we understand social differences and distinctions in term of a logic of

---

[147] Nelson Maldonado-Torres, "Outline of ten theses. . .," 22.
[148] Eduardo Mendieta, "Critique of Decolonial Reason: On the Philosophy of the Calibans," *Graduate Faculty Philosophy Journal*, forthcoming *Philosophy and Coloniality* special issue, 41. No.1 (2020), 146.
[149] Indeed, more that the solution provided, formulating the question "Can the subaltern speak?" is the most enduring legacy of Spivak's seminal essay with the same name (Gayatri Spivak, "Can the Subaltern Speak?," in *Marxism and the Interpretation of Culture*, ed. Cary Nelson [Basingstoke: Macmillan Education, 1988]).

curdling, which is always impure.[150] As Lugones observes, every separation is always and necessarily an exercise in more or less purity: You divide the two substances, the white from the yolk, and make sure neither part contains any fragment of the other.[151] But separation in the form of curdling, as when making mayonnaise, separates into some yolky oil and some oily yolk.[152] There are no fragments understood as unrelated pieces, parts that do not fit together, but rather, in our own terms, only transindividualities. In the impurist logic of curdling, the social world is complex and heterogenous and each of its inhabitants is multiple, non-fragmented, embodied; according to the purist logic of splitting, the social world is both unified and fragmented, homogeneous and divided into pieces that can be hierarchically ordered.[153] Thus, whereas the curdle-separation thrives in multiplicity and *mestizaje*, the split-separation responds to an urge to fragment and thereby control the multiplicity.

By *mestizaje*, we do no not mean racially mixed, but rather a different form of consciousness, one that, as Gloria Anzaldúa defined it, is capable of holding multiple perspectives together, and has thus a certain tolerance for ambiguity.[154] Opening up to a *mestiza* consciousness is necessary to develop the capacity for seeing multiple sources of oppression, being able to perceive them under the surface of things, and navigating through them without responding to the logic of purity that invites their ranking. This is what Anzaldúa called "*la facultad.*"[155] "Those who are punched on the most have it the strongest—the females, the homosexuals of all races, the darkskinned, the outcast, the persecuted, the marginalized, the foreign."[156] This is no faculty born out of pure intellectual exercise: It is very impure and very embodied, because it is born in pain. When you

---

[150] Maria Lugones, "Purity, Impurity, and Separation," *Signs* 19, no. 2.

[151] Ibid, 458.

[152] Ibid, 459.

[153] Ibid, 463.

[154] Gloria Anzaldúa, *Borderlands/La Frontera: The New Mestiza* (San Francisco: Aunt Lute Books, 2012), 101.

[155] Ibid, 61.

[156] Ibid, 60. Although Anzaldúa does not call herself an "anarchafeminist," we believe her concept of the *mestiza* consciousness, as the capacity to see multiple sources of oppressions, without raking them, is an example of anarchafeminist consciousness. See also the following statement: "there is a rebel in me—the Shadow-Beast. It is a part of me that refuses to take orders from outside authorities. It refuses to take orders from my conscious will, it threatens the sovereignty of my rulership. It is that part of me that hates constraints of any kind, even those self-imposed" (Ibid, 38).

suffer repeated forms of oppressions, when they accumulate onto your body like different layers of skin, either you become incapable of feeling any pain, or you become hypersensitive to its presence—a slap in your face, either physical or mental, could come any moment and from any angle. You want to avoid yet more pain, and you learn how to sense it around every corner. You therefore become capable of perceiving not just the violence you have suffered, but all possible violence that might be suffered. And then feeling becomes an intuition—a capacity to see what those who have always inhabited the position of the oppressors cannot see.

This is the faculty that is automatically developed by those who live in borderland, in that "vague and undetermined place created by the emotional residue of an unnatural boundary" and that "is in a constant state of transition."[157] "*Los atraversados* live here: the squint-eyed, the perverse, the queer, the troublesome, the mongrel, the mulatto, the half-breed, the half dead: in short, those who cross over, pass over, or go through the confines of the 'normal.'"[158] By inhabiting this space, listening to the voices of those who did, cultivating *la facultad*, we can develop the decolonial and deimperial attitude needed for an anarchafeminist philosophy.

---

[157] Ibid, 25.
[158] Ibid.

8 Somatic communism and the capitalist mode of (re)production

We have seen how supra-individual forces, such as the global racial capitalism so evident over the last five centuries, helps shaping gendered individualities. After this emphasis on the supra-individual level, we will now focus on the inter-individual level, looking at the process of production and reproduction of life from the point of view of inter-actions. As we will see, within individual interactions, capitalism is still the dominant mode of (re-)production, that is, as a mode of production that systematically separates *production* from *reproduction*, and which, precisely on that basis, enables some bodies to accumulate values at the expense of others. Hence, our usage of the term (re)production, highlighting the need to bring the two back together in order to understand how capitalism works.

We will look at these dynamics of value production from the point of view of our philosophy of transindividuality, a philosophy that considers individuals not as already given individualities but as the result of a process of affective association that takes place at different levels. Although the concept of a "philosophy of transindividuality" may appear new, the idea of somatic communism is far from being new. Indeed, many philosophers in the socialist tradition based their communist ideals and political philosophy on some form of somatic communism. In this work, we distinguish between political communism, as the conscious decision to organize society according to the common ownership of the means of production and the abolition of private property, from somatic communism, which can be understood, more broadly, as the idea that bodies come into being and maintain themselves through what they share with one another. Although the two concepts can converge, it is useful to keep them separate because one can claim that, despite the co-origination of all beings, human society should nevertheless be organized along other principles, such as private property and private ownership of the means of production.

Before we analyze those claims, a reference to a few thinkers in the socialist tradition may illuminate what we mean by somatic communism. To begin with, somatic communism must not only be understood diachronically, focusing on what bodies have in common here and now, but also synchronically. What enables bodies to persist in their being is also what generations have accumulated since the appearance of the *Homo sapiens* species. As Pyotr Kropotkin remarked at the beginning of his *The Conquest of Bread*, at the beginning of human presence on this planet, the most one generation could expect from the previous one was a few utensils and a shelter.[1] Now that our species has learned how to drain the marshes, build roads, drill through entire mountains, create complex machinery, steal nature's secrets, and press steam and electricity in its service, every person, from birth, finds ready for their use (if circumstances permit) an immense capital accumulated by those who came before.[2] By quoting the example of the vast prairies of the Americas, and writing in 1892, this Russian-born anarchist observed how 100 men can produce enough wheat to maintain 10,000 people for a whole year, thanks to the aid of machinery and techniques of cultivation invented by people whose name is lost in the history of humankind.[3] More than a century afterwards, we can say that such capital has further and exponentially increased: Hunger, just to give one significant example, is no longer about lack of food, since one-third of the food produced every year is wasted.[4] Today, even more than in 1892

---

[1] Pyotr Kropotkin, *The Conquest of Bread and Other Writings*, ed. Marshall Shatz (Cambridge: Cambridge University Press, 1995), 11.

[2] Pyotr Kropotkin, *The Conquest of Bread,* 11.

[3] Ibid, 12.

[4] Every year, at least one-third of the world's food gets lost or wasted ("Food Loss and Waste Database," Food and Agriculture Organization of the United Nations, http://www.fao.org/food-loss-and-food-waste/flw-data, accessed March 20, 2021), while statistics show that roughly 30 to 40 percent of the food supply in the US alone is wasted ("8 Facts to Know about Food Waste and Hunger," World Food Program USA, https://www.wfpusa.org/articles/8-facts-to-know-about-food-waste-and-hunger/, accessed March 20, 2021). The numbers relating to clothes waste are even more staggering: Every *second*, the equivalent of one garbage truck worth of textiles is sent to landfill or burned ("Putting the brakes on fast fashion," UN Environment Programme, https://www.unep.org/news-and-stories/story/putting-brakes-fast-fashion, accessed November 12, 2018).

when Pyotr Kroptotkin was writing, "truly, we are rich—far richer than we think; rich in what we already possess, richer still in the possibilities of production of our actual mechanical outfit; richest of all in what we might win from our soil, from our manufactures, from our science, from our technical knowledge, were they but applied to bringing about the wellbeing of all."[5] Thus we are not rich because of the wealth that we possess individually, as economic inequalities in society are even larger than they were in Kropotkin's time. We are rich in what we already possess as a species and richer still in the possibilities that would be available if the immense capital accumulated by the human species were applied to the benefit of all.

Think of our cities and how they grew through the centuries as networks bound together by roads and waterways regulating trading between them. If we dig beneath any metropolis, we find remnants of streets, houses, public buildings, cemeteries, and countless layers of human labor accumulated through the centuries and stratified under our feet.[6] We literally walk over that labor and those bodies. Our cities are testaments to somatic communism. Dig under New York's City Hall and Federal Tax Building, and you will find, among other things, the remnants of an African burial ground.[7] Wealth is quite literally built on the enslaved bodies who made this capital. Dig under Brooklyn's streets, and you will find seeds transported here through the ballast of boats that traveled the Atlantic slave routes, bringing forced labor to the city, and leaving plenty of raw material and commodities for Europeans. And if we are careful enough, we do not even need to dig underneath: A plant of African origin unexpectedly flowering between concrete blocks in a New York neighborhood can tell us the story of colonial travels, of the bodies that brought them here, of the labor of those who built the ships, and loaded the cargo—as just one of the innumerable stories of the "botany of colonization".[8]

---

[5] Pyotr Kropotkin, *The Conquest of Bread*, 13.

[6] Ibid, 14.

[7] "Black Gotham," Kamau Studios, http://kamaustudios.com/blackgotham/ (accessed on March 20, 2021). The artist Kamau Ware has developed a multimedia project exploring the "Black Gotham," the sites of Black history that, literally, lie beneath New York City (one old name for which is Gotham). For example, when the IRS building was built in the 1990s, a colonial common grave for the enslaved was discovered in an area that includes part of City Hall.

[8] As artist Maria Thereza Alves observes in the catalogue of their exhibition *Seeds of Change. New York—A Botany of Colonization* (2016–18, Vera List Center for Art and Politics), "the earth you think you are on is not, it is someplace else, the only way you would know the place is the flower." See *Seeds of Change. New York—A Botany of Colonization*, by Maria Thereza Alves, November 3–27, 2017 (New School: Vera List Center for Art and Politics, 2016–18), 12.

And even now, the value of each building, each factory, each warehouse, is only maintained by the presence and labor of legions of humans in that curve of the globe. "Each of the atoms composing what we call the Wealth of Nations owes its value to the fact that it is a part of the great whole," observed Kropotkin many years ago.[9] "What would a London dockyard or a great Paris warehouse be if they were not situated in these great centers of international commerce? What would become of our mines, our factories, our workshops and our railways, without the immense quantities of merchandise transported every day by sea and land?"[10]

A century after Kropotkin's writings, these questions are timelier than ever. As is his conclusion: "There is not even a thought, or an invention, which is not common property, born of the past and the present."[11] These words could be an epigraph for this entire Chapter. What does it mean to argue that, not only there is no material wealth without the labor of legions, but also that there is not a single thought or invention that is not "common property," born of the past and the present? Within a monist ontology, it means emphasizing that thought and matter are not two different and independent substances but simply two attributes of the same substance. Thus, in as much as material wealth is the result of circulation of bodies, so is intellectual richness: circulation and accumulations of modes in thinking that have aggregated and combined through the millennia. Thousands of inventors, known and unknown, have co-operated in the invention of each of the machines which are now seen as the singular result of a unique mind. Similarly, thousands of writers, poets, scholars, and thinkers have labored to produce and share the ideas that are deposited in our authored books. "They have been upheld and nourished through life, both physically and mentally, by legions of workers and craftsmen of all sorts. They have drawn their motive force from the environment."[12]

The concept used by Pyotr Kropotkin to summarize these ideas is that of "mutual aid."[13] Although the notion may mistakenly suggest that wealth is produced by people's desire to help each other, the notion of

---

[9] Pyotr Kropotkin, *The Conquest of Bread*, 14.
[10] Ibid.
[11] Ibid.
[12] ibid, 15.
[13] Ibid, 19, 246; Pyotr Kropotkin, *Mutual Aid: A Factor of Evolution* (London: William Heinemann, 1902).

mutual aid is not rooted in a philosophical anthropology but rather in a philosophy of biology. As the subtitle of Kropotkin's major work points out, mutual aid is "a factor of evolution,"[14] that is, a factor that recurs along with mutual struggle, but that, in the long term, is far more important. Although competition occurs, especially for success in the struggle for survival, mutual aid is a much more significant feature.[15] Significantly, Pyotr does not base his views on examples from human history, but opens his work with an analysis of animals behaviors: from fish to parrots, from cranes to white wagtails (*motacilia alba*), the systems of mutual aid between individual animals is key to their survival and reproduction.

Although many of Kropotkin's arguments in *Mutual Aid* appear outdated today, his fundamental intuitions, as we saw in Chapter 5, have been confirmed by symbiotic biology. The latter even radicalizes that perspective by arguing that we have never been individuals, properly speaking, since, from the point of view of biology, every individual is a "holobiont," an assemblage of the multicellular eukaryote plus all of its symbionts, an ecological unit made by a host and all the species living around it and through it. Once we assume that perspective, as opposed to that of a methodological individualism which considers individuals as the starting point of philosophizing, then the symbiotic nature of life comes to the fore. And if it is true that, as Emma Goldman argues, anarchism is the teacher of the unity of all life, then we should conclude that symbiotic biology is anarchical in its spirit, if not in its letter.

The question then emerges why such somatic communism, which reverberates in the entire unity of life—from our cities to the book you are reading, from animal behavior to the invention of electricity—become invisible. Following Kropotkin, and other socialist writers, one could point to capitalist ideology itself, with its naturalization of the modern bourgeois property owner into the notion of the individual. To use a Marxian expression, we could say that the very idea of an individual separated from all other individuals is a "Robinsonade,"[16] the fantastic representation of an isolated individual, which is nothing but the imaginary representation of the concrete economic development of a

---

[14] Pyotr Kropotkin, *Mutual Aid.*
[15] Ibid, 6.
[16] Karl Marx, "The Grundrisse," in *Marx-Engels Reader*, ed. Robert C. Tucker (New York: Norton, 1978), 221.

specific epoch: the capitalist bourgeois one. We imagine that individuals cast on a desert island, such as in the colonial fantasy of Daniel Defoe's novel *Robinson Crusoe*, are individuals as they were at the beginning of history, alone, separated, and self-subsistent, but they are actually those of history's end, that is, of the capitalist epoch we live in.

But there are even deeper roots to this trend of forgetting the communism of bodies, namely the tendency to perceive the life (in common) from the perspective of death as opposed to the perspective of birth. Whereas we always die alone, and may therefore perceive life as an individual business, we are always born in communion with others (at least one other). This tendency to privilege death over birth is rooted in a specific Western attitude that, according to Italian feminist philosopher Adriana Cavarero, goes back to Ancient Greek philosophy. As she noticed, following Hannah Arendt, (Western) philosophers tended to look at human beings as beings-toward-death. Very rarely did they take the opposite perspective of considering them as beings-after-birth,[17] a puzzling fact on its own, given the ontological priority of birth over death. For while it is true that we are beings-toward-death, it is equally true that we are so because we are beings-after-birth in the first place. Western philosophers like to remind us of the first truth (that we will die) but tend to forget the second truth (that we are born).

This has a crucial consequence for the way life is perceived, because looking at human beings from the perspective of death means looking at them in a specific way, one that, among other things, privileges the perspective of those bodies that will never experience giving birth, and that, having forgotten the fact of having been given birth to, perceive life only from the perspective of its upcoming end. Death is indeed one of the few events in our life when we can be alone, whereas birth is always necessarily in company. I can give death to myself—I can anticipate it and commit suicide—but I cannot give birth to myself. This peculiarity of birth has a twofold significance. First, in order to give birth, one always needs someone other than oneself: at least currently, a sperm and a womb.

---

[17] Among the exceptions in the West, see Hannah Arendt; for instance, Hannah Arendt, *Love and Saint Augustine* (Chicago: Chicago University Press, 1996), 54–5, 146–8; and Hannah Arendt, *The Promise of Politics* (New York: Schocken, 2005), 126–7. See also Adriana Cavarero, *Nonostante Platone: Figure femminili nella filosofia antica* (Verona: Ombre Corte, 2009); and, Anne O'Byrne, *Natality and Finitude* (Bloomington: Indiana University Press, 2010).

Second, whereas death is something that I can give myself, birth is something that I can only give to somebody else. Things may change in the future, if promises about human cloning are fulfilled, but even that would not affect the fundamental fact that the very act of giving birth always involves an other: This may even be an other who is exactly like us, a perfect duplicate, but it will still be an other, distinguished from us in space and time.

In sum, the body that can die alone is always born by somebody else. Surprisingly enough, despite the peculiarity of death, it is the moment on which most Western political philosophers—from Thomas Hobbes to contemporary theorists of biopolitics—have concentrated their attention.[18] Not by chance, beginning with Ancient Greek philosophy, the term "mortals" (*brotoi*) became a synonym for human beings.[19] According to Cavarero, Greek philosophers privileged death over life because they saw philosophy as an activity that unties the soul from the bodily imprisonment deriving from birth itself. While ciswomen are confined in the space of the body, philosophy becomes the activity that prepares cismen for the liberation of the soul from such imprisonment and thus, ultimately, for death. It is because of a deeply entrenched body-soul dualism, which all too often helped to relegate women to the sphere of bodily needs, that Western philosophers have so consistently privileged death over birth. Their doing so reproduces what, as we have seen, Sylvia Wynter called the dogma of the "nonhomogeneity of substance."[20]

However, if we take the opposite approach and look at human beings as beings-after-birth, a completely different perspective emerges, one that could be called "geneapolitical" in order to oppose it to the "thanatopolitical" paradigm that dominated in Western political philosophy.[21] On a more general philosophical level, it becomes evident that life has always been at the center of politics, not only because life and its needs are crucial

---

[18] We have discussed this point at length in Chiara Bottici, "Rethinking the Biopolitical Turn: From the Thanatopolitical to the Geneapolitical Paradigm," *Graduate Faculty Philosophy Journal* 35, no. 1 (2015), 175–97.

[19] The fact that "mortals" is still often used as a synonym for "human being" is a signal of how entrenched this prejudice is in our culture. See Adriana Cavarero, *Nonostante Platone,* 21–39, 55, 75.

[20] Sylvia Wynter, "Unsettling the Coloniality of Being/Power/Truth/Freedom: Towards the Human, After Man, Its Overrepresentation–An Argument," *CR: The New Centennial Review* 3, no. 3 (2003), 274.

[21] Chiara Bottici, "Rethinking the Biopolitical Turn."

political issues, but also because birth, as Hannah Arendt puts it, is the political moment *par excellence*.[22] If it is true that death is the moment where we can be alone, whereas birth is always in common, then birth, rather than death, should be at the center of our political thinking. In Arendt's view, natality, in which the capacity for action is ontologically rooted, is "the miracle that saves the world, the realm of human affairs, from its normal, natural ruin."[23] The fact that newborns constantly come into the world not only explains how the new is possible, but also why and how the plurality of humans, without which there cannot be any politics, comes about.[24]

If birth comes well before death as the crucial political moment, then politics, *pace* Michel Foucault, has always been to a certain extent biopolitical: what is authentically political is life itself, not because it is *killable*, as Giorgio Agamben argued,[25] but because it is *born(e)*. From Hobbes to Agamben, Western political philosophers have too often conceived politics in relationship to the possibility of inflicting death, and have consistently done so through the fiction of a non-gendered individual. Obsessed with the death as the defining feature of our existential horizon, modern philosophers have been unable to find a better justification for the existence of sovereign political power other than attributing to it the guarantee of our security *vis-à-vis* the possibility of death.[26] This

---

[22] As already mentioned, this is the point developed by Arendt in her reading of Augustine (see for instance Hannah Arendt, *Love and St. Augustine*, 54–5, 146–8; and, Hannah Arendt, *The Promise of Politics*, 126–7), and more recently developed by Adriana Cavarero in *Nonostante Platone*.

[23] Hannah Arendt, *The Human Condition* (Chicago: The University of Chicago Press, 1958), 247.

[24] We should, however, note that Arendt is not very consistent in her treatment of natality, which at times seems to coincide with biological birth itself but in other cases seems to come to full fruition in what she calls the "second birth," the moment when new beginners are witnessed in words and deeds (see Hannah Arendt, *The Human Condition*, 176). In our view, this is the consequence of her overall conceptual apparatus and very specific conception of politics, which does not allow her to fully take into account the political role of the gendered body. On the "second birth," see for instance Peg Birmingham, *Hannah Arendt and Human Rights: The Predicament of Common Responsibility* (Bloomington: Indiana University Press, 2006), who emphasized that to be born is always to be welcomed, and thus to be given a name, so that the second birth is never simply laid over the first, but both happen at once.

[25] Giorgio Agamben, *Homo Sacer: Sovereign Power and Bare Life*, trans. Daniel Heller-Roazen (Stanford: Stanford University Press, 1998).

[26] For this critique of Hobbes's philosophy, see Giorgio Agamben, *Homo Sacer*. We have discussed this more at length in Chiara Bottici, "Rethinking the biopolitical turn."

thanatolopolitical gaze has led to neglecting the crucial political role that both the production and the reproduction of life has always had. There is today an increasing talk about "bio-politics" to denote important changes in the relevance of life (bios) to political life. As we have seen, Foucault introduced the term "biopolitics" to denote the change he perceived in the nature of modern political power: whereas traditional sovereignty has always been a power aimed at controlling life by threatening it with the possibility of death, the new form of power that emerges in the mid-nineteenth century is that of a power aimed at inciting and preserving life.[27] Whereas the sovereign power—not by chance, symbolized by the sword—was essentially the power to kill, the power to take life or let it die, the new biopower he identified would manifest itself as a power to *make* live and let die.[28]

The emergence of the term "biopolitics" does signify a change in the nature of political power that happened with the formation of modern states, those formidable power apparatuses that have the capacity to map, control and discipline the lives of their citizens, which by far surpass that of any other political formations in the history of *Homo sapiens*. And yet, the persistence of this thanatopolitical attitude leads us to forget that the (re)production of life and its needs have always been at the centre of our life in common, so much so that we can say that, to a certain degree, politics has always been biopolitics.

Even in Aristotle, the distinction between the household (*oikos*) and the sphere of the city-state (*polis*) does not mean that life has no role to play in the *polis*. Life and its needs are central to politics because without them there could not be any life in common in the first place. It is not by chance that Aristotle insists that the *polis* derives from the satisfaction of needs, that is, from the fact that we are incapable of providing for our life and our most basic needs in isolation.[29] Aristotle was very well aware of the centrality of life, so when he defines man as the *zoon politikon*, he uses an expression *zoon*, which literally means "living being." The Latin rendering of *zoon* as "animal" is misleading because the term animal has

---

[27] Note, however, that this chronology is uncertain and changes from one text to another. In Michel Foucault, *The History of Sexuality, Volume I: An Introduction,* trans. Robert Hurley (New York: Vintage, 1990), he seems, for instance, to place the beginning of this process much earlier.

[28] Ibid, 136; cf. Michel Foucault, *"Society Must Be Defended": Lectures at the Collège de France, 1975–1976,* trans. David Macey (New York: Picador, 2003), 241.

[29] See *Republic,* 368b; *Politics,* 1252b30.

a connotation of inferiority. On the contrary, *zoon* (from *zoe,* life itself) simply means every "en-souled" or living being.[30] Even Aristotle understood that that we can be *political* beings only because we are *living* beings, that is, because we are born.

When we abandon the thanatopolitical gaze and adopt a geneapolitical one, life comes to the centre of our political thinking, not because it is killable, but because it is borne and therefore (re)produced. This is the core of somatic communism described above, a communism of bodies that, in a transindividual perspective, goes beyond the plurality Arendt emphasized. Birth needs not only a plurality of humans, but also a plurality of other transindividual bodies. The individual dies, but something of its transindividuality always remains. And when we follow all of the infinite networks of affective association and dissociation that makes up any transindividuality, we must conclude that there is something eternal in each transindividuality.[31] We will focus on the infra-actions in Chapter 9, but even while we remain at the level of the inter-actions between humans, it is evident that the (re)production of human life happens through a form of somatic communism.

This is the reason why, according to Pierre-Joseph Proudhon and many socialist thinkers of his time, property is robbery. As the French anarchist put it at the beginning of his 1840 *Qu'est-ce que la propriété?* (*What is Property?*): "If I had to answer the following question, 'What is slavery?', and if I should respond in one word, 'It is murder,' my meaning would be understood at once. I should not need a long explanation to show that the power to deprive a man of his thought, his will, and his personality is the power of life and death. So why this other question, 'What is property?' should I not answer in the same way, 'It is theft,' without fearing to be misunderstood, since the second proposition is only a transformation of the first?"[32]

---

[30] See Hans Jonas, "Zwischen Nichts und Ewigkeit: Zur Lehre vom Menschen," in *Die Grundlegung der Politischen Philosophie bei Aristotles*, ed. Günther Bien (Freiburg: Karl Alber, 1973), 123.

[31] This is in my view the sense in which Spinoza's controversial claim about the eternity of the mind must be interpreted: Even when a body dies, something of its power to affect and being affected remains *sub species aeternitatis*. See, in particular, Part V of Spinoza's *Ethics* (EV P23).

[32] Pierre-Joseph Proudhon, *What Is Property?*, eds. Donald R. Kelley and Bonnie G. Smith (Cambridge: Cambridge University Press, 1993), 13.

This is a text rooted in its own time, including the sexism of Proudhon and his generation of early socialists: "Man" stands here for both the neutral and a specific gender, and for reasons that should be clear at this point, we will not correct this. But we can still read this passage through a transindividual philosophy, which emphasizes how both a human being and a property are trans-individualities that cannot be appropriated by a single external individual without a denial of such individuality, be it in the form of murder or theft.

Although we can connect this argument to more recent critiques of property both inside and outside the West, it is useful to go back to early socialist texts such as this because they were written at a time when the memory of the collective ownership of land, forests, and waterways was still alive. One of the main arguments against communism is usually that it is an impossible utopia, but this argument does not take into account that, if we consider the history of *Homo sapiens*, the collective ownership of land and means of subsistence has been the rule rather than the exception. Even in the West, after Roman law introduced the notion of private property, communism continued to be practiced at different levels, from early Christian communities to medieval villages.[33]

Pierre-Joseph Proudhon's lucid arguments against private property still feel fresh. In the West, the definition that has been most influential is that provided by Roman law: property is the *ius utendi et abutendi re sua, quatenus juris ratio patitur*, that is, the right to use and abuse a thing, within the limits of the law.[34] From this definition, a contrast emerges between possession, which is a matter of fact, and property, which is a matter of law:[35] whereas possessing a thing (*res*) is a question of what empirically happens, a claim to property implies the recognition of the law (*ius*), and thus of a juridical apparatus that can implement such a right. This is why the existence of private property is inseparable from the state, defined as "corporation of citizens united under a common law by an act of society."[36] It is the existence of the state that guarantees property, as opposed to mere possession: "This one his field, another his vineyard, a third his rents, and the bondholder, who might have bought real estate but who preferred to come to the assistance of the treasury, his bonds."[37] Thus,

---

[33] Pyotr Kropotkin, *The Conquest of Bread*, 4.
[34] Pierre-Joseph Proudhon, *What Is Property?*, 35.
[35] Ibid, 36–7.
[36] Ibid, 37.
[37] Ibid, 41.

without the state, understood as the agency that guarantees the legitimacy of property claims, there cannot be any private property system.

But are those claims legitimate? Pierre-Joseph provides a wealth of arguments, most often put in the form of a detailed rebuttals of his adversaries, but they can be summarized by two main claims: possession does not justify property because the earth is finite, and labor does not justify private property since the capital produced by labor is always collective. Possession is just a matter of fact. Humans constantly come into the world and inhabit the earth, but the earth is finite, and the number of humans who are going to be born is infinite: the tension between the two is at the heart of the self-contradictory nature of private property. Proudhon makes this argument by recovering Cicero's famous comparison of the Earth to a theater: everybody who exists within that theater has the right to a seat as long as they occupy just that one, but they have no right to claim it for their heirs nor a right to claim other seats that they are not occupying. No one has a right to more than they need: *suum quidque cujusque sit*, to each one that which belongs to them, meaning each human should be entitled to what is needed to enjoy a seat in the theater of life, without occupying additional ones.[38]

> Every occupant is, then, necessarily a possessor or usufructuary, a condition that excludes proprietorship. The right to usufructuary is such that he is responsible for the thing entrusted to him; he must use it in conformity with general utility, with a view to the preservation and development of the thing; he has no power to transform it, to diminish it, or to change its nature; he cannot divide the usufruct so that another performs the labor while he receives the product. In a word the usufructuary is under the supervision of society and subject to the condition of labor and the law of equality. Thus is annihilated the Roman definition of property, 'the right to use and abuse', an immorality born of violence, the most monstrous pretension that the civil law ever sanctioned. Man receives his usufruct from the hands of society, which alone possesses it in a permanent way. The individual passes away, but society never dies.

Some thinkers argued that things such as air and light belong to the entire society and are thus common property because they are

---

[38] Ibid, 44.

inexhaustible. Besides the fact that "the light of the stars, the atmosphere of the earth, and the water contained in the sea and oceans"—which in 1840 were still considered "to exist in such great quantities that men cannot create any perceptible increase or decrease"[39]—have proved more limited than was then believed, the main thrust of Proudhon's argument is not about quantity. Water, air, and light are not communal property because there is a lot of each, but because they are needed for the survival of every occupant of a seat in the theater of life: "Water, air and light are common things not because they are inexhaustible but because they are indispensable, and indeed so indispensable that nature seems to have created them in quantities almost infinite so that their plentifulness might prevent their appropriation. Similarly, the land is indispensable to our existence, thus a common thing and insusceptible of appropriation; but land is much scarcer than the other elements, and so its use must be regulated not for profit of a few but in the interest and for the society of all. In short, equality of rights is proved by the equality of needs."[40]

It is because each spectator needs their own seat that the common property of life's necessities is justified. The theater is finite so spectators can use their seat insofar as they occupy it and by respecting the equal right to the seats of all other occupants who are currently there or may come in the future. Private property cannot be a natural right because it is based on a mathematical contradiction between the finite nature of things on this planet, and the unknown, potentially infinite number of its potential occupants. Nor is the labor done within our seats in the theater of life a justification for such a right.

It is a common view that we have the right to keep what is the result of our labor: All humans have this psychological tendency. But that tendency must not be mistaken for a right. In fact, all the wealth apparently produced by individual labor is always socially generated—whether we perceive it as such or not. This is not only because, when one arrives in the theater of life, one already finds there all the wealth and capital accumulated by previous generations of laborers: the streets and the tunnels, the bridges and the buildings, the inventions and the techniques, the machines and the medicines, the languages and the books, the textiles and the textures, to name only a few. But this capital accumulated across the millennia is the result of an effort that cannot be reduced to the sum

---

[39] Ibid, 72.
[40] Ibid, 73.

of the labor performed by each individual worker. For example, 200 workers raised the obelisks at the Temple of Luxor on their foundations in a few hours, but it would take a single worker many years to accomplish the same task (if they could do it at all). Similarly, a house to build, a factory to run, a book to write—all these are obelisks to erect, mountains to move, tasks that are possible only through collective endeavor, and not through the sheer sum of individual labor.[41]

This is the nature of human work: "The production of each involves the production of all,"[42] so no matter how individual it may appear, labor is always collective. Therefore, it cannot be repaid as individual labor: "A force of a thousand men working for twenty days has been paid the same as a force of one working fifty-five years; but this force of one thousand has done in twenty days what a single man, working continuously for a million centuries, could not accomplish: is this exchange equitable? Once more, no; for when you have paid all the individual forces, you have still not paid the collective force. Consequently, there always remains a right of collective property which you have not acquired and which you enjoy unjustly."[43] Thus, when a laborer is paid for her work, this should be understood not as a reward for the work done, because that work is always collective.[44] "As the traveller does not appropriate the highway which he travels, so the farmer does not appropriate the field which he cultivates; [. . .] all capital, whether material or mental, is the result of collective labor and so is collective property."[45] When this collective capital is appropriated as private property, it is, therefore, literally stolen.

And so when the capitalist is said to have paid the laborer a "daily wage," it should more properly be said that the capitalist has paid as many times "one day's wage" as he has employed laborers each day, which is not the same thing at all. "For he [the capitalist] has paid nothing for that immense power which results from the union and harmony of laborers and the convergence and simultaneity of their efforts. [. . .] The smallest fortune, the slightest establishment, the beginning of the lowest industry, all demand the combination of so many different kinds of labor and skill that one man could not possibly execute them all."[46] In other words,

---

41 Ibid, 91.
42 Ibid, 115.
43 Ibid, 93.
44 Ibid, 115.
45 Ibid, 114.
46 Ibid, 91.

production demands the power emerging from somatic communism, for, as Spinoza stated, when you join more individuals of the same nature, you do not obtain just a summation of these powers (*potentia*) but an exponential increase of such power.

To sum up, the social nature of value production derives both from the collective nature of labor itself (the production of one is the production of all), and from the division of labor (one can focus on a certain task because other people take care of all other tasks). And yet the capitalist economy, based on the two institutions of the private property and the market, enables only a few to accumulate value at the expense of all others.

As Karl Marx further explained, there are some core features to the capitalist economy that enable this form of exploitation to happen: private property, self-expanding nature of value, a free labor market, and the market allocation of surplus.[47] The first defining feature is the private ownership of the means of production, which, in its turn, generates a class distinction between those who own such a means and those who produce. In contrast to a now vanished world in which, through the commons, people had access to the means of subsistence and to those of production, within a capitalist society there is a class divide between those who have such access and those who have to go through labor markets in order to gain access. The existence of free labor markets is the second defining feature of capitalism, but intimately linked to the first: Because workers have access to the means of subsistence only through the market, they are subjected to its rule, and thus have to sell their labor for a wage, which, in turn, is also determined by the market. This, according to Marx, is what is visible in the sphere of exchange: But if we follow the capitalist into the "hidden abode of production,"[48] we discover that the value produced by the workers is appropriated by the capitalist, who sells the commodities produced at an exchange value, which vastly exceeds the wage paid to the workers. We need to look beyond what appears at the level of market exchange as a "free" exchange and explore the "hidden abode of production" to discover the unfreedom of capitalist accumulation. Capitalism is thus

---

[47] In this reconstruction, we follow Nancy Fraser's insightful and concise reconstruction of Marx's analysis of capitalism (Nancy Fraser, "Behind Marx's Hidden Abode," *New Left Review* 86, 57–60).

[48] Karl Marx, *Capital: A Critique of Political Economy, Volume I*, trans. Ben Fowkes (London: Penguin, 1976), 279.

an essentially exploitative system because based on the systemic extraction of surplus value from the workers labor and its concomitant accumulation in the form of capital. Hence, as Nancy Fraser noted, the third core feature of capitalism, the self-expanding nature of value, for no matter what the intentions are, both capitalists and workers become pawns of capital and its drive to infinite expansion.[49]

Notice here that, precisely because it is an economic system based on the endless expansion of profit, capitalism is literally "utopian": The accumulation of capital is always predicated on this "*eu*"(good) or "*ou*"(no) "*topos*" (place), that is, according to the etymology of the term "utopia," on the idea of a somewhere that does not exist as yet, but will be a good place to reach in the future. It is in this compulsory push towards a place that is both "good" and "not yet there" that the self-expanding nature of capital thrives. We can thus see how the "hidden abode" of production not only obscures the way in which goods are produced, but also hides the way in which desires are produced and (re)produced. It does not appear to be an exaggeration to speak of a "capitalist unconscious" that has its own specific fantasies.[50]

This leads us to the fourth defining feature of capitalism: the specific role of the markets. While markets have existed in many forms in human history, in a capitalist economy they play a double role: They serve to allocate the major inputs to commodity production, because markets allocate labor, real estate, goods, raw materials and credit, but also serve to allocate a society's specific surplus capacity, that is, to distribute the social energies exceeding those required to reproduce a society. As Nancy Fraser said, drawing on an expression by Piero Sraffa, capitalism is a system for the "production of commodities by means of commodities."[51] But, as she also notes, this does not mean that capitalism necessarily leads to a total commodification of life. Quite on the contrary, as Fraser rightly points out, the commodification of certain aspects of social life goes hand in hand with the non-commodification of others: and particularly when seen in a feminist perspective, it is clear that the latter provides the conditions for the former.

---

[49] But, as Proudhon also pointed out, private property can expand infinitely, and thus an economic system based on private property tends to produce endless expansion.
[50] We use this expression in the most general sense of the term. Tomšič uses the expression to frame his investigation of the links between Marx's political economy and Lacan's psychoanalysis. Samo Tomšič, *The Capitalist Unconscious: Marx and Lacan* (London: Verso, 2015).
[51] Nancy Fraser, "Behind Marx's Hidden Abode," 58.

In Volume I of *Capital*, Marx takes us from the apparently free sphere of market exchange into the "hidden abode" of production, where we discover the secret of capital accumulation: Accumulation occurs via exploitation, through the non-compensation of a portion of the worker's labor time. At the end of that volume, however, we discover an even more secret abode, where primitive or original accumulation[52] happens. The condition for the existence of "free markets," and thus for the exploitation of workers via extraction of surplus-value from their labor-time, is indeed the sheer violence and theft that characterizes the original accumulation of capital.[53] While unpacking such violence, Marx focused on the dispossession of peasants, land enclosure, and expropriations of raw material, but a very different—and much more persuasive—understanding of primitive accumulation is provided by feminist scholars who focus not simply on production, but also on reproduction. As Fraser remarks, there is a veritable "epistemic shift" happening here: The amount of care work, material, and "affective labor" needed to (re)produce workers, work that ranges from providing food to educating and socializing young people, which can be summarized as work of social reproduction, is one of the main background conditions for the very existence of a capitalist mode of production.[54] Which is why capitalism necessarily relies on the oppression of women and all those performing the work of social reproduction: Unlike those Marxists who saw the oppression of women as a result of feudal relations, feminists such as Nancy Fraser, Silvia Federici, Leopoldina Fortunati, and Mariarosa Dalla Costa have long since pointed out that women's unpaid domestic labor is the pillar upon which the exploitation of waged labor, or "wage slavery," has been built, and thus the secret of its very productivity.[55] This does not mean that patriarchy did not exist before capitalism, but rather that capitalism

---

[52] Karl Marx, *Capital*, 873–7.

[53] Nancy Fraser, "Behind Marx's Hidden Abode," 61.

[54] Fraser expands the list of background conditions to include also earth ecology and political power (ibid, 66ff). On the centrality of social reproduction work for the existence of capitalism, see also Maria Mies, *Patriarchy and Accumulation on a World Scale: Women in the International Division of Labour* (London: Zed Books, 1986). More recent accounts include Shahrzad Mojab (ed.), *Marxism and Feminism* (London: Zed Books 2015), and Cinzia Arruzza, *Le relazioni pericolose: matrimoni e divorzi tra marxismo e femminismo* (Vicenza: Neri Pozza Editore, 2010), both of which are devoted to discussing the history of encounters and separation between feminism and Marxism.

[55] Mariarosa Della Costa, *Potere Femminile e Sovversione Sociale* (Venice: Marsilio Editore, 1972), 31ff.

re-signified, transformed, and—where it did not already exist—imported patriarchal ideas about the inferiority of women and the superiority of the first sex.

As Silvia Federici showed in her *Caliban and the Witch*, if we understand the process of primitive accumulation in this expanded view, it becomes clear that this is not a one-off, but rather an *ongoing* extraction of value from women's bodies that is accompanied by the devaluation of women's work through the very denial of its status as "labor." As Silvia puts it: "The power differential between women and men in capitalist society cannot be attributed to the irrelevance of housework for capitalist accumulation—an irrelevance belied by the strict rules that have governed women's lives—nor the survival of timeless cultural schemes. Rather it should be interpreted as the effect of a social system of production that does not recognize the production and reproduction of the worker as a social-economic activity, and a source of capital accumulation, but mystifies it instead as a natural resource or a personal service, while profiting from the wageless condition of the labor involved."[56]

Thus, ideals of women as being careful, sensitive, nurturing—in sum, as the angels of the hearth—are not timeless norms, but very time- and space-specific demands. Indeed, Federici's magnificent work shows how the transition to capitalism was accompanied by the emergence of both the "witch" and the "Caliban" persecution, where the former is the symbol of the women whose labor had to be devalued in order to become exploitable, and the latter is the symbol of the anti-colonial rebel, whose work and land had to be expropriated for an original accumulation to happen. Following others before her, Federici carefully reconstructs how the witch-hunts of the Early Modern period were essential for the transition to capitalism. Before becoming "angels of the hearth," women were literally demonized as witches, tortured and persecuted in order to delegitimize their role in knowledge-production and their control over reproduction. Whereas for centuries women had been the source of intergenerational knowledge about the use of plants, medicines, and techniques in (re)production control, these large-scale witch-hunts stripped women of the legitimacy of those skills and knowledge, and often burnt them at the stake as heretics.[57]

---

[56] Silvia Federici, *The Caliban and the Witch: Women, the Body and Primitive Accumulation* (New York: Autonomedia, 2004), 8.

[57] Ibid, 92–4, 102–03.

The criminalization of women's control over procreation was perpetrated through one of the most insidious and systematic attacks on women's bodies for which we have historical records. Whereas Michel Foucault's notion of biopolitics simply registers an intensification of the political and state control over life, but leaves it unexplained, feminist theorists showed (well before him) how such an intensification was nothing but the other side of the expropriation of women's control over procreation, a criminalization that was necessary for capitalism to emerge. "Foucault's analysis of the power techniques and disciplines to which the body has been subjected has ignored the process of reproduction, has collapsed female and male histories into an undifferentiated whole, and has been so disinterested in the 'disciplining' of women that it never mentions one of the most monstrous attacks on the body perpetrated by the modern era: the witch-hunt."[58]

If, instead of adopting the fiction of a gender-neutral subject and its concomitant thanatopolitical perspective, one focuses on the ontogenesis of gendered individuals, then it becomes evident that the witch-hunts were accompanied by a process of redefining gender roles in a binary direction that was essential to the new capitalist mode of production. After the demonization, and thus extermination, of women as witches, those very same subjects could be turned into "angels," and a binary opposition between submissive, passive, chaste women and dominating, audacious, and sexually active men could be established. Throughout sixteenth- and seventeenth-century Europe, women lost ground in every area of social life and experience, including a veritable process of legal infantilization that made them more and more dependent on men.[59] The witch-hunts of the fifteenth century were thus followed by the so-called *querelle de femmes*, on whose significance Federici wrote at length:

How the new sexual division of labor reshaped male–female relations can be seen from the broad debate that was carried out in the learned and popular literature on the nature of female virtues and vices, one of the main avenues for the ideological redefinition of gender relations in the transition to capitalism. Known from an early phase as '*la querelle des femmes*', what transpires from this debate is a new sense of curiosity for the subject, indicating that the old norms were breaking down, and

---

[58] Ibid, 8.
[59] Ibid, 100.

the public was becoming aware that the basic elements of sexual politics were being reconstructed. Two trends within this debate can be identified. On the one hand, new cultural canons were constructed maximising the differences between women and men and creating more feminine and more masculine prototypes.[60] On the other hand, it was established that women were inherently inferior to men— excessively emotional and lusty, unable to govern themselves—and had to be placed under male control.[61]

By re-signifying old Western Christian stereotypes that portrayed women as a mere derivation of a male body (at best), and instigator of original sin (at worst), this new ideological apparatus was reproduced across different intellectual lines. Popular literature, humanists, Protestants reformers, and counter-reformation Catholics alike all cooperated in the systematic vilification of women. A significant historical record of this process is the vast amount of literature that accuses women of being unreasonable, vain, and incapable of keeping their tongues in check. "But the main female villain was the disobedient wife, who, together with the 'scold,' the 'witch,' and the 'whore' was the favourite target of dramatists, popular writers, and moralists."[62]

Figure 8.1, the image of a woman wearing a scold's bridle and being paraded in the streets, aptly captures the attack on women's independence, including that of their speech. The illustration comes from a 1655 book that describes the punishments inflicted on "scolds" by local magistrates in seventeenth-century Newcastle, England. "Scold" was a term used to describe those who disturbed social life with their "chiding and scoulding" and other supposedly unruly behavior.[63] The punishment for those who used their voice to scold was being forced to wear a metal "bridle" or "branks," an instrument of torture which trapped their head while penetrating and inflicting pain in their mouths. It is significant to note, with Silvia Federici, that a similar device was used by European slave traders in Africa to subdue their captives and carry them to their ships.

---

[60] Leopoldina Fortunati, "La ridefinizione della donna," in *Il grande Calibano: Storia del corpo sociale ribelle nella prima fase del capitale,* eds. Silvia Federici and Leopoldina Fortunati (Milano: Franco Angeli, 1984).

[61] Silvia Federici, *The Caliban and the Witch*, 101.

[62] Ibid.

[63] From the British Library Catalogue: https://www.bl.uk/collection-items/a-woman-wearing-a-scolds-bridle-1655 (accessed on March 25, 2021).

FIGURE 8.1 Ralph Gardiner (*b*. 1625–?) and Francis Hargrave (*c*. 1741–1821). A woman wearing a scold's bridle from *England's Grievance Discovered in Relation to the Coal-trade. With the Map of the River of Tine and Situation of the Town and Corporation of Newcastle. The Tyrannical Oppression of Those Magistrates, Their Charters and Grants, the Several Tryals, Depositions, and Judgements Obtained against Them, Etc.* [With plates.] MS. notes [by F. Hargrave, and others.] 1655. Public Domain. © British Library Board, shelfmark: 1029.b.4., p. 110.

As a consequence, it is not an exaggeration to state, as she does, that women were the "savages of Europe":[64] While the inhabitants of the colonized lands were being expropriated of their labor, land, and riches, and heralded as "savages" and "primitives," women were expropriated of their labor via the denial of the status of work, and concomitantly denigrated as "scolds"—too emotional, too vain, too unreasonable.

The change in the nature of political power that Foucault diagnosed with the helpful term of "biopolitics" must therefore be understood as the intensification of the state control and discipline over life that happened at the expense of women, who were dismissed from their role as experts in

---

[64] Silvia Federici, *The Caliban and the Witch*, 100.

reproduction—a role sanctioned by a transmission of knowledge across thousands of years, and countless generations. The emergence of the state system is indeed another background condition for the existence of capitalism. The state is the apparatus that punishes "scolds," guarantees private property, enforces contracts, adjusts disputes, quells anti-capitalist rebellions, and maintains the "full faith and credit" of the money supply that constitutes capital's life blood.[65] The paradox of the "free" market is that markets are anything but "free," dependant as they are on an extremely complex legal apparatus both for their emergence and for their maintenance,[66] an apparatus that necessarily relies on the modern state, i.e., on the dominion over a people that is territorially defined and characterized by the successful claim of the monopoly of legitimate coercion. As Marx's and Engels' succinctly put it, the state is the tool whereby the bourgeoisie has "agglomerated population, centralized means of production, and has concentrated property in a few hands."[67] The functioning of a capitalist

---

[65] Nancy Fraser, "Behind Marx's Hidden Abode," 64.

[66] Bernard Harcourt speaks insightfully of "the illusion of free market" (*The Illusion of Free Markets: Punishment and the Myth of Natural Order* [Cambridge, MA: Harvard University Press 2012]).

[67] Karl Marx and Friedrich Engels, *The Communist Manifesto,* trans. Samuel Moore (London: Verso, 1998), 35, 40. Political theorists have been pointing to this nature of the modern state for quite some time, well before Marx and Engels. Within the West, for instance, this was clearly articulated by Jean-Jacques Rousseau, when he wrote: "If we follow the progress of inequality through these different revolutions, we will find that the establishment of the Law and Right of property was its first term; the institution of Magistracy, the second; the conversion of legitimate into arbitrary power the third and last; so that the state of rich and poor was authorized by the first Epoch, that of powerful and weak by the second, and by the third that of Master and Slave, which is the last degree of inequality, and the state to which all the others finally lead, until new revolutions either dissolve the Government entirely, or bring it closer to legitimate institution" (Jean-Jacques Rousseau, *The Discourses and Other Early Political Writings*, ed. Victor Gourevitch, [Cambridge: Cambridge University Press, 1997], 182). Marx and Engels' critique of the state as a tool whereby a minority rules over a majority is reminiscent of Rousseau and anarchist thinkers such as Proudhon. Whereas Marxists considered at times that it was possible to use the state apparatus through a dictatorship of the proletariat aimed at a communist revolution, anarchist theorists, from Mikhail Bakunin to Emma Goldman, were relentless in their critique. As Bakunin wrote, when contesting the idea of a dictatorship of the proletariat: "The only difference between revolutionary dictatorship and the state is in external appearances. Essentially, they both represent the same government of the majority by a minority in the name of the presumed stupidity of the one and the presumed intelligence of the other. Therefore they are equally reactionary, both having the direct and inevitable result of consolidating the political and economic privileges of the governing minority and the political and economic slavery of the masses." (Mikhail Bakunin, *Statism and Anarchy,* trans. Marshall Shatz [Cambridge: Cambridge University Press, 2005], 137).

economy is thus inseparable from the state, because the creation of markets, enforcement of contracts, reproduction of private property, and regulation of labor markets, capitalism in sum, implies the existence of a form of political power that exercises a monopoly of legitimate coercion, a monopoly that itself depends on the use of illegitimate force, since, as Charles Tilly brilliantly put it, state-making came into being through war-making, that is, as organized crime.[68]

It is through the emergence of such a system of sovereign states, which Europe progressively exported worldwide, that the institutional infrastructures needed for the original accumulation described by Silvia Federici and other social reproduction theorists came about. And it is the state, too, that provides the tools for the administration of the modern colonial gender system. The former would be unconceivable without the latter. In other words, the coloniality of power is inseparable from its intensification as biopower, that is as a power to control, incite, and discipline life. As we have seen, the coloniality of gender has both a light and a dark side, and so we can combine Marxist feminists' analysis of primitive accumulation with Maria Lugones' insight that the coloniality of power works differently in different regions of the globe. Although the gender binary embedded by the division of labor of the European mononuclear family has become widespread worldwide, along with associated ideals of progress, modernity, and development, this hegemonic force operates differently in the different contexts, re-signifying old patriarchal stereotypes where they existed, or importing them where gynocracy—if not matriarchy—was the norm. While feminine women, as the submissive angels of the hearth were celebrated in the West, deviant, monstrous, and bestial others were projected onto the colonial "Other." Much of Western feminism has been analyzing insightfully the technologies whereby "feminine subjects" are created, but often fails to emphasize how much such creations relied on the specular creation of their colonial abjects.[69] The exhibition of the monstrous, hairy, bestial bearded-woman, as in the case of Julia Pastrana, is nothing but the "dark" side of the modern colonial gender system that produces well-groomed, depilated, submissive women on its "light" side.

---

[68] Charles Tilly, "War Making and State Making as Organized Crime," in *Bringing the State Back In*, ed. Peter Evans, et al. (Cambridge: Cambridge University Press, 1985).

[69] As Julia Kristeva observed, the creation of a subject is psychologically dependent on the creation of its abject (Julia Kristeva, *Powers of Horror: An Essay on Abjection*, trans. Leon S. Roudiez [New York: Columbia University Press, 1982]).

Foucauldian inspired feminists have for instance systematically explored the role that medicine, beauty techniques, and fashion styles play in shaping feminine subjects. Sandra Bartky, for example, considered how discipline-based practices such as dieting and fitness regimes create the ideal feminine body, in the same way the military creates the ideal soldier via training.[70] Through an exhaustive regulation of women's body size, dieting, fitness, posture, regimentation of what is appropriate to show (or not), hairstyle, skin care, and make-up, women's bodies are turned into the "docile and compliant companions of men."[71] Notice here how many of these technologies of the self produce "femininity" through infantilization. Skin care products make sure women look "forever young;" the disciplining or complete elimination of hair from the places where it appears as of puberty (armpits, legs, and pubic area) makes sure women's bodies look like those of pre-pubescent girls;[72] and hairstyles and coloring techniques whisk away any signs of aging appearing on a well-groomed head. Whereas youth is valued across the gender spectrum, there is no doubt that, at least in the West, there is a systematic association of "femininity" with the literal removal of all signs of aging, such as wrinkles and grey hair. A man is viewed as even more masculine when his hair turns gray, but a woman becomes less feminine if she does not dye or depilate. Refusal to comply is met with a powerful system of social sanctions, which range from being doomed as sexually undesirable, and the attendant loss of sexual capital, to being dubbed as deviant or anti-social, risking the loss of all one's human capital. Indeed, particularly today, having well-manicured hands and a certain hairstyle can enhance

---

[70] Sandra Lee Bartky, "Foucault, Femininity, and the Modernization of Patriarchal Power," in *Writing on the Body: Female Embodiment and Feminist Theory*, eds. Katie Conboy, Nadia Medina, and Sarah Stanbury (New York: Columbia University Press, 1997); Sandra Lee Bartky, "Suffering to Be Beautiful," in *Gender Struggles: Practical Approaches to Contemporary Feminism*, eds. Constance L. Mui and Julien S. Murphy (Lanham: Rowman & Littlefield Publishers, 2002).

[71] Sandra Lee Bartky, "Foucault, Femininity, and the Modernization of Patriarchal Power," 143.

[72] In a study of depilation practices among American college students, Breanne Fahs documented the systemic association between femininity and hair removal and how people assigned male at birth practicing it were seen as being gay or queer. In particular, the study concludes that "those with male partners—whether male or female—felt more pressure to shave in order to comply with cultural demands for hairlessness" (Breanne Fahs, "Shaving it all off: Examining social norms of body hair among college men in a women's studies course," *Women's Studies* 42, 563: 2013).

one's career.[73] The fear of losing male patronage helps explaining why patriarchy still persists, and is so resilient despite multiple waves of feminist fightback.[74]

Clearly, such techniques—which quite often require extremely painful hair-removal procedures, exhausting dieting regimes, invasive surgeries, and expensive beauty treatments—are frequently embraced with ambivalence, but still perceived as a necessary evil in order to be "beautiful." In Sandra Bartky's revealing phrase, it is widely accepted that a little bit of suffering is necessary to be beautiful.[75] And very few ask themselves why we accept this association of feminine beauty with suffering. Women embrace suffering-towards-beauty and even feel empowered by its demands. That is because, within a patriarchal world that systematically portrays women as the "second sex," by turning themselves into "feminine" subjects, women guarantee themselves male patronage, and thus all the human capital they would otherwise be denied. Besides the pleasure of complying with gender norms, and thus reproducing the expected feminine-female and masculine-men binary, there is the added consolation of not transgressing them, and so avoiding the social stigma associated with whoever interrupts the modern colonial gender system.

Despite its emancipatory potential (Western) psychoanalysis itself has often worked as a technology of the self, aimed at producing docile female subjects. Feminists have systematically explored the way in which Freudian psychoanalysis, for instance, often reproduced a phallogocentric discourse that reduced femininity to lack, thereby turning woman into "this sex which is not one," to use Luce Irigaray's expression. As early as 1892, Sigmund Freud speculated that "the essentially repressed element is always what is feminine," but failed to address the extent to which his own psychoanalytic theory and practice helped to perpetrate that repression.[76] From his writings on female sexuality to those on religion and culture,

---

[73] On this point, see Johanna Oksala, "The Neoliberal Subject of Feminism," *Journal of the British Society for Phenomenology* 42, no. 1 (2011), 115.

[74] The fear of losing male patronage is one of the reasons that explains the persistence of menocracy, even in contexts where one would expect patriarchy to have disappeared. See Carol Gilligan and Naomi Snider's *Why Does Patriarchy Persist?* (Cambridge: Polity Press, 2018).

[75] Sandra Lee Bartky, "Suffering to Be Beautiful."

[76] Jill Gentile, "The Missing Signifier and the Malfunctioning Paternal Law" (forthcoming in *The Routledge Handbook of Psychoanalysis and Philosophy*, Aner Govrin & Tair Caspi, eds.).

Freud operated a sort of *reductio ad penem*,[77] where everything revolves around the figure of the father and that of the mother is persistently marginalized.[78] The entire Freudian theory of the libido reflects this bias, which is also patent in his incapacity to explain female sexuality without using male sexuality as the yardstick for assessing sexuality as such and the development of the libido more generally.[79] Apart from Freud's biography, this certainly reflects the patriarchy of the epoch, which Freudian theory embodies so well.[80]

Although psychoanalytic feminists have criticized psychoanalysis' phallocratic symbolic economy and successfully embarked in a search for the "missing signifier" since its very beginning,[81] the discipline, as a whole, has continued to perpetuate a hetero- and cisnormative view of sexuality that portrayed homo- and trans-sexuality as pathologies until very recently. Hence, as Patricia Gherovici argued, the call for psychoanalysis itself to go through a sex change and revisit the way in which it has systematically reproduced gender binarism and pathologized sexualities that deviated from the standard.[82] Yet, along with a sexual change, psychoanalysis also needs to undergo a racial one, if it wants to deliver on

---

[77] The operation is indeed a form of *reductio ad unum*, that is of reduction to the one, but with the important qualification that the one is the development of the libido in males.

[78] Feminist psychoanalysts have emphasized this aspect of Freudian theory for a very long time. See, for instance, Karen Horney, "On the Genesis of the Castration Complex in Women," *International Journal of Psychoanalysis* 5, no. 1 (1924); Luce Irigaray, *This Sex Which Is Not One* (Ithaca: Cornell University Press, 1985), 23; Julia Kristeva, *Revolution in Poetic Language* (New York: Columbia University Press, 1984), 46; more recently, see Jill Gentile, *Feminine Law: Freud, Free Speech, and the Voice of Desire* (London; Karnac, 2016).

[79] For instance, in Freud's (in)famous essay on female sexuality, which he begins to address with reluctance before ultimately concluding that it is a "puzzle to be left to poets." Sigmund Freud, *New Introductory Lectures to Psychoanalysis* (New York: Norton & Norton, 1965), 167. Freud nevertheless presents an entire reconstruction of female sexuality from the point of view of the development of the libido in males, leading to his very controversial statements about women's supposed penis envy.

[80] Recently, Joel Whitebook, in his innovative intellectual biography of Freud, adduces new historical evidence as to why Freud himself could not really deal with feminine sexuality. Joel Whitebook, *Freud: An Intellectual Biography* (Cambridge: Cambridge University Press, 2017), 52. According to Whitebook, Freud's mother suffered from a chronic depression that left little Sigmund in an emotional vacuum that was only partially filled by his Czech nanny (Joel Whitebook, *Freud*, 43).

[81] Gentile, "The Missing Signifier and the Malfunctioning Paternal Law," 11.

[82] Patricia Gherovici, "Psychoanalysis Needs a Sex Change," *Gay and Lesbian Issues and Psychology Review* 7(1), (2011). See also: Patricia Gherovici, *Transgender Psychoanalysis: A Lacanian Perspective on Sexual Difference* (London: Routledge, 2017).

its emancipatory promise of an analysis of the psychical structures of domination. Most of its conceptual tools reflect not only the phallogocentric tendency to reduce women to "lack" (per Irigaray), but also the Eurocentric propensity to present complexes arising from the European nuclear family as universals, projecting them as the standard for a normal psychic development. One case in point is the concept of an Oedipus complex, generated by the incest taboo, which is intrinsically linked to the Western family structure and the economico-libidinal organization of familial bounds that the latter presupposes, so much so that, as we have seen, it cannot be systematically registered outside of the West. To paraphrase Frantz Fanon, psychoanalysts such as Freud and Jung may think they have found the key to unveil childhood traumas, and thus reached the depth of the infancy of humanity, but it may well turn out they have reached only the infancy of Europeans.

In 1930, John Carl Flügel, a British psychoanalyst and translator of Freud's works, published a book devoted to the psychology of clothes, where he mixed Freudian psychoanalysis with fashion history. Flügel used psychoanalytic tools to identify one of the most extraordinary changes that happened in the history of human fashion and destined to have long and extensive consequences. Around the end of the eighteenth century, he wrote, "men gave up their right to all the brighter, gayer, more elaborate, and more varied forms of ornamentation, leaving this entirely to the use of women, and thereby making their own tailoring the most austere and ascetic of the arts. Sartorially, this event has surely the right to be considered as 'The Great Masculine Renunciation'. Man abandoned his claims to be considered beautiful henceforth aimed at being only useful. So far as clothes remained of importance to him, his utmost endeavor could lie only in the direction of being 'correctly' attired, not of being elegantly or elaborately attired."[83] Men, after such an epochal transformation, would choose their clothes only to be properly/appropriately dressed, not to attract attention to their bodies and display their exhibitionism.

Flügel ascribes the causes of such a monumental change to the Industrial Revolution and the emergence of industrial and commercial ideals that conquered class after class, "until they became accepted even by the aristocrats of all the more progressive countries,"[84] and then by all

---

[83] John Carl Flügel, "The Great Masculine Renunciation," in *The Rise of Fashion: A Reader*, ed. Daniel Leonhard Purdy (Minneapolis: Minnesota University Press, 2004), 103.
[84] Ibid, 104.

the elites around the globe. From a change that originally happened in Western Europe, the two-piece suit became the signifier for a global masculinity that endorsed modern, progressive views. According to John Carl, this "democratization in clothes" reflected ideals of "freedom, equality, fraternity" (*liberté, égalité, fraternité*) born out of the French Revolution: The uniformity in clothing gave a powerful, visible impetus to the doctrine of the "brotherhood of man."[85] Now all wearing the same dark-two-piece suit with the same accentuating tie, men belonging to different classes could feel they belong to the same group. This, Flügel further observed, "could only be achieved by a greater uniformity of dress, a uniformity achieved by the abolition of those distinctions which had formerly divided the wealthy from the poor, the exalted from the humble, and since these distinctions consisted largely in greater elaboration and costliness of aristocratic costume as compared to that of the lower classes, the change in question implied at the same time a greater simplification of dress, by a general approximation to more plebeian standards that were possible to all."[86] Thus, whereas upper-class European men had indulged for centuries in the display of the most extravagant wigs, laces, and sartorial eccentricity, within a century these fripperies had all disappeared and a literal army of bodies all sporting the same sober attire started to populate salons, streets, theaters, public schools and public spaces.

The question then becomes why did (European) men embark on such a renunciation, which implies, among other things, repressing or at least transforming the exhibitionistic tendency in which the European upper classes had so long indulged. John Carl's response is multiple—and yet is singularly sexist and Eurocentric, as we will see. First, the men who underwent the Great Masculine Renunciation are not "men" as a universal category, but, originally at least, Western European men, so the very fact that such attire became hegemonic worldwide as the signifier of masculinity and modernity deserves much more scrutiny than that he accords them. Second, Flügel connects this transformation with a naturalized understanding of sexual difference that sees women as intrinsically more exhibitionist because more narcissistic, as more prone to sexual rivalry because less interested in social life, without realizing of how much of that theory is an import of a Freudian

---

[85] Ibid, 104–05.
[86] Ibid, 104.

phallologentric apparatus, which systematically portrays women as marked by a lack and by the consequent drive to cover such supposed castration through embellishments. Indeed, Flügel states that, through the Great Masculine Renunciation, men gained a renewed sense of brotherhood, since wearing the same general style of clothes produced a sense of community. However, he also observed that this also produced a greater sense of distinction from those who have not gone through such a renunciation, and thus the Great Masculine Renunciation became the main signifier for sexual difference.[87] Whereas man's modern clothing abounds in features that symbolize his devotion to duty, self-control, and other phallic attributes (the tie being the most obvious example), women's varied and much more elaborate clothes, according to Flügel, better respond to their innate narcissism, envious nature, and drive towards sexual competition, of which laces, bright colors, and excessive adornments would be a symptom.[88]

Although Flügel's approach is marked by a phallogocentrism and phallophilia that problematically transforms an historically situated drive configuration into a naturalized sexual difference, his analysis remains very valuable as both an historical document of the formation of the modern colonial gender system, and as a tool for its analysis—particularly when combined with a feminist decolonial and deimperial attitude. Today, two centuries after it began, the effects of the Great Masculine Renunciation are still visible, both as signifier of gender binary, and of the dialectical relationship between the light and the dark side of the modern/colonial gender system. Indeed, it is still the case that men's clothes tend to reproduce those very same values of utility and simplicity, and much greater uniformity, whereas womanhood is associated with a much greater release of exhibitionist drives and proliferation of ornamentation. Furthermore, it is still true that, as the British psychoanalyst observed, the gender binary works psychologically through a transformation of men's exhibitionistic desires into active scoptophilia, from the passive pleasure of being seen to the active one of seeing. The very same men who happily embrace the Great Masculine Renunciation will usually feel an increased desire to contemplate women's sartorial exhibitionism and will feel particularly proud to appear with a "well-dressed woman," since the latter satisfies both their desire to see and, via identification, provides a vicarious satisfaction for their repressed

---

[87] Ibid, 105.
[88] Ibid, 107.

exhibitionism.[89] Thus, despite the enormous changes in society, it is still the case that while women's fashion has varied rapidly and enormously, men's attire has remained much more stable, particularly as it comes to signify a certain position within the modern colonial gender system. The Great Masculine Renunciation has become a signifier of the gender binary because it has become a signifier for the ethno-class of the bourgeois "Man." Wearing a sober two-piece suit and tie became a signifier of belonging to a certain global ethno-class, and that is the reason why from Calcutta to Saigon, from London to Nairobi, Rio to Tokyo, businessmen, politicians, bankers, and educators, can be unified under the same visual and sartorial order. Adopting the clothes that signify such a renunciation has also become a signifier of whiteness—not in the sense of *"blancura,"* that is of biological whiteness, but of *"blanquitud,"* that is of ethical and civilizational whiteness.[90] In other words, the suit became a symbol of internalization of a certain capitalist ethos, one that values waged work, and the consumption of Western commodities, lifestyles, and intellectual products.

We can therefore read the Great Masculine Renunciation as a specific technology of the self within the modern/colonial gender system, one that is particularly powerful because it is global and imaginal at the same time: While looking at world politicians gathered at the United Nations, we perceive the "brotherhood" of (Westernized) men, all united by the same suit and phallic symbol (tie), and thereby distinguished *both* from "women," who are supposed to wear different colors and more elaborate adornments to cover their castration, and from those men who wear "traditional clothes," thereby signifying their position in the imaginal order of *"blanquitud."*[91] To have a sense of the imaginal impact of such

---

[89] Ibid, 108.

[90] On the distinction between the two, see the analysis of modernity inspired by the Frankfurt school by Bolívar Echeverría, *Modernity and "Whiteness"* (Cambridge: Polity Press, 2019), in particular p. 36.

[91] For instance, according to the formal dress code for meetings at the United Nations: "All clothing must portray professionalism as expected in diplomatic settings. If attire is deemed inappropriate by NMUN staff, individuals may be asked to leave the session and return with appropriate attire. Professional business attire is a business jacket, dress shirt, tie, slacks/skirt/dress, and dress shoes. Professional dress expectations require that dresses and skirts be knee length. Delegates should be dressed in professional business attire that reflects their self-identified gender. Traditional dress is permitted only for delegations in whose home countries it is considered professional business dress." ("Conduct Expectations," National Model United Nations, https://www.nmun.org/conduct-expectations.html#:~:text=Delegates%20should%20be%20dressed%20in,%2C%20athletic%20wear%2C%20and%20sunglasses, accessed March 20, 2021).

renunciation in terms of the unconscious organization of desire, compare the two images below.

Figure 8.2 depicts a portrait of Louis XIV,[92] displaying both the power of his monarchy and the French men's fashion as it was before the Renunciation. Notice the abundance of adornments, all the colorful types of lace, merlettes, wigs, furs, and feathers (to name but a few), and the

FIGURE 8.2 Hyacinthe Rigaud, portrait of Louis XIV (1701–02) from Château de Versailles, Wikipedia Commons, Public Domain, CC0, Source: WikiCommons: https://commons.wikimedia.org/wiki/File:Hyacinthe_Rigaud_-_Louis_XIV,_roi_de_France_(1638-1715).jpg)

---

[92] Hyacinthe Rigaud artist QS:P170,Q49898 (https://commons.wikimedia.org/wiki/File: Hyacinthe_Rigaud_-_Louis_XIV,_roi_de_France_(1638-1715).jpg), "Hyacinthe Rigaud: Louis XIV, roi de France (1638–1715)," marked as public domain; more details on Wikimedia Commons: https://commons.wikimedia.org/wiki/Template:PD-old (accessed March 7, 2021).

FIGURE 8.3 Heads of delegations at the 2015 United Nations Climate Change Conference (COP21), which led to the signing of the Paris Agreement. Date: 30 November 2015. Author: Presidencia de la República Mexicana Source: Wiki-Commons (under Creative Commons Attribution 2.0 Generic license): https://commons.wikimedia.org/wiki/File:COP21_participants_-_30_Nov_2015_(23430273715).jpg

explicit emphasis on the body itself, with the king's legs prominently displayed, propped up by high heels, and one tilted slightly to add emphasis and project the entire body forward. Power and authority are displayed through sartorial and physical exhibitionism. Compare this spectacle of authority with one that took place just a few centuries later in another historic moment in the very same country.

Figure 8.3 portrays politicians from around the world at the 2015 United Nations Climate Change Conference, which led to the signing of Paris Agreement.[93] The politicians here are also mainly men, but, most importantly, even the few women present here exhibit a similar sartorial uniformity: All figures are dressed in the same black, dark gray, or dark blue "professional attire," like soldiers of the same army—an army of bodies embodying the Great Masculine Renunciation, mourning all the colors and feathers, merlettes and lace they have lost. All men wear a tie, again with the exception of women and those who are exempted from such enforced dress codes because they can claim to be wearing their

---

[93] Source: Presidencia de la República Mexicana (https://commons.wikimedia.org/wiki/File:COP21_participants_-_30_Nov_2015_(23430273715).jpg), "COP21 participants, 30 Nov 2015 (23430273715)," https://creativecommons.org/licenses/by/2.0/legalcode (accessed March 7, 2021).

"traditional clothes." In contrast to their seventeenth-century precursors, these modern politicians display their authority while mourning their exhibitionism, but thereby also celebrating their phallic status and their shared brotherhood.

Although this is a visual order that is literally enforced by official dress codes and regulation in powerful international organizations and business corporations, it is also an imaginal order unconsciously (re) produced by individual choices and styles. The Great Masculine Renunciation is thus one of the most powerful catalysts for the (re) production of the modern/colonial gender system, on par with other technologies, such as beauty techniques and surgeries. Besides the already-mentioned case of eye surgery, largely performed in Asian countries, and which make eyes look more Western, skin care products are another crucial tool for the production of a feminine "*blanquitud.*" With a detailed analysis of women's magazine in translational Indonesia, L. Ayu Saraswati, for instance, showed how certain products that claim to make Indonesian women look more Western, feed on and at the same time reproduce the desire to belonging to a cosmopolitan whiteness: they are technologies of the self that invite you to "perceive beauty, while sensing race".[94]

The capitalist mode of (re)production is thus inseparable from a division between productive and reproductive labor, and the consequent production of bodies, desires, and images of those who perform the former because they are supposedly naturally predisposed to them, and those who perform the latter, which is also considered a matter of natural predisposition. Although this division of labor has been at the center of Western feminist theorizing for a very long time, theorists have often ignored how the production of the "light" side of the modern/colonial gender system goes hand in hand with its "dark" one. In the United States, for instance, the imaginal production of the feminine mystique of the devout, chaste, and submissive "angel of the hearth" has often been accompanied by the portrayal of women of African descent as jezebels, emasculating matriarchs, and mammies.[95]

---

[94] L. Ayu Saraswati, *Seeing Beauty, Sensing Race in Transnational Indonesia* (Honolulu: University of Hawai'i Press, 2013), 83–108.

[95] For a detailed analysis of such stereotypes, see Patricia Hill Collins, *Black Feminist Thought: Knowledge, Consciousness, and the Politics of Empowerment* (New York: Routledge, 2000), in particular pages 69–97.

Hortense J. Spillers analyzed the American grammar of "mama's baby, papa's maybe," showing how, in a society characterized by patriarchal values and a patrilinear line of descent, African Americans have often been portrayed as backwards and inept because they are considered to be stuck in a matriarchal family structure. According to the 1965 Moynihan Report analyzed by Hortense: "In essence, the negro community has been forced into a matriarchal structure, which, because it is so far out of line with the rest of American society, seriously retards its progress of the groups as a whole, and imposes a crushing burden on the negro male, and, in consequence, on a great many negro women as well".[96] In this racialized fantasy, the problems of the negro community would therefore ultimately lie in the fact that the "negro family" has no Father, the absence of his Name, his Law, and his Symbolic function marking the impressive missing agency in the Black community. This, in turn, would conveniently explain why their children underperform in standardized examinations, matriculations in school, and life in general.[97]

Using an impressive array of history and psychoanalytic tools, Spillers shows how such a widespread American grammar is rooted in that extraordinary event and long-lasting effect of the Atlantic slave trade. The captive body is not only deprived of gender, but family ties are severed because neither father nor mother can claim their child, and no child can claim its parents. Ever since the first slave ships arrived in the territory of what would become the United States, the enslaved Black carried this material and symbolic stripping of the gender and family ties that still reverberate, 500 years later, in the American grammar of the missing paternal law: "Mama's baby, papa's maybe." This grammar, which relies on the opposition between the a-gendered enslaved Black body and the white gender binarism, between the patriarchal world operating under the name of the Father and the emasculating matriarchy operating under the name of the Mother, is the grammar of the modern/colonial gender

---

[96] Hortense Spillers quotes here the words of a very influential report written in the 1960s on what was then referred to as the "negro family," and which identified the sources of the problems encountered by people of color as lying in its matriarchal structure (Hortense J. Spillers, "Mama's Baby, Papa's Maybe: An American Grammar Book," *Diacritics* 17, no. 2 (1987), 65). See also: Daniel P. Moynihan, "The Moynihan Report" [The Negro Family: The Case for National Action. Washington, D.C.: U.S. Department of Labor, 1965]. *The Moynihan Report—The Politics of Controversy: A Transaction Social Science and Public Policy Report*, ed. Lee Rainwater and William L. Yancey, Cambridge, MA: MIT Press (1967).
[97] Lee Rainwater and William L. Yancey, *The Moynihan Report—The Politics of Controversy*, 66.

system operating in the United States of America. From an historical perspective, it is a grammar based on a fatal "misnaming," because it assigns a matriarchal value where it does not belong, and is doubly false: False because the enslaved female had no right to claim her child, and false again because "motherhood" is not perceived as a legitimate line for cultural inheritance in the current social climate.[98]

In sum, as Hortense Spillers put it, "this differential cultural text actually reconfigures, in historically ordained discourse, certain *representational* potentialities for African-Americans: 1) motherhood as female blood-rite is outraged, is denied, at the very same time that it becomes the founding term of a human and social enactment; 2) a dual fatherhood is set in motion, comprised of the African father's *banished* name and body and the captor father's mocking presence. In this play of paradox, only the female stands in *flesh*, both mother and mother-dispossessed. This problematizing of gender places her, in my view, *out* of the traditional symbolics of female gender, and it is our task to make a place for this different social subject. In doing so, we are less interested in joining the ranks of gendered femaleness than gaining the *insurgent* ground as female social subject".[99] An insurgency that, Spillers adds, must begin by embracing the monstrosity of a female with the potential to name.

Finding such an insurgent ground, in turn, implies, as we have seen, unpacking the capitalist mode of (re)production and overcoming the logic of exploitation upon which it rests. This mode of (re)production emerged 500 years ago when, thanks to the emergence of capitalism as a global system, it became possible to *externalize* or *exteriorize* those whom the new patriarchs could exploit: the colonized as savages, women as witches, and nature as external to culture and society.[100] That is why colonization and housewifization necessarily went hand in hand, coalescing with the reduction of the non-human world to mere "nature" to be subsumed under capital. Precisely because the capitalist mode of production relies on the externalization of its costs in at least three directions (race, gender, nature), one cannot aspire to non-racialized capitalism, to feminist capitalism or, even less so, to green capitalism: "the privileges of the exploiters can never become the privileges of all."[101] If

---

[98] Ibid, 80.
[99] Ibid, 80.
[100] Maria Mies, *Patriarchy and Accumulation on a World Scale,* 75.
[101] Ibid, 76.

the wealth of the centers of the capitalist global system is based on the exploitation of its peripheries, then the peripheries cannot achieve wealth unless they also create their own exploitable peripheries. Similarly, if the emancipation of men from social reproductive labor is based on the subordination of women, then women cannot achieve equality with men, because that necessarily includes the right to exploit others. When this happens, it is because some privileged women become exploiters of less fortunate ones, who then carry a double load of women's work. Thus, as Maria Mies wrote: "a feminist strategy for liberation cannot but aim at the total abolition of all these relationships of retrogressive progress. This means it must aim at an end of all *exploitation* of women by men, of nature by man, of colonies by colonizers, of one class by another. As long as exploitation of one of these remains the precondition for the advance (development, evolution, progress, humanization, etc.) of one section of people, feminism cannot speak of liberation or socialism."[102]

Consequently, feminism does not mean that women should come to occupy the position of power enjoyed by (some) men, which is impossible without creating other forms of exploitation. Feminism cannot be achieved by "equality in privileges,"[103] but only through the abolition of all such privileges and the construction of a non-hierarchical, non-exploitative society, where no elites live by dominating others and where all can therefore equally be free. In other words, feminism can only achieve its goal of women's liberation by becoming anarchafeminism.

---

[102] Ibid, 77.

[103] Ibid, 37. Mies wrote: "It is, therefore, wrong as many fear, that feminist only want to replace male dominance by female dominance, because that is what 'equality' means for them: equality of privileges. But the feminist movements is basically an anarchist movement which does not want to replace one (male) power elite by another (female) power elite, but which wants to build up a non-hierarchical, non-centralized society where no elite lives on the exploitation and dominance over others."

9 The environment is us: ecofeminism as queer ecology

We have explored the ontogenesis of gendered and sexed individualities by focusing on supra-individual forces, as they are shaped by their geo-political contexts, and on inter-individual relations, as they emerge in the capitalist mode of (re)production. In this last chapter, we will focus on the same processes through the prism of the infra-level: How does the coming into being of sexed and gendered individuals appear when looked at from the point of view of infra-individual bodies and their intra-actions?

To begin with, this will require reconsidering the very notion of production and reproduction, or, as we prefer to phrase it, of (re) production, to emphasize that the former cannot exist without the latter. Whereas many authors in the socialist tradition have understood that a capitalist mode of production is impossible without the reproduction of the laborer as a living being, and have therefore addressed the importance of social reproductive work, most have ignored the generative capacity of animals, plants, and other living beings, and thus not considered them.[1] For these thinkers, nature was the mere provider of "raw material" to be subsumed under the capitalist mode of production, seen as something external to the sphere of society itself. This externalization of nature is

---

[1] See for instance Michelle Murphy, who remarks that even Karl Marx understood that the labor force needed to be reproduced, and so mentioned women and children as supplementary labor, but completely ignored the generative power of plants and animals as also necessary for reproduction. See Michelle Murphy, "Reproduction," in *Marxism and Feminism*, ed. Shahrzad Mojab (London: Zed Books, 2015), 289.

one of the background conditions for the functioning of capitalism, and must therefore be at the center of any contemporary rethinking of it.[2]

In this chapter, we explore how animals, plants, and other living and non-living beings contribute to the (re)production of sexed and gendered individuals. In doing so, we will discuss not only the separation of nature and culture, and the segregation of animals, plants, and other living beings from society, but also the very separation between "living" and "non-living matter," focusing on the transindividual insight that all beings are, to some extent, animate: Within such a philosophical perspective, the environment cannot be considered as something external, outside there, but becomes constitutive of our own being, inside here. To put it bluntly, "the environment is us,"[3] and thus beyond the inside/outside distinction. This move will substantiate the two main claims of this concluding chapter: First, that anarchafeminism is by definition ecofeminism, because by aiming to abolish all forms of exploitation it cannot but also oppose the exploitation of the natural world; and that, second, from this perspective, ecofeminism becomes itself a form of queer ecology, necessarily aimed at questioning the boundaries of any *scala naturae*: man>woman>slave>animal>plant> inanimate life.

What do we mean by "the environment is us"? At a basic level, this signals the relevance of environmental concerns for our own survival. In the last few decades, there has been an increasing awareness that the reproduction of our lives depends on such common resources as the air we breathe and the water we drink. In November 2015, for instance, we experienced the first truly "global climate strike"—organized action that was global not only in the sense that it addressed "global issues" but also in the sense that it took place in different parts of the world at more or less the same time. A significant feature of this strike, and those that followed it, was its anti-capitalist critique: Environmental concerns about global warming and the survival of the human species converged with the strike—that is, with a praxis and mode of protest typical of the socialist and anarchist tradition. In a way, those global strikes showed a deep awareness that, to paraphrase Murray Bookchin, the very notion of

---

[2] On this point and the notion of "background" conditions for capitalism, see Nancy Fraser, "Behind Marx's Hidden Abode," *New Left Review* 86 (2014), 60–6.
[3] As mentioned before, we borrow this expression from Stacy Alaimo's *Bodily Natures: Science, Environment, and the Material Self* (Indianapolis: Indiana University Press, 2010), 11.

a domination of nature by Man stems from the very real domination of human by human,[4] and that there is therefore no way to tackle the ecological challenge we are facing without addressing the culture of domination and exploitation generated by an economic mode predicated on the endless expansion of profit. Although ecology has now become a buzzword for many capitalist projects, it is crucial to ask: If one accepts the premises of a capitalist mode of production and ethos, is it ever going to be enough to just make it "green"? Can there be such a thing as a "sustainable" capitalism?

There cannot be any such thing as a "green capitalism": It can only be an ideological illusion because there is a systemic contradiction between an economic system based on the unlimited accumulation of capital and a planet in which resources necessary for the reproduction of life are limited. Whereas capital has a self-expanding logic, there is only one Earth and, as climate protesters made clear: "There is no planet B."[5] In other words, at the very heart of capitalism there is a contradiction between exchange value and use value that creates a "schizophrenic state" for the individuals who live within it. People have to produce goods for markets, and thus goods that have exchange value, such as pesticides and cars. In order to survive, however, they need goods that have use value, such as unpolluted air and water.[6] This is only one of the many contradictions of capitalism, and only one of those tensions that generate those crises that are typical of this mode of production, but one that is particularly vital because it directly affects the survival of life, in general, and of human life, in particular.

Yet, while addressing this environmental challenge, we should not forget the other contradictions we have seen, in particular the fact that capitalism needs to externalize its costs on women and colonies. Ecofeminists such as Vandana Shiva and Maria Mies have done illuminating work in showing how patriarchy and ecological catastrophe go together: The war on women and the war on nature have gone hand in

---

[4] See Murray Bookchin, *The Ecology of Freedom: The Emergence and Dissolution of Hierarchy* (Oakland: AK Press, 2005), 65. We use "Man" in Sylvia Wynter's sense of the term as an ethno-class, thus adding a feminism perspective which is not central to Bookchin's argument.

[5] Sign circulating at the New York City Climate Strike on September 20, 2019.

[6] Maria Mies, "The Myth of Catching-up Development," in *Ecofeminism*, eds. Maria Mies and Vandana Shiva (London: Zed Books, 2014), 57.

hand from the very beginning of capitalism.[7] This is shown clearly in the international division of labor: Women produce more than half of the world's food and provide more than 80 percent of food needs in food-insecure households and regions, but a capitalist mode of production focused on capital accumulation systematically renders this work invisible.[8] Since the calculation of the yearly Gross Domestic Product (GDP) of each country—the total value of the goods and services produced within a country's geographic boundaries—only takes into account the value subsumed into the market economy, but not the labor done in order to sustain the laborer, women's work is literally hidden in the economics that drive most of the international development agencies and programs nowadays.

The consequence is not only that women, as the performers of that reproductive labor, are devalued (which also explains why gender violence is so widespread), but that the natural ecosystems from which women have derived food for millennia are being systematically destroyed. This is evident in former colonies such as India, where colonizers imported their industrialized farming (monocultures), enabling the production of capitals for the market economy, but at the same time deprived Indigenous people of the ecosystems on which their subsistence depended, and thereby also deprived women of their role as biodiversity experts. What multinational corporations such as Monsanto perceive as weeds to eliminate are often gardens that Indigenous people used for millennia in order to feed themselves. And women have historically been biodiversity experts because they knew how to derive food, seeds, and medicines from natural biodiversity. When women are dispossessed of those ecosystems, their labor become much harder and thus even more invisible.[9] Many colonized countries were stripped of their subsistence economies and ended up in sheer deprivation. But the former is a very different thing from the latter: A subsistence economy, which may appear as (cultural) poverty to the colonizers, is very different

---

[7] Among their early work, see Maria Mies, *Patriarchy and Accumulation on a World Scale: Women in the International Division of Labour* (London: Zed Books, 1986), and Vandana Shiva, *Staying Alive: Women, Ecology, and Development* (Berkeley: North Atlantic Books, 1999). The two have also co-authored a very influential volume on ecofeminism, from which many of the following insights derive: Maria Mies and Vandana Shiva (eds.), *Ecofeminism* (London: Zed Books, 2014).

[8] Vandana Shiva, *Staying Alive*, xiii.

[9] Ibid, xviii–xx.

from actual poverty and deprivation, that is occupying a low physical quality of life.[10] And yet, the imaginal representation of the former leads to the actual creation of the latter.

There is indeed a self-fulfilling logic at the basis of colonialism "civilizing mission" and of neocolonial "development programs": By deeming certain ways of life as "savage" and "underdeveloped," industrial farming and monocultures producing capital for the global market are introduced and justified, thereby destroying the ecosystems from which Indigenous people gleaned their subsistence, and thus creating real misery. At the same time, women's unwaged work is projected as non-work, deprived of any value, thus producing even more misery. From the perspective of the international division of labor, these three processes are inseparable: the displacement of women from socially recognized economic activities is intimately linked with the destruction of natural resources and the categorization of some people as "savages" and "underdeveloped."

When seen in this global perspective, it is evident that patriarchy is not just a pre-modern phenomenon, destined to be swept away by modernization: As the knowledge and agricultures of women have been replaced by industrial farming and monocultures, women are less needed and thus less valued. Certainly this does not mean that patriarchy begins with capitalism, but that the latter has resignified patriarchy where it already existed, or imported it where it did not. The search for an *archē*, for one single origin of patriarchy is a misleading one: Whether patriarchy derives from early pastoral tribes, such as those that produced Judaism or Christianity, or whether it was introduced by the capitalist mode of production,[11] does not really matter. The oppression of women has many threads, and must therefore be tackled through an anarchafeminist perspective aimed at the abolishment of all forms of oppression and exploitation. And so, the equation of anarchafeminism and ecofeminism is valid in both directions: Not only is anarchafeminism by definition ecofeminist, but ecofeminism is, or should be, anarchafeminist, since it is not possible to address the intermeshing of patriarchy and ecological catastrophe without addressing other forms of oppressions, beginning

---

[10] Ibid, 9.
[11] For a reconstruction of this debate on the origins of patriarchy search, see for instance Cinzia Arruzza, *Le relazioni pericolose: matrimoni e divorzi tra marxismo e femminismo* (Rome: Alegre, 2010), 71–89.

with colonialism and the neo-colonial logic of development.[12] As we have seen, Emma Goldman hinted at this clearly when she argued that anarchism is the teacher of the unity of life: It is because every individuality comes into being through webs of affecting relations that takes place at different levels, that one cannot abolish one form of oppression without tackling all others.

Hence the reason why ecofeminists such as Maria Mies and Vandana Shiva have been calling for a movement that addresses ecological challenges through decolonization. When not accompanied by decolonization, apocalyptic theories of the global ecological catastrophe risk revamping the old colonial argument of the "white man's burden." We must not forget that the early days of colonization were accompanied by the Christian theological idea of saving "savages" from damnation as infidels, the later phases by the ideology of the capitalist duty to bring development and modernity to the "underdeveloped" societies: In both cases the science of the time was invoked as the moral reason for the white man's universal duties and the call to dictate policies to and take decisions on the (presumptively inferior) other.[13] Today's invocation of the universal duty to protect humanity from extinction risks turning into yet another form of the "white man's burden" argument. As we have seen, globalization without decolonization is just another justification for imperial conquest. And we can already see how this plays out in the many programs of agencies such as World Bank and IMF, which rely on apocalyptical environmental scenarios to justify their duty, and thus their right to "protect the environment" and therefore impose their policies of "sustainable development" without any consideration of other form of injustice.

For instance, from the point of view of Native Americans, awareness of the ecological catastrophe did not begin a century ago, when the first global-warming alarms were issued, but rather in 1492, when their ecosystems, lives, and cultures were attacked. By insisting on the novel character of the current global warming ecological catastrophe, with its

---

[12] While not all ecofeminists make this connection, so we cannot say that ecofeminism has always been explicitly anarchist, notice that Maria Mies clearly states that feminism is an "anarchic movement." See in particular Maria Mies, *Patriarchy and Accumulation on a World Scale*, 37–8.

[13] Vandana Shiva, "Decolonizing the North," in *Ecofeminism*, eds. Maria Mies and Vandana Shiva (London: Zed Books, 2014), 264.

imminent threat to human lives, the contemporary focus risks erasing the existence of a form of ecological catastrophe that has been going on for at least five centuries, threatening all forms of lives, but with the native people paying the first and highest price. As Kyle Whyte, put it, settler colonialism is a form of ecological domination, because it disrupts Indigenous people's "collective continuance":[14] It is a form of environmental injustice and catastrophe because it is the process whereby one society tries to establish its collective continuance at the ongoing expense of another. And Native American people have been fighting against that since 1492.

The risk, therefore, with the current neo-colonial policies of the IMF and World Bank is that the environmental crisis becomes a justification for the implementation of "sustainable development" policies that privilege the collective continuance of some affluent Western societies at the expense of other communities. The idea of a "sustainable development" is, however, a contradiction in terms: The notion of "development" without further qualification implies an endless, infinite increase in profits, an ever-growing GDP, whereas that of "sustainability" evokes the idea of limits, of a reproduction of life in a condition where there is "no planet B." As previously suggested, capitalism is a perversely utopian economic system, because it always managed to find new "worlds" to exploit: As the globe became saturated with material commodities, capitalism moved to the immaterial world of finance and the tertiary, becoming so abstract that it turned into an image. As the visionary Guy Debord put it half a century ago, capital can accumulate to such a level of abstraction that it becomes an image, turning society into a society of the spectacle, that is, into a "spectacle" that does not simply denote what one sees, but the social relation themselves.[15] Fifty year after Debord's prediction, financialization has completely fulfilled it, having reached such proportions that most of the wealth produced every year is now immaterial in nature—a pure society of the spectacle in which "speculative communities" navigate uncertainties and anxieties, some literally making profit out of that, and others paying all the price of such speculations, in the form of debts,

---

[14] Kyle Whyte, "Settler Colonialism, Ecology, and Environmental Injustice," *Environment & Society* 9, no. 1 (2018).
[15] Guy Debord, *The Society of the Spectacle*, trans. Donald Nicholson-Smith (New York: Zone Books, 1995).

anxiety and food insecurity.[16] And yet, even the very imaginal world of finances, with its immaterial spectacle of derivatives, endless prediction of new markets to exploits, and the constant supply of yet more capital, needs social (re)production work to reproduce laborers, as well as the extraction of natural resources to (re)produce electricity and material infrastructures where immaterial data are stored and processed.

Hence the ecofeminist proposal to move from the notion of a "sustainable development" to that of a "subsistence perspective,"[17] that is, to one that abandons the *telos* of an endless increase of value for the market economy and privileges instead that of life-producing and life-preserving work. Vandana Shiva invokes the notion of a "democracy of all life"[18] to point not only to the intrinsic values and right of all species to exist, but also to the fact that no (re)production of human life is possible without the generative power of animals, plants, seeds, and all other life forms. And if it is true that anarchism is the teacher of the unity of life, then we have to conclude that ecofeminism is, in spirit, if not always in its phrasing, anarchafeminist. It is not by chance that Mies and Shiva refer to another central idea of the anarchist tradition, that of the "individuality of freedom." The latter means not only that, as Gandhi observed, the oppressed of the world are one, but also that the "oppressors" too are caught in the culture of oppression, which is oppressive for everybody.[19] Thus, whereas the myth of the "catching-up development" portrays the lifestyle of urban northern elites as the model for "development" and a "good life," using it to impose its "developmental" logic, this myth also hides the fact that such lifestyles are far from being ideal, and that they favor, in the best scenario, only a tiny minority of extremely wealthy elites.[20]

---

[16] See, in particular, Aris Komporozos-Athanasiou, *Speculative Communities: Living With Uncertainty in a Financialized World* (Chicago: The University of Chicago Press, 2022 [forthcoming]). The author develops Debord's insights through an analysis of how "speculative communities" proliferate: The enormous success of contemporary social media is indeed inseparable from the emergence of financialization, that is, from the incredible polarization of wealth produced by the abstraction of capital from materiality, and the feeling of uncertainty created by lives that are structured by debt and financial uncertainty.

[17] Maria Mies, "The Need for a New Vision: The Subsistence Perspective," in *Ecofeminism*, eds. Maria Mies and Vandana Shiva (London: Zed Books, 2014), 298–9.

[18] Vandana Shiva, "Decolonizing the North," in *Ecofeminism*, 264.

[19] Ibid. Needless to say, this also means that decolonization is as relevant for the colonizers as it is for the colonized.

[20] Maria Mies, "The Myth of Catching-up Development."

The ecofeminist concept of the "democracy of all life" underscores the systematic link between patriarchy and the destruction of natural resources, and thus questions the dichotomy of nature *versus* culture, the idea that nature is something outside "there," and not also (and inevitably) something inside "here." Paradoxically, the romantic celebration of Nature as pristine and immaculate is nothing but the other side of the drive to subject and dominate it, precisely in the same way in which the idealization of the feminine woman, as a wonder to be admired in her beauty, is nothing but the other side of the Great Masculine Renunciation that accompanied modern patriarchy—the celebration of immaculate purity is an invitation to disavowal. The nature that a sixteenth-century eccentric Marrano philosopher could still celebrate as synonymous with the unique substance, *deus sive natura*, and argue on that basis that every being is to some extent animate, has been transformed into a realm separate from society and culture, and thus into a perfectly exploitable external Other. Indeed, the transformation of nature into Nature (capital N) went hand in hand with the "death of nature," that is with the removal of all organic assumptions about the cosmos and the transformation of nature into a system of dead, inert particles, moved by external rather than internal forces.[21] The modern mechanistic view that transformed organic life into quantifiable laws reduced nature to mere material for exchange value, suitable for subsumption into capital.

It would, however, be a mistake to extend this critique of modern mechanicism to a critique of all modern science as such. Ecofeminists such as Vandana Shiva seem, however, to have taken that road: Instead of dismantling only this specific mechanist view of modern science, Vandana criticizes modern science in its entirety, viewing it as being in opposition to what she terms the "feminine principle." In her view, whereas modern science necessarily operates with a reductivist logic, nature must be understood as a living and creative process from which we all spring, and is therefore identified with the feminine principle.[22] However, by insisting on this identification of women with that principle, on women as "an intimate part of nature," one reproduces that very essentializing dichotomy between (feminine) women and (masculine) men that, as we have seen, is at the core of the modern/colonial gender system.

---

[21] Vandana Shiva, "Decolonizing the North," 267. Shiva quotes here a passage from Carolyn Merchant's work on "The Death of Nature."
[22] Vandana Shiva, *Staying Alive,* 40–3.

If women are essentialized as an eternal feminine principle, then they are relegated once again to the natural realm, as they have been for so long, and to their detriment: That nature has, in its turn, been situated in the horizon of death. And what if nature turns out to be not that static realm that enables us to separate the feminine from the masculine, let alone nature from culture? If we understand nature as synonymous with the unique substance and conceive of individualities as transindividualities, then the boundaries between nature and culture, as well as those between men and women, human and animal, as well as animate and inanimate life, become fluid.

Although ecofeminists such as Mies and Shiva have done pivotal work in providing a philosophico-political framework to address how patriarchy has marched in lockstep with colonialism and the death of nature, to them we must echo Judith Butler's admonition: "It is not enough to inquire into how women might become more fully represented in language and politics. Feminist critique ought also to understand how the category of 'women', the subject of feminism, is produced and restrained by the very structure of power through which emancipation is sought."[23] In other words, while providing a framework for the liberation of women, the ecofeminist identification of women with nature, and with the feminine principle, risks imprisoning women into the hetero- and cisnormative matrix that is at the basis of the modern/colonial binary gender system, and which has not proved to be liberatory for women. This not only makes female masculinity, as well as transwomen's experiences, invisible, but also transforms the historically contingent modern/colonial gender system into a metaphysical framework from which there is no exit.

This does not mean that feminism should abandon femininity. As Jack Halberstam notes, it means that femininity must be rethought in the context of "trans* feminism"—an expression where "the asterisk modifies the meaning of transitivity, by refusing to situate transition in relation to a destination, a final form, a specific shape, or an established configuration of desire and identity."[24] The trans* can thus become a name for not-yet determined forms of difference, and the refusal of an identity politics predicated upon separating out the many kinds of experience that

---

[23] Judith Butler, *Gender Trouble* (London: Routledge, 1990), 2.
[24] Jack Halberstam, *Trans*: A Quick and Quirky Account of Gender Variability* (Berkeley: University of California, 2018), 4.

actually blend together, intersect, and mix, and thus for a refusal to seal women into the eternally feminine principle and men into the eternally masculine one.[25] Paradoxically, if we follow this transindividual perspective, then feminism can be enriched, rather than feel threatened, by "femininity" and by the femininities of women who were not born female. Whereas there have been separatist feminists who denied access to their spaces to women who were not assigned female at birth, in a trans*feminist perspective, feminism becomes broad enough to recognize how femininity is co-constructed and co-inhabited across bodies that are male and female, trans and cis, and thus through variegated sexualities and genders.[26] Far from abandoning femininity, a trans* perspective can actually rescue its meaning from notions of weakness and dependence imposed on it by centuries of patriarchy.[27]

This co-inhabitation becomes even more evident if we focus not only on inter-actions, but also on infra-actions. Whereas transindividuality does not mean transgender, a philosophical framework that explores the ontogenesis of individualities through the supra-, inter-, and infra-individual level, throws a different light on gender transition, too: Far from being an anomaly, or deviation from a supposed norm, transitioning becomes one of the infinite possible modes of ontogenesis, that is, of coming into being as individuated being.

In cases such as those described by Paul B. Preciado, transitioning can also be the site of political experimentation and resistance to the modern/colonial gender system: The experience of one single person's transition from female to male by taking testosterone can become the magnifying glass through which one can perceive the infinite network of affective links created by what Preciado terms the current "pharmaco-pornographic regime." Preciado's *Testo Junkie*, which records such a political experiment, is thus not simply partly a memoir of a transition and partly an essay on the late capitalist mode of (re)production, but rather an attempt to show that one cannot exist without the other:[28] all bodies—not just transgender

---

[25] Ibid, 5.

[26] On the history of the conflict between separatist feminisms and gender variant folks in the United States, see ibid, 107–12.

[27] On this point, see ibid, 119–20, which draws on Julia Serrano, *Whipping Girl: A Transexual Woman on Sexism and the Scapegoating of Femininity* (Berkeley: Seal Press, 2007).

[28] Beatriz Preciado, *Testo Junkie: Sex, Drugs, and Biopolitics in the Pharmacopornographic Era* (New York: The Feminist Press, 2013).

ones—are co-originated with other bodies situated at the infra-, inter-, and supra-individual level. As Beatriz wrote while becoming Paul: "I'm not interested in my emotions insomuch as their being mine, belonging only, uniquely to me. I'm not interested in their individual aspects, only in how they are traversed by what isn't mine, in what emanates from our planet's history, the evolution of the living species, the flux of economics, remnants of technological innovations, preparations for wars, the trafficking of organic slaves and commodities, the creation of hierarchies, institutions of punishments and repression, networks of communications and surveillance, the random overlapping of market research groups, techniques and blocs of opinion, the biochemical transformation of feeling, the production and transformation of pornographic images."[29]

As this long list of transindividual processes already suggests, the framework of this political experiment is that of post-Fordism. The passage from a Fordist mode of production, centered on the mechanical production of goods, to a post-Fordist one, centered on financialization, services, and knowledge, has disclosed new markets for capitalism, increasingly turning it into a form of biocapitalism, that is, a mode of production that infiltrated the intimate processes of (re)production to such a molecular and intimate level that it became one and the same thing with life (*bios*) itself. As new hormonal and molecular discoveries in the fields of chemistry and medicine have entered society, the production of psychosomatic affective states has become a central piece of contemporary cognitive capitalism and its mode of (re)production. Thus, whereas the disciplinary regimes of the eighteenth and nineteenth centuries inaugurated a new biopolitics through the invention of "sex" as nature, the systematic mapping of sexual difference on anatomical dimorphism, and the consequent invention of the category of "homosexuals," the "pharmaco-pornographic regime" that currently dominates the Western sexual epistemology is centered on the production of subjectivities through the dual prism of pornographic images and the hormonal and biomolecular management of bodies.[30] The "pharmaco" is thus inseparable from the "pornographic" because the manipulation of molecules goes hand in hand with that of neurotransmitters as two sides of the same coin.

---

[29] Ibid, 77.
[30] Ibid, 77.

Rather than "pharmaco-pornographic," we prefer to speak of a "pharmaco-imaginal" regime, to underline the fact that images can be more or less pornographic, but that they relentlessly work to produce a certain type of subjectivity—whether they circulate on pornographic sites, social medias, or the culture industry more in general.[31] If the means whereby power was exercised in the classical model of sovereignty was the sword, and in the disciplinary regimes were state apparatuses, today's technologies of the body operate with soft, viscous technologies such as telecommunications, endocrinology, genetic engineering, biotechnologies, molecules that can be incorporated into and penetrate daily life at a level unimaginable before: from a cell phone to the bio-engineering of food production.

As Paul B. Preciado put it: "The real stakes of capitalism today is the pharmacopornographic control of subjectivity, whose products are serotonin, techno-blood and blood products, testosterones, antiacids, cortisone, techno-sperm, antibiotics, estradiol, techno-milk, alcohol and tobacco, morphine, insulin, cocaine, living human eggs, citrate and sildenafil (Viagra), and the entire material and virtual complex participating in the production of mental and psychosomatic states of excitation, relaxation, and discharge, as well as those of omnipotence and total control."[32] Within the West, this shift took hold at the end of the Second World War. Helped by wartime technological advancements, major developments in science and technologies in the 1950s led to the discovery of the Pill and other hormonal treatments that enabled the separation of sex and heterosexuality from reproduction, while the first plastic surgeries allowed bodies to be changed in their morphology in ways that would have been inconceivable before. It is also around that time that pornography started to enter into popular culture and "gender" was invented as a biotech industrial artifact. The first person to employ the grammatical category of gender as a diagnostic tool was John Money, a child psychologist, who used the term in 1955 as a tool to diagnose the problems he encountered in treating "hermaphrodites" and "intersex" babies. The invention of the

---

[31] We have analyzed the convergence of biopolitical and imaginal production of subjectivities and desire, in Chiara Bottici, *Imaginal Politics: Images Beyond the Imagination and Beyond the Imaginary* (New York: Columbia University Press, 2014). For a discussion of that thesis, see also Suzi Adams and Jeremy Smith, ed., *Debating Imaginal Politics* (Lanham, MD: Rowman & Littlefield, 2022, forthcoming).

[32] Ibid, 39.

category of gender is thus far from being the creation of a feminist agenda, but fully belongs to the biotechnological discourse that appeared in the US medical and therapeutic industries in the 1950s, and peaked during the Cold War, "just like canned food, computers, plastic chairs, nuclear energy, television, credit cards, disposable ballpoints pens, bar codes, inflatable mattresses, or telecommunication satellites."[33]

This does not mean that the production of affective-psychosomatic states characteristic of contemporary biocapitalism has supplanted the production of material goods, but rather that it has become the model for other forms of production: From agrarian biotechnologies to the high-tech industries of communications, the techno-management of bodies, whether inter-individual or infra-individual, increasingly accompanies the flow of capital.[34] Preciado pushes the argument as far as to state that the contemporary transformation of capitalism entails such a mutation of the sex-gender order that we may be approaching the twilight of heterosexuality: If white heterosexual femininity is above all an economic function referring to a specific position within biopolitical relationships of production and exchange, then we can conjecture that today pharmaco-pornographic regime may be leading to a post-sexual era, in which all forms of sexuality and production of pleasure will be legitimate and normal(ized), in as far as they are subject to the same molecular and digital technologies.[35]

This is one possible direction. But, even within our current "pharmaco-imaginal" regime, it is also possible that a surgically adapted, hormonally re-produced, compulsory heterosexuality be re-signified, without losing its hegemonic appeal. Whether or not Preciado is right in predicting the twilight of heterosexuality as an institution, we can certainly agree with the deep change that this process has had on the configuration of the mononuclear family. The advances in contraception and hormonal treatment that, as noted above, have separated heterosexuality from reproduction, and of in vitro fertilization techniques, along with the emergence of the dual-wage household system, have deeply changed the traditional configuration of the family. After the frontal attacks to the family launched by feminisms of different sorts, as well as by other social movements in the 1960s and 1970s, some have claimed that the family is

---

[33] Ibid, 99.
[34] Ibid, 40.
[35] Ibid, 122.

now "back." Even within LGBTQI+ and two-spirit communities, and thanks to the legalization of same-sex marriage in some Western countries, the family does indeed seem to have returned center stage. Even if we are facing the twilight of heterosexuality as an institution, this does not seem to have affected the institution of the family as a whole.

First, at least in certain countries and cities, there has been an eclipse of the traditional patriarchal family: As fathers ceased to be the sole breadwinner in a household, they also ceased to be its uncontested single head. This, however, does not automatically mean more freedom for women: Although the model of the two-wage household is increasing, it is still the case that women are the main performers of care work, even in such economically egalitarian (leaving aside pay disparities) households.[36] Phenomena like the so-called "double-shift," which stacks paid work on top of reproductive labor for (the ideology of) love and places it firmly on women's shoulders, are indeed very common: Far from leading to more freedom, the entrance into the waged-labor market meant that many women were doubly oppressed.[37]

Second, if by "patriarch" we mean the male head of the family, then we have to conclude that the patriarchal family is under attack on two fronts, both because fathers are no longer the sole "head" of the family, and because they are not necessarily "male." Same-sex marriages and unions, as well as IVF and other innovations in fertility procedures, have further challenged the identification between the male and the head of the family, while the growing rates of divorce by choice have questioned traditional stereotypes about "single mothers"—an expression, that, as we have seen, is a contradiction in terms which makes sense only from the point of view of a heteronormative imaginary according to which a mother without the complementary companion (preferably of the opposite sex) is merely "single."

---

[36] The pay gap between men and women is a global phenomenon: 2020 statistics say that women are on average paid 63 percent of what men are paid for the same job ("Global Gender Gap Report 2020," World Economic Forum, https://www.weforum.org/reports/global-gender-gap-report-2020, accessed December 16, 2019).

[37] On the transformation of the nuclear family in postindustrial society, see Nancy Fraser, *Fortunes of Feminism: From State-managed Capitalism to Neoliberal Crisis* (London: Verso, 2013), 111–35. As Fraser notes, post-industrial families are less conventional and more diverse for a variety of reasons: heterosexuals are marrying less often and later in life while also divorcing more and sooner; gays and lesbians are pioneering new kinds of domestic arrangements; and women's employment and single mother families are now incresingly common. Despite all of that, women are still paid far less than men (ibid, 112–13).

Some have welcomed this queering of the family, while others have indulged in paranoid thinking about a new "fatherless generation," or even a "fatherless society" that leaves children adrift and in an emotional vacuum.[38] Whatever direction this reconfiguration of the family will take, we can provisionally conclude that the family is indeed back, but what came back is certainly very different from what went away.

Although this is a significant change, it has not necessarily been accompanied by a decline in the power asymmetries between men and women, as well as those between men and other second sexes. The patriarch may have been toppled, the traditional father figure could be challenged, but cismen are still the "first sex"[39]—both in the West and globally. Not only do men still occupy most of the positions of power, both economic and political, but they are also not the object of the relentless gender violence that is exercised systematically on women, feminine bodies, transvestis, and nonbinary genders.[40] In comparison to cismen, women, two-spirited, third gender, and LGBTQI+ folks all occupy the position of the "second sex." We include all of them into the category of "second sex" not to deny existing differences between them, but to point out that in the current predicament they are all excluded from the category of "first sex," and that they are thus mainly the object rather than the perpetrators of gender violence.

---

[38] See, for instance, these two blog pieces about the "fatherless society" (David Blankenhorn, "Fatherless America," *American Experiment* [January 3, 1993], https://www.americanexperiment.org/reports-books/fatherless-america/) and the "fatherless generation" (Rosemary K.M. Sword and Philip Zimbardo, "The Fatherless Generation," *Psychology Today* [August 6, 2018], https://www.psychologytoday.com/us/blog/the-time-cure/201808/the-fatherless-generation), accessed February 25, 2020. Theories about the eclipse of patriarchy began as early as the beginning of the twentieth century, when women started to enter the waged-labor market and obtain political rights in many Western countries. See, for instance, Patrick J. Quinn, *Patriarchy in Eclipse: The Femme Fatale and the New Woman in American Literature and Culture, 1870–1920* (Cambridge: Cambridge Scholars Publishing, 2015).

[39] The implicit reference is the fortunate title of Simone de Beauvoir's masterpiece, *The Second Sex*, which remains (unfortunately) very timely as women are still largely the second sex to men (Simone de Beauvoir, *The Second Sex* (New York: Vintage Books, 2011).

[40] According to statistics provided by the United Nations, 35 percent of women worldwide have experienced physical or sexual violence ("Facts and figures: Ending violence against women," UN Women [updated November 2020], https://www.unwomen.org/en/what-we-do/ending-violence-against-women/facts-and-figures) while there are 140 million missing girls from the global populations, as a consequence of gender violence and gender biased sex-selection ("Gender-biased sex selection," United Nations Population Fund, https://www.unfpa.org/gender-biased-sex-selection, [accessed on 24 March 2021]).

The eclipse of the traditional patriarchal family is, however, a significant phenomenon, which requires further consideration, and for this reason we propose adding the concept of "menocracy" to the old term "patriarchy." "Menocracy" signals that, even in those contexts where there are no more patriarchs, cisgendered men are still the first sex. Whereas "patriarchy" literally means the rule (*archē*) of the patriarch, the male head of the family, that of "menocracy" points to the power (*cratos*) that men exercise in general over those who do not belong to the first sex/gender—a power that, as we have seen, is political, economic, imaginal, ideological, and ecological. As such, it suggests that even in contexts where the patriarch is no longer in charge of ruling (*archē*), men continue to exercise their power through other means. Menocracy can thrive even where patriarchy seems to be in decline. Given that it is not tied to the concept of the family, "menocracy" is a much more malleable tool to travel across different social and cultural contexts, including those, both inside and outside of the West, where, as we have seen, the family is not gendered at all. If Oyèrónkẹ Oyěwùmí is right that white feminism is like a snail, because wherever it goes it brings with it the assumptions derived from the Western nuclear family, then moving towards the concept of menocracy is a way to leave some of those assumptions behind and travel more lightly.

Another way to do this is by looking at the shifting regimes in sexual epistemology through an emphasis on infra-individual bodies and their infra-actions. As the notion of a "pharmaco-imaginal regime" suggests, looking at bodies not from the outside, but from the inside, so to speak, enables us to perceive the capacity of affecting and being affected that even the smallest molecules of matter possess. This produces a very different lens for seeing global inequalities: The difference between the light and the dark side of the modern/colonial gender system thus becomes that between those who have access to the pharmaco-pornographic regime, and those who are excluded from the fluidity it affords, while paying the highest cost for it. Besides the exploitation arising from market inter-actions, there is also the oppression created by the accumulation of toxic waste under the skin, in the very very "hidden abode" of capitalist (re)production. The point is not only that wealthy countries often legally or illegally use poorer countries as trash cans for industrial waste that cannot be processed. More broadly, at the infra-individual level, the asymmetry is that while some bodies can be voluntarily intoxicated with testosterone, citalopram, sertraline, and other common substances to produce pleasurable psycho-somatic effects, other bodies get involuntarily intoxicated with sulphur, endusulfan, mancozeb, and other common pesticides that are used on a massive scale in industrial farming in the global south.

This infra-individual inequality has often gone unnoticed even in those bio-political approaches that are allegedly focused on the political relevance of life. Whereas a lot of biopolitical theories focused only on the supra-individual and inter-individual levels, thereby reproducing a humanist bias,[41] a transindividual philosophy adds emphasis on the infra-individuality that challenges not only anthropocentrism, but any speciesism, and thus any hierarchy between species more generally. The transindividual insight that every being is to some extent animate, which, as we have seen, does not mean that they are all animate in the same way in which humans are, is today reinforced by new materialisms that investigate the capacity of matter, whether organic or not, to affect and being affected.[42] As we have mentioned, Karen Barad's agential realism is the contemporary form of new materialism that has gone the furthest, as it investigates how even at the level of the smallest particles of matter, entities do not precede their inter-actions, such that a new concept of agency that takes into account infra-actions is needed.[43]

The most radical forms of this new materialism literature therefore challenge not only the boundary between nature and culture, but also the boundary between living and non-living matter, which has been the cornerstone of Western metaphysics for several millennia.[44] Even most contemporary biopolitical approaches rely on such a "geontopower," in as far as they have mainly investigated how political power has increasingly

---

[41] Mel Y. Chen, *Animacies: Biopolitics, Racial Mattering, and Queer Affects* (Durham: Duke University Press, 2012), 6.

[42] Examples include Mel Y. Chen's *Animacies*, which systematically investigates the notion of animacy; Jane Bennett's *Vibrant Matter: A Political Ecology of Things* (Durham: Duke University Press, 2010), which applies the notion of affect to more-than-human bodies, showing that it is a constitutive part of each body's materiality, or Stacy Alaimo, *Bodily Natures*.

[43] Karen Barad, *Meeting the Universe Halfway: Quantum Physics and the Entanglement of Matter and Meaning* (Durham: Duke University Press, 2007).

[44] See, for instance, Diana Coole and Samantha Frost (eds.), *New Materialism: Ontology, Agency, and Politics* (Durham: Duke University Press, 2010). Notice here that some forms of new materialism, such as Braidotti's *Post-humanism* are however deeply entrenched in a vitalistic philosophy that reinforces, instead of questioning, the life *versus* non-life binary (Rosi Braidotti, *The Posthuman* [Cambridge: Polity, 2013]).

been concerned with disciplining life, without considering how the very division between life (*bios*) and the non-life of the earth (*geos*) has itself become a mode of governance of both the human and the more-than-human.[45] Most Western ontologies are indeed "biontologies," being metaphysics that measure all forms of existence by the quality of one form of existence (whether it is *bios*, the qualified biological life, or *zoe*, the bare life).[46] Deprived of any interesting place within them, stones become the epitome of dead matter, just as the Stone Age is concomitantly projected as the epitome of barbarism.

The notion of "geontopower" enables us to look at the *scala naturae* from the end of its spectrum. The hierarchy of man>woman>slave>animal> plant>inanimate life is indeed constructed according to an "over-representation of Man"[47] that classifies individualities according to how closely they resemble the top of the scale. It is not by chance that most environmental ethics focus on animal liberation, with comparatively very little attention paid to plants. The latter mostly enter environmental philosophy when their essential role in reproducing animality is in question, not as beings in their own right and thus deserving a philosophical meditation on their own.[48] Dogs and cats respond to our solicitations, so they become more easily an extension of human narcissism, whereas plants exhibit a "sovereign indifference" to us, for which they pay with their systematic neglect by most Western philosophers.[49] And yet, they literally make the world, because they constitute 90 percent of the eucaryote bio-mass of the planet, thereby constantly transforming and shaping the environment they inhabit, including through their own (often incognito) traveling. As Emanuele Coccia put it: "our world is a vegetal fact well before being an animal one."[50] But if plants are too dissimilar from Man to be given extensive attention, then stones and minerals are, not unsurprisingly, barely given any epistemological, let alone agential, consideration.

---

[45] Elizabeth A. Povinelli, *Geontologies: A Requiem to Late Liberalism* (Durham: Duke University Press, 2016), 4.

[46] Ibid.

[47] See Sylvia Wynter, "Unsettling the Coloniality of Being / Power/ Truth/ Freedom: Towards the Human, After Man, Its Overrepresentation—An Argument," *CR: The New Centennial Review* 3, no. 3 (2003).

[48] Things have started to change recently. See in particular, the Emanuele Coccia, *La vie des plantes: Une métaphysique du mélange* (Paris: Éditions Rivage, 2016).

[49] Ibid, 17.

[50] Ibid, 21.

Philosophies inspired by new materialism are now challenging the status quo, while environmental activities on the ground call for the recognition of the rights of inanimate objects such as rivers, forests, and even the entire globe itself. The *pachamama*, a Quechua and Aymara word for nature, was recognized as a legal subject of rights by the 2008 Ecuadorian Constitution,[51] while the Whanganui River in New Zealand has been a legal person since 2017.[52] According legal personhood to rivers means that they must be treated as living being. The Māori tribes that live along the Whanganui have always seen the river as such, since its waters have nourished and blessed their people throughout the 700 years they've spent on its banks, but the river's life had been threatened by pollution and so activists called for its legal recognition as the only way to save the river in both its actual and symbolic meaning. When the New Zealand parliament passed the Te Awa Tapua Act, featuring the Māori concept, a legal framework was set to recognize the rights not simply of the river itself, but of the Te Awa Tupua region as a whole, comprising the Whanganui River from the mountains to the sea, incorporating its tributaries as well as all its physical and meta-physical elements.[53] These are major shifts towards a truly transindividual ecological awareness.

Whereas it is through the prism of quantum theory or Māori cosmologies, there is an increasing awareness not only that all beings are to some extent animate, but also that they are so because of their inter-, supra-, and also infra-dependence. An awareness that was already present in the French anarchist geographer Élisée Reclus, who in 1869, embarked on the ambitious project of writing the history of a river, *Histoire d'un ruisseau*, opening the work with the stunning observation that the history of a river is the history of the infinite. What is a river if not the history of all the drops of water that compose it, of all the mineral molecules it transports, of the snow on top of its mountains, of the vapor of the clouds above it, of the sun that make them evaporate, a history of the European

[51] María Valeria Berros, "The Constitution of the Republic of Ecuador: Pachamama Has Rights," Environment & Society Portal, *Arcadia* 11 (2015).
[52] Eleanor Ainge Roy, "New Zealand River Granted Same Legal Rights as Human Being," *The Guardian* (March 16, 2017), https://www.theguardian.com/world/2017/mar/16/new-zealand-river-granted-same-legal-rights-as-human-being.
[53] Jeremy Lurgio, "Saving the Whanganui," *The Guardian* (November 29, 2019), https://www.theguardian.com/world/2019/nov/30/saving-the-whanganui-can-personhood-rescue-a-river.

mountains, but also that of the African deserts, passing by the fountains in the valleys, the watermills, the vapor in the sky, not less than all the human labor and irrigation systems across the globe?[54] Like other anarchists, who looked at the world beyond artificial geo-political boundaries, Élisée Reclus could see what methodological individualism hides from sight: *"L'histoire d'un ruisseau, même de celui qui naît et se perd dans la mousse, est l'histoire de l'infini. [...]"* and we do not need to look at the entire globe to perceive it: *"Tous les agents de l'atmosphère et de l'espace, toutes les forces cosmique ont travaillé de concert à modifier incessamment l'aspect et la position de la gouttelette imperceptible; elle aussi est un monde comme les astres énormes qui roulent dans le cieux, et son orbite se développe de cycle en cycle par un mouvement sans repos."*[55] It is, and we are, a never-ending movement of the elements, the planets as well as the smallest particles of matter, but one that also includes the incessant inter- and infra-actions with human history. There is no difference between human and natural history: There is just history. And it is infinite.

From the very different angle of the Anishinaabe philosophies, Kyle Whyte has recently put forward a very similar argument. Whereas the French geographer quoted books and experimental observations, Kyle Whyte quotes oral sources, as convenient to a tradition—the Native American one—where thinking often takes place through collective storytelling, discussions, and other oral performances. Whyte introduces the Anishinaabe's concept of interdependence by quoting Chief Ayeetapepetung's 1871 statement that "he was made of the land," as well as the Anishinaabe's elder Tobasonakwut's saying that "his people were the lake, and the lake was them."[56] As Kyle observes, this statement does not simply mean that they depended on the lake for their survival, but that by living off the lake's waters, fish, animals, and plants, they were literally—cell by cell—composed of the lake and the lake's islands. This awareness, in turn, implies the recognition of a system of responsibility, as the land then becomes a *emingoyak*, "that which has been given to us,"

---

[54] Élisée Reclus, *Histoire d'un ruisseau* (Arles: Actes Sud, 1995), 7.

[55] "The story of a stream, even one that is born and lost in the moss, is the story of the infinite. [...] All the agents of the atmosphere and of the space, all the cosmic forces have worked in concert to constantly modify the aspect and the position of imperceptible droplet; the latter too is a world like the enormous stars which move in the heavens, and its orbit develops from cycle to cycle by a movement without rest." Ibid (translation ours).

[56] Kyle Whyte, "Settler Colonialism," 127.

a gift that must be reciprocated.[57] Instead of owning the land, the latter is an invitation to a seasonal round, that is to a type of governance in which the major social and economic institutions shift in shape and organization throughout the year, precisely in order to follow change in the land and through the land.[58] If the land is not something to be exploited according to a never-ending logic of accumulation, but a gift to be reciprocated, then linear time becomes spiral time, while a migration responding to changes in the environment becomes the best tool to achieve what Kyle Whyte calls "collective continuance." It is "continuance" and it is "collective" because it denotes "a society's capacity to self-determine how to adapt to change in ways that avoid reasonably preventable harms,"[59] and differs from the similar concepts of "continuity" because it emphasizes that survival happens *through* the collective response to change, and not *despite* it. In this sense, the Anishinaabe's notion of collective continuance can, and indeed does, inform a new ecological sensibility, and one that is particularly timely today, as a sensibility that is capable of engendering a sense of responsibility tied to one's own identity and constitution. In our transindividual terminology, we could say that when Tobasonakwut states that "his people were the lake, the lake was them," they are pointing to the awareness that two are co-originated, being two sides of the same inter-, supra-, and infra- dependence that includes both humans and other-than-humans.

All these developments confirm the transindividual philosophy insight that every being is endowed with the capacity to affect and to being affected, and that is how they strive to persist in their being. The notion of "affecting"[60] is indeed central to a transindividual philosophy. Within this framework, "ecology" is thus nothing but co-affectivity, whereas "ecological thinking" is nothing but the thinking of such co-affectivity as co-origination. This move does not collapse ecology into an all-encompassing-organicism, where the whole determines its parts:

---

[57] Ibid.
[58] Ibid, 130.
[59] Ibid, 131.
[60] Whereas Spinoza distinguishes between "affects" (*affectus*) and "affections" (*affectiones*), understood as modification of the susbtance, the English literature tends to unify both concepts in the english term "affect". This is partly due to the fact that "affection" in English means both a bodily condition but mostly the emotional response to individual people and thus the caring for others. Similarly to Latin, the Italian language distinguishes between *affetti* and *affezioni*. We use "affecting" to avoid confusion and to emphasize processuality.

Co-affectivity is co-origination without an *archē*. It is "e-co-affectivity,"[61] understood as the capacity of affecting and of being affected by every single being, without implying any *telos* nor any hierarchical organizing of such an infinite web of affecting.

The notion of affecting is thus central to a "politics of renaturalization,"[62] where nature is brought back to the center of philosophico-political thinking, but not as Nature with capital letter, something that is capitalized at the very moment that is alienated from us, and thus rendered exploitable. An anarchafeminist approach to ecology is one *without* Nature,[63] in that alienated form, but *through* nature, in its meaning of the unique infinite substance. An ontology of transindividuality enables us to both retain and distinguish between different individualities, while according none of them any type of ontological superiority: stones, as well as pets or any other candidate for our "animal chauvinism,"[64] are to some extent animate. Along with hierarchies, all rigid boundaries between "man" and "woman," "human" and "animal," "animals" and "plants," "life" and "non-life" are also questioned. A transindividual ecology is indeed a form of ecology where our industrial waste ceases to be outside of nature, and becomes itself a living organism, where the molecules we inhale or encompass become literally constitutive of our being, whether they are alive or not—in sum, it is a queer ecology.

We use the term "queer ecology" not simply to mean that anarchafeminism implies a form of ecology that questions the intersections of sex and nature.[65] Much more broadly, this means a form of ecology that questions the boundaries between the discrete individualities, let alone the hierarchy between them. The term "queer" is here both an adjective and a verb, both a description of the queer nature of most of the living

---

[61] We borrow the expression from Marjolein Oele, *E-Co-Affectivity: Exploring the Pathos at Life's Material Interfaces* (Albany: SUNY Press, 2020). Notice, however, that Marjolein Oele mainly focuses on interfaces between living organs such as skin and placenta.

[62] This insight comes from Hasana Sharp, who emphasized the centrality of this notion in Spinoza's philosophy (Hasana Sharp, *Spinoza and the Politics of Renaturalization* [Chicago: University of Chicago Press, 2011]).

[63] On the notion of an "ecology without nature," see Timothy Morton, *The Ecological Thought* (Cambridge, MA: Harvard University Press, 2010a), 3–4. Morton is obviously considering only a certain type of nature—that is, the alienated nature.

[64] We take this term from Emanuele Coccia, *La vie des plantes*, 16. Coccia refers to earlier usages by W. Marshall Darley and J. L. Arbor.

[65] For this definition, see Catriona Mortimer-Sandilands and Bruce Erickson, *Queer Ecologies: Sex, Nature, Politics, Desire* (Indianapolis: Indiana University Press, 2010), 5.

matter and an exhortation to queer the established hierarchies between different forms of being.[66] Thus queer ecology is not (only) the ecology thought and practiced by people who define themselves as queer, but a questioning of heteronormativity and cisnormativity that is part of a more general attempt at questioning all kinds of hierarchies.

Many authors have noticed some affinities between ecology and queer theory, with some even stating that "fully and properly, ecology is queer theory and queer theory is ecology."[67] Both queer theory and ecology have a vocation towards questioning established hierarchies, classifications, and the rigid boundaries between the inside and the outside. But questioning boundaries does not mean to eliminate distinctions, nor to give up individualities: It simply means conceiving them as transindividualities. Thus, whereas Tim Morton's insights that queer theory is ecology is based on the notion of the mesh, as a "nontotalizable, open-ended concatenation of interrelations that blur and confound boundaries at practically any level,"[68] a transindividual philosophy frames queer ecology as one that examines boundaries and topples hierarchies while maintaining distinctions. The reason for this is easy to see: If ecological thinking means that boundaries are confounded at "practically any level," and that we are thereby invited to "becoming open, radically open—open forever, without the possibility of closing again,"[69] then not only do we end up in a night where all cows equally look gray, but also open the door to the idea that anything is therefore up for grabs by anybody. This is not only a caricature of a queer theory, but also a theoretico-political dangerous move that potentially justifies violence against queer bodies. To question boundaries does not mean to state that one is "open forever."

---

[66] This is slightly different from Catriona Mortimer-Sandilands and Bruce Erickson's definition, who write: "Queer, then, is both noun and verb in this project: ours is an ecology that may begin in the experiences and perceptions of non-heterosexual individuals and communities, but is even more importantly one that calls into question heteronormativity itself as part of its advocacy around issues of nature and environment—and vice versa" (ibid.). For them, "queer ecology" remains linked to the questioning of heteronormativity, whereas for us the expression suggests the questioning of boundaries and established categories more in general.

[67] Timothy Morton, "Queer Ecology," *PMLA* 125, no. 2 (2010), 281.

[68] Ibid. For a longer discussion of the "mesh," see also Timothy Morton's *The Ecological Thought*, 28–38.

[69] This is the expression used as "opening moves" in Timothy Morton's *The Ecological Thought*, 8.

Although Morton's understanding of queer ecology problematically brings it to a terrain where most queer people may actually be uncomfortable, it still points to a possible tension within queer theory itself: How can we rethink the questioning of boundaries without ending up in a confusing mesh where everything is available for grabbing? The notion of transindividuality can here be very useful, precisely to point out that emphasizing the inter-, supra-, and even infra-dependence of every being does not mean abandoning individualities and distinctions. It means conceiving every individuality as trans-individuality, as the result of a process of affecting and being affected that takes place at multiple levels, as one that individualizes, so to speak, in single concrete formations and in different spaces and times. It is a social ontology that enables us to perceive what happens beyond the threshold of somebody else's skin, but also one that does not invite us to violate that threshold if uninvited.

If, from constitutional law to queer theory, from quantum physics to Indigenous philosophies, there is a growing awareness that we are individual because we are transindividual, the question emerges of why it is so hard to perceive transindividuality before, after and inside individuality. The individualist ideology that accompanies modernity is certainly a part of the answer. The conditions of modern life tend to separate us from all that would enable the perception of such transindividuality: The air we breathe is taken largely for granted as plants only appear as accidental adornments in our cities, despite the fact that they literally constitute the breath of the world. There is a logic of alienation that governs capitalist modernity, which goes hand in hand with a logic of separation and classification.[70]

The classification of *eros* into different forms of sexualities did go hand in hand with the classifications of people around the globe according to their phenotypes, and of the different life species according to modern taxonomies. Indeed it is revealing that, historically, the rise of evolutionary thought in the wake of Charles Darwin generally coincided with the rise of sexological thought following Richard von Krafft-Ebing's classification of sexual pathologies: "new forms of biological and environmental knowledge jostled with new ideas about sex, and their commingling has

---

[70] On the modern logic of classification, and the feeling of loss of meaning it generates, see the Weberian meditations of Dimitri D'Andrea, *L'incubo degli ultimi uomini. Etica e politica in Max Weber* (Carocci: Roma 2005). On the concept of alienation and its contemporary relevance, see Rahel Jaeggi, *Alienation* (New York: Columbia University Press, 2013).

had lasting effect."[71] Sex became a matter of being fit and individual attributes could be evaluated based on their apparent adaptiveness to an organism-reproductive capacity.[72] It is not by chance that the invention and medicalization of homosexuality arose at the same time as eugenics and scientific racism:[73] As we have seen, all express the same obsession with the control of (re)production. Whereas cultural attitudes towards *eros* varied before modernity, with the emergence of the modern/colonial gender system, the pathologization of homosexuality and transgenderism became structurally functional to the maintenance of the "man-on-top binary gender system."[74]

The development of the modern/colonial gender system is indeed inseparable from the modern/colonial drive to name, classify, and discipline both the life of the various populations and the life of the different species. In as much as pastoralism, and thus the habit of matching domesticated animals for the sake of reproduction, makes us blind to the queer nature of most ways in which life is reproduced, by falsely projecting heterosexuality as the norm,[75] so the modern/colonial drive towards classification and disciplining of the different life species makes us blind to our transindividual nature. Equally it makes us forget that, if it is true that property is theft, then we must conclude that we steal not only from other humans, but also from the generative capacity of the more-than-human.[76]

In all and every single breath, we literally only exist through others.[77] The Other is not only Other human beings, without whom we certainly

---

[71] Catriona Mortimer-Sandilands and Bruce Erickson, *Queer Ecologies,* 7.

[72] Ibid, 10.

[73] pattrice jones, "Eros and the Mechanisms of Eco-Defense," in *Ecofeminism: Feminist Intersections With Other Animals & the Earth*, eds. Carol J. Adams and Lori Gruen (New York: Bloomsbury Academic, 2014), 99.

[74] Ibid, 178.

[75] Ibid.

[76] Mitchell Verter, "The Flow of the Breath: Levinas Mouth-to-Mouth with Buddhism," in *Levinas and Asian Thought*, eds. Leah Kalmanson, Frank Garrett, and Sarah Mattice (Pittsburgh: Duquesne University Press, 2013). In a beautiful passage quoting Buddhadasa Bhikkhu, Verter writes: "Throughout our lives we have been thieves. We have been stealing things that exists naturally—in and belonging to nature—namely the conditions (*sankhara*). We have plundered them and taken them to be our selves and our possessions" (pp. 236–7). Verter's meditations combines Buddhist philosophy with that of Emmanuel Levinas. The path of this book is different, but reaches similar conclusions.

[77] Mitchell Verter, "The Flow of the Breath," 228. And also Emanuele Coccia, *La vie des plantes*, 21.

would not exists, but also other Others, that is the other-than-human—
including the plants through which we breathe and the toxic waste
molecules that circulate in our bodies. To care for ourselves means to care
for the world: "*la cura del mondo.*"[78] Anarchism is thus not only the teacher
of the unity of life, as Emma Goldman suggested, but also the teacher of
the unity of being: It is because every being is a transindividual being, co-
originated through an infinite process of co-affectivity, that we cannot
abolish one form of oppression without abolishing all of them. If the
Other that constitutes ourselves is not only the other human being but
also the other-than-human, then anarchafeminism becomes truly
"infinitely demanding."[79] An infinite and impossible task, yet all the more
necessary to accomplish, along with the awareness that, even when one's
body dies in its individuality, something of its transindividuality will
always remain, at least under some sort of eternity—*sub specie aeternitatis.*

---

[78] Elena Pulcini, *La Cura del Mondo* (Turin: Bollati Boringhieri, 2009). Eng. trans. *Care of the World* (New York: Springer, 2012).

[79] The expression "infinitely demanding" comes from Simon Critchley, who, in the face of the political disappointment that characterizes contemporary liberal democracies, calls for anarchism as an ethical practice and tool for remotivating political engagement. See Simon Critchley, *Infinitely Demanding: Ethics of Commitment, Politics of Resistance* (London: Verso, 2007).

CODA

An ongoing manifesto

We live under a global menocracy. Maybe patriarchy is declining, maybe men are no longer the single head of the family, but they are still everywhere the first sex. Menocracy can thrive even where patriarchy is declining. And it is thriving. Now. Women, third-gender and LGBTQI+ people, are still oppressed all over the world, and all over themselves. In a time when the world has become a global village, when information and viruses travel worldwide in seemingly the blink of an eye, we cannot pretend we did not know, and so we know. What do we know? We know that women and gender-noncoforming people are politically, economically, socially, and sexually oppressed. No matter which sources of oppression one focuses on—race, class, gender, empire—the second sex is always at the bottom. And cismen are on top.

There are many tools by which cismen exercise their privilege, but a useful, although temporary, list includes the following: death, the state, capital, and the imaginal. Death because women are the object of a worldwide gendercide, the state because the sovereign state is an instrument of the sovereign sex, capital because its economic logic exploits some genders more than others, and the imaginal because the global menocratic imaginary constantly produces and reproduces images that are detrimental and oppressive for women and other second sexes.[1]

---

[1] A first version of this manifesto was published as an invitation to collective manifesto writing on Public Seminar (https://publicseminar.org/2020/05/anarchafeminist-manifesto-1-0/), and subsequently translated into Turkish (https://www.catlakzemin.com/anarkafeminist-manifesto-1-0/?fbclid=IwAR3ZaCLfyUGDzmemRCX7sxnn8l3bnr1jv2RHQL4HdQEn5lJAw M2PBIljOBA), Hungarian (https://aszem.info/2021/02/anarchafeminista-manifesztum-1-0/) and Spanish (*La maleta*: forthcoming). The 1.0 of the title points to the fact that we plan many different versions of such manisfesto, one that will incorporate all suggested changes to it.

1. A worldwide gendercide

There is a war going on globally and that war is waged against women, two-spirit, and LGBTQI+ people.

Why are there more men than women on the planet, despite the fact that women tend to live longer? Where are all the missing girls? The "missing girls" are not counted in the hundreds, or thousands, but in the millions. As of today, there are at least 140 million girls missing from the global population as a consequence of sex-selective abortion, infanticide, and inequalities of care.[2] Violence against women's bodies does not stop after birth: One in every three women knows it, and she knows it because she has experienced it herself—in the form of physical or sexual violence, or, very often, a combination of both. Women are not the only object of gendercide: at least sixty-nine countries worldwide have national laws criminalizing same-sex relations between consenting adults, while some have laws directly targeting transgender and gender-nonconforming folks, leading to an uninterrupted flow of violence against them.[3] Homes, as we learned during the Covid-19 pandemic, are not safe for women nor for all other exponents of the second sex: As lockdowns wore on, gender violence went up.[4]

Against femicide and feminicide,[5] against all forms of gender violence, we anarchafeminists call for the liberation of the second sex. Either all of us, or none of us will be free. *Ni una menos!*[6] Not one less!

---

[2] These are UN estimates: "Gender-biased sex selection," United Nations Population Fund, https://www.unfpa.org/gender-biased-sex-selection (accessed March 24, 2021).

[3] http://internap.hrw.org/features/features/lgbt_laws/

[4] https://www.theguardian.com/global-development/2020/apr/28/calamitous-domestic-violence-set-to-soar-by-20-during-global-lockdown-coronavirus (accessed March 24, 2021).

[5] Whereas "femicide" means the killing of *femina* (the Latin term for "women"), "feminicide," like "women's gendercide," points to the killing of women with direct state responsibility, either in the form of soft delayed legal punishment or impunity. The Kurdish women's movement uses "feminicide" as a comprehensive, structurally anchored war against women—both in armed conflicts and in everyday life. This war takes place on a physical, military level as well as on an ideological and psychological level" ("100 reasons to prosecute the dictator," Kurdish Women's Movement of Europe [TJK-E], https://100-reasons.org/call/ [accessed March 24, 2021]).

[6] We use here both the English expression "not one less!" and the Spanish "*Ni una menos*" to recognize how inspiring the slogan of the Argentinian eponymous movement has been for us.

2. The sovereign state is an instrument of the sovereign sex

Men are the sovereign sex because, like sovereign states, they do not have to recognize any (sex) superior to themselves. The world is currently divided into states, meaning there is no single piece of land to which we can escape. So we are forced to live under state rule which, in turns, also means we are forced to live under men's rule: Across 149 states assessed (some did not even agree to submit any data), the number of women heads of state or women occupying key political roles was meager.[7] Other genders were not even taken into statistical consideration. Thus, it is largely men who ultimately decide what is legal and what is illegal, who/how and when taxes have to be paid, who/how and when employment is offered, marriages made, property inherited, healthcare assured, kindergartens built, and abortion legalized—or not.

If the sovereign state is an instrument of the sovereign sex, we can understand why, in the US alone, 16 percent of transgender people have been incarcerated at least once in their life, while, in the case Black transwomen, the number of incarcerations reaches the astounding number of 47 percent of them.[8]

Furthermore: Given that we live under men's rule, are we surprised to hear that, globally, women are paid on average 63 percent of what men earn?[9]

No, we are not surprised.

Does this mean that we should fight to have a woman president?

No, this means we should fight to have no president at all.

Be under no illusion: There cannot be a feminist state because feminism means the liberation of all women, and the state is the tool via which a minority of people rules over the vast majority. But feminism cannot mean the liberation of just a few women. We have another name for that: elitism. As He-Yin Zhen put it more than a century ago: "When

---

[7] https://www.weforum.org/reports/global-gender-gap-report-2020

[8] https://transequality.org/sites/default/files/docs/resources/NCTE_Blueprint_for_Equality2012_Prison_Reform.pdf (accessed on 21 May, 2021).

[9] The data are from "Global Gender Gap Report 2020," World Economic Forum, https://www.weforum.org/reports/global-gender-gap-report-2020, accessed December 16, 2019.

a few women in power dominate the majority of powerless women, unequal class differentiation is brought into existence. If the majority of women do not want to be controlled by men, why would they want to be controlled by a minority of women?"[10] Instead of competing with men for power, women should strive for overthrowing men's rule: Anarchafeminism is the best tool we can use to achieve this because it is the best antidote against the possibility of feminism becoming simply elitism or, even worse, white privilege.

In an age when the election of a single woman as president is often presented as liberation for *all* women, when "feminism" risks becoming a fashion brand, the fundamental message of anarchafeminists of the past is more urgent than ever: "Feminism does not mean female corporate power or a woman president: it means no corporate power and no president."[11]

Against the violence perpetrated by sovereign states in order to maintain the sovereign sex's privilege, we anarchafeminists call for the liberation of the entire second sex. Not one less! Either all, or none of us will be free.

3. In the beginning was movement

Anarchism does not mean absence of order, but rather searching for a social order without an orderer.[12] The main orderer of our established ways of thinking about politics is the state, and the main tool via which states control the population within their territories is the policing of borders. It is also through the bureaucratic apparatus of the state that gender identity becomes attached to us from the time we are assigned a sex at birth: once doctors and nurses determine our "sex," it gets inscribed

---

[10] He Zhen, "Women's Liberation," in *Anarchism: A Documentary History of Libertarian Ideas – Volume I,* ed. Robert Graham (Montreal: Black Rose Books, 2005), 341.

[11] Peggy Kornegger, "Anarchism: The Feminist Connection," in *Quiet Rumors* (California: AK Press, 2012), 25.

[12] In other words, we could say that anarchism means searching for "an order," understood as spontanous sociality, without "the order," as command. Those who reject anarchy as synonimous with chaos and disorder often conflate the two meanings of the term "order": order as the recurrence of certain patterns of behavior, without which no social life would be possible, and order as command, or injunction, as in expression such as "this is an order!".

in our medical records and state papers, such as passports, and will remain with us for the rest of our lives (except for those who undergo a sex change). But why does the state need to know and monitor our sex/gender? Political regimes of the past, for instance, may not have been ideal places to live in, but they did not feel the need to systematically map and monitor the gender of its citizens. Why do we now take for granted that states have the right to do it? To what purpose? What is the biopolitical apparatus that governs us by making sure our gender conforms to our supposed nature (or sex)? There cannot be a truly feminist struggle without taking into account the role of the state in maintaining a binary gender system that maps it onto an imaginal biological dimorphism, and without taking into account how state boundaries discipline the flux of bodies, labor forces, and ideas.

It is because we are so accustomed to living in sovereign states and their security apparatuses that we tend to perceive the migration of bodies across the globe as a problem.[13] On the contrary, we should remember that, whereas sovereign states are a relatively recent historical phenomenon (for most of human history people have lived under other types of political formations),[14] human beings have been migrating across Earth since the very appearance of so-called *Homo sapiens*.[15] The *Homo sapiens* is also the *Femina sapiens*, the knowing woman, and from the very beginning an *Esse migrans*, a migrating being. Human beings did not cross state borders: It was the state border that, to begin with, crossed *them* and their movement. Hence, the need for a form of feminism before, beyond, and thus without borders.[16]

---

[13] "Historical evidence indicates clearly that, well into the nineteenth century, people routinely regarded as 'foreign' those from the next province every bit as much as those who came from other 'countries'" (John Torpey, *The Invention of the Passport: Surveillance, Citizenship and the State* [Cambridge: Cambridge University Press, 2018], 11–12).

[14] See Gianfranco Poggi, *The Development of the Modern State: A Sociological Introduction* (Stanford: Stanford University Press, 1978), particularly Chapter V, wherein the "modern state" is specifically located within the nineenth century.

[15] See Peter Bellwood, "Introduction," in *The Global Prehistory of Human Migration* (Hoboken: Wiley Blackwell, 2014). As Peter Bellwood argued, by combing the records of biology, archaeology and comparative linguistics, we find evidence of perpetual migration from "the initial migrations of the incipient genus *Homo,* around two million years ago, to the relatively recent but still prehistoric migrations of populations such as the Eastern Polynesians and Thule Inuit."

[16] We borrow the term from Chandra Talpade Mohanty, *Feminism Without Borders: Decolonizing Theory, Practicing Solidarity* (Durham: Duke University Press, 2003).

Against the violence perpetrated in the name of state boundaries and the racism they support, against the historical amnesia that leads us to forget that at the beginning was movement, we anarchafeminists call for the liberation of all women. Not one less! Either all, or none of us will be free.

4. Capital sins

If we liberate ourselves from the intellectual yoke of state boundaries and take the entire globe as our framework, the first striking datum to emerge is that people have not always been "doing" gender, and, moreover, even if they did it, they did it on very different terms. It is only with the emergence of a worldwide capitalist system that the rigid gender binary dividing bodies into masculine men and feminine women became so hegemonic worldwide. This does not mean that sexual difference did not exist before global capitalism, nor that capitalism invented patriarchy from scratch. It simply means that capitalism reoccupied previous forms of patriarchy, eradicating matriarchy where it existed, thereby giving menocracy a new strength and a new formidable impetus. In sum, it means that capitalism is inseparable from the "modern/colonial binary gender system." Capitalism needs "women," because it needs the assumption that women are not "working" when they wash their children's socks and cook their meals: It needs them to believe that they are just being good wives and good mothers. If a capitalist had to pay wages for all the cleaning, cooking, feeding, caring, baby-sitting, and child-raising labor that "good wives" and "good mothers" do for free, then there would be no capitalism at all because there would be a limit to the limitless expansion of profit that defines capitalism as an economy.

But along with the extraction of unwaged labor from women and those who occupy that position, capitalism also needs to extract free natural resources from the environment and create mechanisms to regulate labor flows. This is the reason why, from the very beginning, capitalism has gone hand in hand with colonialism, land occupations, and ecological catastrophes. As a system devoted to the endless accumulation of profit, capitalism relies on boundaries to regulate the movement of labor force and the extraction of natural resources, but it also relies on racism to make sure that some bodies are more exploitable than others. This is where intersectionality is most evident, because being a woman of color means being exploitable in a way that cannot simply be explained by the quality of being a woman *plus* being a person of color, and being an indigenous woman, whose environment has been destroyed and waters poisoned, means being exploited to such a degree that no monthly check can ever pay back. Something very peculiar happens in those intersections of capital's sins, and that is where "the coloniality of gender"[17] thrives.

Against this systematic intertwinement among capitalist exploitation, racial classification of bodies, and environmental destruction, against this boundary drawing that separate women and two-spirit from other genders in order to make them more exploitable, we anarchafeminists call for the liberation of all women. Not one less! Either all, or none of us will be free.

5. Another woman is possible

At this point one might ask: Why insist on anarchafeminism and not just call this anarchism? If the purpose is to dismantle all types of hierarchies, should we not also get rid of the gender binary, which opposes "women" to "men," and thus imprisons us in a cisgendered and heteronormative matrix?

By drawing insights from an ontology of the transindividual, we respond that bodies in general, and women's bodies in particular, must not be considered as individuals, as fixed, unchangeable objects, but rather as processes. Women's bodies, like all bodies, are bodies in plural because they are processes constituted by mechanisms of affects and associations that occur at the *inter-*, *infra-*, and the *supra-*individual level. Our bodies come into being through an *inter-*individual encounter, they are shaped by *supra-*individual forces, such as their geographical locations, and they are made up by *infra-*individual bodies such as the molecules we breathe, the hormones we absorb, or the images we process every day. A "woman" comes into being not just through "inter"-actions, but also through "intra"-actions.

Properly speaking we are not, and never have been, individuals: We are, literally, transindividual processes, accidental sites of a process of

---

[17] Maria Lugones, "The Coloniality of Gender," in *The Palgrave Handbook of Gender and Development*, ed. Wendy Harcourt (London: Palgrave Macmillan, 2016).

becoming that takes place at different levels. We are relations, not substances. Processes, not things. Only if we consider skin boundaries as the ultimate boundaries, can we classify bodies as males and females. However, if we look beyond those boundaries and consider the totality of the cells comprising human bodies, we find out that 95 percent of them escape that dichotomy: Most living matter is actually queer.[18] If we adopt this transindividual perspective, can we speak about "womanhood" outside of the modern/colonial gender system, and thus use that very term in order to include all those who identify themselves as women: feminine women, masculine women, transwomen, AFAB women, AMAB women, lesbian women, bisexual women, intersex women, ciswomen, asexual women, queer women, and so on and so forth. All the way up to ways of being woman that have not yet been invented because another woman is not just possible: it has also, always, already begun.

Against the violence perpetrated in the name of gender binarism, homophobia, and transphobia, we anarchafeminists call for the liberation of the entire second sex: women, two-spirit, third-gender, gender fluid, trans and queer bodies, and so on and so forth. Not one less! Either all, or none of us will be free.

6. Transindividual ecology

Every being is endowed with the capacity to affect and to being affected, and that is how they strive to persist in their being. We persist in our being not despite others, but through others: other humans, as well as through the other-than-human. As a consequence, "ecology" is nothing but *co-affectivity*, whereas "ecological thinking" is nothing but the thinking of co-affectivity as co-origination. We do not want to collapse ecology into an all-encompassing organicism, where the whole determines its parts: Co-affectivity is co-origination without an *archē*. Anarchafeminism is the revindication of "e-co-affectivity,"[19] understood as the capacity to affect and of being affected by every single being, without implying any hierarchical organizing of such an infinite web of affecting.

---

[18] Myra Hird, "Naturally Queer," *Feminist Theory* 5, no. 1 (2014), 85–8.
[19] Marjolein Oele, *E-Co-Affectivity: Exploring the Pathos at Life's Material Interfaces* (Albany: SUNY Press, 2020).

Are we calling for a return to nature? We want to bring nature back to politics, but what is coming back is not the same thing that went away: Our nature is not Nature with a capital letter, something that is capitalized at the very moment that is idealized, and thus sadistically made exploitable.[20] An anarchafeminist approach to ecology is one *without* Nature, in that alienated form, but *through* nature, in its meaning of the unique infinite substance we all express. In sum, it is a transindividual ecology.

An ontology of transindividuality enables us to both retain and distinguish between different (trans)individualities, while according none of them any type of ontological superiority, and questioning rigid boundaries between them. We consequently refuse any form of "animal chauvinism"[21] and proclaim that every being is to some extent animate and that it can be so in radically different ways from which humans are. We therefore challenge all systems that have classified life according to the hierarchy of "man (on top of)>woman (on top of)>slave (on top of)>animal (on top of)>plants (on top of)>dead matter," because they are done from the perspective of "Man" as the yardstick for value. We reject this menocratic hierarchy, and fight for animal, plants, and even for mineral liberation. There is no such thing as "dead matter," because every type of matter is to some extent "living matter": The environment is not simply something outside there, the inert surrounding of our being—the environment is us. An anarchafeminist ecology is thus a transindividual ecology according to which industrial waste is not outside of nature, but a living organism, whereas the molecules we inhale or the minerals we encompass are literally constitutive of our being—in sum, it is a queering of ecology.

Against the violence perpetrated in the name of that contradiction in terms called "green capitalism," against that menocratic hierarchy man>woman>slave>animal>plant>inanimate matter, we anarchafeminists state that all matter is to some extent animate, so there cannot be a liberation of the second sex without a liberation of the planet. Not one less! Either all, or none of us will be free.

---

[20] This is the nature that anarchafeminists, like xeno-feminists, reject. We are referring here to Laboria Cuboniks, *The Xenofeminist Manifesto: A Politics for Alienation* (London: Verso, 2018), which rejects nature as a source of injustice.

[21] Emanuele Coccia, *La vie des plantes: Une métaphysique du mélange* (Paris: Éditions Rivages, 2016), 16. Coccia refers to earlier usages by W. Marshall Darley and J. L. Arbor.

7. Technologies of the self

The imaginal apparatus that sustains the global menocracy has infiltrated even the process of becoming a woman. Women's bodies are everywhere the object of a process of disciplining whose very purpose is not simply to govern bodies but to instill in us the idea that our bodies need to be governed. Images and rituals of health, beauty, and care change a lot from one context to another, but they are everywhere powerful sites for the exercise of menocratic technologies of the self. This is how docile subjects are created: not (only) through the imposition of rules from the outside, but through the voluntary and, at times, even joyful participation in one's own submission.

We therefore reject the imaginal fashion that perpetrates the modern/colonial gender system. Since the nineteenth century—that is, the time of the emergence of factories and compulsory military service—European men have undergone their "Great Masculine Renunciation"[22]: They gave up all the colors, laces, and adornments to wear the sober, dark two-piece suit sported today by all important businessmen, from Nairobi to Shanghai. But the "European men's" great masculine renunciation of the past is the "men's" great masculine renunciation of our global present. This has certainly increased men's attire functionality as well as their solemnity, particularly when the jacket opens up to reveal that imponderable adornment hanging down in the middle of the chest and called a "tie". By renouncing all other adornments, except the phallus on the chest, men made it clear that they did not need any of them, precisely because they are already so important by themselves, whereas women, who incessantly need to prop themselves up, are consequently invited to carry all the burden of colors, laces, and fusses. It is women who are most expected to wear "make-up": why do we have to carry the burden of "making it up"? What do we have to "make up" for? Being women?

But of course it's not just "make-up": Women worldwide carry most of the burden of care, in all senses of the term—from childcare to bodycare, all the way up to healthcare. Women's bodies and sexualities are indeed medicalized and pathologized to a degree inconceivable in the case of

---

[22] John Carl Flügel, "The Great Masculine Renunciation," in *The Rise of Fashion: A Reader*, ed. Daniel Leonhard Purdy (Minneapolis: Minnesota University Press, 2004).

men. Why are women supposed to visit a gynecologist once a year, while most men can lead an entire life without ever having seen a urologist? Why do women's sexual organs need so many more "check-ups" than men's? Are we assuming that something must have gone wrong just because. . . they are women?

And why are women sexual organs so often spoken of as "vagina," which, as the Latin etymology reminds us, means the scabbard? The Christian God created the world by giving out names, and, since then, name-giving has remained the sovereign act *par excellence*. Why describe all that variegated space as a mere "container for the sword"? Where have the clitoris, the vulva, the pubis, the uterus, and the labia gone? All into the "vagina." The whole is reduced to the part—the part that is supposed to give pleasure to the penis.

This is not just a form of terminological reductionism: precisely because female genitalia are named as incomplete as they are, precisely because women are supposed to carry the burden of "make-up," women more compliantly undergo constant rituals of adjustment that may vary enormously but which are relentless in their disciplining effect. For instance, whereas men rarely undergo complete body depilation, women are increasingly expected to have all hair stripped from their bodies in order to be regarded as clean, desirable, and sexy. But why do we need to have hairless, pre-pubescent vulvas in order to be acceptable? If it is true that hair appears on the body when we reach puberty, what is this imaginal order of pre-pubescent vulvas asking us? That we never reach puberty? That we remain "little girls" forever? Can we greet everybody and politely walk away from this menocratic order?

Probably not that quickly. From traditional foot-binding to the more modern wearing of high heels, the control of women's feet is yet another tool for disciplining our bodies. Whether prevented from their natural growth, because small feet were said to be particularly attractive, or seduced into walking on painful high heels, because by walking on pointy little penis substitutes we are said to be particularly "dressed UP," women's feet never seem to be quite right. Why can men be masculine when wearing perfectly comfortable shoes, while women have to be in pain in order to be truly feminine? How have we come to accept this systematic association of the feminine with pain and suffering?

Against menocratic technologies of the self, we anarchafeminists call for a global liberation of women—literally from head to toe. We pledge to fight: state fascism and plantar fasciitis, rape and osteoarthritis, phallocracy and metatarsalgia, sexual harassment and bunions, brain wash and pump bump, unpaid housework and hammer toes, denial of abortion rights and bone spurs, gender pay gap and ankle sprains, feminicide and foranimal stenosis, gender mutilation and stress fractures, lower back pain, and cramps and spasms. . . . In sum, we want all women to be able to walk—free.

8. Just do it

Begin your revolution now. No site is ever too small to start, because the tyrant is not only outside but also inside. Aiming to seize state power first, or asking for recognition from it, means reproducing that very power structure that needs to be questioned in the first place. On the contrary, "just do it" means that at least a little bit of freedom is within everybody's reach. No rebellion is ever too small or too big, and most importantly, rebellions are not mutually exclusive: Resist gender norms, play with them, refuse to comply, disobey, boycott, fight capitalism, practice radical democracy, be a "gender pirate"[23] in a different way. Even in ways that have not been invented yet. If you cannot build an anarchafeminist society in your country, build it in your neighborhood. If you cannot build it in your neighborhood, build it in your household. If you cannot build it in your household, build it within yourself. These actions are not simply "individualist strategies," as some have labeled them. They are prefigurations of a different world. They are political acts *per se*, which are the other side of collective projects, such as the increasing examples of mass mobilization, grassroots organizations, general strikes, occupations, communal and queer living that are proliferating around the globe and aimed at abolishing capitalism and the authoritarian state. The feminist international[24] begins with the feminist transindividual, but it does not stop there. Local and even infra-individual acts may be necessary but clearly not sufficient. Global is the oppression, so global has to be the fight.

---

[23] We borrow the expression from Beatriz (now Paul B.) Preciado, *Testo Junkie* (New York: The Feminist Press, 2013), 55.
[24] Verónica Gago, *Feminist International: How to Change Everything* (London: Verso, 2020).

9. The end is the means

There cannot, and should not, be any definitive fully-fledged program for an anarchafeminist manifesto, because freedom is the end and it is an outright contradiction to think of reaching it through anything except freedom itself. Anarchism is a method, and not a blueprint. This does not mean that there cannot be any site-specific and time-limited programs and "to do lists." There can and there should be many of them. In the same way in which bodies are plural and plural is their oppression, plural must also be the strategies to fight such an oppression. If freedom is both the means and the end, then one could also envisage a world free from the very notion of gender as well as the oppressive structures that it generates. Because gendered bodies are still the worldwide objects of exploitation and domination, we need an anarchafeminist manifesto here and now. Urgent times call for urgent means and manifestos are an expression of that urgency. But the latter should be conceived of as a ladder that we may well abandon once no longer needed. Indeed, it is implicit in the very process of embarking on such an anarchafeminist project that we should strive for a world beyond the compulsory binary opposition between men and women and thus, in a way, also beyond feminism itself.

Bibliography

Abbagnano, Nicola (1971) *Dizionario di filosofia*. Turin: UTET.

Ackelsberg, Martha A. (2005) *The Free Women of Spain. Anarchism and The Struggle for the Emancipation of Women*. Oakland: AK Press.

Adams, Suzi, and Jeremy Smith, eds (2022, forthcoming) *Debating Imaginal Politics: Dialogues with Chiara Bottici*. Lanham, MD: Rowman & Littlefield.

Agamben, Giorgio (1998) *Homo Sacer: Sovereign Power and Bare Life*, trans. Daniel Heller-Roazen. Stanford: Stanford University Press.

Agamben, Giorgio (2017) *Creazione ed anarchia. L'opera nell'età della religione capitalista*. Vicenza: Neri Pozza Editore.

Alaimo, Stacy (2010) *Bodily Natures: Science, Environment, and the Material Self*. Bloomington: Indiana University Press.

Alatas, Syed Farid, and Vineeta Sinha (2017) *Sociological Theory Beyond the Canon*. London: Palgrave Macmillan.

Allen, Amy (2008) *The Politics of Our Selves: Power, Autonomy, and Gender in Contemporary Critical Theory*. Columbia University Press.

Alves, Maria Thereza (2017) *Seeds of Change. New York – A Botany of Colonization*, November 3–27, New School: Vera List Center for Art and Politics 2016–18.

Amadiume, Ifi (1987) *Male Daughters, Female Husbands: Gender and Sex in an African Society*. London: Zed Books.

Anderson Barbata, Laura, and Donna Wingate, eds. (2017) *The Eye of the Beholder: Julia Pastrana's Long Journey Home*. Seattle: Lucia Marquard.

Anderson Barbata, Laura (2017) "The Repatriation pilgrimage of Julia Pastrana," in Laura Anderson Barbata and Donna Wingate (eds.), *The Eye of the Beholder: Julia Pastrana's Long Journey Home*. Seattle: Lucia Marquard, 131–54.

Anselm, Saint, Archbishop of Canterbury (2007) *Anselm: Basic Writings*. Trans. Thomas Williams. Indianapolis: Hackett Publishing.

Anzaldúa, Gloria (2012) *Borderlands/La Frontera: The New Mestiza*. San Francisco: Aunt Lute Books.

Arendt, Hannah (1996) *Love and Saint Augustine*. Chicago: Chicago University Press.

Arendt, Hannah (1998) *The Human Condition*. Chicago: The University of Chicago Press.

Arendt, Hannah (2005) *The Promise of Politics*. New York: Schocken.

Aristotle (1932) *Politics*. Trans. H. Rackham, *Loeb Classical Library*, 264. Cambridge: Harvard University Press.

Aristotle (1957) *On the Soul; Parva Naturalia; On Breath*. Trans. W. S. Hett. Cambridge: Harvard University Press.

Arruzza, Cinzia (2010) *Le relazioni pericolose: matrimoni e divorzi tra marxismo e femminismo*. Roma: Alegre.

Arruzza, Cinzia, Tithi Bhattacharya, and Nancy Fraser (2019) *Feminism for the 99%: A Manifesto*. London: Verso.

Bakunin, Mikhail (1972) *Bakunin on Anarchy: Selected Works by the Activist-Founder of World Anarchism*. New York: Vintage Books.

Bakunin, Mikhail (1872) "Letter to La Liberté." Available at: http://www.marxists.org/reference/archive/bakunin/works/1872/la-liberte.htm (accessed July 25, 2020).

Bakunin, Mikhail (1970) *God and the State*. New York: Dover Publications.

Bakunin, Mikhail (1972) *Bakunin on Anarchy: Selected Works by the Activist-Founder of World Anarchism*. New York: Vintage Books.

Bakunin, Mikhail (1974) 'The political theology of Mazzini', in *Selected Writings*. New York: Grove, 214–31.

Bakunin, Mikhail (1996) *Tre conferenze sull'anarchia*. Roma: Manifestolibri.

Bakunin, Mikhail (2000) *La libertà degli uguali*. Milan: Eleuthera.

Bakunin, Mikhail (2005a). *Statism and Anarchy*. Trans. M. Shatz. Cambridge: Cambridge University Press.

Bakunin, Mikhail (2005b) "Bakunin: Against Patriarchal Authority," in Robert Graham (ed.), *Anarchism: A Documentary History of Libertarian Ideas, Vol. I*. Montreal: Black Rose Books, 236–8.

Balibar, Étienne (1997) "Spinoza: From Individuality to Transindividuality," in *Medelingen vanwege het Spinozahauis*. Delft: Heburon, 3–36.

Balibar, Étienne (1998) *Spinoza and Politics*. London: Verso.

Balibar, Étienne (2018) "Philosophies of the Transindividual: Spinoza, Marx, Freud," *Australasian Philosophical Review* 2(1): 5–25.

Balibar, Étienne and Vittorio Morfino, eds. (2014) *Il transindividuale*. Milan: Mimesis.

Barad, Karen (2007) *Meeting the Universe Halfway: Quantum Physics and the Entanglement of Matter and Meaning*. Durham, Duke University Press

Barkawi, Tarak (2010) "Empire and Order in International Relations and Security Studies," in Robert Allen Denemark (ed.), *The International Studies Encyclopedia*. Hoboken: Wiley-Blackwell, p. 1360.

Bartky, Sandra Lee (1997) "Foucault, Femininity, and the Modernization of Patriarchal Power," in Katie Conboy, Nadia Medina, and Sarah Stanbury (eds.), *Writing on the Body: Female Embodiment and Feminist Theory*. New York: Columbia University Press, 129–154.

Bartky, Sandra Lee (2002) "Suffering to Be Beautiful," in Constance L. Mui and Julien S. Murphy (eds.), *Gender Struggles: Practical Approaches to Contemporary Feminism*. Lanham, MD: Rowman & Littlefield.

Bellwood, Peter (2014) "Introduction," in *The Global Prehistory of Human Migration*. Hoboken: Wiley Blackwell.

Bennett, Jane (2010) *Vibrant Matter: A Political Ecology of Things*. Durham: Duke University Press.

Benovsky, Jiri (2018) *Mind and Matter: Panpsychism, Dual-Aspect Monism, and the Combination Problem*. Switzerland: Springer.

Bernasconi, Robert, and Tommy Lee Lott (2000) *The Idea of Race*. Indianapolis: Hackett Publishing.

Bernini, Lorenzo (2017) *Queer Apocalypses*. London: Palgrave.

Bernini, Lorenzo (2020) *Queer Theories: An Introduction*. New York: Routledge.

Bernier, Francois (2000) "A New Division of the Earth," in Robert Bernasconi and Tommy Lott (eds.), *The Idea of Race*. Indianapolis: Hackett Publishing, 1–4.

Bernstein, Sara (2020) "The Metaphysics of Intersectionality," *Philosophical Studies* 177(2): 321–35.

Berros, María Valeria (2015) "The Constitution of the Republic of Ecuador: Pachamama Has Rights," Environment & Society Portal, *Arcadia* 11.

Berthier, René (1991) *Bakounine politique*. Paris: Edition du Monde Libertaire.

Bey, Marquis (2020) *Anarcho-Blackness: Notes Towards a Black Anarchism*. Oakland: AK Press.

Bilge, Sirma (2013) "Intersectionality Undone: Saving Intersectionality from Feminist Intersectionality Studies," *Du Bois Review* 10(2): 405–24.

Birmingham, Peg (2006) *Hannah Arendt and Human Rights: The Predicament of Common Responsibility*. Bloomington: Indiana University Press.

Blankenhorn, David (1993) "Fatherless America," *American Experiment*, https://www.americanexperiment.org/reports-books/fatherless-america/ (accessed February 5, 2020).

Blaut, James Morris (1993) *The Colonizer's Model of the World: Geographical Diffusionism and Eurocentric History*. New York: Guilford Press.

Blumenberg, Hans (1975) *Work on Myth*. Trans. Robert M. Wallace. Cambridge, MA: MIT Press.

Blumenfeld, Jacob (2018) *All Things Are Nothing to Me: The Unique Philosophy of Max Stirner*. Winchester: Zero Books.

Blumenfeld, Jacob, Chiara Bottici, and Simon Critchley, eds. (2013) *The Anarchist Turn*. London: Pluto Press.

Bohannan, Paul (1963) *Social Anthropology*. New York: Holt, Rinehart & Winston.

Boehm, Omri (2014) *Kant's Critique of Spinoza*. Oxford: Oxford University Press.

Bondeson, Jan (2017) "The Strange Story of Julia Pastrana," in Laura Anderson Barbata and Donna Wingate (eds.), *The Eye of the Beholder: Julia Pastrana's Long Journey Home*. Seattle: Lucia Marquard, 9–24.

Bookchin, Murray (2005) *The Ecology of Freedom: The Emergence and Dissolution of Hierarchy*. Oakland: AK Press.

Bottici, Chiara (2007) *A Philosophy of Political Myth*. Cambridge: Cambridge University Press.

Bottici, Chiara (2009) *Men and States: Rethinking the Domestic Analogy in a Global Age*. Trans. Karen Whittle. Basingstoke: Palgrave Macmillan.

Bottici, Chiara (2011) "Anarchy," in G. T. Kurian (ed.), *The Encyclopedia of Political Science*. Washington DC: Sage, 52–4.

Bottici, Chiara (2012) "Another Enlightenment: Spinoza on Myth and Imagination," *Constellations* 19(4): 1–19.

Bottici, Chiara (2014) *Imaginal Politics: Images Beyond Imagination and the Imaginary*. New York: Columbia University Press.

Bottici, Chiara (2015) "Rethinking the Biopolitical Turn: From the Thanatopolitical to the Geneapolitical Paradigm," *Graduate Faculty Philosophy Journal* 35(1): 175–97.

Bottici, Chiara (2017) "Bodies in Plural: Towards an Anarcha-feminist Manifesto," *Thesis Eleven* 142(1): 91–111.

Bottici, Chiara (2018) "From the Transindividual to the Imaginal: A Response to Balibar's 'Philosophies of the Transindividual: Spinoza, Marx, Freud'", *Australasian Philosophy Review* 2(1): 69–76.

Bottici, Chiara (2020) "Philosophy, Coloniality and the Politics of Remembrance," special issue "Philosophy and Coloniality", *Graduate Faculty Philosophy Journal* 41(1), 87–125.

Bottici, Chiara (2022) *A Feminist Mythology*. London: Bloomsbury.

Bottici, Chiara, and Benoît Challand (2010) *The Myth of The Clash of Civilizations*. New York: Routledge.

Bottici, Chiara, and Benoît Challand (2013) *Imagining Europe: Myth, Memory, and Identity*. Cambridge: Cambridge University Press.

Bottici, Chiara, and Benoît Challand (2020) "Europe after Eurocentrism?," *Crisis & Critique* 7(1): 57–87.

Bottici, Chiara, and Miguel de Beistegui (2018) "Spinoza and the Hydraulic Discipline of Affects: From the Theologico-political to the Economic Regime of Desire," in A. K. Kordela and Dimitris Vardoulakis (eds.), *Spinoza's Authority, Volume II*. London: Bloomsbury, 167–92.

Braidotti, Rosi (2013) *The Posthuman*. Cambridge: Polity.

Brown, L. Susan (1990) "Beyond Feminism: Anarchism and Human Freedom," in D. I. Roussopoulos (ed.), *The Anarchist Papers 3*. New York: Black Rose Books, 201–10.

Brüntrup, Godehard, and Ludwig Jaskolla, eds (2017) *Panpsychism: Contemporary Perspectives*. Oxford: Oxford University Press.

Bull, Hedley (1977) *The Anarchical Society*. London: Macmillan.

Butler, Judith (1990) *Gender Trouble*. New York: Routledge.

Butler, Judith (1993) "Imitation and Gender Insubordination," in Henry Abelove, Michèle Aina Barale, and David M. Halperin (eds.), *The Lesbian and Gay Studies Reader*. New York: Routledge, 307–20.

Butler, Judith (2011) *Bodies That Matter: On the Discursive Limits of "Sex."* New York: Routledge.

Calla, Pamela, and Nina Laurie (2006) "Desarrollo, poscolonialismo y teoria geografica politica," in Nina Laurie and Maria Esther Pozo (eds.), *Las displicencias de genera en los cruces del siglo pasado al nuevo milenio en los Andes*. Cochabamba, Bolivia: CESU-UMSS.

Call, Lewis (2002) *Postmodern Anarchism*. Lanham: Lexington.

Castiglioni, Luigi, and Scevola Mariotti. (1966) *Vocabolario della lingua latina*. Turin: Loescher.

Castillo, Marco, Ragan Petrie, and Maximo Torero (2012) "Beautiful or White? Discrimination in Group Formation," *GMU Working Paper in Economics*, No. 12–29.

Castoriadis, Cornelius (1987) *The Imaginary Institution of Society*. Cambridge: Polity.

Castoriadis, Cornelius (1988) *Political and Social Writings*. Trans. David A. Curtis. Minneapolis: University of Minnesota Press.

Cavarero, Adriana (1997) *Relating Narratives: Storytelling and Selfhood*. Trans. P. Kottman. London: Routledge.

Cavarero, Adriana (2009) *Nonostante Platone: Figure femminili nella filosofia antica*. Verona: Ombre Corte.

Cavazzini, Andrea (2014) "'Cellule, Organismi, Comunita': Il transindividuale nelle scienze della vita contemporanee',' in Étienne Balibar and Vittorio Morfino (eds.), *Il transindividuale*. Milan: Mimesis, 231–52.

Chakrabarty, Dipesh (2000) *Provincializing Europe: Postcolonial Thought and Historical Difference*. Princeton: Princeton University Press.

Challand, Benoît (2009a) "1989, Contested Memories and the Shifting Cognitive Maps of Europe," *European Journal of Social Theory* 12(3): 397–408.

Challand, Benoît (2009b) *Palestinian Civil Society*. London: Routledge.

Chalmers, David J. (1995) "Facing Up to the Problem of Consciousness," *Journal of Consciousness Studies* 2(3): 200–19.

Chalmers, David J. (1996) *The Conscious Mind: Towards a Fundamental Theory*. New York: Oxford University Press.

Chanter, Tina (2006) *Gender: Key Concepts in Philosophy*. London: Continuum.

Chen, Kuan-Hsing (2010) *Asia as Method. Toward Deimperialization*, Durham: Duke University Press,

Chen, Mel Y. (2012) *Animacies: Biopolitics, Racial Mattering, and Queer Affect*. Durham: Duke University Press.

Cherokee Women's Councils (2018) "'Petitions to the Cherokee National Council.' Cherokee Lands; May 2, 1817, June 30, 1818, and October 17, 1821," in Penny A. Weiss (ed.), *Feminist Manifestos: A Global Documentary Reader*. New York: New York University Press, 47–50.

Ching, Julia (1978) "Chinese Ethics and Kant," in *Philosophy East and West*, Apr., 1978, 28(2): 161–72.

Chomsky, Noam (2005) *Chomsky on Anarchism*. Oakland: AK Press.

Coccia, Emanuele (2016) *La vie des plantes: Une métaphysique du mélange*. Paris: Éditions Rivage.

Collins, Patricia Hill (2000) *Black Feminist Thought: Knowledge, Consciousness, and the Politics of Empowerment*. New York: Routledge.

Collins, Patricia Hill (2019) *Intersectionality as Critical Social Theory*. Durham: Duke University Press.

Collins, Patricia Hill, and Margaret L. Andersen, eds. (2012) *Race, Class and Gender: An Anthology*. Belmont: Wadsworth Publishing.

Collins, Patricia Hill, and Sirma Bilge (2016) *Intersectionality*. Cambridge: Polity.

The Combahee River Collective (1982) "A Black Feminist Statement," in Gloria T. Hull, Patricia Bell Scott, and Barbara Smith (eds.), *But Some of Us Are Brave: Black Women's Studies*. New York: The Feminist Press, 13–22.

Combes, Muriel (2013) *Gilbert Simondon and the Philosophy of the Transindividual*. Cambridge: MIT Press.

Coole, Diana, and Samantha Frost, eds. (2010) *New Materialism: Ontology, Agency, and Politics*. Durham: Duke University Press.

Cornell, Drucilla (1995) *The Imaginary Domain: Abortion, Pornography and Sexual Harassment*. London: Routledge.

Craib, Raymond, and Barry Maxwell (2015) *No Gods, No Masters, No Peripheries*. Oakland: PM Press.

Cremins, Robert, (2019) "Is There a Political Myth of Settler Homosexuality?," MA Thesis submitted to the Philosophy Department of The New School.

Crenshaw, Kimberlé (1989) "Demarginalizing the Intersection of Race and Sex: A Black Feminist Critique of Antidiscrimination Doctrine, Feminist Theory and Antiracist Politics," *The University of Chicago Legal Forum*, 140: 139–67.

Critchley, Simon (2001) *Continental Philosophy: A Very Short Introduction*. Oxford: Oxford University Press.

Critchley, Simon (2007) *Infinitely Demanding: Ethics of Commitment, Politics of Resistance*. London: Verso.

Critchley, Simon (2013) "Introduction," in Jacob Blumenfeld, Chiara Bottici, and Simon Critchley (eds.), *The Anarchist Turn*. London: Pluto Press, 1–5.

Crowder, George (1992) *Classical Anarchism: The Political Thought of Godwin, Proudhon, Bakunin, and Kropotkin*. Oxford: Clarendon Press.

Cuboniks, Laboria (2018) *The Xenofeminist Manifesto: A Politics for Alienation*. London: Verso.

Curd, Patricia, ed. (2010) *A Presocratics Reader: Selected Fragments and Testimonia*. Indianapolis: Hackett Publishing.

D'Andrea, Dimitri (2005) *L'incubo degli ultimi uomini. Etica e politica in Max Weber*. Carocci: Roma.

Daannaa, H.S. (1994) "The Acephalous Society and the Indirect Rule System in Africa," *The Journal of Legal Pluralism and Unofficial Law* 26(34): 61–85.

Damasio, Antonio (2003) *Looking for Spinoza: Joy, Sorrow, and the Feeling Brain*. Orlando: Harcourt Inc.

Dark Star Collective (2012) *Quiet Rumor: An Anarchafeminist Reader*. Oakland: AK Press.

Davis, Angela (1981) *Women, Race and Class*. New York: Random House.

Dean, Carolyn (2001) "Andean Androgyny and the Making of Men," in Cecilia Klein (ed.), *Gender in preHispanic America*. Washington, D.C.: Dumbarton Oaks, 143–182.

Debord, Guy (1995) *The Society of the Spectacle*. Trans. Donald Nicholson-Smith. New York: Zone Books.

De Beauvoir, Simone (2011) *The Second Sex*. New York: Vintage Books.

De Cleyre, Voltairine (2001) "They Who Marry Do Ill," in Peter Glassgold (ed.), *Anarchy! An Anthology of Emma Goldman's Mother Earth*. Washington, DC: Counterpoint, 103–13.

De La Boétie, Étienne (2015) *The Politics of Obedience: The Discourse of Voluntary Servitude*. Auburn: Mises Institute.

Dalla Costa, Mariarosa (1972) *Potere Femminile e Sovversione Sociale*. Venice: Marsilio Editore.

De Sousa Santos, Boaventura (2014) *Epistemologies of the South: Justice Against Epistemicide*. Boulder: Paradigm Publishers.

De Sousa Santos, Boaventura (2018) *The End of the Cognitive Empire: The Coming of Age of Epistemologies of the South*. Durham: Duke University Press.

Deleuze, Gilles (1992) *Expressionism in Philosophy: Spinoza*. Trans. Martin Joughin. New York: Zone Books.

Deleuze, Gilles (1985) *Spinoza et le problème de l'expression*. Paris: Éditions de Minuit.

Deleuze, Gilles, and Félix Guattari (1987) *A Thousand Plateaus: Capitalism and Schizophrenia*. Trans. Brian Massumi. Minneapolis: University of Minnesota Press.

Dodd, James (2017) *Phenomenology, Architecture and the Built World: Exercise in Philosophical Anthropology*. Leiden: Brill.

Donaldson, Laura E., ed. (1992) *Decolonizing Feminisms: Race, Gender, and Empire Building*. Chapel Hill: UNC Press.

Dunbar-Ortiz, Roxanne (2012) "Quiet Rumors: An Introduction to This Anthology," in Dark Star Collective (eds.), *Quiet Rumors: Anarcha-feminist Reader*. Oakland: AK Press, 11–13.

Dunbar-Ortiz, Roxanne (2014) *An Indigenous Peoples' History of the United States*. London: Beacon Press.

Dussel, Enrique (1995) *The Invention of the Americas: Eclipse of "the Other" and the Myth of Modernity*. Trans. Michael D. Barber. New York: Continuum.

Echeverría, Bolívar (2019) *Modernity and "Whiteness."* Cambridge: Polity Press, 2019.

Ehrlich, Carol (2007) "Anarchism, Feminism and Situationism," in Robert Graham (ed.), *Anarchism: A Documentary History of Libertarian Ideas. Volume Two: The Emergence of the New Anarchism (1939–1977)*. Montreal: Black Rose Books, 492–9.

Ehrlich, H. J. (2013) "Toward a General Theory of Anarchafeminism," in H. J. Ehrlich and a. h. s. boy (eds.), *The Best of Social Anarchism*. Tucson: See Sharp Press, 51–6.

Eisenstein, Zillah R. (ed.) (1979) *Capitalist Patriarchy and the Case for Socialist Feminism*. New York: Monthly Review Press.

Elden, Stuart, and Mendieta, Eduardo, eds. (2011) *Reading Kant's Geography*. Albany: SUNY Press.

Eng, David, Jack Halberstam, and José E. Muñoz (2005) "What's Queer About Queer Studies Now?," *Social Text* 23(3–4): 1–17.

Fahs, Breanne (2013) "Shaving It All Off: Examining Social Norms of Body Hair Among College Men in a Women's Studies Course," *Women's Studies* 42: 559–77.

Fanon, Frantz (1967) *Toward the African Revolution: Political Essays*. Trans. Haakon Chevalier. New York: Grove Press.

Fanon, Frantz (2004) *The Wretched of the Earth*. Trans. Richard Philcox. New York: Grove Press.

Fanon, Frantz (2008) *Black Skin, White Masks*. Trans. Richard Philcox. New York: Grove Press.

Farrow, Lynne (2012) "Feminism as Anarchism," in Dark Star Collective (eds.), *Quiet Rumors: Anarcha-feminist Reader*. Oakland: AK Press, 19–25.

Farvid, Panteá (2015) "Heterosexuality," in Christina Richards and Meg John Barker (eds.), *The Palgrave Book of the Psychology of Sexuality and Gender*. London: Palgrave Macmillan, 92–108.

Farvid, Panteá, and Virginia Braun (2020) "A Critical Encyclopedia of Heterosexuality," in Kira Hall and Rusty Barrett (eds.), *The Oxford Handbook of Language and Sexuality*. Oxford: Oxford University Press.

Federici, Silvia (2004) *The Caliban and the Witch: Women, The Body and Primitive Accumulation*. New York: Aunotomedia.

Federici, Silvia (2012) *Revolution at Point Zero: Housework, Reproduction, and Feminist Struggle*. Oakland: PM Press.

Ferguson, Susan J. (2013) *Race, Gender, Sexuality, and Social Class: Dimensions of Inequality and Identity*. London: Sage.

Feyerabend, Paul (1993) *Against Method*. London: Verso.

Fleury, Cynthia (ed.) (2006) *Imagination, imaginaire, imaginal*. Paris: PUF.

Flügel, John Carl (2004) "The Great Masculine Renunciation," in D. Purdy (ed.), *The Rise of Fashion: A Reader*. Minneapolis: Minnesota University Press, 102–08.

Fortunati, Leopoldina (1984) "La ridefinizione della donna," in Silvia Federici and Leopoldina Fortunati, *Il grande Calibano: Storia del corpo social ribelle nella prima fase del capitale*. Milan: Franco Angeli.

Foucault, Michel (1980) *Power-Knowledge*. New York: The Harvester Press.

Foucault, Michel (1988) *Technologies of the Self: A Seminar with Michel Foucault*. Amherst: University of Massachusetts Press.

Foucault, Michel (1990) *The History of Sexuality*. New York: Vintage Books.

Foucault, Michel (2003) *"Society Must be Defended": Lectures at the Collège de France, 1975–1976*. Trans. David Macey. New York: Picador.

Fraser, Nancy (2013) *Fortunes of Feminism: From State-managed Capitalism to Neoliberal Crisis*. London: Verso.

Fraser, Nancy (2014), "Behind Marx's Hidden Abode," *New Left Review* 86: 55–72.

Fraser, Nancy, and Axel Honneth (2003). *Redistribution or Recognition? A Political-Philosophical Exchange*. London: Verso.

Freud, Sigmund (1965) *New Introductory Lectures to Psychoanalysis*. New York: Norton & Norton.

Friedan, Betty (1963) *The Feminine Mystique*. New York: W. W. Norton.

Friedman, Jonathan (1992) "Myth, History and Political Identity," *Cultural Anthropology* 7(2): 194–210.

Fromm, Erich (1989) "Psychoanalysis and Sociology" and "Politics and Psychonalaysis," in Stephen Eric Bronner and Douglas MacKay Kellner (eds.), *Critical Theory and Society: A Reader*. New York: Routledge.

Fromm, Erich (2009) *Beyond the Chains of Illusion: My Encounter with Marx and Freud*. New York: Continuum.

Gago, Verónica (2020) *Feminist International: How to Change Everything*. London: Verso.

Garland-Thomson, Rosemarie (2017) "Julia Pastrana, the 'Extraordinary Lady,'" in Laura Anderson Barbata and Donna Wingate (eds.), *The Eye of the Beholder: Julia Pastrana's Long Journey Home*. Seattle: Lucia Marquard, 31–60.

Gatens, Moira (1996) *Imaginary Bodies: Ethics, Power and Corporeality*. London: Routledge.

Gatens, Moira, and Genevieve Lloyd (1999) *Collective Imaginings: Spinoza, Past and Present*. London, Routledge.

Gearhart, Sally Miller (1982) "The Future—If There Is One—Is Female," in Pam McAllister (ed.), *Reweaving the Web of Life: Feminism and Nonviolence*. Philadelphia: New Society Publisher, 266–85.

Gentile, Jill (2016) *Feminine Law: Freud, Free Speech, and the Voice of Desire*. London: Karnac.

Gentile, Jill (2022 forthcoming) "The Missing Signifier and the Malfunctioning Paternal Law," forthcoming in Aner Govrin & Tair Caspi (eds.), *The Routledge Handbook of Psychoanalysis and Philosophy*. New York: Routledge.

Gherovici, Patricia (2011) "Psychoanalysis Needs a Sex Change," *Gay and Lesbian Issues and Psychology Review* 7(1): 3–18.

Gherovici, Patricia (2017) *Transgender Psychoanalysis. A Lacanian Perspective on Sexual Difference*. New York: Routledge.

Gherovici, Patricia (2019) "Transgender Expressions and Psychosis: Towards an Ethics of Sexual Difference," *British Journal of Psychotherapy* 35(3): 417–30.

Gilbert, Scott F., Jan Sapp, and Alfred I. Tauber (2012) "A Symbiotic View of Life: We Have Never Been Individuals," *The Quarterly Review of Biology* 87(4) (December 2012): 325–41.

Gilligan, Carol and Naomi Snider (2018) *Why Does Patriarchy Persist?* Cambridge: Polity.

Goff, Philip (2019) *Galileo's Error: Foundations for a New Science of Consciousness*. New York: Pantheon Books.

Goff, Philip, William Seager, and Sean Allen-Hermanson (2020) "Panpsychism," *The Stanford Encyclopedia of Philosophy*. Available at: https://plato.stanford.edu/archives/sum2020/entries/panpsychism/ (accessed July 25, 2020).

Goldman, Emma (1923) *My Disillusionment in Russia*. Garden City: Doubleday, Page & Company.

Goldman, Emma (1931) *Living My Life*. New York: Alfred A. Knopf.

Goldman, Emma (1969) *Anarchism and Other Essays*. New York: Dover
   Publications.
Gourgouris, Stathis 2013, *archē*, in *Political Concepts: A Critical Lexicon*, https://
   www.politicalconcepts.org/arche-stathis-gourgouris/
Graeber, David (2004) *Fragments of an Anarchist Anthropology*. Chicago: Prickly
   Paradigm Press.
Graham, Robert, ed. (2005) *Anarchism: A Documentary History of Libertarian
   Ideas, Volume One: From Anarchy to Anarchism (300 CE to 1939)*. Montreal:
   Black Rose Books.
Graham, Robert, ed. (2009) *Anarchism: A Documentary History of Libertarian
   Ideas, Volume Two: The Emergence of the New Anarchism*. Montreal: Black
   Rose Books.
Guaman Poma de Ayala, Felipe (2009) *The First New Chronicle and Good
   Government: On the History of the World and the Incas up to 1615*. Austin:
   University of Texas Press.
Guérin, Daniel (1999) *Ni Dieu, ni Maître: Anthologie de l'anarchisme*. Paris:
   La Découverte.
Gunn Allen, Paula (1992) *The Sacred Hoop: Recovering the Feminine in American
   Indian Traditions*. Boston: Beacon Press.
Halberstam, Jack (2018) *Trans*: A Quick and Quirky Account of Gender
   Variability*. Oakland: University of California Press.
Harcourt, Bernard (2012) *The Illusion of Free Markets: Punishment and the Myth
   of Natural Order*. Cambridge, MA: Harvard University Press.
He Zhen (also known as He-Yin Zhen), (2005) "Women's Liberation," in Robert
   Graham (ed.), *Anarchism: A Documentary History of Libertarian Ideas, Vol. 1*.
   Montreal: Black Rose Books, 336–41.
He Zhen (2013a) [1907] "On the Question of Women's Liberation," in, Lydia H.
   Liu, Rebecca E. Karl, and Dorothy Ko (eds.), *The Birth of Chinese Feminism.
   Essential Texts in Transnational Theory*. New York: Columbia University
   Press, 52–71.
He Zhen (2013b) [1907] "Feminist Manifesto," in Lydia H. Liu, Rebecca E. Karl,
   and Dorothy Ko (eds.), *The Birth of Chinese Feminism. Essential Texts in
   Transnational Theory*, New York: Columbia University Press, 52–71.
Hershock, Peter D. (2012) *Valuing Diversity: Buddhist Reflection on Realizing a
   More Equitable Global Future*. Albany: SUNY Press.
Hewitt, Marsha (2007) "Emma Goldman: The Case for Anarcho-feminism,"
   in Penny A. Weiss and Loretta Kensinger, L. (eds.) *Feminist Interpretations of
   Emma Goldman*. University Park: Pennsylvania State University Press,
   312–18.
Hill, Mike, and Warren Montag (2014), *The Other Adam Smith*. Stanford:
   Stanford University Press.
Hillman, James (2005) *Healing Fictions*. Putnam: Spring.
Hippler, Thomas (2011) "Spinoza's Politics of Imagination and the Origins of
   Critical Theory," in Chiara Bottici and Benoît Challand (eds.), *The Politics of
   Imagination*. London: Routledge, 55–73.
Hird, Myra J. (2004) "Naturally Queer," *Feminist Theory* 5(1): 85–9.

Hobbes, Thomas (1839) *Malmesburiensis Opera Philosophica Quæ Latine Scripsit Omnia in Unum Corpus Nunc Primum Collecta Vol. II*, Studio et Labore Gulielmi Molesworth. London: Joannem Bohn.

Hodos, William, and C.B.G Campbell (1969) "Scala Naturae: Why there is no theory in Comparative Psychology," *Psychological Review* 76(4): 337–50.

Holmes, Brooke (2010) "Marked Bodies (Gender, Race, Class, Age, Disability, Disease)," in Daniel H. Garrison (ed.), *A Cultural History of the Human Body, Vol. 1: In Antiquity*. Oxford: Berg, 159–83.

Honneth, Axel (1995) *The Struggle for Recognition: The Moral Grammar of Social Conflict*. Cambridge: Polity.

hooks, bell (1999) *Feminist Theory: From Margin to Center*. Boston, MA: South End Press.

hooks, bell (2010) *Understanding Patriarchy*. Louisville: Anarchist Federation.

hooks, bell (2015) *Talking Back: Thinking Feminist, Thinking Black*. New York: Routledge.

Horney, Karen (1924) "On the Genesis of the Castration Complex in Women," *International Journal of Psychoanalysis* 5(1): 50–65.

Horswell, Michael J. (2003) "Toward an Andean Theory of Ritual Same-Sex Sexuality and Third-gender Subjectivity," in Pete Sigal (ed.), *Infamous Desire: Male Homosexuality In Colonial Latina America*. Chicago: The University of Chicago Press.

Husserl, Edmund (1970) *The Crisis of European Sciences*. Trans. David Carr. Evanston: Northwestern University Press.

Israel, Jonathan (2001) *Radical Enlightenment: Philosophy and the Making of Modernity 1650–1750*. Oxford: Oxford University Press.

Irigaray, Luce (1985) *This Sex Which Is Not One*. Ithaca: Cornell University Press.

Jaeggi, Rahel (2013) *Alienation*. New York: Columbia University Press.

Jingyan, Bao (2005) "Neither Lord Nor Subject," in Robert Graham (ed.), *Anarchism: A Documentary History of Libertarian Ideas. Volume One: From Anarchy to Anarchism (300 CE to 1939)*. Montreal: Black Rose Books, 1–4.

Johannes, Fabian (1983) *Time and the Other: How Anthropology Makes its Object*. New York: Columbia University Press.

Jonas, Hans (1973) "Zwischen Nichts und Ewigkeit: Zur Lehre vom Menschen," in Günther Bien (ed.), *Die Grundlegung der Politischen Philosophie bei Aristotles*. Freiburg: Karl Alber.

jones, pattrice (2014) "Eros and the Mechanisms of Eco-Defense," in Carol Adams and Lori Gruen (eds.), *Ecofeminism:Feminist Intersections with Other Animals and the Earth*. New York: Bloomsbury Academic, 91–108.

Kant, Immanuel (2000) "On the Different Human Races," in Robert Bernasconi and Tommy Lee Lott (eds.), *The Idea of Race*. Indianapolis: Hackett Publishing, 8–22.

Kardas, Goran (2015) "From Etymology to Ontology: Vasubandhu and Candrakīrti on Various Interpretations of pratītyasamutpāda," *Asian Philosophy* 25(3): 293–317.

Kelly, Mark G. E., and Dimitris Vardoulakis (2018) "Balibar and Transindividuality," *Australasian Philosophical Review* 2(1): 1–4.

Kensinger, Loretta (2007) "Speaking with Red Emma: The Feminist Theory of Emma Goldman," in P. A. Weiss and L. Kensinger (eds.), *Feminist Interpretations of Emma Goldman*. University Park: Pennsylvania State University Press, 255–82.

Kerner, Ina (2018) "Postcolonial Theories as Global Critical Theories," in *Constellations* 25: 614–28.

Kinna, Ruth (2010) "Anarchism," in M. Bevir (ed), *Encyclopedia of Political Theory*. London, Sage, 34–7.

Klein, Kerwin Lee (2000) "On the Emergence of Memory in Historical Discourse," *Representations* 69: 127–50.

Komporozos-Athanasiou, Aris (2022) [forthcoming] *Speculative Communities: Living With Uncertainty in a Financialized World*. Chicago: The University of Chicago Press.

Kornegger, Peggy (2012) "Anarchism: The Feminist Connection," in Dark Star Collective (eds.) *Quiet Rumors: Anarcha-feminist Reader*. California: AK Press.

Koselleck, Reinhart (2000) "Gebrochene Erinnungen? Deutsche und polnische Vergangenheiten," in *Jahrbuch der Deutschen Akademie fuer Sprache und Dichtung*. Goettingen: L. Schneider, 19–32.

Kristeva, Julia (1982) *Powers of Horror: an Essay on Abjection*. New York: Columbia University Press.

Kristeva, Julia (1984) *Revolution in Poetic Language*. New York: Columbia University Press.

Kristeva, Julia (1987) *Tales of Love*. New York: Columbia University Press.

Kristeva, Julia (2002) "Motherhood According to Giovanni Bellini," in *The Portable Kristeva*. New York: Columbia University Press.

Křížek, Michal (2012) "Dark Energy and the Anthropic Principle," *New Astronomy* 17(1): 1–7.

Kropotkin, Pyotr (1902) *Mutual Aid: A Factor in Evolution*. London: William Heinemann.

Kropotkin, Pyotr (1970) *Anarchism: A Collection of Revolutionary Writings*. New York: Dover Publications.

Kropotkin, Pyotr (1976) *The Essential Kropotkin*. London: Macmillan.

Kropotkin, Pyotr (1995) *The Conquest of Bread, and other Writings*, Cambridge University Press

Kropotkin, Pyotr (2001) 'Sterilization of the unfit', in Glassgold, P. (ed.) *Anarchy! An Anthology of Emma Goldman's Mother Earth*. Washington DC: Counterpoint, pp.120–123.

Kropotkin, Pyotr (2002) *Anarchism: A Collection of Revolutionary Writings*. New York: Dover Publication.

Kuehner, Angela (2008) *Trauma und Kollektives Gedächtnis*. Giessen: Psychosozial-Verlag.

Kuranga, David Oladipuno (2012) *The Power of Interdependence: Lessons From Africa*. London: Palgrave.

Lacan, Jacques (2006) *Écrits*. Trans. Bruce Fink. New York: W. W. Norton & Company.

Lacan, Jacques (2014) *The Seminar of Jacques Lacan, Book X: Anxiety*. Trans. A. R. Price. Cambridge: Polity.

Landucci, Sergio (1993) "Idea," in Gianni Vattimo, Maurizio Ferraris, and Diego Marconi (eds.), *Enciclopedia di filosofia*. Milan: Garzanti, 515–16.

Lara, María Pía (1998) *Moral Textures: Feminist Narratives in the Public Sphere*. Cambridge: Polity.

Lara, María Pía (2021) *Beyond The Public Sphere. Film and the Feminist Imaginary*. Evanston/Illinois: Northwestern University Press.

Lazar, Hillary (2016) "Until All Are Free: Black Feminism, Anarchism, and Interlocking Oppression," *Perspectives on Anarchist Theory* 29: 35–50.

Lazar, Hillary, et al., eds. (2020) *Anarchafeminisms, Perspectives on Anarchist Theory*, No. 29. Oakland: AK Press.

Lentin, Alana (2008) *Racism: A Beginner's Guide*. Oxford: Oneworld.

Liddell, Henry George, and Robert Scott (2015) *Liddell and Scott's Greek-English Lexicon, Abridged*. Mansfield Centre, CT: Martino.

Liu Lydia H., Rebecca E. Karl, and Dorothy Ko (2013) "Introduction: Towards a Transnational Feminist Theory," in Lydia H. Liu, Rebecca E. Karl, and Dorothy Ko (eds.), *The Birth of Chinese Feminism. Essential Texts in Transnational Theory*. New York: Columbia University Press: 1–25.

Loick, Daniel (2019) *A Critique of Sovereignty*. London: Rowman & Littlefield.

Long Chu, Andrea (2019) *Females*. London: Verso.

Lorde, Audre (1984) "Age, Race, Class, and Sex: Women Redefining Difference," in *Sister Outsider: Essays and Speeches*. Berkeley: Crossing Press, 114–23.

Lorde, Audre (2017) *The Master's Tools Will Never Dismantle the Master's House*. London: Penguin.

Lovejoy, Bess (2017) "Lives on Show, Bodies behind Glass: Julia Pastrana's Parallels in Museum Collections," in Laura Anderson Barbata and Donna Wingate (eds.), *The Eye of the Beholder: Julia Pastrana's Long Journey Home*. Seattle: Lucia Marquard, 155–76.

Lovejoy, Arthur O. (1936) *The Great Chain of Being. A Study of the History of an Idea*, Cambridge, MA: Harvard University Press.

Lugones, Maria (1994) "Purity, Impurity, and Separation," *Signs: Journal of Women in Culture and Society* 19(2): 458–79.

Lugones, Maria (2007) "Heterosexualism and the Colonial/Modern Gender System," *Hypathia* 22: 186–209.

Lugones, Maria (2010) "Towards a Decolonial Feminism," *Hypathia* 25: 742–69.

Lugones, Maria (2016) "The Coloniality of Gender," in W. Harcourt (ed.), *The Palgrave Handbook of Gender and Development*. New York: Palgrave Macmillan, 13–33.

Lurgio, Jeremy (2019) "Saving the Whanganui," *The Guardian* (November 29, 2019), https://www.theguardian.com/world/2019/nov/30/saving-the-whanganui-can-personhood-rescue-a-river (accessed April 9, 2021).

Macherey, Pierre (1998) *In a Materialist Way*, ed. Warren Montag. London: Verso.

Malatesta, Errico (2001) *L'anarchia*. Roma: Datanews.

Maldonado-Torres, Nelson (2006) "Toward a Critique of Continental Reason: Africana Studies and the Decolonization of Imperial Cartographies in the Americas," in Lewis Gordon and Jane Anna Gordon (eds.), *Not Only the Master's Tools: African-American Studies in Theory and Practice*. London: Routledge, 51–84.

Maldonado-Torres, Nelson (2016) "Outline of Ten Theses on Coloniality and Decoloniality." Available at: http://fondation-frantzfanon.com/outline-of-ten-theses-on-coloniality-and-decoloniality/ (accessed July 25, 2020).

Maldonado-Torres, Nelson (2020) "What is Decolonial Critique?," forthcoming in special issue "Philosophy and Coloniality," *Graduate Faculty Philosophy Journal*, 40 (1), 157–83.

Marcos, Sylvia (2006) *Taken from the Lips: Gender and Eras in Mesoamerican Religions*. Leiden and Boston: Brill.

Marcucci, Nicola, and Luca Pinzolo, eds. (2010) *Strategie della relazione. Riconoscimento, transindividuale, alterità*. Rome: Meltemi.

Margulis, Lynn (1998) *Symbiotic Planet, A New Look at Evolution*. New York, Basic Books.

Marquez-Grant, Nicholas (2017) "The Repatriation of Julia Pastrana: scientific and ethical dilemmas," in Laura Anderson Barbata and Donna Wingate (eds.), *The Eye of the Beholder: Julia Pastrana's Long Journey Home*. Seattle: Lucia Marquard, 101–30.

Marshall, Peter (1992) *Demanding the Impossible: A History of Anarchism*. London: HarperCollins.

Marso, Lori Jo (2007) "A Feminist Search for Love: Emma Goldman on the Politics of Marriage, Love, Sexuality and the Feminine," in P. A. Weiss and L. Kensinger (eds.), *Feminist Interpretations of Emma Goldman*. University Park: Pennsylvania State University Press, 71–89.

Marx, Karl (1976) *Capital: A Critique of Political Economy, Volume I*, trans. Ben Fowkes. London: Penguin.

Marx, Karl (1978a) "The Economic and Philosophical Manuscripts of 1844," in R. C. Tucker (ed.), *Marx-Engels Reader*. New York: Norton, 66–125.

Marx, Karl (1978b) "On the Jewish Question," in R. C. Tucker (ed.), *Marx-Engels Reader*. New York; Norton, 26–52.

Marx, Karl (1978c) "The Grundrisse," in R. C. Tucker (ed.), *Marx-Engels Reader*. New York; Norton, 221–468.

Marx, Karl (1978d) "Critique of the Gotha Program," in R. C. Tucker (ed.), *Marx-Engels Reader*. New York; Norton, 525–41.

Marx, Karl, and Friedrich Engels (1975) "The Holy Family, or Critique of Critical Criticism: Against Bruno Bauer and Company," in *Karl Marx and Frederick Engels Collected Works*, Volume 5. London: Lawrence and Wishart, 1–540.

Marx, Karl, and Friedrich Engels (1976) "The German Ideology," in *Karl Marx and Frederick Engels Collected Works*, Volume 4. London: Lawrence and Wishart, 1–211.

Marx, Karl, and Friedrich Engels (1978) "Manifesto of the Communist Party," in R. C. Tucker (ed.), *Marx-Engels Reader*. New York: Norton, 469–500.

Marx, Karl, and Friedrich Engels (1998) *The Communist Manifesto*. Trans. Samuel Moore. London: Verso.

Matarrese, Sabino, et al., eds. (2011) *Dark Matter and Dark Energy: A Challenge for Modern Cosmology*. Dordrecht: Springer.

May, Todd (1994) *The Political Philosophy of Poststructuralist Anarchism*. University Park: Pennsylvania State University Press.

Mazure, Alain (2012) *Matter, Dark Matter, and Anti-Matter: In Search of the Hidden Universe*. Switzerland: Springer.

Mbah, Sam, and I. E. Igariwey (1997) *African Anarchism: The History of a Movement*. Tucson, See Sharp Press.

McCall, Leslie (2005) "The Complexity of Intersectionality," *Signs: Journal of Women in Culture and Society* 30(3): 1771–1800.

McCumber, John (2001) *Time in the Ditch: American Philosophy and the McCarthy Era*. Evanston: Northwestern University Press.

McLaughlin, Paul (2002) *Mikhail Bakunin: The Philosophical Basis of His Anarchism*. New York: Alogra Publishing.

Mendieta, Eduardo (2007) *Global Fragments. Globalizations, Latinamericanism, and Critical Theory*. Albany: SUNY Press.

Mendieta, Eduardo (2020) "Critique of Decolonial Reason: on the Philosophy of the Calibans," forthcoming in special issue on "Philosophy and Coloniality," *Graduate Faculty Philosophy Journal*, 40 (1) 127–54.

Mies, Maria (1986) *Patriarchy and Accumulation on a World Scale: Women in the International Division of Labour*. London: Zed Books.

Mies, Maria (2014) "The Myth of Catching-up Development," in *Ecofeminism*, (eds.) Maria Mies and Vandana Shiva. London: Zed Books.

Mies, Maria (2014) "The Need for a New Vision: The Subsistence Perspective," in Maria Mies and Vandana Shiva (eds.), *Ecofeminism*. London: Zed Books.

Mignolo, Walter D., ed. (2000) *Local Histories/Global Designs: Coloniality, Subaltern Knowledges, and Border Thinking*. Princeton: Princeton University Press.

Mignolo, Walter D., ed. (2001) *Capitalismo y geopolítica del conocimiento: el eurocentrismo y la filosofía de la liberación en el debate intelectual contemporáneo*. Buenos Aires: Ediciones del Signo/Duke University.

Mitchell, Juliet, and Jacqueline Rose, eds. (1982) *Feminine Sexuality: Jacques Lacan and the école freudienne*. London: Macmillan Press.

Mohanty, Chandra Tolpade (2003) *Feminism Without Borders: Decolonizing Theory, Practicing Solidarity*. Durham: Duke University Press.

Mojab, Shahrzad (2015) *Marxism and Feminism*. London: Zed Books.

Montag, Warren, ed. (1998) *In a Materialist Way: Selected Essays by Pierre Macherey*. London: Verso.

Montague, W. P. (1905) "Panpsychism and Monism," *The Journal of Philosophy, Psychology, and Scientific Methods* 2(23): 626–9.

Morfino, Vittorio (2010) "Transindividuale e/o riconoscimento: ancora sull'alternativa Hegel/Spinoza," in N. Marcucci and L. Pinzolo (eds.), *Strategie della relazione. Riconoscimento, transindividuale, alterità*. Rome: Meltemi, 179–200.

Morfino, Vittorio (2014) *Plural Temporality: Transindividuality and the Aleatory Between Spinoza and Althusser*. Leiden: Brill.

Morris, Brian (2014) *Anthropology, Ecology, and Anarchism: A Brian Morris Reader*. Oakland: PM Press.

Mortimer-Sandilands, Catriona, and Bruce Erickson (2010) *Queer Ecologies: Sex, Nature, Politics, Desire*. Indianapolis: Indiana University Press.

Morton, Timothy (2010) "Queer Ecology," *PMLA* 125(2): 273–82.

Morton, Timothy (2010a) *The Ecological Thought*. Cambridge, MA: Harvard University Press.

Muñoz, José Esteban (1999) *Disindentifications: Queers of Color and the Performance of Politics*. Minneapolis: Minnesota University Press.

Muñoz, José Esteban (2009) *Cruising Utopia: The Then and There of Queer Futurity*. New York: New York University Press.

Murphy, Michelle (2015) "Reproduction," in Shahrzad Mojab (ed.), *Marxism and Feminism*. London: Zed Books.

Myung, Yun Soo (2005) "Holographic Principle and Dark Energy," *Physics Letters B* 610(1–2): 18–22.

Naess, Arne (2005) "Spinoza and the Deep Ecology Movement," in Alan Drengson (ed.), *The Selected Works of Arne Naess*. New York: Springer, 2662–87.

Nandy, Ashis (1983) *The Intimate Enemy: Loss and Recovery of Self Under Colonialism*. Delhi: Oxford University Press.

Nash, Jennifer C. (2018) *Black Feminism Reimagined: After Intersectionality*. Durham: Duke University Press.

Negri, Antonio (1991) *The Savage Anomaly: The Power of Spinoza's Metaphysic and Politics*. Minneapolis: University of Minnesota Press.

Newman, David M. (2001) *Identities and Inequalities: Exploring the Intersections of Race, Class, Gender, and Sexuality*. New York: McGraw Hill.

Newman, Saul (2016) *Postanarchism*. Cambridge: Polity.

Nietzsche, Friedrich (1966) *Beyond Good and Evil: Prelude to a Philosophy of the Future*. Trans. Walter Kaufmann. New York: Vintage Books.

Nietzsche, Friedrich (1976) *The Portable Nietzsche*. Trans. Walter Kaufmann. New York: Penguin Books.

Nietzsche, Friedrich (1994) *On the Genealogy of Morals*. Trans. C. Diethe. New York: Cambridge University Press.

Nietzsche, Friedrich (1998) *Twilight of the Idols; or, How to Philosophize With a Hammer*. Trans. Duncan Large. Oxford: Oxford University Press.

Nikulin, Dmitri, ed. (2015) *Memory: A History*. Oxford, Oxford University Press.

Nikulin, Dmitri (2017) *The Concept of History*. London: Bloomsbury.

O'Byrne, Anne (2010) *Natality and Finitude*. Bloomington: Indiana University Press.

Oele, Marjolein (2020) *E-Co-Affectivity: Exploring the Pathos at Life's Material Interfaces*. Albany: SUNY Press.

Oksala, Johanna (2011) "The Neoliberal Subject of Feminism," *Journal of the British Society for Phenomenology* 42(1): 104–20.

Oliver, Kelly (2010) "Animality," in Mark Bevir (ed.), *Encyclopedia of Political Theory*, Vol 1: 50–3.

Onions, C. T., ed. (1936) *The Shorter Oxford English Dictionary on Historical Principles*. Prepared by William Little, H. W. Fowler, and J. Coulson, Revised and Edited by C. T. Onions. Oxford: Clarendon Press.

Ortega, Mariana (2017) "Decolonial Woes and Practices of Un-knowing," *The Journal of Speculative Philosophy* 31(3): 504–15.

Oyewùmí, Oyèrónkè (1997) *The Invention of Women*. Minneapolis: University of Minnesota Press.

Oyewùmí, Oyèrónkè (2002) "Conceptualizing Gender: Eurocentric Foundations of Feminist Concepts and the Challenge of African Epistemologies," *A Journal of Culture and African Women Studies* 2(1): 1–9.

Pavon, Diego (2005) "Holographic Dark Energy and Cosmic Coincidence," *Physics Letters B* 628: 206–10.

Park, Peter K. J. (2014) *Africa, Asia, and the History of Philosophy: Racism in the Formation of the Philosophical Canon 1780–1830*. Albany: SUNY Press.

Perspectives Editorial Collective (2016) *Anarchafeminism: A Special Issue of Perspectives on Anarchist Theory*. Portland: Eberhardt Press.

Plato (2004) *Republic*. Trans. C.D.C. Reeve. Indianapolis: Hackett Publishing.

Poggi, Gianfranco (1978) *The Development of the Modern State: A Sociological Introduction*. Stanford: Stanford University Press.

Poggi, Gianfranco (1990) *The State: Its Nature, Development, and Prospects*. Cambridge: Polity.

Pozo, Maria Esther, and Jhonny Ledezma (2006) "Genera: trabajo agricola y tierra en Raqaypampa." In *Las displicencias de genera en las cruces del siglo pasado al nuevo mile nio en las Andes*, ed. Nina Laurie and Maria Esther Pozo. Cochabamba, Bolivia: CESU-UMSS.

Povinelli, Elizabeth A. (2016) *Geontologies: A Requiem to Late Liberalism*. Durham: Duke University Press.

Preciado, Beatriz (2013) *Testo Junkie: Sex, Drugs, and Biopolitics in the Pharmacopornographic Era*. New York: The Feminist Press at CUNY.

Preciado, Paul B. (2018) *Counter-Sexual Manifesto*. Columbia: Columbia University Press.

Preciado, Paul B. (2019) *An Apartment on Uranus*. Cambridge: Semiotext(e).

Prichard, Alex, et al. (2017) *Libertarian Socialism: Politics in Black and Red*. Oakland: PM Press.

Proudhon, Pierre-Joseph (1994) *What is Property?* Cambridge: Cambridge University Press.

Puar, Jasbir (2007) *Terrorist Assemblages: Homonationalism in Queer Times*. Durham: Duke University Press.

Pulcini, Elena (2009) *La Cura del Mondo*. Turin: Bollati Boringhieri.

Putnam, Hilary (2002) *The Collapse of the Fact/Value Dichotomy and Other Essays*. Cambridge: Harvard University Press.

Quijano, Aníbal (2000a) "Coloniality of Power, Eurocentrism, and Latin America," *Nepantla: Views from the South* 1(3): 533–80.

Quijano, Aníbal (2000b) "Colonialidad del Poder y Clasificacion Social," Festchrift for Immanuel Wallerstein, Part 1, *Journal of World System Research*, V. xi(2), Summer/Fall: 342–386.

Quinn, Patrick J. (2015) *Patriarchy in Eclipse: The Femme Fatale and the New Woman in American Literature and Culture, 1870–1920*. Cambridge: Cambridge Scholars Publishing.

Rainwater, Lee, and William L. Yancey (1967) *The Moynihan Report the Politics of Controversy: A Transaction Social Science and Public Policy Report*. Cambridge, MA: MIT Press.

Rapp, John A. (2012) "Daoism and Anarchism Reconsidered," in *Daoism and Anarchism: Critiques of State Autonomy in Ancient and Modern China*. London: Continuum, 19–50.

Rawes, Peg (2015) "Spinoza's Geometric and Ecological Ratios," in Manuel Shvartzberg and Matthew Poole (eds.), *Politics of Parametricism*. London: Bloomsbury, 213–30.

Read, Jason (2016) *The Politics of Transindividuality*. Chicago: Haymarket Books.

Reclus, Élisée (1995) *Histoire d'un ruisseau*. Arles : Actes Sud.

Rich, Adrienne (1980) "Compulsory Heterosexuality and Lesbian Existence," *Signs: Journal of Women in Culture and Society* 5(4) : 631–60.

Ricœur, Paul (2000) *La mémoire, l'histoire, l'oubli*. Paris: Editions du Seuil.

Rodney, Walter (1984) *How Europe Underdeveloped Africa*. Enugu, Nigeria: Ikenga Publishers.

Rogue, J., and Abbey Volcano (2012) "Insurrection at the Intersections," in Dark Star Collective (eds.), *Quiet Rumors: Anarcha-feminist Reader*. Oakland: AK Press, 43–7.

Rousseau, Jean-Jacques (1997) *The* Discourses *and other early politics writings*. Ed. and trans. Victor Gourevitch. Cambridge: Cambridge University Press.

Rovelli, Carlo (2014) *Sette brevi lezioni di fisica*. Milan: Adelphi.

Rovida, Giorgio (1997) "Anarchismo," in Gianni Vattimo, Maurizio Ferraris, and Diego Marconi (eds.), *Enciclopedia di filosofia*. Milan: Garzanti, 30–1.

Roy, Eleanor Ainge (2017) "New Zealand River Granted Same Legal Rights as Human Being," *The Guardian* (March 16, 2017), https://www.theguardian.com/world/2017/mar/16/new-zealand-river-granted-same-legal-rights-as-human-being (accessed April 9, 2021).

Ruíz, Elena (2017) "Framing Intersectionality," in *The Routledge Companion to the Philosophy of Race*. London: Routledge, 335–8.

Saar, Martin (2013) *Die Immanenz der Macht, Politische Theorie nach Spinoza*, Berlin: Suhrkamp.

Sakai, Naoki (2000) "'You Asians': On the Historical Role of the West and Asia Binary," *South Atlantic Quarterly* 99(4): 789–817.

Sanders, Robert H. (2010) *The Dark Matter Problem: A Historical Perspective*. Cambridge: Cambridge University Press.

Santhosh, Mathew (2014) *Essays on the Frontiers of Modern Astrophysics and Cosmology*. Switzerland: Springer.

Saraswati, Ayu L. (2013) *Seeing Beauty, Sensing Race in Transnational Indonesia*. Honolulu: University of Hawai'i Press, 2013.

Saraswati, Ayu, and Barbara L. Shaw, eds. (2020) *Feminist and Queer Theory: An Intersectional and Transnational Reader*. Oxford: Oxford University Press.

Sargent, Lydia, ed. (1981) *Women and Revolution: A Discussion of the Unhappy Marriage of Marxism and Feminism*. Boston: South End Press.

Schürmann, Reiner (1986) "On Constituting Oneself an Anarchist Subject," *Praxis International* 3: 294–310.

Schürmann, Reiner (1987) *Heidegger on Being and Acting: From Principles to Anarchy*. Trans. Christine-Marie Gros. Bloomington: Indiana University Press.

Scott, James C. (2009) *The Art of Not Being Governed: An Anarchist History of Upland Southeast Asia*. Yale: Yale University Press.

Sedgwick, Eve Kosofsky (2008) *Epistemology of the Closet*. Berkeley: University of California Press.

Serano, Julia (2016) *Whipping Girl: A Transsexual Woman on Sexism and the Scapegoating of Femininity*. Berkeley: Seal Press.

Shannon, Deric (2009) "Articulating a Contemporary Anarcha-feminism," *Theory in Action* 2(3): 58–74.

Sharp, Hasana (2011) *Spinoza and the Politics of Renaturalization*. Chicago, Chicago University Press

Shiva, Vandana (1999) *Staying Alive: Women, Ecology, and Development*. Berkeley: North Atlantic Books.

Shiva, Vandana (2014) "Decolonizing the North," in Maria Mies and Vandana Shiva (eds.), *Ecofeminism*. London: Zed Books.

Shohat, Ella, and Robert Stam (1994) *Unthinking Eurocentrism: Multiculturalism and the Media*. London and New York: Routledge.

Shulman, Alix Kates (2007) "Dancing in the Revolution: Emma Goldman's Feminism," in Penny A. Weiss and Loretta Kensinger (eds.), *Feminist Interpretations of Emma Goldman*. University Park: Pennsylvania State University Press, 241–53.

Silko, Leslie Marmon (2006) *Ceremony*. New York: Penguin Books.

Silverblatt, Irene (1990) *Taller de historia oral Andina. La Mujer Andina en la historia*. Chukiyawu: Ediciones de! THOA.

Silverblatt, Irene (1998) *Moon, Sun, and Witches*. Princeton: Princeton University Press.

Simondon, Gilbert (1964) *L'individu et sa genèse physico-biologique*. Paris: Presses Universitaires de France.

Simondon, Gilbert (1989) *L'individuation psychique et collective*. Paris: Aubier.

Simondon, Gilbert (2005) *L'individuation à la lumière des notions de forme and d'information*. Grenoble: Edition Million.

Simpson, John, and Edmund Weiner (1989) *The Oxford English Dictionary*, Vol. 2. Oxford: Oxford University Press.

Sinha, Vineeta, and Syed Farid Alatas (2017) *Sociological Theory Beyond the Canon*. London: Palgrave Macmillan.

Slotkin, Richard (1985) *Regeneration Through Violence: The Mythology of the American Frontier 1600–1860*. Norman: University of Oklahoma Press.

Smith, Andrea (2010) "Queer Theory and Native Studies: The Heteronormativity of Settler Colonialism," *GLQ: A Journal of Lesbian and Gay Studies* 16(1–2): 42–68.

Spillers, Hortense J. (1987) "Mama's Baby, Papa's Maybe: An American Grammar Book," *Diacritics* 17(2): 65.

Spinoza, Baruch (1925) *Opera* (4 vols.). Heidelberg: Winter.

Spinoza, Baruch (1994) *A Spinoza Reader*. Trans. Edwin Curley. Princeton: Princeton University Press.

Spivak, Gayatri (1988) "Can the Subaltern Speak?," in Cary Nelson and Lawrence Grossberg (eds), Marxism and the Interpretation of Culture. Basingstoke: Macmillan Education, 271–313.

Spivak, Gayatri (1999) *A Critique of Postcolonial Reason*. Cambridge, MA: Harvard University Press.

Stevenson, Angus, and Lesley Brown (2007) *Shorter Oxford English Dictionary on Historical Principles*. Oxford: Oxford University Press.

Stirner, Max (2017) *The Unique and Its Property*. Berkeley: Ardent Press.

Stoler, Ann Laura (2017) *Duress: Imperial Durabilities in Our Times*. Durham & London: Duke University Press.

Stryker, Susan (2020) "Transgender Studies: Queer Theory's Evil Twin," in L Ayu Saraswati and Barbara L Shaw (eds.), *Feminist and Queer Theory: An Intersectional and Transnational Reader*. Oxford: Oxford University Press, 70–2.

Sword, Rosemary K.M., and Philip Zimbardo (2018) "The Fatherless Generation," *Psychology Today*, https://www.psychologytoday.com/us/blog/the-time-cure/201808/the-fatherless-generation) (accessed February 25, 2020).

TallBear, Kim (2013a) "Genomic Articulations of Indigeneity," *Social Studies of Science* 43(4): 509–33.

TallBear, Kim (2013b) *Native American DNA. Tribal Belonging and the False promise of Genetic Science*. Minneapolis and London: University of Minnesota Press.

Tanenbaum, Julia (2016) "To Destroy Domination in All its Forms: Anarchafeminist Theory, Organization and Action, 1970–1978," in Perspectives Editorial Collective, *Anarchafeminism: A Special Issue of Perspectives on Anarchist Theory*. Portland: Eberhardt Press, 13–34.

Teerikorpi, Pekka, et al. (2009) *The Evolving Universe and the Origin of Life: The Search for Our Cosmic Roots*. Cham: Springer.

Tegos, Spyridon (2018) "Identification with Authority and the Transindividual in Rousseau: Critical Comments on Balibar's Concept of the Transindividual," *Australasian Philosophical Review* 2(1): 94–100.

Tilly, Charles (1985) "War Making and State Making as Organized Crime," in Peter Evans et al. (eds.), *Bringing the State Back In*. Cambridge: Cambridge University Press.

Tomšič, Samo (2015) *The Capitalist Unconscious: Marx and Lacan*. London: Verso.

Torpey, John (2018) *The Invention of the Passport: Surveillance, Citizenship and the State*. Cambridge: Cambridge University Press.

Trump, Ivanka (2017) *Women Who Work: Rewriting the Rules for Success*. New York: Penguin.

Tuck, Eve, and K. Wayne Yang (2012) "Decolonization Is Not a Metaphor," *Decolonization: Indigeneity, Education & Society* 1(1): 1–40.

Van Norden, Bryan W. (2017) *Taking Back Philosophy: A Multicultural Manifesto*. New York: Columbia University Press.

Vattimo, Gianni, Maurizio Ferraris, and Diego Marconi, eds. (1993) *Enciclopedia di filosofia*. Milan: Garzanti.

Vardoulakis, Dimitris (2020) *Spinoza, the Epicurean. Authority and Utility in Materialism*. Edinburgh: Edinburgh University Press.

Verter, Mitchell (2013) "The Flow of the Breath: Levinas Mouth-to-Mouth with Buddhism," in Leah Kalmanson, Frank Garrett, and Sarah Mattice (eds), *Levinas and Asian Thought*. Pittsburgh: Duquesne University Press.

Vinyeta, Kirsten, Kyle P. Whyte, and Kathy Lynn (2016) "Indigenous Masculinities in a Changing Climate: Vulnerability and Resilience in the United States," in Elaine Enarson and Bob Pease (eds.), *Men, Masculinities and Disaster*. New York: Routledge. 140–8.

Voss, Daniela (2018) "Immanence, Transindividuality and the Free Multitude," *Philosophy and Social Criticism* 44(8): 865–887.

Waltz, Kenneth (1979) *Theory of International Politics*. Boston: McGraw-Hill.

Wark, McKenzie (2020) *Reverse Cowgirl*. Cambridge, MA: Semiotext(e).

Warner, Michael (2001) "Introduction: Fear of a Queer Planet," *Social Text* 29: 3–17.

Warner, Michael (2012) "Queer and Then? The End of Queer Theory," *The Chronicle for Higher Education*, January 1, 2012. Available at: https://www.chronicle.com/article/QueerThen-/130161 (accessed January 22, 2020).

Weber, Max (1958) *Politik als Beruf*. Munich und Leipzig: Duncker and Humblot.

Webster, Jamieson (2019) *Conversion Disorder: Listening to the Body in Psychoanalysis*. New York: Columbia University Press

Weiss, Penny A. with Megan Brueske (2018) *Feminist Manifestos: A Global Documentary Reader*. New York: New York University Press.

Wehling, Jason (2007) "Anarchy in Interpretation: The Life of Emma Goldman," in Penny A. Weiss and Loretta Kensinger (eds.), *Feminist Interpretations of Emma Goldman*. University Park: Pennsylvania State University Press, 19–38.

Weiss, Penny A., and Loretta Kensinger, eds. (2007) *Feminist Interpretations of Emma Goldman*. University Park: Pennsylvania State University Press.

Wendt, Alexander (1992) "Anarchy Is What States Make It: The Social Construction of Power Politics," *International Organization* 46: 391–425.

Wexler, Alice (1984) *Emma Goldman: An Intimate Life*. New York: Pantheon Books.

Whitebook, Joel (2017) *Freud: An Intellectual Biography*. Cambridge: Cambridge University Press.

Whittle, Stephen Thomas (2005) "Gender Fucking or Fucking Gender?" in Iain Morland and Dino Willox, Dino, *Queer Theory*. London: Palgrave, 115–30.

Whyte, Kyle (2017) "Featured philosopher: Kyle Whyte." Available at: https://politicalphilosopher.net/2017/02/03/featured-philosopher-kyle-whyte/ (accessed July 25, 2020).

Whyte, Kyle (2018) "Settler Colonialism, Ecology, and Environmental Injustice," *Environment and Society: Advances in Research* 9(1): 125–44.

Wight, Martin (1960) "Why Is There No International Theory?" in Herbert Butterfield and Martin Wight (eds.), *Diplomatic Investigations: Essays in the Theory of International Politics*. London: Macmillan, 17–34.

Williams, Caroline (2007) "Thinking the Political in the Wake of Spinoza: Power, Affect and Imagination in the Ethics," *Contemporary Political Theory* 6: 349–69.

Williams, Eric (1944) *Slavery and Capitalism*. Chapel Hill: University of North Carolina Press.

Wokler, Robert (2007) "Rites of Passage and the Grand Tour: Discovering, Imagining and Inventing European Civilization in the Age of Enlightenment," in Anthony Molho, Diogo Ramada Curto, and Niki Koniordos, eds. *Finding Europe: Discourses on Margins, Communities, Images; ca. 13th-ca. 18th Centuries*. New York: Berghahn Books, 205–22.

Woodcock, George (1987) *Pierre-Joseph Proudhon: A Biography*. Montreal: Black Rose Books.

Wynter, Sylvia (2003) "Unsettling the Coloniality of Being/ Power/ Truth/ Freedom: Towards the Human, After Man, Its Overrepresentation—An Argument," in *CR: The New Centennial Review* 3(3): 257–337.

Yeates, Nicola (2009) *Globalizing Care Economies and Migrant Workers: Explorations in Global Care Chains*. New York: Palgrave Macmillan.

Yovel, Yirmiyahu (1989) *Spinoza and Other Heretics: The Marrano of Reason*. Princeton: Princeton University Press.

Zepf, Siegfried (2007) "The Relationship Between the Unconscious and Consciousness: A Comparison of Psychoanalysis and Historical Materialism," *Psychoanalysis, Culture and Society* 12: 105–23.

Index

waged labor 17, 190, 191, 201 n.77,
204, 240, 274, 275 n.38
Ware, Kamau 226 n.7
Wallerstein, Immanuel 190
Warner, Michael 87 nn.30–1, 93 n.53
Weber, Max 48 n.19
Webster, Jamieson x, 160 n.17
Wehling, Jason 74 n.119
Weiss, Penny A. 73 n.116, 74,
74 n.118, 214 n.121
Weiss, P.A., Kesinger, L. 60 n.55
Wells, Ida B. 34
Wendt, Alexander 48 n.18
Western
bio-logic 204–5
civilization 183, 187–8
metaphysical dualism 133
organization of time 183, 185
Western feminism, critique of 246
Wexler, Alice 71 n.101, 71 n.104,
74 n.119
What is Property? (Proudhon)
50 n.27, 233, 233 n.32,
234 n.34
white
gaze 191
privilege 4, 32, 34, 37, 82, 290
theory 37
Whitebook, Joel 249 n.80
whiteness 32, 191, 193, 253, 256
blancura vs *blanquitud* 253
Whittle, Stephen Thomas 91 n.44,
92 n.46
Whyte, Kyle 216 n.125, 266, 266 n.14,
280, 280 n.56, 281
Wight, Martin 46 n.14
Williams, Caroline 128 n.43
Williams, Eric 195 n.56
witch 241, 243
witch-hunts 241–2
Wokler, Robert 185 n.10
Wollestonecraft, Mary 60 n.55
womb 65, 96 n.59, 158, 229

women
"angels of the hearth" 241, 246
biodiversity experts 263
bodies 19, 20, 154, 163– 4, 241–2,
247, 288, 293, 296
see also body
condition 40, 71
as processes 21, 154–5
"the savages of Europe" 244
snail 206, 208, 221, 276
see also Oyěwùmí
traffic in 72
Women, Race and Class (Davis) 39,
39 n.41
Women who Work (Trump) 83,
83 nn.18–19
Women's Suffrage (Goldman) 69–70
womanhood 3, 9, 17, 19, 21–2, 169,
172–4, 215, 252, 294
Black womanhood 29–30
as narrating self 154, 166
naturalized understanding of 96
spectacle of 174
Woodcock, George 48 n.20
World Bank 265–66
writing styles, multiplicity of 22
Wynter, Sylvia 105, 105 n.9, 197–8,
230, 230 n.20, 262 n.4,
278 n.47
coloniality of being 197, 197 n.63,
197 n.65

Yeates, Nicola 86 n.28
Yovel, Yirmiyahu 111 n.5, 116 n.16

Zambrano, Maria 155
Zhen, He-Yin 5, 5 n.9, 79, 82,
82 n.17, 83, 84, 84 n.20, 86,
207 n.97, 289, 290 n.10
critique of Western feminism 207
nannü 208–9
nüxing and *nanxing* (woman and
men) 208